LIBRARY OF HEBREW BIBLE/ OLD TESTAMENT STUDIES

704

Formerly Journal for the Study of the Old Testament Supplement Series

Editors
Claudia V. Camp, Texas Christian University, USA
Andrew Mein, Durham University, UK

Founding Editors
David J. A. Clines, Philip R. Davies and David M. Gunn

Editorial Board
Alan Cooper, Susan Gillingham, John Goldingay,
Norman K. Gottwald, James E. Harding, John Jarick, Carol Meyers,
Daniel L. Smith-Christopher, Francesca Stavrakopoulou,
James W. Watts

ANONYMOUS PROPHETS AND ARCHETYPAL KINGS

Reading 1 Kings 13

Paul Hedley Jones

LONDON • NEW YORK • OXFORD • NEW DELHI • SYDNEY

T&T CLARK
Bloomsbury Publishing Plc
50 Bedford Square, London, WC1B 3DP, UK
1385 Broadway, New York, NY 10018, USA
29 Earlsfort Terrace, Dublin 2, Ireland

BLOOMSBURY, T&T CLARK and the T&T Clark logo
are trademarks of Bloomsbury Publishing Plc

First published in Great Britain 2021
This paperback edition published 2022

Copyright © Paul Hedley Jones, 2021

Paul Hedley Jones has asserted his right under the Copyright, Designs and Patents Act, 1988, to be identified as Author of this work.

Cover design: Charlotte James

All rights reserved. No part of this publication may be reproduced or transmitted in any form or by any means, electronic or mechanical, including photocopying, recording, or any information storage or retrieval system, without prior permission in writing from the publishers.

Bloomsbury Publishing Plc does not have any control over, or responsibility for, any third-party websites referred to or in this book. All internet addresses given in this book were correct at the time of going to press. The author and publisher regret any inconvenience caused if addresses have changed or sites have ceased to exist, but can accept no responsibility for any such changes.

A catalogue record for this book is available from the British Library.
Library of Congress Control Number: 2019956638.

ISBN:	HB:	978-0-5676-9526-0
	PB:	978-0-5676-9962-6
	ePDF:	978-0-5676-9527-7

Series: Library of Hebrew Bible/Old Testament Studies, volume 704
ISSN 2513-8758

Typeset by: Forthcoming Publications Ltd

To find out more about our authors and books visit www.bloomsbury.com
and sign up for our newsletters.

For Anakatrina

Contents

Preface	ix
Acknowledgements	xi
Abbreviations	xiii

Chapter 1	
INTRODUCTION	1
Chapter 2	
KARL BARTH'S EXEGESIS OF 1 KINGS 13	11
Introduction	11
Form	14
The Elected/Rejected Status of the Two Prophets/Nations	16
Division of the Kingdoms	18
Prohibition of Fellowship between North and South	19
Genuine Dialogue between North and South	20
The Disobedience of the Man of God and of Judah	21
The Exilic 'Tomb' of the Prophets and of the Nations	22
Content	22
The Double-Picture on the Right	23
The Double-Picture on the Left	24
The Whole Picture: The Relation between Judah and Israel	25
Context	30
Barth's Hermeneutical Context	30
Barth's Doctrinal Context: Election	39
Summary of Barth's Contribution	48
1 Kings 13 as Narrative Analogy	48
Reading 1 Kings 13 Synchronically	48
Chapter 3	
MARTIN A. KLOPFENSTEIN	51
Klopfenstein's Evaluation of Barth's *Exegesis* (1966)	51
Zur Einzelexegese	53
Konfrontation und Würdigung	57
Klopfenstein's Impact upon Subsequent Scholarship	63

Chapter 4
SEVENTY YEARS OF SCHOLARSHIP — 67
- The Question of Genre — 69
- Variant Readings of 1 Kings 13 — 70
    - Discernment of True and False Prophecy: James Crenshaw (1971) — 77
    - The Efficacious Word of God: Jerome T. Walsh (1989, 1996) — 85
    - Anti-North Polemic: Van Seters (1999, 2000) — 93
    - Political Allegory: Roland Boer (1996, 1997) — 106
- Summary and Conclusions — 113

Chapter 5
HERMENEUTICAL AND METHODOLOGICAL ISSUES — 116
- Barth and Klopfenstein: Divergent Approaches to Scripture — 116
- Author-Hermeneutics and Text-Hermeneutics — 117
- Historical-Critical and Canonical Approaches — 121
- Synchronic and Diachronic Priorities — 130
- 'Scripture is' and 'scripture as' — 137

Chapter 6
BOSWORTH: REVISITING BARTH — 141
- David Bosworth: Revisiting Barth — 141
- 1 Kings 13 as *mise-en-abyme* (2008) — 144
    - (a) The Threefold Command — 147
    - (b) The Man of God Reneges — 147
    - (c) Role-reversal — 149
    - (d) The Lion — 149
    - (e) A Shared Grave — 150
- Appraisal of Bosworth — 150
- A Literary or Theological Analogy? — 151
- Christological Focus — 154
- *Mise-en-abyme* — 156

Chapter 7
ANONYMOUS PROPHETS AND ARCHETYPAL KINGS:
A LITERARY-THEOLOGICAL READING OF 1 KINGS 13 — 159
- Historical Frame of Reference — 160
- Literary and Theological Shaping — 163
- Literary Function — 165
    - The Framing of 1 Kings 13 — 166
    - The Function of 1 Kings 13 — 169
    - 1 Kings 13 as Opening Bookend — 172
- A Literary-Theological Reading of 1 Kings 13 — 181
    - 1 Kings 12.25-32 — 182
    - 1 Kings 12.33–13.5 — 184
    - 1 Kings 13.6-10 — 189

1 Kings 13.11-19	194
1 Kings 13.20-22	203
1 Kings 13.23-25	205
1 Kings 13.26-32	210
1 Kings 13.33-34	214
2 Kings 23.15-20	218
Conclusion: Anonymous Prophets and Archetypal Kings	221
Theological Context	222

Chapter 8
CONCLUSION 227
  Summary 227
  Implications 229
    (a) Hermeneutics 229
    (b) Literary Approaches 230
    (c) Redaction Criticism 230
    (d) Theology of the DH 232
    (e) Canonical Shaping 232
    (f) Figural Reading 233

Bibliography 235
Index of References 245
Index of Authors 250

Preface

Old Testament scholars often like to up the ante for their work by claiming that that particular part of the biblical text which they are studying is unusually difficult, maybe even one of the most difficult texts in the whole biblical canon. Whatever one makes of that recurrent trope, there can be little doubt that 1 Kings 13 really *is* one of the most difficult passages in the whole Old Testament, one that consistently baffles and bewilders readers in a way that few other passages do. What on earth is going on, and why is it here? Does it just show that the Old Testament is weird?

The biblical interpretations of Karl Barth elicit a wide range of responses, and their quality does indeed vary greatly. Yet reading Barth on 1 Kings 13 has been one of my memorable "aha" moments as a biblical scholar. His key insight is that the story is in some way a symbolic depiction of the history of the divided kingdoms of Israel and Judah, whose division has just been recounted in the previous chapter. Thus this strange story starts to make sense when it is taken as a particular way of seeing all that follows in 1 and 2 Kings. Moreover, it illustrates something of the deep theological logic of God's election of Israel and Judah as his people. Barth is so suggestive here that I had sometimes thought about trying to follow it up for myself; but I never managed to get round to it.

When Paul Jones decided that 1 Kings 13 would be a good focus for doctoral research he saw that Barth's insight was the appropriate starting point. It would of course need scrutiny in its own right, but nonetheless it offered the prospect of a fresh way of reading Kings in line with the priorities of those responsible for shaping and preserving the histories of the kingdoms. Jones has done all the necessary work not only in critical evaluation of Barth's insight but also in developing it in ways that stay closer to the world of the Old Testament text, and Old Testament scholarship, than Barth himself did. His work is exemplary for how one can learn from, criticise, and further develop a brilliant insight in a way that its original author could not, or would not. What Barth would have made of this reading of 1 Kings 13 I'm not sure, as he could be unpredictable. For myself, I find all Jones' key moves in reading 1 Kings 13 to be fully persuasive. He has made sense of this difficult biblical text in a way that no one else (whom I have read) has. I commend *Anonymous Prophets* as a model of what good Old Testament scholarship can look like.

Walter Moberly,
Abbey House,
Palace Green,
Durham

ACKNOWLEDGEMENTS

It's been almost ten years since I wandered unknowingly into the otherworldly forest of 1 Kings 13. When I commenced my PhD studies at Durham University under the supervision of Professor Walter Moberly, I naively expected to solve the riddle of this text within three years and emerge more or less unscathed. But as I examined the paths that previous interpreters had taken, it soon became apparent that there are a number of ways to navigate this unusual chapter, some leading to illuminated glades and others to brambled impasses. As it turns out, *Anonymous Prophets and Archetypal Kings* is as much about the importance of navigational and hermeneutical self-awareness as it is about the ultimate meaning of a certain story.

A number of organisations and individuals have encouraged and enabled this project. I am immensely grateful to the small charity organisation in NSW (who wish to remain anonymous) that sponsored a significant portion of my PhD expenses, and to Trinity College Queensland for funding a period of study leave that made it possible for me to revise my dissertation for publication. I was pleased to be able to finish the book in February 2020, just prior to our early (and rather hasty) return to Brisbane in response to Covid-19.

I am especially thankful for my supervisors, and I could not have hoped for better, given my interests in hermeneutics and theological interpretation of the Old Testament. I'm grateful for regular opportunities to converse with Richard Briggs over warm pints of English ale and a bowl of salted cashews. Whether we spoke of 1 Kings 13, hermeneutics, preaching, or family life, I always returned home with a fresh appreciation for Richard's humility, humour and wisdom. I am equally indebted to Walter Moberly, who remains an exemplar for me in so many ways. From his fervent spiritual life and deep sincerity to his punctilious academic mind, I have benefited so much simply from being around him. (To be perfectly honest, I continue to ask myself in challenging situations: 'What would Walter do?')

Finally, I am eternally grateful to my wife, Katy, whose friendship and encouragement have sustained me over the past twelve years in more ways than I can now recall, and to Sofi and Eden, our gorgeous daughters, who are yet to grasp what 'daddy's work' is really all about. To the three of you, all my thanks and love.

Paul Hedley Jones
Trinity College Queensland
Brisbane

ABBREVIATIONS

AB	Anchor Bible
ATANT	Abhandlungen zur Theologie des Alten und Neuen Testaments
BAT	Die Botschaft des Alten Testaments
BEThL	Bibliotheca Ephemeridum Theologicarum Lovaniensium
BHS	*Biblia hebraica stuttgartensia*
BibInt	Biblical Interpretation
BKAT	Biblisches Kommentar zum Alten Testament
BO	Berit Olam: Studies in Hebrew Narrative and Poetry
BZAW	Beihefte zur Zeitschrift für die alttestamentliche Wissenschaft
CBQ	*Catholic Biblical Quarterly*
CBQMS	Catholic Biblical Quarterly Monograph Series
CBR	*Currents in Biblical Research*
CD	The Church Dogmatics
DH	Deuteronomistic History (some scholars use DtrH)
Dtr	(the) Deuteronomist
EQ	*The Evangelical Quarterly*
ExAud	Ex Auditu
FAT	Forschungen zum Alten Testament
FOTL	Forms of the Old Testament Literature
FRLANT	Forschungen zur Religion und Literatur des Alten und Neuen Testaments
HSM	Harvard Semitic Monographs
HTR	*Harvard Theological Review*
HUCA	*Hebrew Union College Annual*
Int	*Interpretation*
ITC	International Theological Commentary
JBL	*Journal of Biblical Literature*
JESOT	*Journal for the Evangelical Study of the Old Testament*
JETS	*Journal of the Evangelical Theological Society*
JPS	Jewish Publication Society
JSOT	*Journal for the Study of the Old Testament*
JSOTSup	Journal for the Study of the Old Testament, Supplement Series
JTI	*Journal of Theological Interpretation*
KD	Die Kirchliche Dogmatik
LHBOTS	Library of Hebrew Bible/Old Testament Studies
LXX	Septuagint
MT	Masoretic Text

NASB	New American Standard Bible
NCBC	New Century Bible Commentary
NIB	New Interpreter's Bible
NIBC	New International Biblical Commentary
NICOT	New International Commentary on the Old Testament
NIV	New International Version
NRSV	New Revised Standard Version
OBT	Overtures to Biblical Theology
OTL	Old Testament Library
SAT	Die Schriften des Alten Testaments
SBL	Studies in Biblical Literature
SBTS	Sources for Biblical and Theological Study
SemeiaSt	Semeia Studies
SJOT	*Scandinavian Journal of the Old Testament*
TB	*Tyndale Bulletin*
Them	*Themelios*
TOTC	Tyndale Old Testament Commentaries
VT	*Vetus Testamentum*
VTSup	Vetus Testamentum, Supplement Series
WBC	Word Biblical Commentary
WUNT	Wissenschaftliche Untersuchungen zum Neuen Testament
ZAW	*Zeitschrift für die alttestamentliche Wissenschaft*

Private Collection © Look and Learn/Bridgeman Images.

1

INTRODUCTION

I was given this bit of advice when I commenced my doctoral studies: 'If you want to keep your friends, don't talk to them about your area of research. More importantly, do not – *under any circumstances* – discuss your research with your spouse!' I soon discovered that there was a degree of wisdom in that counsel, perhaps the voice of experience. However, I also distinctly remember that when my wife was suffering from some insomnia during that time, she asked me late one night to tell her all about my research... Generally speaking, however, when anyone mustered the courage to inquire about my studies, I sought to keep things light-hearted by responding in this way: 'Well, have you heard the one about two prophets, a donkey and a lion...?' This retort became something of a standing joke (at least to me), but it also become clear over the course of writing my dissertation that there is a sense in which this may be just the right question to ask. For whatever the nature of one's engagement with the strange story in 1 Kings 13, the question of whether one has really *heard* it, for all it has to say, is an important one.

Karl Barth is well known for stressing the importance of fully hearing the biblical text. While he acknowledged that historical reconstructions of the world behind the text are of some merit, Barth urged interpreters to press beyond this 'preparatory' phase in order that all of the words and details of the received text may be properly heard in accordance with their *Sache*.[1] This, in turn, raises a critical question, since one of the biggest challenges faced by interpreters of 1 Kings 13 has been precisely that of

---

1. On Barth's emphasis on *hearing* as a Spirit-superintended activity, see Karl Barth, *Church Dogmatics I.1: The Doctrine of the Word of God*, trans. G. T. Thomson (Edinburgh: T. & T. Clark, 1936), 183; also Richard E. Burnett, *Karl Barth's Theological Exegesis: The Hermeneutical Principles of the* Römerbrief *Period* (Grand Rapids: Eerdmans, 2001), 62–4, 239.

determining the story's primary subject matter, or *Sache*. Indeed, the only consensus scholars appear to have reached is that the story is 'strange'[2] and 'enigmatic'[3] in character. Almost every detail concerning both the composition and the meaning of the narrative remains contested.

Is 1 Kings 13 a 'prophetic story', based on two distinct narratives (Würthwein) or just one (DeVries)? Is it illustrative of the prophetic office (Klopfenstein) or the inexorable word of God (Long)? Is it a prophetic legend that establishes the criteria (Dozeman), or lack thereof (Crenshaw), for discerning between true and false prophets? In terms of its literary value, is 1 Kings 13 'a fairly crass piece of anti-Samaritan religious propaganda constructed with little narrative skill or sensitivity to religious and moral issues' (Van Seters),[4] or, given its literary context, does this tale of two anonymous, prophetic figures from north and south provide a subtle and sophisticated commentary on the division of the kingdom (Barth)? Even these few questions reveal considerable variance in the queries and aims interpreters bring to 1 Kings 13. Consequently, as one might expect, studies of the narrative have produced wide-ranging results.

It is largely due to my own interests that what follows is an interdisciplinary study engaging with the theological exegesis of Karl Barth, narrative-critical method, and contemporary hermeneutics. My aim in this book is to present a coherent reading of 1 Kings 13 that is attentive to literary, historical, and theological issues and that does not preclude insights from any sub-discipline. Most obviously, this requires a detailed exegesis of the text and engagement with a variety of other interpreters. But it is also my intention that this study reflect a significant degree of self-consciousness regarding the interpretive aims, hermeneutical assumptions, and theological priorities that undergird and support various readings, including the one put forth here in Chapter 7. But before I outline the contents of this book, let us consider the narrative of 1 Kings 13 and its epilogue (2 Kgs 23.15-20) in brief outline:

> In Bethel, King Jeroboam is about to make a sacrifice on an altar of his own making when suddenly a man of God from Judah appears 'by the word of the LORD'. The man of God prophesies not against the king, but directly against the altar, naming Josiah as a future Judean king who will sacrifice

---

2. Gene Rice, *1 Kings: Nations Under God*, ITC (Grand Rapids: Eerdmans, 1990), 110.

3. Walter Brueggemann, *1 & 2 Kings* (Macon, GA: Smyth & Helwys, 2000), 167.

4. John Van Seters, 'On Reading the Story of the Man of God from Judah in 1 Kings 13', in *The Labour of Reading: Desire, Alienation, and Biblical Interpretation*, ed. Robert C. Culley et al. (Atlanta: Scholars Press, 1999), 233.

priests of the high places on the very same altar. Offended by the prophetic oracle, Jeroboam reaches his hand out towards the intruder and commands his men to 'seize him!' The hand of the king withers immediately. The man of God from Judah is then asked to intercede, which he does, and the king's hand is immediately restored to him. For whatever reason, the king then invites the man of God to eat with him, whereupon the man of God reveals that he is under a threefold, divine prohibition: 'For thus I was commanded by the word of the LORD: You shall not eat food, or drink water, or return by the way that you came' (v. 9). The man of God leaves Bethel in obedience to the divine command, such that the first part of the story (vv. 1-10) is more or less resolved.

The plot thickens in v. 11 with the introduction of an old prophet in Bethel who hears of these events from his sons and sets his heart on tricking the man of God into disobedience. (His motive for doing so is not made explicit.[5]) He sets out in pursuit of the Judean man of God on his donkey and, upon finding him under 'the oak', offers the same invitation that King Jeroboam had done. The man of God initially responds just as he had to Jeroboam, holding fast to the divine decree, but the Bethelite prophet deceives him, claiming that an angel has more recently given a contrary word. The man of God is taken in by the ruse and he returns to the Bethelite prophet's house to eat and drink. It is there that the story takes an unexpected turn.

Having successfully duped the man of God, the Bethelite prophet receives a genuine word of prophecy: 'Thus says the LORD: Because you have disobeyed the word of the LORD, and have not kept the commandment that the LORD your God commanded you, but have come back and have eaten food and drunk water in the place of which he said to you, "Eat no food, and drink no water", your body shall not come to your ancestral tomb' (vv. 21-22). The man of God leaves and is promptly killed by a lion, which consumes neither the dead man's corpse nor his donkey. What's more, the lion remains standing with the donkey near the dead man of God – a sight which captures the attention of passers-by (v. 25). When news of the strange sight reaches the Bethel prophet, he offers up an explanation: 'It is the man of God who disobeyed the word of the LORD; therefore the LORD has given him to the lion, which has torn him and killed him according to the word that the LORD spoke to him' (v. 26).

Once again, the prophet from Bethel sets out on a donkey (apparently he owned at least two of them) to find the man of God. Having done so, he returns to Bethel with the corpse of the Judean and buries him in his own grave. He mourns over the man of God and requests that he himself

---

5. See my 'Deceiving the Man of God from Judah: A Question of Motive', in *Characters and Characterization in the Book of Kings*, ed. Keith Bodner and Benjamin J. M. Johnson (London: T&T Clark, 2020), 83–102.

be buried alongside him in the course of time. The Bethel prophet then confirms the Judean's prophecy from the beginning of the story (regarding the destruction of the altar in Bethel), but adds to it 'all the high places of Samaria' as well (v. 32).

The concluding verses return the focus to King Jeroboam, who, in spite of 'this thing' (הדבר הזה) – whether the prophecy, the sign, or indeed, the entire saga between the two prophets – does not return from his evil way but goes on appointing priests from among the people. The narrator's final words in v. 34 are conclusive in their judgment; 'This matter became sin to the house of Jeroboam, so as to cut it off and to destroy it from the face of the earth'.

Three hundred years later, after acquainting himself with the recently discovered Book of the Law, King Josiah proceeds to tear down numerous places of idolatry and false worship around Jerusalem before also heading north to Bethel. There he destroys the altar that was built by Jeroboam son of Nebat and burns bones from local tombs upon it in order to defile it. In doing so (and apparently without realising it), Josiah acts according to the word of the LORD spoken by the man of God from Judah.

Seeing the tomb in which the man of God was buried, Josiah asks about its significance (presumably, it had been marked in some way), and the inhabitants of Bethel explain to him, 'It is the tomb of the man of God who came from Judah and predicted these things that you have done against the altar at Bethel' (2 Kgs 23.17b). Josiah then commands that the bones in this particular tomb be left alone, and consequently, the bones of both 'the man of God who came from Judah' and 'the prophet who came from Samaria' are left undisturbed.

From there, Josiah proceeds to 'all the cities of Samaria', doing to them as he had done in Bethel and thereby fulfilling the old Bethelite's amplification of the prophecy (1 Kgs 13.32) in addition to the man of God's original decree against the altar (1 Kgs 13.2). Josiah removes the high places, sacrifices the high priests upon their altars, and defiles them before returning to Jerusalem (2 Kgs 23.20).

Arguably the best-known interpretation of 1 Kings 13 with a distinctively theological accent is the one presented by Karl Barth in his *Church Dogmatics* II.2.[6] Although Barth's interpretation remains one of the most evocative, it was not well-received by his contemporaries, largely because his methodology and the critical questions that he brought to the text

---

6. Karl Barth, *Church Dogmatics II.2: The Doctrine of God*, trans. G. W. Bromiley et al. (Edinburgh: T. & T. Clark, 1957), 393–410. Translated from *Die Kirchliche Dogmatik II; Die Lehre von Gott 2* (Zollikon-Zürich: Evangelischer Verlag A.G., 1942), 424–53. References hereafter are to the English translation (*CD*), unless reference is made to the original German (*KD*).

were deemed inappropriate. Our study begins in Chapter 2 with a detailed examination and appraisal of Barth's exegesis, first published (in German) in 1947.

Barth's sophisticated analysis establishes and elucidates a pair of *Doppelbildern* (double-pictures), through which he accentuates a reciprocal dynamic between the man of God and the Bethel prophet in 1 Kings 13 that is also reflected in the mutual interdependence of Judah (the elect) and Israel (the rejected) in the ensuing history. Like other dyads in the Old Testament (Abel and Cain; Isaac and Ishmael; Jacob and Esau; Leah and Rachel; David and Saul; Judah and Israel), Barth argues that the anonymous prophets of 1 Kings 13 present a clear illustration – perhaps even the clearest – of God's differentiating election. For the division of the kingdom is perceived as the culmination of a series of moments and relationships in Israel's history that stress the theme of distinction-within-unity, uniquely expounded 'in title-form' in 1 Kings 13. Thus, in Barth's view, the two anonymous – and morally ambiguous – prophetic figures (together with their corresponding kings) are representatives of Israel and Judah divided, and yet, paradoxically, this internal distinction in God's people is a necessary step towards God's eschatological will for the *union* of the elect and rejected, which is fully made known in Christ.[7]

For a proper understanding of Barth's exegesis, it is necessary not only to explore the doctrinal context (election) of Barth's treatment of 1 Kings 13, but also to understand certain hermeneutical conventions that characterise Barth's work – notably, intertextuality, synchrony and Christology. Therefore, each of these is explored in Chapter 2 with reference to Barth's theological exegesis of the story.

The first scholar to seriously engage with Barth's exegesis was Martin Klopfenstein, whose criticisms had long-lasting impact. Klopfenstein's lengthy engagement with Barth is therefore assessed in Chapter 3, where we explore the methodological divergence between Barth's overtly theological interpretation and Klopfenstein's (strictly) historical-critical approach. Klopfenstein offers his own detailed exegetical treatment of 1 Kings 13, but he also clearly sets out his 'main question…namely, whether the text itself proves Barth right in understanding [1 Kgs 13] as a witness for God's electing and rejecting, rejecting and electing, and their peculiar juxtaposition'.[8] Klopfenstein is especially critical of Barth's

---

7. Barth, *CD* II.2, 403.
8. M.A. Klopfenstein, '1. Könige 13', in *ΠΑΡΡΗΣΙΑ: K. Barth zum achtzigsten Geburtstag*, ed. E. Busch, J. Fangmeier, and M. Geiger (Zurich: EVZ-Verlag Zurich, 1966), 667.

delineation of a series of (five) reversals in the story that are indicative of the interdependence of Israel and Judah within his theological schema. Rather, Klopfenstein makes the 'purely *exegetical* objection' (rein *exegetisch* einzuwenden) that the narrative contains a *single* turning point (in v. 20).[9] The same concern, i.e. the introduction of external categories, lies behind Klopfenstein's disagreements with Barth's *Überinterpretation* of the lion and the shared grave as well. But while Klopfenstein is critical of Barth for imposing a dialectical scheme of thought into his interpretation, he nonetheless ultimately agrees that election is an important theme for understanding the narrative, and he commends Barth for the theological accent of his exposition. In spite of any positive remarks in closing, however, it would appear that the negative criticisms of Klopfenstein (and subsequently, of Noth) had a marked detrimental impact upon subsequent scholarship, especially upon those who share the methodological priorities of Klopfenstein's historical-critical approach.

Chapter 4 reviews the past seventy years of scholarship, from Barth's exegesis (1947) through to the present (2019). In order to show that different readings emerge from distinct inquiries and their associated methodologies, I group scholars into four categories, based on their determination of the story's primary subject, and scrutinise one example from each category. The categories are these: (i) *the discernment of true and false prophecy* (Crenshaw); (ii) *the efficacious word of God* (Walsh); (iii) *anti-north polemic* (Van Seters); and (iv) *political allegory* (Boer).

James Crenshaw's reading of 1 Kings 13 addresses the issue of *prophetic discernment* within a larger work[10] that seeks to explain the decline and demise of prophecy in Israel. Crenshaw begins with a psychological consideration of the phenomenon of prophecy and argues for a particular sociological perspective regarding ancient Israel's deteriorating attitude towards prophecy. He uses selected phrases and elements of 1 Kings 13 to support his theses, though I argue that as a whole (when select phrases are not extracted from the whole to suit a particular purpose) 1 Kings 13 does not actually address the issue of prophetic discernment.

Jerome Walsh understands the narrative to promote *obedience to the inexorable word of God*, and his essays and books are of special interest for their deliberation upon hermeneutical questions. Walsh reads 1 Kings 13 within three different contexts – 'as two self-contained narratives, as a component of the story of Jeroboam, and as an element in

---

9. Klopfenstein, '1. Könige 13', 668 (emphasis original).
10. James L. Crenshaw, *Prophetic Conflict: Its Effect Upon Israelite Religion* (Berlin: de Gruyter, 1971).

the Deuteronomistic History of the two kingdoms'[11] – to ascertain how shifting literary horizons impact upon meaning. The exercise is illuminating, as one might expect, and Walsh's narrative-critical insights are characteristically sharp, though I think he leans rather too heavily on certain structural patterns that he identifies as being 'fundamental to the text'.[12]

Van Seters treats 1 Kings 13 as an *anti-north polemic*, albeit one that is difficult to understand because its post-Deuteronomistic author is literarily incompetent. He identifies sixteen problematic elements in the story in an effort to show that 1 Kings 13 (and 2 Kgs 23.15-20) 'is incoherent throughout'.[13] Moreover, because of this incoherence, Van Seters warns against drawing theological or moral lessons from 1 Kings 13. I address these sixteen problems and argue that they are much less disconcerting than Van Seters suggests. In a second essay, he focuses on the redaction seams around 1 Kings 13 and addresses the purpose of redaction-criticism. At the same time, he endeavours to disprove Cross's double-redaction theory by arguing that 1 Kings 13 was composed in the exilic period and that Josiah's reforms never actually occurred in Bethel and Samaria. These issues are addressed further in Chapter 5.

Finally, Roland Boer reads 1 Kings 13 as a *political allegory*. He identifies tensions within the narrative as pointers to broader ideological concerns. Thus, within a framework that highlights the reliability of the divine word (*viz.* 1 Kgs 11–14), 1 Kings 13 sows doubt with a contradictory word from a deceptive 'brother' so that the Deuteronomistic theme of prophecy–fulfilment is brought under fire. In addition, via the themes of hospitality and the threefold command, the narrative simultaneously legitimates the North and undermines divine favour upon the South. These elements of conflict in the narrative offer an imaginary resolution to the perplexing co-existence of North and South in Israel.[14] Overall, Boer's reading strategy is impressively self-aware and yields counter-intuitive insights.

I conclude Chapter 4 with some observations about how each of these interpreters utilises methods that suit their particular questions or issues. Perhaps, in theory, this is to be expected, but it is interesting nonetheless – and instructive – to see this pattern unfold. The survey of approaches and

---

11. Jerome T. Walsh, 'The Contexts of 1 Kings XIII', *VT* 39 (1989): 355–70.
12. Walsh, 'Contexts', 369.
13. Van Seters, 'On Reading', 230.
14. Roland Boer, *Jameson and Jeroboam*, Semeia Studies (Atlanta: Scholars Press, 1996), 174.

methods in Chapter 4 paves the way for a more theoretical discussion in Chapter 5 regarding some hermeneutical dichotomies that tend to surface regularly in disputes about biblical exegesis. These are: author- and text-hermeneutics; historical-critical and canonical approaches; and synchronic or diachronic priorities.

These three dichotomies are explored with reference to the exegetical works discussed in previous chapters. My purpose is neither to pigeon-hole nor polarise the interpreters under scrutiny, but rather to stress the importance of self-consciously locating one's work within a particular set of concerns or angle of enquiry, so that meaningful conversation may ensue. The point, at least in part, is that textual, historical, and theological issues can be resolved in different ways, depending on what drives the project: a precise date may or may not affect one's interpretation of a text; redaction-criticism can be utilised to understand the text in its final form or as a means of retrieving a core work; what one reader sees as a narrative gap to be filled, another sees as evidence of disparate source materials; and so on and so forth. Hermeneutical issues such as these are discussed in an effort to show that the dichotomisation of differing approaches is, in many cases, neither helpful nor necessary. One's approach generally serves one's interpretive interests. Ultimately, I concur with Richard Briggs' observation that many (though not all) divisive issues can be resolved by learning to speak of 'scripture *as...*' rather than bluntly insisting on what 'scripture *is*'.[15]

Having reviewed methodological differences and their implications for interpretation, we turn in Chapter 6 to the work of David Bosworth, a recent interpreter who has sought to assimilate Barth's reading within contemporary, mainstream scholarship. His project is evaluated in light of its goal: to advocate and support Barth's exegesis. Bosworth's reading is certainly interesting and worthwhile, albeit less consistent with Barth's enterprise than he perhaps recognises. Bosworth leaves the theme of election aside and refrains from christological interpretation, and although he draws on Barth's multiple reversals, he interprets them in a way that is more literary and chronological than theological. Bosworth's angle of enquiry is thus quite original, and his understanding of 1 Kings 13 as a *mise-en-abyme* proves illuminating and provocative.

---

15. Richard S. Briggs, 'Biblical Hermeneutics and Scriptural Responsibility', in *The Future of Biblical Interpretation: Responsible Plurality in Biblical Hermeneutics*, ed. Stanley E. Porter and Matthew R. Malcolm (Milton Keynes: Paternoster, 2013), 36–52.

Finally, in Chapter 7 I offer my own interpretation of 1 Kings 13, drawing on certain key observations made by Barth while resisting other aspects of his interpretation. In response to Barth's final question about 1 Kings 13 – 'Where else is its fulfilment to be found if not in Jesus Christ?' – my answer is 'Josiah'. That is to say, I conclude that the narrative's function and meaning may be understood within an Old Testament (or more particularly, a Deuteronomistic) frame of reference rather than seeing Christ as the story's only conceivable *telos*. One of my main criticisms of Barth's reading is that he identifies 2 Kgs 23.15-20 as the 'epilogue' of the story in 1 Kings 13, but then fails to actually develop this, preferring instead to resolve the theological tension in the narrative by pointing to Easter. Of course, readers are free to choose the contextual parameters for interpreting (as stated above), but in this instance Barth appears to deviate from his own stated hermeneutical pattern of remaining within the Old Testament world unless no resolution can there be found.[16]

I find that reading 1 Kings 13 as a narrative analogy and through a 'Josianic lens' not only accentuates the thematic priorities of the Deuteronomist (Dtr) throughout the history of the kingdoms, but also untangles much of the complexity of 1 Kings 13 in particular. My literary-theological reading of 1 Kings 13 takes seriously the analogical dimension of the text, and interprets the chapter as a proleptic parable that anticipates Josiah of Judah as the ideological antithesis of Jeroboam I of Israel. Represented by two anonymous prophetic figures, these two archetypal kings are juxtaposed in the narrative in a way that accents the theological significance of their actions as national leaders. In this sense, 1 Kings 13 is found to have both a retrospective and a prospective function, not unlike Dtr's speeches, as per Wellhausen and Noth. Moreover, the reading proffered in Chapter 7 recognises that the hopeful denouement of 1 Kings 13 is of significance for Deuteronomistic theology. Even the unjust death of the man of God from Judah (preempting the tragic death of Josiah) leads to a hopeful portent of reunification as the Judean man of God and the Samarian prophet together await the fulfilment of their shared prophecy concerning the end of cultic malpractice and the coming of a Davidic scion.

What, then, is the ultimate value of this study? Broadly speaking, it provides a model for how one might engage hermeneutically with a troublesome Old Testament narrative, using 1 Kings 13 as a case study. Many of my findings have wider application and will, I hope, prove useful for students and scholars seeking reading strategies for other perplexing

---

16. E.g., Barth, *CD II.2*, 389 (see the discussion in Chapter 2).

Old Testament texts. Although my interpretation of 1 Kings 13 borrows elements from Barth's overtly theological construal of the text, I have sought to remain within the literary world depicted by Dtr. The reading in Chapter 7 is thereby demonstrative of an interpretive method that sustains interest in theological motifs such as prophecy, covenant fidelity, leadership, and hope, without failing to also account for the author's historical frame of reference and the literary shape of the whole. To put it otherwise, this work seeks to demonstrate that insights garnered from literary, historical, and theological methodologies can be harnessed and brought together to expound a given text.

As for my conclusions, I have sought to highlight the literary *function* of 1 Kings 13 (as a narrative analogy) within the larger corpus rather than identifying a particular moral to the story, as many scholars have done. My reading thereby opens the door for comparable texts to also be interpreted as narrative analogies; i.e. as seemingly independent stories that provide commentary on their wider literary contexts (e.g., Judg. 9; 1 Sam. 25; 1 Kgs 20). Related to this, my reading of 1 Kings 13 as an 'opening bookend' to the history of the divided kingdom has significance for synchronic studies of Dtr's historiographical and ideological peculiarities, as well as for diachronic studies of redaction theories pertaining to the Deuteronomic History (DH). That is to say, the interpretation of 1 Kings 13 offered here is relevant to readers with an interest in literary-structural studies of the DH in its received form, as well as those interested in the compositional history of these books. But we shall return to these observations in the eighth and final chapter, where the implications of this study are spelt out in greater detail.

2

Karl Barth's Exegesis of 1 Kings 13

Introduction

Karl Barth, who describes 1 Kings 13 as 'the richest and most comprehensive prophetic story in the Old Testament',[1] interprets the story as an 'illustration of the differentiating [*unterscheidende*] election of God'.[2] His exegesis of the passage appears in volume II.2 of his *Church Dogmatics* in concert with two other Old Testament texts that also illustrate the doctrine of election: the sacrificial animals in Leviticus 14 and 16, and Israel's elected and rejected kings, David and Saul. Significantly, Barth does not understand 1 Kings 13 to be about prophecy per se. Rather, in his judgment, the 'peculiar theme of the chapter is the manner in which the man of God and the prophet belong together, do not belong together, and eventually and finally do belong together; and how the same is true of Judah and Israel'.[3] That is to say, the man of God and the Bethel prophet are perceived by Barth as representative figures for their respective kingdoms, and the primary subject of the narrative is the reciprocal nature of their relationship. Moreover, in light of its literary context – 1 Kings 13 immediately follows the division of Israel as a divine response to Solomon's idolatry – Barth understood the self-contained narrative to illuminate the record of the divided kingdom that follows. Again, citing Barth: 'In view of the context of 1 K. 13, we are almost tempted to say...that the prophetic problem is raised only in order to illustrate the problem of the kingdoms, and therefore that it is only a background to that problem'.[4]

---

1. Barth, *CD* II.2, 409.
2. *CD* II.2, 393 (*KD* II.2, §35, 434).
3. Ibid.
4. Ibid., 399.

Although the majority of biblical scholars appear to have largely ignored Barth's exegesis of this passage, a significant few have critically engaged with it,[5] and some have even sought to develop his ideas.[6] According to Brevard Childs,

> major credit goes to Karl Barth, who in his exegesis…first opened up the real theological dimension of the biblical text. He observed at the outset the paradigmatic significance of the chapter's being placed at the division of the two kingdoms in order to function almost as a superscription for the remaining history of the divided kingdom. He also correctly noted that the story is not merely about two prophets, but relates to far larger theological issues.[7]

Barth's exegesis of 1 Kings 13 first appeared in his *Kirchliche Dogmatik* II.2 (1942)[8] under the heading of election, and was published again as a stand-alone piece as volume 10 of *Biblischer Studien* (1955), with an adulatory foreword by Hans-Joachim Kraus.[9] The English translation of *Church Dogmatics* II.2 was then published in 1957. In order to elucidate the substantive content of the passage, Barth begins by dividing the story into five sections and an epilogue. A taut summary of his analysis is offered here in order to highlight certain accents in his reading. We shall then give full consideration to his exegesis below.

> vv. 1-5:
> The Judean man of God comes to Bethel and denounces Jeroboam's false worship in the strongest terms. The king, who stands 'at the head of his unlawful priesthood' (394), seeks to arrest him and loses control of his hand.
>
> vv. 6-10:
> Jeroboam is surprised at this demonstration of power and asks to be restored, but when the man of God complies, Jeroboam understands the healing of his withered hand to suggest 'a cancellation of the threat of judgment that had

---

5. See the discussion of Klopfenstein in Chapter 3.
6. David Bosworth is the most notable exception in this regard; see Chapter 6.
7. Brevard Childs, *Old Testament Theology in a Canonical Context* (Philadelphia: Fortress, 1985), 142. In spite of this endorsement, Childs does not develop Barth's notion of election as the 'real theological dimension' of 1 Kings 13. Rather, he understands the narrative to offer 'a theocentric perspective' concerning 'the fulfilment of God's word of judgment which will not tolerate any softening or compromise' (143).
8. Barth, *Die Kirchliche Dogmatik II*, 424–53.
9. Karl Barth, 'Exegese von 1. Könige 13', in *Biblische Studien, Heft 10*, ed. H.-J. Kraus (Neukirchen-Vluyn: Neukirchener Verlag, 1955), 12–56.

been pronounced' (394). In his mind, 'amicable compromise' (394) becomes a real possibility. But the Judean man of God's commission explicitly forbids him fellowship with anyone at Bethel.

vv. 11-19:
'The conflict itself emerges in the third section (vv. 11-19)' (395), where the 'professional' prophet of Bethel, upon hearing about the altercation, takes up Jeroboam's cause. As Barth puts it, the Bethel prophet 'takes the place of the king in relation to the stranger's word' (395). His pursuit of the man of God suggests that 'he has perceived the importance of the refusal given to Jeroboam...and that he is determined to reverse it at any price' (395) because 'he has grasped the fact that for the greater Israel everything depends upon ending this emphatic refusal by Judah in the name of God, and upon bringing about the fellowship between Jerusalem and Bethel, the toleration and compromise, which had been the goal of Jeroboam's invitation' (395). At the end of v. 18, 'the whole issue now rests on a razor's edge' (395), for there are two purported words from the LORD, and obedience to either one necessitates infringement of the other.

vv. 20-26:
In the fourth section, the liar from Bethel becomes God's harbinger of truth, and the Judean man of God 'is put to death because he made a peace which God did not will and had not made...God did not intend peace between Jerusalem and Bethel' (397).[10]

vv. 27-32:
This reversal of roles is not the end, however. After fetching the Judean's body and making arrangements to be buried with him, the Bethel prophet proceeds to affirm the very word spoken 'against himself and the cause which he represents' (397), explicitly reiterating the man of God's prophecy and including also the high places in Samaria (13.32). Barth suggests that he does so to secure his own preservation in his (shared) grave when the Judean's prophecy is fulfilled three centuries later.

vv. 33-34:
The 'provisional epilogue' links these events back to Jeroboam so that the strange sequence of events explains why Jeroboam's house was cut off from the face of the earth. But the 'real epilogue', says Barth, is found in 2 Kgs 23.15-20, where Josiah fulfils the prophecy in detail (397).[11]

---

10. Similarly, Jerome T. Walsh, *1 Kings*, Berit Olam (Collegeville, MN: Liturgical Press, 1996), 203: 'The political separation of Judah and Israel is acceptable; religious schism of the two territories is not'.

11. Despite Barth's reference to 2 Kgs 23.15-20 as 'the real epilogue' to 1 Kgs 13, he declines to offer an exegetical treatment of these verses. I will have more to say about this.

The theological context of election for Barth's exegetical treatment of the passage is vital, and will be examined below. But first, let us consider Barth's analysis of the *form* and *content* of this perplexing story.

Form

Barth's exegesis of 1 Kings 13 sidesteps the priorities of historical-critical enquiry, as was his wont, and suggests rather that the chapter serves, together with a range of other Old Testament texts, to elucidate the theme of election. No claims are made regarding the authorship or origins of 1 Kings 13. Barth is content simply to offer a few general remarks about the chapter's apparent redaction as 'a fragment of ancient tradition':

> The passage appears to be drawn from another source than its context. This can hardly be the same, but it is perhaps similar to the Elisha-cycle at the beginning of 2 Kings…the parallels to the Book of Amos are so remarkable and distinctive that it is not impossible that what we have here – not in form, but in substance – is a fragment of ancient tradition concerning the nature of the Israelite prophet and the relationship between the two Israelite kingdoms.[12]

According to Barth, the story in 1 Kings 13 was adopted from a distinct source and inserted where it now stands as a reflection on 'the nature of the Israelite prophet and the relationship between the two Israelite kingdoms'. Thus, Barth's few comments on the origins of this narrative are consistent with the findings of contemporary scholarship.

In spite of the fact that the story's main characters are both prophets, Barth avers that the narrative is not about prophecy per se. Nor is it about Jeroboam in particular, nor even the cult established at Bethel. Rather, one of Barth's most striking exegetical contributions is his suggestion that the northern prophet and the man of God from the south represent the kingdoms whence they come. Thus, while Barth interprets the narrative on its own terms and reads it with full, imaginative seriousness as a story about the interplay between two prophets, he consistently has in mind the implications of this reciprocity for the nations represented. He therefore posits that tensions in the narrative between the northern and southern prophets are mere reflections, or indicators, of the real issue: the nature of the relationship between Israel and Judah.

---

12. *CD* II.2, 393. Klopfenstein notes that Barth leaves the question of dating open ('1. Könige 13', 641). Regarding Barth's introductory words cited above, Klopfenstein writes, 'In these two sentences, Barth obviously summarised what emerged to him as the result of studying academic commentaries' (ibid., 640, my translation)

> When we consider the complex nature of this story we may well ask, but cannot decide, what the real problem is. Is it the contrast between the real man of God and the man of the prophetic guild, or is it between the realms of Judah and Israel? – for both problems are so interwoven in the story that we obviously have to consider both in order to understand it. Unmistakably, the prophetic problem is in the foreground. But the problem of the two kingdoms is undeniably more than merely accessory to it. In view of the context of 1 K. 13, we are almost tempted to say the opposite, that the prophetic problem is raised only in order to illustrate the problem of the kingdoms, and therefore that it is only a background to that problem.[13]

Barth assumes an apparent conflict 'between professional and original prophets'.[14] However, he says relatively little about it since any tension relating to (true or false) prophecy is thought only to accentuate the primary issue of political distinction. In his view, it is *the nature of the relationship between north and south* that is in focus, as it appears in 1 Kings 13 'in title-form' and then also in 'the whole ensuing history of the two separated kingdoms of Israel'.[15] This foundational insight concerning the function of 1 Kings 13 – that the text be read as what might now be called a *narrative analogy*[16] – has been accepted and appropriated by subsequent biblical scholars to a much greater extent than Barth's emphasis on election.[17] What Barth ultimately proposes is that the distinction made in the narrative between the Bethelite prophet of the north and the man of God from Judah is not primarily intended to identify one as illegitimate and the other as legitimate, but rather to illustrate the interdependence of both the Elect and Rejected as equally requisite parts of the one, true Israel.

13. *CD* II.2, 397–8.
14. Ibid., 404. Barth's distinction 'between professional and original prophets' is not well supported in Kings. In 1 Kgs 13, the commissioned (authentic) man of God disobeys and the lying (professional) prophet in Bethel speaks a genuine word of prophecy. More broadly, in the history of the divided kingdoms, much attention is paid to the legitimacy of northern prophets such as Elijah, Elisha, and Micaiah, which calls into question Barth's labelling of northern prophets as 'professional', 'institutional' and 'false'. See Chapter 4 under 'Discernment of True and False Prophecy'.
15. Ibid., 403.
16. Robert Alter, *The Art of Biblical Narrative* (New York: Basic Books, 1981), speaks of 'narrative analogy, through which one part of the text provides oblique commentary on another' (21; cf. 180). See Chapter 7 under 'The Function of 1 Kings 13'.
17. See esp. Peter Leithart, *1 & 2 Kings*, Brazos Theological Commentary on the Bible (Grand Rapids, MI: Brazos, 2006); Walsh, *1 Kings*; David A. Bosworth, *The Story within a Story in Biblical Hebrew Narrative*, CBQMS 45 (Washington: Catholic Biblical Association of America, 2008).

The representative function of these prophetic figures segues directly into Barth's profound theological argument concerning the nature of election because, for Barth, the issue of form is intrinsically linked to the question of *Sache*.

Having established that the two prophets serve representative roles within the narrative, Barth proceeds to describe how the dynamics between the prophets in 1 Kings 13 are analogous to the dynamics between the nations in the history of the divided kingdom. In Barth's terms, 1 Kings 13 'constitutes a kind of heading'[18] over the history of the kingdoms, highlighting numerous points of connection between 1 Kings 13 and the broader history that follows. The parallels are not set out as a sequence of events in the shorter narrative that correspond chronologically with the history of the kingdoms, nor can they easily be tied to specific texts within the book of Kings. They are more general and theological in nature. Some of the more salient points are the following:

The Elected/Rejected Status of the Two Prophets/Nations

The first and most obvious feature of Barth's proposal is that each representative prophet shares his elected or rejected status with a kingly figure (mentioned by name) and a corresponding nation. As Barth pictures it, we see on the right 'the man of God from Judah, with the figure of Josiah at a distance behind him: authentic, divinely commissioned prophecy, as a representative of the authentic Davidic monarchy and kingdom'.[19] In sum: man of God; Josiah; Judah. Conversely, on the left is the Bethel prophet, Jeroboam, and Israel – described by Barth as 'the people who have rejected God as their king'.[20] Moreover, Barth claims that 'it is the prophet of Bethel, and not the king, who is the real representative of this dark kingdom'.[21]

This stark dichotomy in Barth's interpretation applies not only to the particular kings and prophets mentioned in 1 Kings 13, but also to the north and the south in a more general sense. That is, the elected and rejected status of the prophets (together with their respective kings and nations) correlate with authentic or professional prophecy. The man of God represents not only the elect nation of Judah, but as we noted above, 'authentic, divinely commissioned prophecy'.[22] Conversely, the Bethel prophet is consistently labelled 'professional' (in a pejorative sense),

18. *CD* II.2, 403.
19. Ibid., 398.
20. Ibid., 400.
21. Ibid.
22. Ibid., 398.

'institutional', and even 'false', in Barth's exegesis.[23] To be sure, he generalises about the falsehood of *all* northern prophets:

> But confession is shown to be characteristic of the south, and profession of the north, and the light naturally falls upon the former, and the shadow upon the latter. The shadow which lies upon the professional *Nabi*-ism is…representative of the Israelite form of the Canaanite vitalism, the religion of blood and soil, which, according to the will of the God of Sinai and Jerusalem, is the very opposite of the life demanded of his people. It is thus no accident that this prophetic order has to the northern kingdom…the affinity which is proper to it in the story.[24]

While there are perhaps good reasons for thinking that the Bethel prophet shares Jeroboam's agenda, it is nonetheless worth noting that the Bethel prophet is not explicitly identified with Jeroboam in the text. He resides in Bethel, where Jeroboam has built an altar and set up a golden calf, but no mention is made of a positive association between the old prophet and Israel's king. In fact, without Barth's dialectical framework, one could argue that the Bethelite's introduction in v. 11 as 'a certain older prophet' may be understood as an attempt to distance him and his credentials from the recently crowned King Jeroboam, whose arbitrary appointment of priests is decidedly unorthodox. One could also draw a similar inference from the narrator's observation that it is the prophet's sons who attend Jeroboam's ceremony and not the Bethel prophet himself. The reason for the old prophet's absence from the ceremony is a narrative gap, left open to conjecture. In any case, my point is simply that readers should not be hasty to assume that the Bethel prophet is in league with Jeroboam just because he hails from Bethel. Barth's dichotomy between north and south is convincing in many respects, though not as self-evident as his exegesis implies. After all, in the immediate context of this narrative, God makes profound promises (of Davidic proportions!) to Jeroboam (1 Kgs 11) before then pronouncing judgment upon him (1 Kgs 14) through a northern prophet, namely Ahijah the Shilonite. But in any case, regardless of whether the text supports the notion, we note that Barth associates the man of God with authentic prophecy in Judah, and the Bethel prophet with professional prophetism in Israel. And while he recognises that kings more naturally lend themselves to representative roles in historical literature, in 1 Kings 13 it is the Bethel prophet who is identified as 'the real Satan of the story'.[25]

23. Ibid., 405, 409.
24. Ibid., 400.
25. Ibid., 402.

Division of the Kingdoms

A second clue regarding the symbolic, or parabolic, form of 1 Kings 13 pertains to the importance of the division of the kingdoms within God's overarching purposes. When Barth considers the relation between Judah and Israel on his imagined right and left, he begins by stating that 'the very significant position...of 1 K. 13 in relation to the historical record of the Old Testament must not pass unobserved'.[26] Here Barth indicates that 1 Kings 13 provides an interpretive clue for the preceding narrative as well as for the history of the kingdoms that follows. In his words, 1 Kings 13 'comes directly after the account of the disruption under Rehoboam and Jeroboam, *and in some sense explains it*'.[27] But how exactly does 1 Kings 13 explain the division of the kingdoms? To understand this, we must hear what he has to say about the history that follows.

Whatever sociological or historical explanation one might give to the dissolution of the Israelite amphictyony,[28] Barth suggests that the record of Israel's history offered in Kings posits a *theological* explanation for the political fracture. In summary, God wills a holy and unified people who will serve him, and he therefore wills this division in Israel for the sake of a better unity. Since 'the real subject of the whole ensuing history... is obviously the unity of the will of God for the whole people whom he led out of Egypt', and since God also wills to sanctify this people by excluding and cutting off their sin, Barth asserts that 'the separation of the kingdom into David's kingdom and the national monarchy of Samaria' are the inevitable consequence of 'this distinction of the will of God itself'.[29] In Barth's view, it is precisely because of their deficiencies that the peoples, kings and prophets of Israel and Judah 'become completely authentic occasions for authentic revelations of God, and as such reveal the authentic meaning of the existence of Israel'.[30] These revelations of God are manifested in the interplay between the elect and the rejected (which is only possible because of the division between them), and as we shall see, the responsibility goes both ways.

In light of this perceived theological dynamic, 1 Kings 13 may be understood to posit an explanation for the disruption under Rehoboam and Jeroboam that occurs in 1 Kings 12. God's desire for an obedient

---

26. Ibid., 403.
27. Ibid. (emphasis added).
28. See, e.g., Martin Noth, *The History of Israel*, trans. P. R. Ackroyd, 2nd ed. (London: A. & C. Black, 1960), 85–109, esp. 90–1.
29. CD II.2, 403.
30. Ibid.

and unified people is realised in part by the division of the kingdom that occurs in response to Solomon's idolatry (1 Kgs 11), since the opposition that ensues between Rehoboam and Jeroboam in 1 Kings 12, and between Judah and Israel in 1 Kings 14, elucidates the theological motifs of election and rejection. In 1 Kings 13 then, at this critical juncture in the book, Barth asserts that 'separation and opposition in Israel's course and destiny are necessary',[31] and that 'because of the division there are now authentic relations in the history of Israel'.[32] Barth's propensity for dialectical theology comes to the fore most clearly at this point, and as we shall see, it is this overtly theological view of history that is subjected to severe criticism by Klopfenstein and others (see Chapter 3).

Prohibition of Fellowship between North and South

A third point of correspondence between our story and the larger history is suggested by the threefold prohibition governing the man of God's actions. Barth interprets the man of God's prohibition from eating and drinking in Bethel, together with Jeroboam's invitation in v. 7, to represent the divine prohibition of fellowship between north and south:[33]

> What Jeroboam would like is reconciliation, tolerance, amicable compromise between himself and the divinely commissioned bearer of the word from Judah. For his own part, he sees no reason why they could not shake hands, or why Jerusalem and Bethel could not settle down alongside one another. It is precisely that which the man of God from Judah refuses to concede by refusing the invitation. It is precisely that which God has forbidden him to do...[34]

Barth thus understands the threefold prohibition to highlight the distinction between elect Judah and reprobate Israel (though he does not comment on the third prohibition specifically). Judah and Jerusalem worship God rightly whereas Israel and Bethel do not. 'In Jeroboam it is immediately apparent why God says No to this altar and this throne, to this religion and this politics'.[35] Moreover, since Israel's worship is false,

---

31. Ibid.
32. Ibid.
33. Barth makes no particular comment about what the third command ('do not return by the way that you went') might mean.
34. Ibid., 394.
35. Ibid., 400.

> [God] does not will the worship paid Him in Bethel, or the whole nation which is assembled with its king about that altar, even although this people is called (with particular emphasis) 'Israel', even although its king did not reach his throne apart from God and the call of a prophet of God. For their apostasy from the house of David is simply a concealed or flagrant apostasy from Himself. His people have ceased here to be His people. The man of God from Judah is the herald of this divine displeasure. So, too, is the whole being of Judah in its contrast to that of Israel.[36]

The threefold prohibition thereby reinforces that the man of God and the nation of Judah stand for God's will, as surely as Jeroboam and Israel stand against it – both in 1 Kings 13 and in the history that follows. But the prohibition from fellowship is not, according to Barth, the only relational dynamic between Israel and Judah,[37] for election entails not just abstaining from corruption, but also heeding the call to speak against it.

Genuine Dialogue between North and South

In spite of the prohibition from having fellowship with compromised Israel, Barth goes on to state: 'It is only by going to the north with this Word that the man of the south can confirm and justify his own election'.[38] That is to say, extending this principle to the kingdoms represented, 'the true Israel in the south has no right to an existence which is tranquil and settled in itself. It cannot possibly rejoice or boast in its election to the derogation of the false Israel in the north.'[39] The very purpose of the division, from Barth's perspective, is to clarify the two nations' respective roles as speaker and hearer,[40] not to be confused with a facile fellowship that blurs the need for any distinction in the first place. Again, Barth draws a parallel between the man of God in the story and Judah in the broader history; just as the man of God is commissioned to confront Jeroboam and yet to abstain from having fellowship in Bethel, so Judah must demonstrate her election not only by resisting compromise, but also by confronting her neighbour, Israel, with the truth:

---

36. Ibid., 398.
37. Barth makes no reference to other narratives about fellowship between north and south in the book of Kings, even in spite of the fact that such narratives nearly always lead directly to disaster in a way that would appear to strengthen his argument (e.g. 1 Kgs 22; 2 Kgs 3). We will return to this in Chapter 6.
38. Ibid., 404.
39. Ibid.
40. Ibid.

> The true Israel must converse with the false Israel just because it is not a stranger to the latter's guilt, because everything that separates Israel as a whole from God has simply been made explicit in the northern people, sundered from the house of David and the temple in Jerusalem. It is not from a secure elevation, but from the depths of the same distress, sustained by the unmerited grace of God alone, that Judah addresses and necessarily must address Israel by the mouth of its prophets, and must speak to it the one Word, i.e., the Word of God, which is its own support… The Word of God must be spoken and heard.[41]

Again, Barth's exegesis leans heavily toward theological conclusions; if there is to be any fellowship between Israel and Judah, God wills that it take the shape of a prophetic voice, speaking truth in love.

The Disobedience of the Man of God and of Judah

The points of contact between this introductory narrative and the history of the kingdoms are further supplemented by a general alignment between the fates of the man of God and the nation of Judah. Barth draws a further analogy between the Bethel prophet's deception of the man of God and the manner in which Samaria lures Judah into sin:

> And it is not only the genuine prophet who here becomes a traitor and denier, but in him and like him Jerusalem, the city of David and of God… All Jerusalem and Judah will do as this man of Judah has done. They will weigh the commission entrusted to them, and heard and clearly proclaimed by them, against the alleged commission of another. They will listen to supposed angelic voices from far and near. And their decision, too, will be false. They will become tolerant and then disobedient. They will eventually fall into every form of apostasy. They will become almost or altogether indistinguishable from the Northern Kingdom, at least in that which they desire and do…they will do that which displeases the Lord in monstrous contradiction of their commission, just as this man of God did in a first and hardly noticeable step.[42]

Barth not only observes that Judah follows Israel into sin and ultimately shares the same fate, buried in a foreign land, but he also highlights the fact that Judah is *deliberately* led astray. That is, the Bethel prophet's act of deceit 'smacks of truth although it is definitely a lie, so that the man of God yields to him (as Jerusalem and Judah were later to succumb to

---

41. Ibid.
42. Ibid., 399.

the temptation to tolerance, and eventually to end as Samaria ended).'[43] Israel's culpability for Judah's downfall is thus accented by Barth as yet another element that features in both 1 Kings 13 and the ensuing history.

The Exilic 'Tomb' of the Prophets and of the Nations

Although Barth does not use the word 'exile' to describe the shared tomb at the end of the story, this is clearly what he has in mind when he speaks of a 'common grave':

> Both here and in the whole sphere of the Old Testament history of kings and prophets there can be no visible consummation of the restored fellowship other than this common grave. It is Israel's grave into which Judah itself is first laid, and then Israel. The historical conclusion brings a reversal in the actual sequence of events. But either way, it is in this grave that the reunion of the separated brothers is completed.[44]

Barth's comment about 'the historical conclusion' (Israel before Judah) being a reversal of what happens in 1 Kings 13 (Judah before Israel)[45] reinforces his perception of the Bethel prophet and the man of God as portents for the shared exilic demise of Israel and Judah. Thus, the final theological parallel Barth identifies between 1 Kings 13 and its broader context is that both nations share the same fate.

Content

Having established the way in which 1 Kings 13 functions within its wider context as a kind of focal lens, let us consider how Barth elucidates the theological substance of the story. In the main body of his exegetical argument, Barth paints a pair of complex 'double-pictures' (*Doppelbildern*) from the narrative. He uses this term because each double-picture – Judah on the right and Israel on the left – refers to a kingdom, north or south, as well as a form of prophecy, false or true,[46] and because there is a positive

---

43. Ibid., 401.
44. Ibid., 406.
45. Barth appears to refrain from being explicit about 'exile' in order that the image of a grave may sustain further referents. He proceeds by accenting the manner in which this common grave – not just of the man of God and the Bethel prophet, but of every one of us – is answered in Christ (409).
46. Although I do not find Barth's suggestion that the man of God be equated with genuine prophetism and the prophet with professional (i.e. false) prophetism convincing, my purpose for the time being is simply to outline Barth's reading as it stands.

and a negative aspect to each double-picture. All of these variables merge to form a comprehensive picture overall. We will examine each part in turn.

The Double-Picture on the Right

'The double-picture on the right is that of the man of Judah, with the figure of Josiah at a distance behind him.'[47] The positive dimension of this portrait is that the man of God from Judah represents Davidic (divinely legitimated) kingship, heralding God's displeasure at Israel's apostasy under Jeroboam I. But more than this, the positive aspect of the double-picture pertaining to Judah also highlights the fundamental importance of Judah's (com)mission to address Israel. For Judah 'cannot possibly rejoice or boast in its election to the derogation of the false Israel in the north. Nor can it come to terms with it and accept it without at once addressing itself afresh to this Israel'.[48] On the contrary, Judah 'is under obligation to Israel'.[49] The very election and *raison d'être* of the true Israel consists of this responsibility toward the false Israel. If Judah fails to appropriate this calling, Judah fails to be elect; 'It has repulsed the grace which made it an elect and called people'.[50]

The negative aspect of the Judean man of God consists of the fact that the Judean betrays his calling and reveals his unworthiness when put to the test. He listens to the lie and betrays his God-given cause, even in spite of the tremendous clarity with which he reiterated the threefold command to Jeroboam and the older prophet. Citing Jesus' words from Luke 12, Barth says, 'Much is required of him to whom much is given. Much was given to the man of Judah, infinitely more than to Jeroboam or the prophet of Bethel. Therefore nothing less than his life can now be required of him.'[51]

However, even when he falls prey to the Bethel prophet's coercion and breaks God's command, Barth insists that the man of God's fate represents that of the nation of Judah in that he is killed by a lion (representing YHWH) but not devoured. 'The stock of David, hewn down to the ground, is preserved'[52] – in spite of being buried in a foreign grave. Jerusalem is never entirely forgotten.

47. Ibid., 398.
48. Ibid., 404.
49. Ibid.
50. Ibid., 405.
51. Ibid.
52. Ibid., 399–400.

The Double-Picture on the Left

The negative aspect is more dominant in the double-picture on the left, where king and prophet stand together behind Jeroboam's 'new political and religious creation'.[53] Barth stresses, however, that the prophet of Bethel, representing the 'professional' prophetism that is characteristic of the North, comes off worse than the king:

> It is because this man is a prophet that he is more aware than the king of the need for a theological justification of the North-Israelite Kingdom and cult which are challenged at the altar by the word of the man of God from Judah, and which would be rehabilitated by his eating and drinking at Bethel... Thus the professional prophet becomes that which is impossible for the king of Israel – the true and successful tempter and destroyer of the man of God...he is the real and the worse representative of the kingdom of darkness in this story. That is why what Jeroboam does looks only grey compared to what this professional does.[54]

Barth then explains how the negative aspect of the left double-picture leads quite naturally into its positive aspect:

> But this fact – the fact that the false Israel becomes the tempter and destroyer of the true – is still far from being the end of the story. On the contrary, the story now moves on to its sequel, that the very tempter and destroyer must now take up the flag which the other had let fall. The fact that the false Israel had not ceased to be the Israel of God is now revealed, to the terrible shame but also to the supreme consolation, of the true Israel. For the Word of God cannot be silenced...[55]

The positive aspect of this left-hand (Israelite) picture is manifested most clearly when the old prophet 'takes over the office of the genuine man of God'.[56] We shall see below that this reversal of roles has enormous implications for Barth's understanding of the purpose and substantive content of the story. In fact, the overarching purpose of Barth's complex illustration is to show that the positive and negative aspects of the two double-pictures converge within the narrative to highlight the interdependence of Judah and Israel as elect and rejected. It is precisely in this

---

53. Ibid., 401.
54. Ibid., 400–401.
55. Ibid., 405.
56. Ibid., 403.

interplay between the rejected north and the elect south, and between the positive and negative aspects of these *Doppelbildern* that Barth's doctrine of election is elucidated. Put another way, for Barth the reciprocal dynamic of the story *is* the point.

But the other positive dimension of this left-hand picture is expressed in the story's resolution (if we may call it that). Barth concludes that there is a 'strange light which falls on the picture to the left',[57] namely, the way in which 'the necessary punishment of the human trespass...does not fall on Jeroboam...[nor] on the prophet... It falls on the one who is here only the seduced.'[58] Surprisingly, the old Bethelite prophet, 'the most guilty, goes free. He is even preserved beyond his death.'[59]

The Whole Picture: The Relation between Judah and Israel

Having shown how each double-picture, right and left, has a positive and negative aspect, Barth proceeds to explain how both pictures merge to elucidate the relationship between Israel and Judah. 'They are indeed to be seen and understood together. The meaning of both consists precisely in the fact that they mutually complement and confirm one another in the positive as well as in the negative aspects peculiar to both.'[60] To explicate the whole picture, Barth refers to a dialectic movement within the story that is exhibited in a series of five 'reversals' that signal the interdependence of Israel and Judah:

The elect (Judah) initiates the dialectic momentum of the story by bringing word of God's judgment to the rejected (Israel) in Bethel.[61]	
	When the man of God is deceived by the Bethelite prophet, 'the rejected acts on behalf of the elect when he takes over the latter's mission'.[62]

---

57. Ibid.
58. Ibid., 402–3.
59. Ibid., 404.
60. Ibid., 403.
61. Ibid., 404: the man of God's 'mission to Israel already attests that the true Israel in the south has no right to an existence which is tranquil and settled in itself... The true Israel must converse with the false Israel.'
62. Ibid., 406.

Consequently, 'the elect acts on behalf of the rejected when he suffers the latter's punishment'.[63] When Barth speaks of the 'the necessary punishment of the human trespass in this story',[64] he stresses that Jeroboam and the Bethelite were more deserving of death than the man of God.

'similarly, at the end, the rejected acts for the elect by making his own grave a resting-place for the latter.'[65]

Finally, 'the elect acts for the rejected in that the bones of the latter are kept and preserved for his sake, and together with his bones'.[66]

Barth's sophisticated analysis thus places a heavy accent on *the reciprocal dynamic between the man of God and the Bethel prophet* as the central theme that is introduced in 1 Kings 13 which comes to expression throughout the history of the divided kingdom in *the mutual interdependence of Israel and Judah*. This dialectic movement in the story, which powerfully illuminates Barth's doctrine of election, is critical to a proper understanding of his theological interpretation of 1 Kings 13, but it is also perhaps the most divisive element in his reading. Barth's identification of multiple role reversals in 1 Kings 13 has become a catalyst for further development in the minds of some scholars[67] and the focus of severe criticism for others,[68] as we shall see.

Given Barth's understanding of the story as something akin to a narrative analogy (I will say more about this rhetorical device in due course), the implications of these dynamics in 1 Kings 13 are threefold for the nations of Judah and Israel:

i. God wills the obedience and unity of his people;
ii. notwithstanding the ideal of unity, God also wills an 'internal distinction' among his people as a means of cutting off their sin;

---

63. Ibid.
64. Ibid., 402.
65. Ibid., 406.
66. Ibid.
67. So Bosworth; see Chapter 6.
68. So Klopfenstein; see Chapter 3.

iii. in spite of this apparent paradox wherein God desires both unity and division among his people (points i and ii), 'the will of God – and this is the third fact which emerges in the later history – does not cease to be one and the same for all Israel'[69] (i.e. God remains faithful in his promises both to Judah and to Israel).

So while Barth understands separation and opposition between Israel and Judah to play a part in God's unfolding purposes for his people, God's ultimate purpose for a unified and obedient people remains unchanged. In fact, the division within Israel ultimately serves this purpose, since it is in the relations between 'people, kings and prophets' of Israel and Judah that 'the authentic meaning of the existence of Israel' comes to light.[70] 'The man of Judah has not ceased to be the elect, nor has the prophet of Bethel ceased to be the rejected. But in their union as elect and rejected they form together the whole Israel from which the grace of God is not turned away.'[71]

The rich theological landscape against which Barth exegetes 1 Kings 13 permits us to grasp how 'the ways of the two prophets who occupy the foreground are so involved in their manifold intersections that they are unmistakably meant to be taken together'.[72] The interconnection of Barth's two double-pictures thereby seeks to evoke a fuller understanding 'of that which makes divided Israel more than ever His people'.[73] Here we reach the heart of the matter: *As the relationship between Israel and Judah reveals God's will for a united people in the history of the kingdoms, so the relationship between the Bethelite and the Judean reflects this reality in 1 Kings 13.*

Barth's exegesis thus takes one of the most problematic aspects of the narrative and shows how it may be understood as the hermeneutical crux. Numerous scholars have been troubled by the fact that no clear line is drawn between the two prophets in terms of legitimacy; the 'true' man of God breaks his God-given commands, just as the 'false' Bethelite receives a genuine word from the Lord.[74] But as Barth understands the passage

---

69. Ibid., 403.
70. Ibid.
71. Ibid., 406.
72. Ibid., 398.
73. Ibid., 404.
74. E.g., Erhard Blum, 'Die Lüge des Propheten. Ein Lesevorschlag zu einer befremdlichen Geschichte (1 Kön 13)', in *Textgestalt und Komposition: Exegetische Beiträge zu Tora und Vordere Propheten* (Tübingen: Mohr Siebeck, 2010), 319–20.

this blurred ethical line is, in fact, pivotal to a proper understanding of the nature of the relationship between the two prophets/nations. He therefore describes the man of God as 'the seduced...who is struck by the lightning of divine wrath'[75] just as the Bethel prophet 'must now take up the flag that the other had let fall'.[76] The two anonymous figures are, to repeat, 'unmistakably meant to be taken together'.[77]

In accordance with this, Barth can now look back over the whole and point out that the opening scene (vv. 1-10) is precisely about how God's unified will for *all* his people is borne out in the conflict between north and south. It is worth quoting him at length:

> The beginning of the story corresponds to this. That which the king and people of Israel have to hear through the man of God from Judah is their own rejection *a limine* in and with the threat against the Bethel altar. And the rejection is underlined by the strict refusal of the requested table fellowship; the most absolute intolerance. Yet even this event itself has its other side. We have already seen that precisely in this harsh form there is a resumption of contact between Jerusalem and sinful, separated Northern Israel, almost before the latter is aware of its separation. It is not indifference at all events, that encounters Israel from this quarter. At least in the form of judgment the grace of God is not removed from Israel the moment it sins. On the contrary, it has hardly left this kingdom before it returns. The guilt which lies up on it is the common guilt of all Israel. But the word of God which Judah has and Israel does not have is addressed to all Israel, and is, therefore, to be directed by hearing Judah to unhearing Israel. This twofold solidarity is the secret of the beginning of the story, which does not possess for nothing the character of a revelation of the patience of God even in His wrath, which already at the very outset – even though it is a dark and unsatisfactory, tragic beginning – does not speak of an ending, but, on the contrary, of a genuine new beginning of God with His lost people.[78]

We have seen that Barth considers the division within Israel to be necessary in order that there may be genuine dialogue and a sense of mutual accountability between the elect and the rejected. Building on this insight, Barth highlights how the opening scene, an episode of conflict between prophet and king (vv. 1-10), introduces this issue of accountability or 'twofold solidarity' between elect Judah and rejected Israel. At first, the

75. *CD* II.2, 403.
76. Ibid., 405.
77. Ibid., 398.
78. Ibid., 407.

scene seems more or less to resolve itself (as text-critical scholars have observed), but then it segues into a second, related story (vv. 11-32) that elaborates upon the reciprocity between Judah and Israel. The tale of two prophets in the latter part of the chapter is thus perceived by Barth to be set against a theological background not just of election, but of divine grace. God's will for the obedient worship of Israel is expressed in a prophetic confrontation against 'every expectation of salvation from their own skill and power instead of from the fulfilment of [his] promise'.[79] The initial conflict between the man of God and Jeroboam signifies neither that God is for Judah nor against Israel, but rather that he is faithful to *both* Judah and Israel. The distinction that exists between them has been made for the sake of unity. 'Just because of the division there are now authentic relations in the history of Israel.'[80]

It must be said, however, that in making these assertions, Barth fails to offer specific examples from the history of these 'authentic relations' between Judah and Israel. His claim is not supported by the mention of any other narratives (in Kings or elsewhere) that might shed light on the nature of the relations between the kingdoms or that signal their mutual accountability.[81] We are left with the provocative suggestion of a pattern, but without its detailed exposition.[82] Indeed, this gap has fuelled at least one scholarly effort to develop and expand upon Barth's thesis (see Chapter 6). But let us turn to the interpretative contexts for Barth's stimulating exegesis of 1 Kings 13.

---

79. Ibid., 403.
80. Ibid., 403.
81. Perhaps it is reasonable to assume that when Barth states that the relations between peoples, kings and prophets of north and south 'reveal the authentic meaning of the existence of Israel' (ibid., 403), he refers, e.g., to those incidents of prophetic conflict so characteristic of the Elijah and Elisha cycles. However, this is not made explicit.
82. It is well-known, however, that the history of the kingdoms is recounted according to a fairly consistent, alternating pattern whereby the narrator chimes back and forth when reporting on the kings of the northern and southern kingdoms. Jerome Walsh, who is somewhat indebted to Barth's exegesis, writes: 'To tell the history of Judah and the history of Israel as separate histories would belie the unity of the people. To tell the history of Judah and the history of Israel as one history would belie the political separation Yahweh has decreed. In the narrator's view, Yahweh's people is one, but by God's will it lives under the rule of two kings. He arranges his material to do justice to both realities.' Walsh, *1 Kings*, 208.

Context

Although Barth's exegesis of 1 Kings 13 has been read as an independent exegetical piece,[83] his unique interpretation is further illuminated by two contextual frames of reference, one hermeneutical and the other doctrinal. This book cannot possibly provide a comprehensive analysis of Barth's hermeneutics or his *Dogmatics*, but a couple of brief, contextual 'detours' will prove helpful for our understanding and evaluation of Barth's exegetical method.

Barth's Hermeneutical Context

It is not easy to make any kind of programmatic or systematic analysis of Barth's hermeneutics, since Barth was rather reluctant – perhaps even altogether resistant – to offer up a hermeneutical manifesto himself.[84] Nonetheless, endeavours to come to grips with his hermeneutics have generally been approached in one of two ways. One approach has been to understand Barth's hermeneutics by examining the logic and findings of his exegesis. McGlasson and Cunningham, for instance, are each convinced that the workings of Barth's exegesis are more telling than the relatively few, explicit theoretical statements he made about interpretation.[85] A second approach, undertaken most notably by Richard Burnett's examination of draft materials for the first edition of Barth's *Römerbrief* (published in 1919), has sought to show 'that Barth had clear, self-conscious hermeneutical convictions from the very beginning'.[86] It is

---

83. Note its publication as a stand-alone piece in vol. 10 of *Biblischen Studien* (1955).

84. Barth refused to engage in public debate about hermeneutics, since he assumed (wrongly, as it turned out) that the discipline of hermeneutics would be little more than a passing fad. Moreover, he was opposed to the notion of *anthropologising* theology, that is, of asking the question of God from the human standpoint or condition, as Schleiermacher proposed. Barth was convinced that no method *per se* could lead one to encounter God and therefore refused to focus on hermeneutics as a means of revealing God, since knowledge of God comes – *only* – from God. See Burnett, *Theological Exegesis*, 36-9. Notwithstanding this, Barth does offer occasional reflections on hermeneutics in the *Dogmatics* (*CD* I.2, 457–537).

85. Paul McGlasson, *Jesus and Judas: Biblical Exegesis in Barth* (Atlanta, GA: Scholars Press, 1991); Mary Kathleen Cunningham, *What Is Theological Exegesis? Interpretation and Use of Scripture in Barth's Doctrine of Election* (Valley Forge, PA: Trinity Press, 1995).

86. Burnett, *Barth's Theological Exegesis*, 9. In Burnett's view, while the works of McGlasson and Cunningham are valuable for honouring Barth's own priorities – 'exegesis, exegesis, and still more exegesis!' – they ultimately reveal little about his theological exegesis (6).

not my intention to evaluate these different approaches. For our purposes, both methods enable us to see that certain basic principles are consistent throughout Barth's interpretive work. Here I will focus on just three characteristics of Barth's hermeneutics that are particularly relevant to our text.

(i) *Intertextuality*

In her concise and insightful study of theological exegesis, Mary K. Cunningham insists on beginning with Barth's exegesis when examining his methodology, since going from hermeneutics to exegesis 'does not honor the pattern of Barth's thinking...the unsystematic nature of his thought'.[87] According to Cunningham, 'Barth's most crucial exegetical tactic'[88] is the juxtaposition of key texts, his penchant for what has since been labelled intertextuality.[89] Wallace, by the same token, observes that Barth reads the Bible 'as a complicated typological intertext',[90] which is certainly an apt description of the way Barth delineates election via his exegesis of other biblical texts. When Barth consecutively reads Leviticus 14 and 16, the narratives concerning David and Saul, and 1 Kings 13 in his discussion of Old Testament texts pertaining to election, his purpose is not simply to align passages dealing with the same theme in order to strengthen their theological import; it is more than that. Barth interprets one text in light of what has been extrapolated from another. The patriarchal narratives in Genesis, the sacrificial rites in Leviticus 14 and 16, and the David and Saul narratives all precede 1 Kings 13 in *CD* II.2 not just because they come first in the biblical canon, but because they pave the way and provide a foundation for his exegetical observations

---

87. Cunningham, *What is Theological Exegesis?*, 14. McGlasson expresses the same conviction: 'The fact is, the best way to come to grips with Barth's possible contribution to contemporary theological hermeneutics is to focus on his actual biblical exegesis, rather than the less clear contours of his few hermeneutical statements'. McGlasson, *Jesus and Judas*, 2.

88. Cunningham is referring to Barth's juxtaposition of Jn 1.1-2 and Eph. 1.4 in establishing that Jesus Christ is both the subject and object of election. The same 'exegetical tactic' applies to his consideration of the three Old Testament texts outlined below.

89. The term is generally attributed to Julia Kristeva's work in the late 1960s. See 'Bakhtin, le mot, le dialogue et le roman', *Critique* 33 (1967): 438–65 (ET: 'Word, Dialogue and Novel', in *Desire in Language: A Semiotic Approach to Literature and Art*, ed. Leon S. Roudiez, trans. Thomas Gora et al. [New York: Columbia University Press, 1980], 64–91).

90. Mark I. Wallace, *The Second Naiveté: Barth, Ricoeur, and the New Yale Theology* (Macon, GA: Mercer University Press), 7 n. 20.

from 1 Kings 13 regarding Israel and Judah. In this sense, Barth's work resembles a musical composition, as John Webster has observed:

> Commentators often note the musical structure of Barth's major writings: the announcement of a theme, and its further extension in a long series of developments and recapitulations, through which the reader is invited to consider the theme from a number of different angles and in a number of different relations. No one stage of the argument is definitive; rather, it is the whole which conveys the substance of what he has to say.[91]

This means that Barth's interpretation of 1 Kings 13 is intended to be read as the culmination of a number of theological strands in the Old Testament, and of the theme of election in particular. In this narrative, a pattern that has been present from the opening chapters of the Bible reaches something of a climax, at least as far as the Old Testament is concerned. Referring to the distinctions made in Genesis between 'Abel and Cain, Isaac and Ishmael, Jacob and Esau, Leah and Rachel, and so on', Barth declares that '[t]he ceremonies [in Lev. 14, 16] are obviously a comment on the history of Israel as a history of the differing choices'.[92] Like those stories of election in Genesis, the rituals involving two goats and two birds – where the animal pairs are the same in quality but distinct in purpose or calling – are actually about Israel's relationship with God. Similarly, regarding the somewhat puzzling rejection of Saul and the election of sinful David,[93] Barth stresses that these two kings, in their rejection and election, are representative of the people. This dynamic is developed in the books of Samuel until we eventually come to one of the clearest and most striking images that the Old Testament contains concerning the differentiating election of God: 1 Kings 13.[94] Barth's point is that the division of the kingdom in 1 Kings 11 does not come as a bolt from the blue. It ought rather to be 'heard' as a prominent Old Testament theme reaching its crescendo – in anticipation of the Christ event. In the Old Testament's canonical arrangement, the division of the kingdom is presented as the culmination of a series of moments in Israel's history that stress the theme of distinction-within-unity. For this reason, Barth's juxtaposition of these biblical passages is neither arbitrary nor an unconscious 'reading in'. Rather, his musical arrangement of these texts and their recapitulating theme is exegetically consistent with the Old Testament's

---

91. John Webster (ed.), *The Cambridge Companion to Karl Barth* (Cambridge: Cambridge University Press, 2000), 9.
92. *CD* II.2, 358.
93. Ibid., 387.
94. Ibid., 393.

own canonical presentation of narratives and rituals addressing the theme of election. Therefore, when the end of the Deuteronomistic History (DH) recounts a period in Israel's history when a divinely ordained 'internal distinction' in Israel makes it possible for God's elect people to also function as the rejected, what we are witnessing is the culmination of a prominent theological motif whose roots go right back to Genesis 4. When Barth describes the 'real subject'[95] of 1 Kings 13 as the way in which God's will for a unified people is expressed in the relationship between Israel as the rejected and Judah as the elect, he intends for us to hear the maturation of a dominant Old Testament theme *and* to apprehend the theme of election anew, from a fresh angle.

In brief, Barth reads intertextually because the Bible is the inspired Word of God about Jesus, and is intended to be read as a witness to Christ, in accordance with Jn 5.39.[96] He therefore 'reads in' according to a christological hermeneutic, since election is understood through Christ, and not vice versa. Others read intertextually for different reasons. For instance, Brevard Childs does so because of his conviction that the Bible's own historical process of transmission and redaction lends itself to being read that way.[97]

Because his exegesis is intertextual, many of the themes Barth discusses in connection with 1 Kings 13 (e.g., double-pictures, role reversals, complementarity between elect and rejected) are identified and developed because of their relation to preceding texts. By juxtaposing passages of scripture like this, Barth departs from the exegetical practice of historical-critical scholars, who tend to limit the resources for interpreting a text to the parameters of its immediate contexts, both literary and historical. (In the next chapter, this comes to the fore in Klopfenstein's critique of Barth's *Überinterpretation* of the lion in the story.) One key characteristic of Barth's hermeneutics, then, is a freedom to permit scripture to interpret scripture.

(ii) *Synchrony*

A second important aspect of Barth's hermeneutics is his synchronic, rather than diachronic, approach to scripture. Barth is well-known for his resistance to modernity's emphasis on human subjectivity, manifested most notably in his attitude towards historicism. He was never opposed to historical-critical work *per se*, but only its failure to get beyond explaining

---

95. Ibid., 403.
96. 'You search the scriptures because you think that in them you have eternal life; and it is they that testify on my behalf' (NRSV).
97. Childs' canonical approach is discussed further in Chapter 5.

(*Erklärung*) to understanding (*Verstehen*). In his (in)famous prefaces to the *Römerbrief*, Barth stressed that genuine biblical exposition must go beyond merely the recognition and elucidation of historical referents. His goal, rather, was to press beyond historical-critical analysis to a theological grasp of the Bible. Barth disliked historicism's emphasis on the world *behind* the text over and above the world *of* the text, as though biblical texts exist primarily to reveal something other than their own subject matter (*Sache*).[98] A consequence of this approach is that revelation becomes identified with facts outside or beyond the text, a situation that Barth lamented.

This is not to say that Barth was uninterested in questions pertaining to source materials or the formation of the canon. On the contrary, his opening remarks about 1 Kings 13 acknowledge that the story 'appears to have been drawn from another source than its context',[99] and in his discussion of David and Saul, he asks repeatedly why these texts were preserved among a kingless community during the post-exilic period.[100] It is clear that Barth did not avoid such questions altogether. But he chose not to linger on them, saying only what was necessary to clarify his point about the meaning of the text *as it now stands*. In addition, Barth was quite candid about his exegetical priorities being well-suited to his own theological agenda – though few of his critics found this acceptable.

(iii) *Christology*

Finally, at the heart of Barth's hermeneutic is the notion that all of Scripture serves in some way to make Christ known. This is a primary cause for criticism against Barth; that he interprets the parts in light of an already-determined whole. (In the next chapter, we will consider Klopfenstein's argument that the constituent parts of a narrative must be permitted to speak for themselves – via historical-critical analysis – so that theological judgments are not presented as foregone conclusions.) But Barth's 'universal rule of interpretation' was that 'a text can be read and understood and expounded only with reference to and in light of its theme [or *Sache*]'.[101] In his view, this is unavoidable. All interpreters necessarily have some conception of a (theological) 'whole' in place when

---

98. Cf. *CD* I.2, 494.
99. *CD* II.2, 393.
100. Ibid., 385–6.
101. Burnett, *Barth's Theological Exegesis*, 86; cf. Cunningham, *What is Theological Exegesis?*, 70: 'Barth believes…that Scripture is one because Jesus Christ is One'. Cf. Barth, *CD* I.2, 483–5.

they come to consider the (textual or historical) parts. And since Barth presupposes that the Bible's central theme is the self-revelation of God in Jesus Christ, he is quite content to be labelled as someone who 'reads in'. As he put it in one of his preface drafts, 'Whoever does not continually "read in" because he participates in the subject matter [God], cannot "read out" either'.[102] Behind Barth's reason for 'reading in' is his conviction that the entire Bible is about Jesus, and that *participation* in Christ is indispensable for the proper interpretation of biblical texts.

So, to put the matter simply, Barth's identification of Election as the primary subject of 1 Kings 13 arises from his conviction that this text (like all biblical texts) reveals Christ in some way. Yet, this is precisely why Barth's reading of the story – as 'an illustration of the differentiating election of God'[103] – has proven hard for some to swallow, regardless of their preferred exegetical method; it rests on an understanding of Scripture that appears to freely impose categories upon the text from 'beyond' or 'outside', as it were. And yet, while very few scholars have affirmed or developed Barth's claim that 1 Kings 13 pertains to the doctrine of election, one can hardly accuse Barth of ignoring the story's literary and/or historical context. Indeed, it is 'in view of the context' that he ultimately considers 1 Kings 13 to be about the problem of the kingdoms, following immediately after the division of the kingdoms as it does, and from a literary or structural point of view it is hard to find fault with this observation.

Related to Barth's christological emphasis is his particular understanding of the Old Testament as Christian Scripture. In *Church Dogmatics* I.2, where Barth sets out his approach to the Old Testament in christological terms, Barth describes many of the events in the Old Testament as having multiple vantage points.[104] On one hand, Old Testament texts must be understood within their own historical contexts, but on the other, they must also be considered in light of their corresponding fulfilments in the course of time. He seeks to demonstrate this point using a variety of themes, including the people, the land, the temple, lordship, and kingship, in an effort to show that each subject is best understood in terms of a dialectic relationship between its originary particularity and its eschatological fulfilment.[105] This very dynamic is also displayed in the

---

102. Cited in Burnett, *Barth's Theological Exegesis*, 95–6 n. 3 (see Appendix 2, 591–2).
103. Ibid., 393.
104. *CD* I.2, 95.
105. Ibid., 96–101.

way that Barth explores the twin themes of election and rejection in *CD* II.2. In his concluding comments on the three Old Testament texts we have mentioned here, Barth perceives the Christ event as the story's real epilogue in each case. In his conclusion to the section about Leviticus 14 and 16, he states that these sacrificial rites point forward to Christ:

> In the same way, the old exegesis was quite right to find in Lev. 14 the prediction of that which was fulfilled, according to Rom. 4^{25}, in the fact that Christ 'was delivered for our offences, and was raised up again for our justification'.[106]

Then, in his closing remarks about Saul and David, he describes these Old Testament kings as types of Christ:

> The fact that this king takes several forms – at least two, or more precisely four in this case too – and that these forms cannot be reduced to any common denominator, and are full of inner contradictions, characterizes them as prophetic figures in distinction from the fulfilment actualized in the person of Jesus Christ… The King Jesus Christ is the true subject and hero of these stories of the kings.[107]

Finally, as he concludes his treatment of 1 Kings 13, he again refers to the insufficiency of the Old Testament witness:

> But this story, too, does point to one real subject if Jesus Christ is also seen in it, if at the exact point where this story of the prophets breaks off a continuation is found in the Easter story… In this one prophet the two prophets obviously live. And so, too, do the two Israels – the Israels which in our story can finally only die, only be buried, only persist for a time in their bones… What else is 1 K. 13 if it is not prophecy? Where else is its fulfilment to be found if not in Jesus Christ? These are the questions which must be answered by those for whom the suggested result of our investigation may for any reason be unacceptable.[108]

According to Barth, the bones of the two prophets (representing Judah and Israel) that end up in a shared grave at the conclusion of 1 Kings 13 foretell the promise of life for the elect and the rejected that is made possible in the resurrection of Christ. It is because of such statements that Barth has been accused of 'reading in' anachronistically or disrespecting

---

106. *CD* II.2, 365.
107. Ibid., 389, 391.
108. Ibid., 409.

the integrity of the Old Testament's discrete voice. Yet, in fairness, Barth is careful not to import Christ into the Old Testament in ways that violate the plain sense of any given text. Far from seeing christophanies behind every stone and bush in the world of the Old Testament, Barth endeavours to treat these passages within their historical and literary contexts, as we have seen. Only when their witness appears incomplete does he introduce Christ as the true epilogue to the narrative. In his discussion of Saul and David, for instance, which ultimately points to Christ (see above), Barth says this in his own defence:

> So far we have not mentioned His name in our investigation of these passages. We have remained within the Old Testament world and its possibilities. We have tried in this world to bring out and think through what is said there about the elect king, but we have been forced to the conclusion that the entity in question cannot be brought out or apprehended within the Old Testament world.[109]

In an effort to describe this paradoxical character of Barth's exegesis that seeks at once to honour the Old Testament and to read Scripture christologically, Mark Gignilliat writes: 'Barth allows the Old Testament's voice to open up the possibilities for an apostolic exegesis that retrospectively makes sense of the incomplete nature of the Old Testament in light of Jesus Christ'.[110] Regarding 1 Kings 13, then, we note that Barth's sensitivity to the multivalency of the story permits the narrative to have its own historical referentiality (regarding prophecy and the kingdoms) as well as being a witness to Christ.[111] The manner in which he refers to 'the grave' both as an image for the exilic deaths of Israel and Judah and as the place of 'our last human possibility and expectation' is but one example of his theological hermeneutics at work. Barth thus keeps his discussion nuanced in order that he may read the text as commentary on ancient Israel while also permitting the accent to ultimately fall on Christ. It is worth hearing him expound this hermeneutical move at length:

---

109. Ibid., 389.
110. Mark S. Gignilliat, *Karl Barth and the Fifth Gospel: Barth's Theological Exegesis of Isaiah* (Aldershot, England: Ashgate, 2009), 60.
111. Bosworth, somewhat surprisingly, remarks that 'Barth's interpretation of the Old Testament texts can not be characterised as christological. Christological statements are absent from the interpretation of 1 Kings 13.' Bosworth, 'Revisiting Karl Barth's Exegesis of 1 Kings 13', *BibInt* 10 (2002): 372.

> The grave stands only too eloquently at the end of the story of these prophets. And it is not an empty grave, but a grave "which indeed appears beautiful outward, but is within full of dead men's bones, and all uncleanness" (Mt. 23[27]). Certainly it is a grave of prophets, which as such could be built and garnished (Mt. 23[9]), and which obviously was built and garnished, so that much later it was recognized for what it was by Josiah and his people. Yet it is only a grave. And in it the elect and the rejected, the worthy and the unworthy, the confessional and the professional prophet, Judah and Israel, Jerusalem and Samaria, in all their unity, diversity and relatedness, lie finally together in that corruption and decay which is our last human possibility and expectation; buried, and on the third day – forgotten, finished, because our time is over. It is surely remarkable that this story, perhaps the most expressive and at any rate the richest and most comprehensive prophetic story in the Old Testament, should end with this grave...[112]

In contrast to this image of a grave, Barth – not surprisingly – goes on to describe another story with a radically different outcome on the third day, and another, very different grave:

> But this story, too, does point to one real subject if Jesus Christ is also seen in it, if at the exact point where this story of the prophets breaks off a continuation is found in the Easter story... [T]he One lifted up in whose death all was lost, but who in His death was the consolation and refuge of all the lost – this One truly died and was buried, yet He was not forgotten and finished on the third day, but was raised from the dead by the power of God. In this one prophet the two prophets obviously live. And so, too, do the two Israels – the Israels which in our story can finally only die, only be buried, only persist for a time in their bones. They live in the reality and unity in which they never lived in the Old Testament, but could only be attested. They remain in Him, and in Him the Word of God proclaimed by them remains to all eternity.[113]

In summary, one struggles to grasp Barth's counter-intuitive and seemingly undisciplined hermeneutics unless one understands that his interests are (unapologetically) christocentric. Barth understands Christ to be the true *Sache* of all Scripture, and he reads accordingly.[114] I will argue that this is one legitimate framework for interpretation (for Christian readers at

   112. *CD* II.2, 408–9.
   113. Ibid., 409.
   114. Although Barth was influenced greatly by Calvin, he criticised him for being insufficiently christological in his delineation of election and predestination. See *CD* II.2, §32; cf. Eberhard Busch, *Karl Barth: His Life from Letters and Autobiographical Texts*, trans. John Bowden (London: SCM, 1976), 278.

least), although one could question whether Barth is being faithful to his own rules of reading when he points to Christ in this way at the end of his exegesis. In my view, Barth is somewhat inconsistent on two accounts. First, Barth's recognition of 2 Kgs 23.15-20 as 'the real epilogue to the story'[115] appears only to serve a single purpose, namely, to highlight the image of a tomb 'full of dead men's bones, and all uncleanness'. That is to say, Barth neglects to say anything about the remarkable reforms of Josiah, which is undoubtedly the primary focus of this 'real epilogue' (and of 2 Kgs 23 as a whole, actually). Second, Barth's exegetical decision to use 2 Kgs 23.15-20 to highlight the negative image of a grave instead of Josiah's positive actions, neatly paves the way for his climactic, concluding question: 'Where else is its fulfilment to be found if not in Jesus Christ?'[116] But Barth's expressed desire to stay within the world of the Old Testament is undercut by insufficient attention to Josiah in these verses, in spite of the fact that Barth earlier utilised the figure of Josiah (rather effectively) as a backdrop for the unfolding drama of 1 Kings 13. In his closing remarks, Barth claims that the questions he raises are 'if anything, even more difficult to answer if we keep to the confines of Old Testament history'.[117] Yet the case could be made – and will be made in Chapter 7 – that Barth's question ('Where else is its fulfilment to be found...?') can be answered in other ways than by jumping all the way to Easter. Indeed, I will suggest that a significant degree of fulfilment is found precisely in Josiah, to whom 1 Kgs 13.2 points quite explicitly. But we shall return to these details in due course.

In any case, it is clear that Barth's interpretation of the story in 1 Kings 13 is guided by his conviction that all of Scripture serves to make Christ known. By the same token, one cannot fully account for Barth's nuanced reading of 1 Kings 13 without also considering the doctrinal context for his exegesis within the *Dogmatics*. So to that dimension of his exegesis we now turn.

Barth's Doctrinal Context: Election

It is important to consider how Barth's exegesis of 1 Kings 13 informs a larger schema within his *Church Dogmatics* (II.2 §35), since his use of 1 Kings 13 to support a broader argument is the main reason Barth's exegesis has elicited criticism. As noted above, many have perceived Barth to be bringing 'external' concerns to bear upon the narrative.

---

115. *CD* II.2, 397.
116. Ibid., 409.
117. Ibid., 408.

Barth offers exegetical treatments of three Old Testament texts pertaining to election, 1 Kings 13 being the last of these. In his view, each text pertains to the theme of election and each also witnesses to Christ. But there is yet a third common element that Barth draws out in his treatment of each of these passages, a dynamic which facilitates his argument about the elect and rejected Christ that is attested in them. The point Barth repeatedly makes is that the complex relationship that exists between the elect and the rejected is signalled by the interdependence and mutuality of the text's binary subject matter. Barth insists that the sacrificial rites described in Leviticus 14 and 16 be considered together;[118] that 'the first two and mutually alternating Israelite kings, Saul and David' be understood in relation to one another;[119] and in 1 Kings 13, that the series of role reversals and exchanges between the man of God and the old prophet manifest their *interdependence* as representatives of Judah and Israel.

Barth's doctrine of election begins with the statement that Jesus Christ is both promise and fulfilment, both elect and rejected. According to Barth's formulation of the doctrine, God elected himself for rejection from eternity, and then bore that election within history so that humanity could be elect in Christ.[120] In Christ, God himself 'is rejected in order that we might not be rejected'.[121] This interdependence of the elect and rejected is central to a proper understanding of Barth's doctrine of election. Although the following citation precedes his treatment of 1 Kings 13, it nonetheless illuminates Barth's depiction of the relation between the Judean man of God and the Bethel prophet:

> We can no more consider and understand the elect apart from the rejected than we can consider the rejected apart from the elect... The elect are always those whose task it is to attest the positive decree, the *telos* of the divine will, the loving-kindness of God. And the rejected must always accompany them to attest the negative decree, that which God in his omnipotence and holiness and love does not will, and therefore his judgment. But it is always the one will of the one God which both attest. Both attest always the covenant which comprehends both, whose power is neither based upon the faithfulness of the elect, nor to be destroyed by the faithlessness of the rejected, whose fulfilment is indeed proclaimed by the blessing heaped upon the elect but also announced, and therefore not denied but made the subject of a new promise, by the curse heaped upon the rejected. It is for this reason

---

118. *CD* II.2, 363: 'We have to listen to two words in all the distinction which is peculiar to our two passages and their obviously conflicting standpoints'.
119. Ibid., 384, 392.
120. Ibid., 167–8; see also p. 123.
121. Ibid., 167.

that the relationship between faithfulness and faithlessness, blessing and curse, life and death, cannot be measured as if some were simply bearers of the first and others simply bearers of the second. It is for this reason that the functions and directions and ways of the complementary figures intersect, as do also the figures themselves. It is for this reason that in their own way the elect are to be censured, while in their own way the rejected are to be commended that the former are not free from the judgments of God, and the latter do not lack signs of His goodness and patience. It is for this reason that the elect and the rejected, in spite of the greatest dissimilarities, can see that in many respects they are only too similar. It is not merely that in spite of the variety of their functions they operate together. On the contrary, they can exchange their functions.[122]

Barth's notion of election, wherein the old and new covenants are substantiated by both the elect and the rejected, does not polarise the faithful and the faithless but rather sees them operating together and even exchanging functions. In his lengthy treatment of Scripture texts that follows, Barth accentuates this dynamic. Beginning with Genesis 4, where the distinction between Cain and Abel rests solely and simply 'on a decision of God concerning them', Barth notes that Cain's sacrifice is not accepted by God and yet he finds grace in the promise of life and protection. Conversely, Abel initially pleases God with his sacrifice, and yet his lot is 'a determination to death'.[123] Their functions and roles are not straightforward, but are in a sense reversed. Similar observations are made about other figures in the patriarchal narratives, including Ephraim and Manasseh (Gen. 48), Perez and Serah (Gen. 38), and more generally between Israel and neighbouring nations.[124] To paraphrase Barth's argument on this point: sinful Israel attests God's character throughout the Old Testament via revelations that are made possible due to the reality of election and non-election. The theme arises as early as Genesis 4, and can be identified in Israel's sacrificial laws (Lev. 14; 16) and in the dynamics between her kings (Saul and David) and prophets (1 Kgs 13), but it is brought to its fullest expression (at least, as far as the Old Testament is concerned) in the relation between Judah and Israel. Moreover, this relationship between Israel and Judah is so important for a proper understanding of how the divine will is expressed in the Old Testament's historical books that it

122. Ibid., 353–4.
123. Ibid., 355. For other theological readings of this text that resist rationalising Abel's election, see R. W. Moberly, *Old Testament Theology: The Theology of the Book of Genesis* (Cambridge: Cambridge University Press, 2009), 92–101; Levenson, *Death and Resurrection*, 74–5.
124. *CD* II.2, 355–6; also 343–4.

is uniquely introduced in 1 Kings 13. As Barth puts it: 'The fulness of these relations and occasions already emerges, in title-form, in 1 K. 13'.[125] But in order to fully appreciate the substance of 1 Kings 13, it will be helpful to approach that text as Barth does, via other Old Testament texts pertaining to the doctrine of election.

Leviticus 14 and 16

Barth's trilogy of Old Testament texts begins with Leviticus 14 and 16. Leviticus 14.4-7 describes the ceremony (involving two birds) for cleansing a leper, and Lev. 16.5-10 describes the sacrificial rite (involving two goats) to be performed on the Great Day of Atonement.[126] About the animals, Barth says this: 'Two creatures which are exactly alike in species and value are dealt with in completely different ways. The selection of the one for this and of the other for that treatment, seems to be a matter for the priest in Lev. $14^{15f.}$, while lots are cast in Lev. 16^8. In both cases it is obvious that the selection is inscrutable, and that it is really made by God himself.'[127] Barth perceives these rites as commentary on the election stories of Genesis,[128] and in characteristic style he affirms throughout that the sacrificial animals attest to the real *Sache* of the Old Testament; 'Jesus Christ is each of the four creatures in Lev. 14 and 16'.[129] But these sacrificial rites that stress the stark divide between death and life whilst also affirming the unity of God's saving grace also have a deeper significance in that they reveal the operative principle of distinction-within-unity.

Saul and David

This Old Testament motif – Barth calls it 'the differentiating choice of God' – is next picked up 'in the opposition of the figures of Saul and David which constitutes the theme of the Books of Samuel'.[130] Barth notes the tension in the DH between a unified Israel and early 'indications of a division of this totality into Israelite kingdoms'.[131] However, the focus of Barth's exegesis here is his depiction of Israel's first kings,

125. Ibid., 403.
126. For an analysis of Barth's hermeneutics in his exegesis of Lev. 16, see Wallace, *The Second Naiveté*, 16–20.
127. *CD* II.2, 257.
128. Ibid., 358, 366.
129. Ibid., 364.
130. Ibid., 366.
131. *CD* II.2, 366–7: 'For according to Jud. 19–21 the tribe of Benjamin is isolated from all the others when it is threatened with total annihilation and then preserved. Later, of course, it is Judah (2 Sam. 2^{1f}; 1 K. 11^{13}, 12^{20}) which replaces it

Saul and David. Saul is rejected in spite of being 'a choice young man' (1 Sam. 9.2) who carries out 99% of the will of God[132] while David is elect in spite of his sin that is 'flagrant and crimson when compared with that of Saul'.[133] Since the Old Testament is so candid about the gravity of David's sin and somewhat ambiguous about Saul's, Barth asks 'what is and is not to be understood by divine election in this tradition'.[134] Clearly, in these narratives, election and/or rejection have no direct correspondence to the measure of one's sinfulness or faithfulness. On the contrary, 'in the Old Testament, the election of a man is that in spite of himself God makes this kind of man a witness to His will, the will of His grace'.[135] Thus, according to Barth, David's sin with Bathsheba is not contradictory to his elected status but is, in fact, 'absolutely indispensable to this presentation'.[136]

In general terms, Barth describes the two books of Samuel as 'the story of the appointment and reign of the first *two and mutually alternating Israelite kings*, Saul and David, as rooted in the divine election'.[137] He thus identifies a similar dynamic in Samuel to the one in Kings; the two prophets in 1 Kings 13 represent Israel and Judah in much the same way that the two kings, David and Saul, represent the people of Israel in the books of Samuel. But the question that vexes Barth most in his consideration of these kings concerns the unity of God's will. What can it really mean, he asks, for an Israelite king to be divinely elected if that king's life is marked by division and ambiguity?[138] Shouldn't election infer single-minded obedience? Would not the historical records of Saul and David have been more beneficial to the post-exilic community if they had been more straightforward in this regard? Barth's answer is that the open or unresolved character of these texts points to the fact that 'they are to be read and understood as prophecy' whose ultimate subject is Jesus Christ.[139] He puts this most clearly in the following statement:

---

in this special situation.' Cf. James Linville, *Israel in the Book of Kings: The Past as a Project of Social Identity*, JSOTSup 272 (Sheffield: Sheffield Academic Press, 1998), 114.

132. *CD* II.2, 371.
133. Ibid., 371, 381.
134. Ibid., 383.
135. Ibid.
136. Ibid.
137. Ibid., 384; emphasis added.
138. Ibid., 387-8.
139. Ibid., 388.

> If we look at this picture from the standpoint of Jesus Christ, i.e., of its proper subject, we immediately understand why the Old Testament record itself expressly brings out all these reservations and does not take any real offence at them; why its picture of the elect king accepts and indeed emphasizes so strongly the negative aspect, not attempting to balance it with the positive, or to offer the reader a composite picture made up equally of light and shade. Just as the rejected king is always rejected in spite of all the light that falls upon him, so the elect king is always what he is…[140]

Thus, both Saul and David (and Barth includes Jeroboam and Solomon along with them) anticipate the kingship of Christ as *both* Rejected and Elect. Two statements undergird Barth's typological Christology: 'The king of Israel rejected by God, whether he be called Saul or Jeroboam, is the prototype and copy of Jesus Christ',[141] and at the same time, 'Conversely, the king of Israel elected by God, David himself and David's son and in his own way every king of Jerusalem, is the prototype and copy of Jesus Christ'.[142]

1 Kings 13

By the time Barth treats 1 Kings 13, the third Old Testament text in his exposition of election, a number of key themes in 1 Kings 13 have already been established. Consequently, and in characteristic fashion, Barth draws theological principles from these other texts and applies them to (or identifies them within) 1 Kings 13. The notion of interchangeability between elect and rejected has been introduced, as well as the related notion that the elect and rejected function together within God's unified will for his people. The principle wherein one's election has no direct correlation to one's moral standing is also relevant. Moreover, as we have seen, Barth notes regarding all three texts that tensions are left unresolved in a manner that points directly to their fulfilment in Christ. This is so in the case of the Levitical sacrifices, the perplexing complementarity of Saul and David, and the two prophets whose burial together evidently anticipates Easter. Having considered Barth's treatment of Leviticus 14 and 16 and of Saul and David, it becomes apparent just why the series of role reversals between the man of God and the Bethel prophet is so important to Barth's theological interpretation of 1 Kings 13. Whether the dialectical formation by which he interprets 1 Kings 13 is present in

---

140. Ibid., 391.
141. Ibid., 390.
142. Ibid., 391.

the narrative itself, or whether it has been imported from his treatment of prior texts, is a question we leave open for now, since Klopfenstein will address it directly in Chapter 3.

Christ

Finally, since each of the Old Testament texts we have reviewed is illustrative of the elect and rejected Christ, this section would be incomplete without reference to the finale of Barth's masterful composition. Since Barth perceives the final scene of 1 Kings 13 (Josiah's discovery of the tomb in 2 Kgs 23.15-20) to direct readers forward to Christ, perhaps his exegesis of the story can only be fully understood if we consider the *telos* of his argument. As Barth puts it himself, 'What else is 1 K. 13 if it is not prophecy? Where else is its fulfilment to be found if not in Jesus Christ?'[143]

Barth insists that these Old Testament illustrations of God's differentiating election point to Christ, in whom the separation between the elect and the rejected is manifested, and equally, in whom the connection between 'these two peoples' is revealed.[144] In Christ it is made known that any apparent opposition between the elect and the rejected 'can only be relative, because both are in the one absolute hand of God'.[145] This truth is not revealed through the interfacing of the elect and rejected throughout Scripture, but only in the person of Jesus Christ, who is *the* Elect and *the* Rejected.[146] Barth's conviction is that we do not understand Jesus more fully in the light of election or Israel or any other biblical theme, but rather that such themes and doctrines are always best understood through Christ. The retrospective lens takes priority, and this applies particularly to Barth's conception of the elect and rejected:

> For all the great difference between them, both have their true existence solely in Him [i.e. Christ]. It is in Him, who originally is both the Elect and the Rejected that their mutual opposition finds its necessity. But it is not simply the relativity of their opposition which is established in Him, but also the fact that in all their opposition they are brothers, mutually related in their being and function, forming an inalienable and indissoluble unity. As the election of Jesus Christ finds its scope and completion in His representative

---

143. Ibid., 409. Cf. 94–145, 340–54.
144. Ibid., 351.
145. Ibid., 350.
146. Ibid., 352–3.

rejection, and as conversely this very representative rejection confirms His election, so the elect and the rejected do not stand only against one another, but also alongside and for one another.[147]

In keeping with this, Barth's accent on the role reversals between the two prophets in 1 Kings 13 is illuminated (unapologetically) by his Christology. He rejects any talk of certain individuals being appointed or predestined as 'elect' to be blessed with faith and fulness of life whilst others are 'rejected' and consigned to a cursed existence of faithlessness.[148] Rather, he states – and this clearly applies to the man of God and the old Bethelite – that 'the functions and directions and ways of the complementary figures intersect, as do also the figures themselves'.[149] The elect and rejected can only be understood together and in light of their reciprocity, and what they signify together is the 'twofold nature' of the love of God as it has been revealed in Christ. For God has purposed to establish a distinction and opposition between himself and all humanity and then to overcome that distinction through the rejection of Christ. 'God loves us as He makes this distinction. This is how He loves His only Son. This is how He loves us in Him.'[150]

Without doubt, Barth's christological reading is internally coherent, and brilliant in many respects. However, if doubts are to be raised about the manner in which Barth reaches such an overtly christological conclusion, then they ought to be articulated in a way that is fair to Barth's own deliberate decisions regarding his canonical parameters and contextualisation. Simply put, it is unfair to critique Barth according to a set of hermeneutical guidelines that did not govern his exegesis. For instance, Barth's identification of multiple reversals in the story appears to be a by-product of his propensity for dialectical theology and his related conviction (or presupposition) that the Old Testament contains multiple examples of 'God's differentiating election'. To some, these are perceived as external categories that have no rightful place in an exegetical study of this Old Testament text. Yet these tendencies and convictions have been drawn out in Barth's exegetical work because of his close attention to the whole canon of Christian Scripture (read intertextually) and from a text-based hermeneutic that avoids the reductionism of equating truth with historicity. Not to mention the fact that every reader contributes something of themselves to the making of meaning, and Barth's mind

147. Ibid., 353.
148. Contra Calvin; see n. 114 above.
149. Ibid., 353–4.
150. Ibid., 354.

happened to work in such a way that this dialectical pattern was the one he saw. In short, Barth's use of 1 Kings 13 to illustrate his unique doctrine of election is warranted by his distinct methodological proclivities, and the same principle applies to his christological interest. His reading is, by all accounts and for obvious reasons, Barthian! And since Barth reads the Old Testament and New Testament as two parts of a single canon, such that 'Christ is manifest in the Old Testament as the expected one',[151] he can hardly be faulted for reading Old Testament texts in ways that lean into Christ. Another interpreter might wish to do things differently (and be equally clear about his or her method and intentions), but it would unfair – and untrue – to say that Barth's reading is misguided on his own terms. But we shall return to these issues in chapters to come.

As a brief aside, I do not mean to suggest that in our postmodern milieu all readers are now above reproach, or criticism – or to paraphrase Dtr, that each may do what is right in their own eyes because there is no hermeneutical king governing the literary landscape. Readings can be more, or less, faithful to a text; they can be in/consistent by the reader's own prescribed methodology; they can cut corners to reach foregone conclusions; and so on and so forth. Ultimately, of the multiple readings availed by any given text, some will ring true, bear fruit, and make sense, more than others. The proof of the pudding is in the eating, as it were.

My own opinion of Barth's christological reading, as I hinted at earlier, is that by highlighting certain dynamics in the story (such as reciprocity) and images (such as the grave) over others, Barth effectively narrows the interpretive possibilities of the narrative in order to nudge it towards a *particular* christological climax. I am not opposed to christological readings in principle (at all), though it seems to me that Barth jumps the gun somewhat, especially since Josiah's righteous actions in 2 Kings 23, which hardly bear mentioning in Barth's exegesis, pave the interpretive way to Christ with arguably greater clarity (and content) than just the image of a tombstone. The point is, I do not agree with Barth that it is 'difficult' to offer a reading of 1 Kings 13 within the confines of Old Testament history. On the contrary, I will argue that a comprehensive treatment of the text's 'real epilogue' has the potential to illuminate the strange story in 1 Kings 13 *and* to deliver an even greater christological punchline. But we are getting ahead of ourselves. In any case, by way of summary, Barth's ultimate contention that the story functions to illuminate God's salvific work in Christ has given some historical-critical scholars cause to abandon his theological interpretation in its entirety.

151. *CD* II.2, 72.

Summary of Barth's Contribution

Barth's exegesis of 1 Kings 13 has not generally found favour with Old Testament scholars, and in the next chapter we will examine the nature of these disagreements in greater detail. But whatever one's view on certain issues of contention, Barth's theological exegesis of this narrative surely proffers a range of potential gains for biblical scholars, provided that the scholars in question are open to a variety of methodological approaches, and to literary-theological as well as historical insights. We conclude this chapter, then, with a summary of Barth's more significant contributions for the task of reading 1 Kings 13, each of which has been picked up and developed in varying degrees by other exegetes.

1 Kings 13 as Narrative Analogy

Barth's suggestion that the man of God from Judah and the Bethel prophet represent the nations whence they come seems a simple, perhaps even obvious, observation to make. 1 Kings 13 would surely seem out of place were it not for the fact that its literary context addresses the division and enmity between north and south. 1 Kings 12 outlines the division of the kingdoms under Rehoboam and Jeroboam, and the subsequent record of Israel's and Judah's kings (1 Kgs 14–2 Kgs 21) is carefully narrated so as to keep the record balanced. Even so, relatively few interpreters have adopted this insight for their own interpretive endeavours.

Barth's exegesis treats the entire story according to its own internal logic, but at the same time he proposes that 1 Kings 13 is presented as a kind of parable concerning the relational dynamic between Judah and Israel. This has significant implications for scholars interested in the story's original form and its redaction into the DH, but it also has significance for those interested in synchronic analysis. In its received form, does 1 Kings 13 function like the programmatic speeches identified by Wellhausen and Noth as theological markers in the history? We shall return to this question in Chapter 7.

Reading 1 Kings 13 Synchronically

In many ways, Barth was ahead of his time. This can certainly be said of his preference for attending to the final form of 1 Kings 13 over reconstructions of its (hypothetical) pre-Deuteronomistic forms.[152] Barth's

---

152. E.g., Erik Eynikel, 'Prophecy and Fulfillment in the Deuteronomistic History: 1 Kgs 13; 2 Kgs 23, 16-18', in *Pentateuch and Deuteronomistic Studies*, ed. C. Brekelmans and J. Lust, BETL 94 (Leuven: Leuven University Press, 1990),

theological readings of texts have been considered too explicitly religious by those who would prefer to keep biblical scholarship and matters of faith a safe distance from one another. Krister Stendahl, for instance, described Barth's method as one that dissolved the criteria distinguishing what a text *meant* from what it *means*, so that for Barth, 'what is intended as a commentary turns out to be a theological tractate'.[153]

So, while his contemporaries were interested in the meaning and origins of this 'prophetic legend' prior to its (apparent) redaction into the DH, Barth makes it clear that what is at stake in his theological interpretation is the meaning of the text as it stands. Barth had a significant influence on Childs in this regard, and in some ways was a forerunner for Childs' canonical approach.[154] Similarly, while much of Barth's exegesis preceded the 'literary turn' of the late 1960s and early 1970s (he died in December, 1968), Barth's exegetical method has more in common with narratology than with the historical-critical method of many of his contemporaries. In particular, Barth pays close attention to characterisation, plot, dialogue, and the voice of the narrator in 1 Kings 13, and the narratological observations he makes undergird many of his astute theological insights.

In addition to these particular contributions, Barth's distinctively theological reading has been recognised for exposing the 'essential substantive content' (*wesentlichen Aussagegehalt*)[155] of 1 Kings 13. Even

227 37; Werner F. Lemke, 'The Way of Obedience: I Kings 13 and the Structure of the Deuteronomistic History', in *Magnalia Dei: The Mighty Acts of God*, Festschrift for G. E. Wright, ed. F. M. Cross, W. E. Lemke, and P. D. Miller, Jr. (Garden City: Doubleday, 1976), 301–4; Thomas B. Dozeman, 'The Way of the Man of God from Judah: True and False Prophecy in the Pre-Deuteronomic Legend of 1 Kings 13', *CBQ* 44 (1982): 379–93; Walter Gross, 'Lying Prophet and Disobedient Man of God in 1 Kings 13: Role Analysis as an Instrument of Theological Interpretation of an Old Testament Narrative Text', *Semeia* 15 (1979): 100–107. A PhD dissertation submitted in 2012 on Barth's reading of this passage is divided into three parts, the first of which assumes a pre-Deuteronomistic form of the story. See Mark Dwayne Allen, 'The Man of God, the Old Prophet, and the Word of the LORD' (PhD diss., University of Notre Dame, 2012), 11–83.

153. Krister Stendahl, 'Biblical Theology, Contemporary', in *Interpreter's Dictioe nary of the Bible* (Nashville: Abingdon, 1962), 420. The remark was made regarding Barth's *Römerbrief*.

154. Childs recalls some interesting engagements with Barth in Basel in the early 1950s, and his writings credit Barth in numerous ways. See Daniel R. Driver, *Brevard Childs, Biblical Theologian: For the Church's One Bible* (Tübingen: Mohr Siebeck, 2010), 90–1.

155. The phrase is used by Kraus in his foreword to Barth's exegesis (vol. 10 of *Biblische Studien*, 9) and picked up again by Klopfenstein, who commends Barth but

Barth's most thorough critic concludes that he has succeeded in lifting precious treasure from 'the diversely vegetated field of this peculiarly strange chapter of the Old Testament'.[156] To that critic's analysis we now turn.

---

remains uncertain of what comprises this *wesentlichen Aussagegehalt* (Klopfenstein, '1. Könige 13', 671: 'Es bleibt Karl Barths Verdienst, den kostbaren Schatz dieses Zeugnisses aus dem bunt bewachsenen Acker des seltsam fremden alt-testamentlichen Kapitels gehoben zu haben').

156. Klopfenstein, '1. Könige 13', 672.

3

Martin A. Klopfenstein

The previous chapter provided a summary of Barth's theological exegesis of 1 Kings 13. His understanding of the function and content of the story was outlined in light of his hermeneutical priorities and the doctrinal context for his exegesis (vol. II.2 of *Dogmatics*). But while Barth's treatment of this text has been hailed as 'classic'[1] and 'justly famous',[2] very few scholars have proffered a thorough critical appraisal of his exegesis. Martin Klopfenstein is one of the few, and was the first, to do so. Moreover, Klopfenstein made it clear that his primary focus was Barth's exegetical method, so his evaluation of Barth is of special interest for this book given our double agenda, to explore both the how and the what of reading 1 Kings 13. In this chapter, I review Klopfenstein's appraisal of Barth and consider the impact that his essay had upon subsequent scholarship.

Klopfenstein's Evaluation of Barth's Exegesis *(1966)*

Klopfenstein's rigorous critique of Barth's reading of 1 Kings 13 was proffered in a Festschrift celebrating Barth's eightieth birthday in 1966.[3] In his opening comments, Klopfenstein acknowledges that Barth's exegeses of Old Testament texts typically raise stimulating hermeneutical questions, yet he notes his disapproval of Barth's overtly theological method – as the tripartite structure of his essay suggests.[4] Regarding his

---

1. Crenshaw, *Prophetic Conflict*, 40.
2. Walsh, 'Contexts', 368.
3. Klopfenstein, '1. Könige 13', 639–72.
4. Part I, *Barths Exegese von 1. Könige 13* [Barth's exegesis of 1 Kings 13] (ibid., 639–46), is set in juxtaposition with part II, *Hauptzüge einer historisch-kritischen*

purpose, Klopfenstein states: 'By the example of 1 Kings 13, Barth's exegetical approach will be presented, confronted with an historical-critical interpretation, and evaluated'.[5] He thus clarifies from the outset that it is 'Barth's exegetical method' (*Barths exegetische Arbeitsweise*) that is in focus; i.e. the details and conclusions of Barth's exegesis are assessed in order to evaluate his methodology. As Klopfenstein puts it, 'our critical question has more to do with the approach and interpretive method of Barth, which of course manifest themselves very clearly in certain details, which is why they have to be – though not exclusively – assessed from within those details'.[6] Accordingly, Klopfenstein begins his analysis by locating Barth's exegesis of 1 Kings 13 within the broader scheme of the *Dogmatics*:

> These writings are in the larger context of the doctrine of God, more precisely: God's gracious election, (even) more precisely: the election of the individual. Immediately under the headline 'The Elect and the Rejected', the inseparability of God's election and God's non-election is exemplified, how it is brought about in Christ (p. 452f.) and ultimately revealed as reality in Christ. 1 Kings 13 is therefore being scrutinized from the perspective of God's electing and rejecting activity, and interpreted as a testimony to the unity and distinctiveness of (both) election and rejection.[7]

Exegese von 1. Könige 13 [The main features of an historical-critical exegesis of 1 Kgs 13] (ibid., 646–6), leading into a brief synthesis in part III, *Konfrontation und Würdigung* [Confrontation and evaluation] (ibid., 667–72).

5. Ibid., 639: 'Am Beispiel von 1. Könige 13 soll Barths exegetische Arbeitsweise dargestellt, mit der historisch-kritischen Auslegung konfrontiert und gewürdigt werden'. Klopfenstein's critique of Barth bears similarities to those of Walter Baumgartner. See the correspondence between Barth and Baumgartner (between 1940 and 1955) in Rudolf Smend, 'Karl Barth und Walter Baumgartner: Ein Briefwechsel über das Alte Testament', in *Zeitschrift für Theologie und Kirche, Beiheft 6: Zur Theologie Karl Barths Beiträge aus Anlass seines 100. Geburtstags*, ed. Eberhard Jüngel (Tübingen: Mohr Siebeck, 1986), 240–71.

6. Klopfenstein, '1. Könige 13', 667: 'Vielmehr betrifft unsere kritische Anfrage mehr den Ansatz und die Methode der Auslegung Barths, die sich freilich gerade in bestimmten Details besonders deutlich manifestieren und darum zwar nicht nur, aber doch auch von ihnen aus beurteilt werden müssen'.

7. Ibid., 640: 'Die Stücke stehen im größeren Zusammenhang der Lehre von Gott, näher: von Gottes Gnadenwahl, näher: von der Erwählung des Einzelnen. Unter der direkten Überschrift "Der Erwählte und der Verworfene" wird an ihnen das unablösliche Beieinander von Gottes Erwählen und Gottes Verwerten, wie es dann in Christus (S. 452f.) letztgültig offenbare Wirklichkeit geworden ist, exemplifiziert. 1. Könige 13 wird also unter dem Gesichtspunkt des erwählenden und verwerfenden

3. Martin A. Klopfenstein

Klopfenstein is clearly cognizant of the way Barth's exegesis illuminates his doctrine of Election and yet, somewhat unfairly, he proceeds to assess Barth from within an historical-critical paradigm. Rather than accepting that Barth's intertextual and canonical hermeneutics lead him to draw motifs (e.g., election) and patterns (e.g., double pictures) from thematically related texts so as to apply them to 1 Kings 13, Klopfenstein implies from the outset that Barth's reading ought to build on the same foundations as most other biblical interpreters of his time.

The first section of Klopfenstein's engagement with Barth summarises his colleague's reading of the text (as I have done in the previous chapter), making minor comments along the way. Following Barth's divisions of the story, he outlines the two double-pictures and their relation to one another.

Zur Einzelexegese

In part two, 'The Main Features of an Historical-Critical Exegesis of 1 Kings 13' (pp. 646–66), Klopfenstein briefly raises issues concerning the form, unity and origins of the story before presenting an historical-critical exegetical treatment of the narrative under the heading, 'To the single exegesis'.[8] He stresses that he has no intention of providing a full exegetical treatment of the chapter. (For that, readers are referred to the 'recent' commentaries of John Gray and Johannes Fichtner, both published in 1964 [9]) His intention is different: 'I want here to trace the course of the narrative with only a few strokes and to introduce some details that are important for the engagement with Karl Barth'.[10]

Klopfenstein's *Einzelexegese* commences with some speculation about the inevitability of Jeroboam's syncretistic cultus as an attempt to consolidate his independence,[11] and the nature of the distinction between

---

Handelns Gottes befragt und als Zeugnis der Einheit und Unterschiedenheit dieses erwählenden und verwertenden Handelns ausgelegt.'

8. Ibid., 652: 'Zur Einzelexegese'.

9. John Gray, *I & II Kings* (London: SCM, 1964); Joseph Fichtner, *Das erste Buch von den Königen*, BAT (Stuttgart: Calwer, 1964).

10. Klopfenstein, '1. Könige 13', 652: 'Ich möchte hier nur den Gang der Erzählung mit ein paar Strichen nachzeichnen und auf einige Einzelheiten eintreten, die für die Konfrontation mit Karl Barth wichtig sind'

11. Ibid., 653. Similarly, Frank Moore Cross, 'Yahweh and 'El', in *Canaanite Myth and Hebrew Epic: Essays in the History of the Religion of Israel* (Cambridge, MA: Harvard University Press, 1973), 73–5, argues that the sin of Jeroboam is not idolatry or false worship, but the eschewing of Jerusalem.

a 'man of God' and a 'prophet' in the ancient world.[12] Klopfenstein's judgments on these matters anticipate key elements in his delineation of the story, which he reads as a pro-Bethel story defending the presence of truth-bearers in the north as well as in Judah. Central to Klopfenstein's interpretation of 1 Kings 13 is his assertion that the old prophet commits an *intentional* act of deceit on behalf of his king because he understands the gravity of what has occurred in Bethel: the man of God has desecrated Jeroboam's sacrifice, and everything is now at stake. So this prophet from Bethel does what he is specially equipped to do because of his age,[13] simultaneously achieving two ends through his act of deception. On one hand, the Judean's prophecy concerning Bethel 'by the word of the Lord' (v. 2) will be negated if he clearly – and publicly – disobeys the threefold command that was also received 'by the word of the Lord' (vv. 9, 17). On the other hand, the man of God's visit to the house of the Bethel prophet constitutes an acknowledgement of Bethel's equality with Jerusalem; i.e. their shared meal suggests 'community among equals'.[14] In essence, then, the old Bethel prophet aims to vindicate Jeroboam's cultus by upending the man of God's obedience to the word. Klopfenstein understands the Bethel prophet's deceit to thereby accomplish a specific purpose: 'The syncretism of Jeroboam was therefore not rubbish, but rather a legitimate form of Yahweh worship. The old prophet had rescued the cause of Jeroboam'.[15]

In spite of this wilful deception, however, the old prophet makes a startling transition; from representing the cultic concerns of his king to proclaiming a genuine word of prophecy. This twist in the plot is genuinely 'most dramatic and surprising' (*höchst dramatisch und überraschend*) – an important point for Klopfenstein's critique of Barth,

---

12. Klopfenstein, '1. Könige 13', 653–4, concurs with Alfred Jepsen, *Nabi: Soziologische Studien zur alttestamentlichen Literatur und Religionsgeschichte* (Munich: Beck, 1934), 182, who distinguishes between Yahwistic prophets of north and south.

13. I.e. only an aged and experienced prophet will succeed against this Judean opponent [*Gegner*] (Klopfenstein, '1. Könige 13', 657).

14. Ibid., 658: 'die Gemeinschaft unter Gleichberechtigten'.

15. Ibid.: 'Der Synkretismus Jerobeams war also kein Abfall, sondern eine legitime Form des Jahwedienstes. Der alte Nabi hatte die Sache Jerobeams gerettet.' Incidentally, Crenshaw misunderstands the context of this statement in Klopfenstein's argument. He states that Klopfenstein 'goes so far as to argue that the syncretistic cult of Jeroboam was a legitimate form of Yahweh worship' (*Prophetic Conflict*, 44). However, Klopfenstein is not presenting his own view, but rather commenting on the impact or effect of the old prophet's deception. Klopfenstein's view, quite to the contrary, rests entirely on the fact that Jeroboam's cult was *illegitimate* – and was condemned as such by both southern and northern prophets.

since the *schriller Dissonanz* of this moment does not conform to any preconceived dialectic pattern. Whatever false notion of community or equality that may have existed briefly between the two prophets is now shattered by the divine judgment that passes between them.[16] Significantly, the new oracle is spoken by the northern prophet, who now declares that the Judean will be killed by a lion because he has 'rebelled against the mouth of the LORD' (v. 21).[17] In saying this, the Bethel prophet's oracle verifies that the initial proclamation against Jeroboam's altar will certainly be fulfilled in due course. This detail is central to Klopfenstein's reading. 'The point of all of this last section in vv. 20b-32 is in that respect, to make it clear: it is by divine election that real Jahwistic prophets are also in the northern kingdom, and this manifests itself as such in the fact that they reject the cultic schism and the Canaanite-Yahwistic syncretism'.[18] Any doubts concerning whether Jeroboam's cult was sinful in God's eyes are thereby done away with, as attested by the fate of the Judean *and* the subsequent reiteration of his prophecy in v. 32: 'For the saying that he proclaimed by the word of the LORD against the altar in Bethel, and against all the houses of the high places that are in the cities of Samaria, shall surely come to pass'. Thus, the greater goal (*Ziel*) of the narrative is accomplished, as Klopfenstein understands it; namely, to communicate that there are true prophets in the north as well as the south, both of whom have proclaimed God's irrefutable verdict against the cult of Jeroboam.[19]

> 1 Kings 13 is thus a rather dramatic illustration, signifying for these circles of colleagues who approved of the Bethel cult what a true, northern Israelite, Yahwistic prophet was responsible for. At the same time it meant that bearers of truth in this matter are not only found in Judah after all, but also in the northern kingdom.[20]

---

16. Klopfenstein, '1. Könige 13', 658.
17. Following Gray, Klopfenstein understands the verb hrm to mean 'defy authority'. Ibid., 659.
18. Ibid., 659: 'Die Pointe dieses ganzen letzten Abschnittes vv 20b-32 liegt darin, deutlich zu machen: Es gibt kraft göttlicher Erwählung echte Jahweprophetie auch im Nordreich, und als solche zeigt sie sich eben darin, daß sie das kultische Schisma und den kanaanäisch-jahwistischen Synkretismus ablehnt'.
19. Ibid.
20. Ibid., 655: '1. Könige 13 ist dann ein recht drastisches Exempel, mit dem diese Kreise ihren den Kult Bethels billigenden Kollegen bedeuteten, was ein rechter nordisraelitischer Jahweprophet zu vertreten habe, und mit dem sie zugleich zu verstehen gaben, daß die Träger der Wahrheit in dieser Sache immerhin nicht nur in Juda, sondern auch im Nordreich zu finden seien'.

Following this discussion, Klopfenstein proceeds to explore the significance of the lion. He devotes considerable time and space to expressing his disbelief at various hypotheses that are expressed with unmerited certitude.[21] In contrast to various well-known scholars, Klopfenstein finds it difficult to detect any supposed 'qualities' (*Eigenschaften*) in the lion when the narrator speaks only of 'its function, its role in the course of events'.[22] Klopfenstein takes this opportunity (citing Barth, Vischer and others) to warn against interpretations that are overly moralistic or theological because certain readers feel the need to overindulge keywords like 'lion' by searching for something that simply isn't there.[23]

Since Barth understands the elect to suffer on behalf of the rejected, he refers to the lion who strikes the Judean as the 'lion of Judah'.[24] That is to say, the lion represents God who strikes his own on behalf of sinful Israel. Klopfenstein considers this assessment to go well beyond the intended meaning of the text, insisting, rather, that only two simple statements can rightly be made about the lion, both of which express its dual purpose.[25] First – and Klopfenstein stresses that this is intended *theologically* – the lion kills the Judean (vv. 24, 26). As the old prophet puts it in v. 26, 'The LORD has given him to the lion'. The lion's first function, then, is quite simply 'to be the punitive tool of Yahweh'.[26] The second assertion that can safely be made is that the lion stands beside the corpse without consuming it and refrains from harming the donkey (vv. 24, 28). To what end? In Klopfenstein's view, the whole purpose of the lion's action (or inaction) is that passers-by noticing the strange scene are compelled to spread the word concerning the fate of the Judean. That is, the lion's *Abstinenz* thereby makes possible a sequence of events that captures Jeroboam's attention, since no one who has seen the spectacle (including the old Bethel prophet) can in the end harbour any doubt about the divine

---

21. Klopfenstein notes with surprise that Duhm presumes to call the lion (and the donkey) 'righteous' while Gunkel describes it as a 'really brave lion'. But even worse is Greßmann, who treats the entire story under the intolerable, moralising heading: 'the disobedient man of God and the obedient animal of God'

22. Klopfenstein, '1. Könige 13', 660: 'seine Funktion, seine Rolle im Ablauf der Ereignisse'.

23. Ibid., 661–5.

24. *CD* II.2, 407. Barth again interfaces the reference to the lion with other key texts; Gen. 49.9; Amos 1.2; 3.8 (ibid., 397).

25. Klopfenstein, '1. Könige 13', 660: 'Es werden über ihn nur zwei Aussagen gemacht'.

26. Ibid.: 'Das ist seine erste Funktion: Strafwerkzeug Jahwes zu sein'.

rejection of Jeroboam's cultus. When the 'grotesque conspicuousness' (*groteske Augenfälligkeit*) of this scene – a prophet's corpse at the feet of a lion and a donkey – reaches the old Bethel prophet (once again, via his sons), he is prompted to offer up an explanation for the strange turn of events (v. 26). And as the divine judgment that was initially proclaimed by the man of God from Judah is now echoed by a second, more familiar (i.e. northern) voice, Jeroboam can no longer deny that his cultus has in fact been rejected by God. Indeed, as Klopfenstein puts it, 'the old Nabi had turned from cultic friend to cultic foe of the king!'[27]

Finally, in keeping with this, Klopfenstein suggests that the Bethelite seeks neither protection nor atonement in his request to be buried next to the man of God. Rather, his purpose is to further strengthen the unity of their prophetic utterance. 'Anyone should be able to see that he really was side by side, without distance and without reservation, beside the Judean.'[28] This, as it turns out, is the central thrust of Klopfenstein's *Einzelexegese*; that in 1 Kings 13, both the man of God from Judah and the old Bethel prophet give voice to the same proclamation against Bethel.

Konfrontation und Würdigung

In part three of his essay, 'Confrontation and Evaluation',[29] Klopfenstein turns from exegetical details to 'the main question...namely, whether the text itself proves Barth right in understanding it as a witness for God's electing and rejecting, rejecting and electing, and their peculiar juxtaposition'.[30] Klopfenstein seeks ultimately to assess whether Barth is interpreting the story through foreign categories that are not immediately present in the text. Not only does Klopfenstein stick firmly to his historical-critical guns at this point, but he manifests either an unwillingness or a blindness to the possibility of assessing Barth within an alternative set of parameters that include intertextual hermeneutics, dialectic patterns, and a christological framework.

---

27. Ibid., 661: 'der alte Nabi, vom kultischen Freund zum kultischen Gegner des Königs geworden war!'

28. Ibid., 666: 'Jedermann sollte sehen können, daß er wirklich Seite an Seite, ohne Distanz und ohne Vorbehalt, neben dem Judäer lag'.

29. Ibid., 667–72.

30. Ibid., 667: 'so werden wir nur atil die Hauptfrage näher eintreten, auf die Frage nämlich, ob der Text selber Barth das Recht gibt, ihn als Zeugnis für das erwählende und verwerfende, verwerfende und erwählende Handeln Gottes und ihr eigentümliches Beieinander zu verstehen'.

Klopfenstein begins by comparing Barth's exegetical results with those of his own historical-critical analysis, and he notes a manifold compliance between the two outlines with regards to both historic and thematic details. Where differences between Barth's exposition and Klopfenstein's historical-critical analysis exist, these are explained by Barth's propensity for imposing extraneous, critical questions upon the exegetical task. Specifically, he is referring to Barth's explication of multiple role reversals between the elect man of God and the rejected Bethel prophet: 'Barth describes the sequence of events in our narrative as a dialectic movement'.[31] Since this pattern is pivotal to Barth's understanding of the theological significance of 1 Kings 13 for the doctrine of election (as we noted in the previous chapter), Klopfenstein proceeds with a summary of Barth's five reversals:

i. the elect presents God's word of judgement to the rejected at Bethel;
ii. the rejected takes over his mission when the elect succumbs to temptation;
iii. the elect suffers the penalty of death on behalf of the rejected;
iv. the rejected offers the elect his own grave as a resting place;
v. the elect preserves the bones of the rejected when he is laid beside him.[32]

He then explains: 'this juxtaposition is understood as a type of the merging of the Elect and Rejected in the figure of Jesus Christ, in whom the unity of Israel in its eschatological grandeur finds eternal, lasting fulfilment'.[33] But while Barth's reading may have an internal coherence of sorts, Klopfenstein objects to his multiple role reversals and undergirding dialectic pattern on two grounds:

> Two critical questions arise from this. First is the purely *exegetical* objection; there can be no talk of several role changes. The *one*, real turning point in the narrative falls clearly in v. 20. Here *one* surprising role reversal takes place. This is already clear in purely formal terms; only here does God explicitly intervene in the plot and give it a new twist.[34]

---

31. Ibid.: 'Barth schildert den Verlauf der Ereignisse in unserer Erzählung als dialektische Bewegung'.
32. Ibid.
33. Ibid., 667–8: 'dieses Beieinander wird verstanden als Typus jenes Ineinanders von Erwähltem und Verworfenem in der Gestalt Jesu Christi, in der die Einheit Israels als eschatologische Größe ihre in Ewigkeit bleibende Verwirklichung findet'.
34. Ibid., 668 (emphasis original): 'Hier brechen zwei kritische Fragen auf. Zunächst ist rein *exegetisch* einzuwenden, daß von mehreren Rollenwechseln wohl

Klopfenstein's first objection – that the only real turning point in the story occurs in v. 20, where the mission of the man of God passes over to the Bethel prophet – is 'purely exegetical'. He appears to mean by this that only one turning point is referred to explicitly in the text itself (*der Text selber*). Only in v. 20, says Klopfenstein, is it justifiable to speak of the unworthy Nabi crossing over into the sphere of election – where he remains.

Klopfenstein's second objection follows from this: the point of the story's reversal is that the two prophets, elect and rejected though they may be at the beginning of the story, are drawn together – and remain irrevocably together – in such a way that they ultimately share the divine commission to testify against Bethel. To put it differently, what Barth perceives as 'reciprocal advocacy' (*das wechselseitige Eintreten*) between the northern and southern prophets throughout vv. 11-32, Klopfenstein sees as the 'sustenance' (*Durchhalten*) of the Bethel prophet's newly acquired mission, following the story's (single) plot reversal.[35] While Klopfenstein is prepared to acknowledge a degree of complementarity between the prophets from v. 20 onwards, he flatly denies any notion of repeated reversals: 'There can be no denying that the acquired role which the old Nabi has to play in vv. 11-32, is uninterpretable without his peculiar way of being together with the Judean. But in these verses a genuine role reversal is no longer present.'[36]

After the Bethel prophet receives a genuine word from the LORD in v. 20, the next shift of roles, according to Barth's schema, is the man of God's death on behalf of the rejected (iii above). As one might expect, Klopfenstein considers the notion of vicarious suffering to be foreign (*fern*) to the narrative, and he sees no reason to infer additional role reversals from the report of a common grave (iv and v above). On the contrary, Klopfenstein perceives the old prophet's acquired (*übernommene*) election to be established – once and for all – in v. 20 and then sustained in what follows through a series of public incidents:

---

nicht die Rede sein kann. Die *eine* wirkliche Zäsur in der Erzählung fällt deutlich auf v 20. Hier findet der *eine* überraschende Rollentausch statt. Das wird schon rein formal dadurch klar, daß nur hier Gott ausdrücklich in die Handlung eingreift und ihr eine neue Wendung gibt.'

35. Ibid., 668–9.

36. Ibid., 668: 'Es soll nicht geleugnet werden, daß die übernommene Rolle, die der alte Nabi in den vv 11-32 zu spielen hat, ohne das eigentümliche Zusammensein mit dem Judäer nicht deutbar ist. Doch liegt in diesen Versen ein eigentlicher Rollentausch nicht mehr vor.'

> The fact that the Nabi *acquired* the corpse of the man of God proves his role as an *acquired* [i.e. elect; the wordplay is less effective in English], and thereafter precisely this [fact] will be encountered again and again by the Bethel public: first by those passersby, which tell of the grotesque road-scene, then through the transportation of the body, then by the Judean burial in the grave of the old man, finally through the burial of the old man himself at the Judean's side.[37]

Klopfenstein's critique of this imposed series of reversals leads naturally to the matter of the enigmatic lion. Barth's argument – that 'the lion of Judah' strikes the elect instead of the rejected – requires not only that the notion of substitution be imported from Isaiah 53 into 1 Kings 13;[38] it leans on the assumption that the man of God re-assumes his role as the elect after breaking the commandment and departing from the Bethelite's home. But if Klopfenstein is right about a single turning point – i.e. the old prophet maintains his assumed role as the elect until the end – then one cannot properly speak of the lion striking the elect when it kills the man of God from Judah. In other words, Barth's theological identification of the lion must also be deemed foreign to the narrative. Klopfenstein thus seeks to nullify Barth's *Überinterpretation* of the lion by arguing that this animal, in all its ambiguity, 'is quite simply the agent of Yahweh'.[39]

Having made the case that Barth imposes external categories (multiple role reversals and the 'lion of Judah') upon his interpretation of 1 Kings 13, Klopfenstein raises one last critical question concerning Barth's exegetical method. He asks, 'Is not a dialectical scheme of thought, whose self-powered movement insists on a final synthesis of thesis and antithesis, at times couched in Barth's interpretation, which is on the whole very impressive, like an external [alien] force?'[40]

---

37. Ibid., 669 (emphasis added): 'Daran, daß der Nabi die Leiche des Gottesmannes übernimmt, erweist er seine Rolle als eine übernommene, und eben darauf soll das öffentliche Bethel wieder und wieder gestoßen werden: erst durch jene Passanten, die von der grotesken Wegszene berichten, dann durch die Überführung der Leiche, dann durch die Bestattung des Judäers im Grab des Alten, endlich durch die Bestattung des Alten selbst an des Judäers Seite'.

38. Ibid., 669–70.

39. Ibid., 669, 670.

40. Ibid., 670: 'Liegt nicht ein dialektisches Denkschema, das seine aus ihm selber stammende Bewegung in dem auf eine letzte Synthese hindrängenden Wiederspiel von These und Antithese findet, streckenweise wie ein fremder Zwang auf der im Ganzen sehr eindrücklichen Interpretation Barths?'

To illustrate Barth's penchant for dialectics, Klopfenstein cites the following passage, where Barth explains the theological significance of the division between Israel and Judah:

> If the separation and opposition in Israel's ways and stories are necessary, they may and can exist only in such a way that they point beyond themselves. They must still witness to the unity of God's will, and therefore also to the unity of Israel; to the truth which is now eschatological, but which is all the more true for that very reason. And they must do so with a force which was impossible for the undivided kingdom, monarchy and prophecy. For the human division speaks much more loudly than any human solidarity could ever do of God Himself as the real basis of Israel, and not its own kings and prophets. Just because of the division there are now authentic relations in the history of Israel.[41]

In response, Klopfenstein asks:

> Is not the disruption of the initial unity [of Israel] here a necessary transitional stage on the way to better eschatological unity, so that dualism of thought and history are the required conditio sine qua non of a better monism? And is not what will arrive and mature in the final and better unity already all on the way, hidden in thesis and antithesis, and embryonically laid out? But in this view is there still room for new settlements of God and responsible decisions of people, for election and rejection, for faithfulness and sin, in short: for genuine history?[42]

Klopfenstein rightly perceives that Israel's division, presented as the culmination and expression of many other such divisions in the Old Testament, is considered by Barth to be necessary in order that God's unified and eschatological will – for the union of the elect and rejected in Christ – might be fully revealed.[43] But for Klopfenstein, such a view of

---

41. *CD*, 403; *KD*, 446; Klopfenstein, '1. Könige 13', 670.
42. Klopfenstein, '1. Könige 13', 670–1: 'Ist hier nicht das Auseinanderbrechen der anfänglichen Einheit ein notwendiges Durchgangsstadium auf dem Weg zur besseren eschatologischen Einheit, also der Dualismus die denk- und geschichtsnotwendige conditio sine qua non eines besseren Monismus? Und ist nicht, was in der letzten besseren Einheit ankommen und reifen wird, alles schon jetzt in These und Antithese verborgen auf dem Weg und keimhaft angelegt? Ist aber in dieser Sicht noch Raum für neue Setzungen Gottes und zu verantwortende Entscheidungen des Menschen, für Erwählung und Verwerfung, für Treue und Sünde, kurz: für echte Geschichte?'
43. Cf. Barth, *CD* I.2, §14: 45–121.

history is so rigid and preordained that it leaves no room for an authentic response from either people or God, or as he puts it, for 'genuine history' (*echte Geschichte*). Klopfenstein therefore suggests an alternative:

> In contrast, 1 Kings 13 bears witness with its one turnabout to a real progression in the history of new, unexpected stages that are not anticipated by any law of historical movement. And only in their openness to a new and surprising way is the real future eschatological dimension of the stage reached in each case; God on the way with his people. What remains in the end is the assurance that Yahweh cannot be dissuaded by human disobedience from this path and that his judgments and saving words will remain the light on this path.[44]

In the final analysis, then, Klopfenstein is critical of Barth for reading external categories into the narrative both structurally, through his imposition of dialectical theology expressed in multiple reversals, and exegetically, in his interpretation of the lion, for instance. This is especially problematic since Barth's perception of the reciprocal relationship between the prophets is absolutely central to his presentation. If the driving force of Barth's reading is found to have been imposed upon the text, does this not compromise his whole interpretive enterprise? We shall return to this question and reconsider the methodological divergence between Barth and Klopfenstein in Chapter 5, where hermeneutics and methodology are our primary concerns.

In spite of Klopfenstein's criticisms that cut to the heart of Barth's reading, he is by no means dismissive of Barth's exegesis of 1 Kings 13. On the contrary, when Klopfenstein eventually returns to his primary question – whether Barth is right to understand the text as a witness to election and rejection – he expresses an indebtedness to Barth for 'the really proper exposition of the theological witness of 1 Kings 13'.[45] In fact, he goes further, acknowledging that there is truth to Barth's claim

---

44. Klopfenstein, '1. Könige 13', 671 (emphasis original): 'Demgegenüber bezeugt 1. Könige 13 mit seiner *einen* Rollenvertauschung ein wirkliches Fortschreiten in der Geschichte zu neuen, überraschenden Stationen, die nicht nach irgend einem Gesetz geschichtlicher Bewegung zu erwarten sind. Und nur in ihrer Offenheit auf neue, überraschende Zukunft hin liegt die echte eschatologische Dimension der jeweils erreichten Stufe auf dem Weg Gottes mit seinem Volk. Was in allem bleibt, ist die Gewißheit, daß Jahwe sich auch durch menschlichen Ungehorsam von diesem Weg nicht abbringen läßt und daß sein richtendes und rettendes Wort das Licht auf diesem Weg bleibt'.

45. Ibid.: 'die wirklich sachgemäße Darlegung des theologischen Zeugnisses von 1. Könige 13'.

concerning the centrality of election. First, he affirms that Barth's notion of a 'double dispute' (*doppelte Auseinandersetzung*) in 1 Kings 13 (i.e. tensions between the northern and southern kingdoms and between true and false prophecy) is best understood against a theological background of election and rejection. But Klopfenstein also affirms Barth's delineation of what it means in practical terms to be elect: i.e. that the purpose of election is only realised in the service of others, that it is only by staying true to this uncomfortable demand that the elect prove their status.[46]

Klopfenstein concludes with three comments about belonging together (*gehören...zusammen*) that subtly pick up on Barth's summative claim that '[t]he peculiar theme of the chapter is the manner in which the man of God and the prophet belong together, do not belong together, and eventually and finally do belong together; and how the same is true of Judah and Israel'.[47] However, Klopfenstein makes no mention of 'not belonging together' since in his view the multiple reversals are problematic, and he also alters the subject. Instead of Judah and Israel, Klopfenstein speaks of Jerusalem and Bethel, who 'belong together' in danger and in hope, in their God-willed salvation and their utter dependence upon the divine summons to speak a prophetic word, and in their openness toward their future saviour.[48] With a few minor adjustments, Klopfenstein affirms a modified form of Barth's theological exegesis and uses it to bolster his own conclusions. And in spite of being subjected to rigorous criticism, Barth is in the end commended for a reading of 1 Kings 13 that is theologically fruitful.

Klopfenstein's Impact upon Subsequent Scholarship

Barth's exegesis of 1 Kings 13 caused a stir among biblical scholars, renewing interest in this peculiar story and evoking a variety of responses.[49] Klopfenstein was the first to respond in print, and given the thorough and insightful nature of his analysis, it is hardly surprising that his essay had a lasting impact. However, it is unfortunate that the unfavourable aspects of Klopfenstein's analysis appear to have had a more enduring

46. Ibid.
47. *CD* II.2, 393; cited in Klopfenstein, '1. Könige 13', 641.
48. Ibid., 672.
49. Jepsen's essay, 'Gottesmann und Prophet: Anmerkungen zum Kapitel 1. Könige 13', in *Probleme biblischer Theologie: Gerhard von Rad zum 70. Geburtstag*, ed. H. W. Wolff (Munich: Kaiser, 1971), 171–82, begins: 'since K. Barth has treated 1 Kgs 13 so extensively in the context of his doctrine of God, it has become the subject of special discussions on several occasions...' (171).

legacy among historical-critical scholars than his concluding positive endorsement. As a result, the primary elements of Barth's reading have been largely dismissed.[50] Gunneweg could thus state about 35 years after its publication, that 'Barth's exegesis has found no positive response in the field of Old Testament studies'.[51] Uriel Simon thought it 'misleading' to publish Barth's exegesis independently of the *Dogmatics*, since it serves a particular purpose in its context there (to explicate the doctrine of election) and because his exposition 'remains in the class of free theological discourse'.[52] Given the comprehensive nature of Klopfenstein's critique, perhaps fewer scholars have seen any need to engage with Barth at length themselves.[53] Thus, Klopfenstein's criticisms were considerably influential, and appear to have been adopted wholesale, especially by those who share his (historical-critical) interpretive and methodological priorities.

Similarly, the judgments of Martin Noth, a monumental biblical scholar of the twentieth century, have proven highly influential upon subsequent scholars. In his commentary on Kings (1968),[54] Noth cites Klopfenstein and then states categorically:

> When K Barth sees in the actions between the man of God and the Prophet a certain dialectical play of multiple role reversals between 'the elected' and 'the rejected', he goes well beyond what the story actually says or can say or may even be understood to suggest. It does not correspond with the intention of the narrative to relate the terms 'election' and 'rejection' to the two (anonymous) main actors.[55]

50. See Bosworth's similar remarks in 'Revisiting', 373f.
51. A. H. J. Gunneweg, 'Die Prophetenlegende 1 Reg 13 – Mißdeutung, Umdeutung, Bedeutung', in *Prophet und Prophetenbuch: Festschrift für Otto Kaiser zum 65. Geburtstag*, BZAW 185 (Berlin: de Gruyter, 1989), 75: 'Barths Exegese fand in der alttestamentlichen Fachwissenschaft auch kein positives Echo'. Similarly, and more recently, Blum says of Klopfenstein's critique: 'In der Exegese ist Barth damit auf wenig Gegenliebe gestoßen'. Blum, 'Die Lüge des Propheten', 319 n. 2.
52. Uriel Simon, 'I Kings 13: A Prophetic Sign – Denial and Persistence', *HUCA* 47 (1976): 82. Acknowledging Klopfenstein's criticisms, Simon adds: 'But since this theme [election] has no basis in the literal meaning of the biblical text, it cannot be derived therefrom without going back, for support, to symbolization and over-interpretation'.
53. Barth's exegesis is 17 pages long; Klopfenstein's critical evaluation is 24!
54. Martin Noth, *1 Könige, 1*, BKAT 9 (Neukirchen-Vluyn: Neukirchener Verlag, 1968), 306–7.
55. Ibid.: 'Wenn K Barth dann freilich in dem Handeln zwischen Gottesmann und Prophet das dialektische Spiel eines mehrfachen Rollenwechsels zwischen "dem

Noth is explicitly averse to Barth's categories, speaking confidently of 'the intention of the narrative' in ways that are fairly typical of author-hermeneutics. (We will explore this, in contrast to text-hermeneutics, in Chapter 5.) More fundamentally, however, Noth adds that for God to proclaim his word through a prophet is not even necessarily an act of election per se, since God is free to use whomever he wishes. Rather, following Klopfenstein, Noth asserts that the story concludes with both prophets recognising the rejection of Bethel and the election of Jerusalem.[56] Since Noth also understands the text in historical terms, i.e. as a rejection of Jeroboam's cultus, he rejects outright Barth's identification of election and rejection as the central theme, or dynamic, of the story.[57] A survey of subsequent scholarship indicates that Noth has proven especially influential on this point.[58]

To summarise, both Klopfenstein and Noth perceive Barth to be reading the wider concerns of his *Church Dogmatics* into his exegesis of 1 Kings 13, and their criticisms have had a significant impact on subsequent scholarship. Noticeably few studies recognise that Klopfenstein ultimately commends Barth for the theological accent of his exposition.[59]

In more recent years, commentators with literary-theological interests have responded more favourably to Barth's reading of 1 Kings 13.[60] We will attend to some of these works in the next chapter, in a survey of the past seventy years of scholarship on 1 Kings 13, since the publication of *CD* II.2 in 1947. In Chapter 5, we shall return to the methodological divergence between Barth and Klopfenstein and reconsider some of the

Erwählten" und "dem Verworfenen" sieht, so geht er weit hinaus über das, was die Erzählung wirklich besagt oder besagen kann oder auch nur als hintergründigen Sinn zu verstehen gibt. Es entspricht überhaupt nicht der Intention der Erzählung, die Begriffe "Erwählung" und "Verwerfung" auf die beiden (anonymen) Haupthandelnden zu beziehen.'

56. Ibid., 307.

57. Like many other redaction critics who divide vv. 1-10 from vv. 11-32, Noth reads the story in two parts: the first part fits neatly with the concerns of 1 Kgs 12 and 14, within which Jeroboam's kingdom is torn from him via the prophetic judgment of Ahijah; vv. 11-32 are then viewed as a later addition to the narrative, expressing a distinct concern for the theme of prophetic conflict. Cf. Bosworth, 'Revisiting', 365.

58. Bosworth, 'Revisiting', 373–4, observes that Würthwein (1977), Simon (1976), and Gross (1979) each cite Noth in their (negative) evaluations of Barth's exegesis.

59. DeVries overstates when he writes: 'Klopfenstein found no justification for numerous details in Barth's exposition, and for the treatment as a whole' (*1 Kings*, WBC 12, 2nd ed. [Nashville: Nelson, 2003], 172).

60. E.g., Lemke, Walsh, Bosworth and Leithart.

hermeneutical issues raised by the variety of approaches and interpretations outlined in Chapter 4. This will establish a hermeneutical basis for Bosworth's reading in Chapter 6, which seeks to develop Barth's notion of multiple reversals, and for my own interpretation in Chapter 7, which seeks to apprehend the story with full, imaginative seriousness using a motif other than election.

4

Seventy Years of Scholarship

The past seventy years have seen significant shifts in the fields of Old Testament studies and hermeneutics. The hegemony of historical-critical analysis ended with the literary turn of the late 1970s, and methodological pluralism is now widely accepted.[1] In keeping with this, the following survey of interpretations not only covers a range of suggestions concerning the *Sache* of 1 Kings 13, but also a variety of interpretive methods. This, of course, is in keeping with the principle that how one reads depends largely on why one reads, as we have already seen with Barth and Klopfenstein. One significant gain from the increased interest in hermeneutics in recent years is a greater awareness of the impact an interpreter's choices have upon the meaning(s) found in any given text. The interpreter comes to the text with a particular question; the interpreter selects a method of inquiry appropriate to that question; the interpreter chooses to limit the inquiry in terms of literary context, reception history, theological categories; and so it goes. In one sense, indeterminacy is inevitable. Nonetheless, I hope to show that there is yet much to be gained from exploring a range of interpretive

---

1. See, e.g., S. Porter and M. Malcolm, eds, *The Future of Biblical Interpretation: Responsible Plurality in Biblical Hermeneutics* (Downers Grove, IL: InterVarsity, 2013). Craig Bartholomew puts it nicely: 'If we think of modern biblical interpretation as a series of turns, then the historical turn that dominated the twentieth century was followed in the 1970s by a literary turn; this was followed by the postmodern turn, which is now being followed by a theological turn. The turns do not replace the previous ones but significantly alter the landscape of biblical interpretation and raise important questions about the relationship between these different emphases.' Bartholomew, 'Theological Interpretation', in *The Oxford Handbook of Biblical Studies*, ed. Steven L. McKenzie (Oxford: Oxford University Press, 2013), 387.

possibilities whilst keeping our critical faculties attuned to the hermeneutical moves – and the choices – being made.[2]

Similarly, it is worth noting that perceptions and assumptions about the compositional history, present form, and purpose of 1 Kings 13 impact upon a reader's terms of engagement. Not all scholars display an equal willingness to simply get on with reading 1 Kings 13 in its received form, due to its apparent lack of conceptual consistency and its seeming disregard for moral issues. Joseph Robinson, for instance, writes:

> We must frankly say that the view of God's nature underlying this chapter is crude and insensitive, untouched by the spiritual awareness of the best of the Old Testament tradition. All this can be accounted for by understanding the origins of the narrative. It is Midrash, a story used in popular religious teaching. Like all such literature it makes a single point with clarity and force but, in so doing, oversimplifies the issues and distorts truth.[3]

The majority of scholars agree on the importance of biblical themes such as obedience and the efficacy of the divine word, but Robinson is not alone in expressing doubts about the heuristic value of 1 Kings 13.[4] Nor is he the first to defer to 'the origins of the narrative' for a solution.[5] The seemingly amoral quality of the narrative has evoked numerous attempts

---

2. Charles H. Cosgrove, 'Toward a Postmodern *Hermeneutica Sacra*: Guiding Considerations in Choosing between Competing Plausible Interpretations of Scripture', in *The Meanings We Choose: Hermeneutical Ethics, Indeterminacy and the Conflict of Interpretations*, ed. Charles Cosgrove (London: T&T Clark, 2004), 39–61, similarly encourages greater interpretive awareness and hermeneutical scrutiny of 'extra-exegetical' interests, be they theological, moral, correlational or ecumenical.

3. J. Robinson, *The First Book of Kings* (Cambridge: Cambridge University Press, 1972), 162. Robinson's view concerning the 'single point' of 1 Kgs 13 is 'that coming to terms with Canaanite civilization, as they believed the northern kingdom had done, was spiritually dangerous'.

4. E.g. Hugo Gressmann writes, 'This legend is regarded as religiously and morally inferior' ('Diese Legende ist, religiös und sittlich betrachtet, minderwertig'). *Die älteste Geschichtsschreibung und Prophetie Israels (von Samuel bis Amos und Hosea)*, SAT 2/1, 2nd ed. (Göttingen: Vandenhoeck & Ruprecht, 1921), 247. Noth (*I Könige*, 306) also remarks that the author has a penchant for the sensational. See also the views of Crenshaw and Van Seters below.

5. Thus the tendency among scholars to assume what Dozeman refers to as 'the pre-Deuteronomic stage of the legend'. Dozeman, 'The Way of the Man of God', 379.

to redeem it through recourse to hypothetical source material that is less troublesome.[6] But this kind of approach does little to resolve the tensions as they stand in the received text.[7] Therefore, given my own (theological and synchronic) line of enquiry, this chapter focuses on readings that endeavour to account for the narrative complexity of the entire story. I do not agree with Robinson's judgment that 1 Kings 13 is 'untouched by the spiritual awareness of the best of the Old Testament tradition' – but we will come to that in due course.

Current scholarly debate regarding the subject matter or 'moral' of 1 Kings 13 may be divided into four general categories.[8] Barth's exegesis touches on each of these to some extent, but his proposal resists any single category to the exclusion of the others. We shall consider these four majority views in greater depth below by attending to a representative voice from each. Naturally, the categories could be defined in different terms to the ones put forward here, but in my view these represent a helpful cross-section of how scholars approach and understand 1 Kings 13. In addition, I have selected scholars whose disparate conclusions have been reached via different methods, including analyses that are psychological and sociological (Crenshaw), narratological and structural (Walsh), source- and redaction-critical (Van Seters), and political and allegorical (Boer). This serves our dual purpose of evaluating variant readings of 1 Kings 13 whilst also attending to methodological and hermeneutical debates.

The Question of Genre

The determination of a text's subject matter naturally necessitates a discussion of genre, and it is hardly surprising that multiple views have

---

6. The same point is made by Blum, 'Die Lüge des Propheten', 319.
7. Gross, 'Lying Prophet', 108–10, notes a variety of problems encountered by interpreters, not least the moral and religious verdicts that are often reached. He makes the further observation that Barth's dialectic approach helpfully steers away from this moralising tendency.
8. James Mead, 'Kings and Prophets, Donkeys and Lions: Dramatic Shape and Deuteronomistic Rhetoric in 1 Kings XIII', *VT* 49 (1999): 191–2, also adopts four categories to summarise scholarly approaches to 1 Kgs 13. There is some overlap between his categories and mine. Also see Gary N. Knoppers' summary of scholarly opinion regarding the 'moral' of 1 Kgs 13 in *Two Nations Under God: The Deuteronomistic History of Solomon and the Dual Monarchies*, 2 vols (Atlanta: Scholars Press, 1994), 2:57–8.

been put forward regarding 1 Kings 13, including such labels as parable,[9] prophetic legend(s),[10] midrash,[11] prophetic authorisation narrative,[12] and satire.[13] As one might expect, correlations exist between certain terms and their associated methodologies so that 'prophetic legend' is a common answer to source-critical questions, whereas 'prophetic authorisation narrative' or 'satire' constitute attempts to describe the function or purpose of the text – be that for an ancient or contemporary audience. Perhaps the adoption of a canonical approach that seeks to address both diachronic and synchronic questions might lead to more nuanced conclusions regarding literary form. For instance, one might determine that the (hypothetical) source material for 1 Kings 13 is best described as a prophetic legend, but that the narrative now appears to serve a parabolic function in its final form and context.[14]

Variant Readings of 1 Kings 13

The first commonly held view regarding the *Sache* of 1 Kings 13 is that the story addresses *the discernment of true and false prophecy*. Barth touches on this theme when he distinguishes between the 'true' and

---

9. Alexander Rofé, 'Classes in the Prophetical Stories: Didactic Legenda and Parable', in *Studies on Prophecy*, VTSup 26 (Leiden: Brill, 1974), 158; *The Prophetical Stories*, 173; J. Van Seters, *In Search of History: Historiography in the Ancient World and the Origins of Biblical History* (New Haven: Yale University Press, 1983), 304 n. 49; D. W. Van Winkle, '1 Kings XIII: True and False Prophecy', *VT* 29 (1989): 42.

10. Crenshaw, *Prophetic Conflict*, 38; Gray, *I & II Kings*, 318; Eynikel, 'Prophecy and Fulfillment', 227–8; Gwilym H. Jones, *1 and 2 Kings*, ed. Ronald E. Clements, NCBC (Grand Rapids: Eerdmans, 1984), 1:261 ('two independent legends'); Burke O. Long, *1 Kings with an Introduction to Historical Literature*, FOTL 9 (Grand Rapids: Eerdmans, 1984), 150.

11. Julius Wellhausen, *Die kleinen Propheten übersetzt underklärt*, 4th ed. (Berlin: W. de Gruyter, 1963), 277; Klopfenstein, '1. Könige 13', 639; Robinson, *The First Book of Kings*, 162; Lemke, 'The Way of Obedience', 303–4.

12. DeVries, *I Kings*, 169; idem, *Prophet Against Prophet: The Role of the Micaiah Narrative (1 Kings 22) in the Development of Early Prophetic Tradition* (Grand Rapids: Eerdmans, 1978), 59–61.

13. David Marcus, 'Elements of Ridicule and Parody in the Story of the Lying Prophet from Bethel', in *Proceedings of the Eleventh World Congress of Jewish Studies* (Jerusalem, June 22–29, 1993), 68.

14. This is essentially how Barth presents 1 Kgs 13, although his exegesis obviously precedes Childs' formal delineation of a canonical approach. See Barth's opening comments in *CD* II.2, 393.

'original' prophets of Judah in contrast to the 'false' and 'professional' prophets of the north, though this is certainly not his primary emphasis.[15] Advocates of this view include:

James Crenshaw:	'this passage deals the death knell to every attempt to specify absolute criteria by which to differentiate the true from the false prophet'[16]
Thomas Dozeman:	'Our thesis is that the unifying theme of the pre-deuteronomic legend is true and false prophecy'.[17]
Simon DeVries:	'this writer has argued that the major concern is for the authority, and hence authenticity, of the Judahite man of God'.[18]
D. W. Van Winkle:	'1 Kgs xiii is a parable which among other things advances a criterion for discerning the message of a prophet. This criterion is the conformity of the message to the commandment of Yahweh'.[19]
Paul House:	'Basically, 1 Kings 13 continues the book's emphases on proper worship, the prophetic word, and the slow demise of the covenant people. It also begins to analyze the difference between true and false prophecy'.[20]
Roy Heller:	'The question which 1 Kgs 3 asks is "How can we know the word that YHWH has spoken?"'[21]

A second suggestion regarding the 'moral of the story' in 1 Kings 13 – the most common in contemporary scholarship – has to do with *the efficacious word of God*. Such a reading of 1 Kings 13 perceives

---

15. Barth, *CD* II.2, 393, 395, 401–6, 409.

16. Crenshaw, *Prophetic Conflict*, 47. Notably, Crenshaw's reading does not seek to defend certain criteria for discernment, but argues instead that it is ultimately impossible to discern at all.

17. Dozeman, 'The Way of the Man of God from Judah', 379.

18. DeVries, *1 Kings*, 169. DeVries does not explicitly discuss various criteria for prophetic discernment, but he classes the narrative as a 'prophetic authorisation narrative', emphasising that the preacher-prophet's radical obedience is the ultimate mark of authentic revelation.

19. Van Winkle, '1 Kings XIII', 42. Cf. idem, '1 Kings XII 25–XIII 34: Jeroboam's Cultic Innovations and the Man of God from Judah', *VT* 46 (1996): 101–14.

20. Paul R. House, *1, 2 Kings*, NAC 8 (Nashville: Broadman & Holman, 1995), 188–9.

21. Roy Heller, *Power, Politics, and Prophecy: The Character of Samuel and the Deuteronomistic Evaluation of Prophecy*, LHBOTS 440 (New York: T&T Clark, 2006), 37.

God's word itself to be the driving force within the strange world of the narrative; the prophets remain secondary characters, as it were. Barth gives due emphasis to this theme in his conclusion: 'It may well be said that this is in fact the beginning and end, the sum and substance of 1 K. 13 – that the Word of God endures through every human standing and falling...'[22] Scholars advocating this view are divided between those who accent the divine word's innate propensity to achieve its purpose, and those who stress the requirement of obedience to such a word. Scholars who emphasise the inevitable fulfilment of the divine word include the following:

Terence Fretheim:	'the story shows the *tenacity* of the word of God to work in and through deceptions, disobedience, and death – even of prophets – to accomplish God's purposes'.[23]
Brevard Childs:	'The emphasis falls completely on the objective nature of the word of God... The story has to do with the fulfilment of God's word of judgment which will not tolerate any softening or compromise.'[24]
Uriel Simon:	'From beginning to end, the story dwells on a single theme – the fulfillment of the word of the Lord in its due time, having transcended the weakness of its bearer and converted its violators into its confirmants'.[25]
Burke O. Long:	'The divine word will win out, whatever the wayward actions of men, even prophets, may be!'[26]
Richard D. Nelson:	'the main point of chapter 13, as set forth in the final resolution of the story (v. 32): the word against Bethel will come true... This is a story about the word's power to get itself done'.[27]
Gary Knoppers:	'If there is an overarching theme in 1 Kings 13...it is the triumph of YHWH's word over both its subjects and adversaries'.[28]

22. Barth, *CD* II.2, 410.
23. Terence E. Fretheim, *First and Second Kings* (Louisville: Westminster John Knox, 1999), 81 (emphasis original).
24. Childs, *Old Testament Theology*, 143.
25. Simon, 'I Kings 13: A Prophetic Sign', 116.
26. Long, *1 Kings*, 148.
27. Richard D. Nelson, *First and Second Kings*, Interpretation (Louisville: John Knox, 1987), 83, 89.
28. Knoppers, *Two Nations*, 2:58. Knoppers acknowledges an indebtedness to Simon ('I Kings 13: A Prophetic Sign') and Long (*1 Kings*) on this point.

Iain W. Provan:	'True prophecy will bring forth the judgment it promises; even prophets cannot escape if they are disobedient. And if prophets cannot escape, neither can kings'.[29]
Mordechai Cogan:	'the lesson of 1 Kgs 13: the word of YHWH is trustworthy… Yet the word of YHWH…is self-fulfilling; even centuries later, it finds its object.'[30]

Among those who stress the importance of *obedience* to the word of the LORD are:

Jerome T. Walsh:	'since, as we shall see, both the prophet and the man of God are emblems of larger realities, and since the thrust of the tale is the inexorability of the divine word, the narrator centers our attention on the issues of obedience and disobedience to the word'.[31]
James Montgomery:	The story has its moral in the theme of the disobedient prophet; cf. the Balaam story and that of Jonah'.[32]
Werner Lemke:	'this story revolves around two dominant motifs: a polemic against the cultic establishment of Jeroboam [vv. 1-10] and a discursive narrative about the importance of obedience to the divine word [vv. 11-32]'.[33]
Gene Rice:	'There is no more ringing affirmation in the Bible of the importance of obedience, particularly in the "little things," than in the tragic fate of the man of God from Judah'.[34]
Robert Culley:	'The punishment sequence is clear. Disobey Yahweh, it implies, and the consequences will be disastrous'.[35]

---

29. Iain W. Provan, *1 and 2 Kings*, NIBC (Peabody, MA: Hendrickson, 1995), 115.

30. Mordechai Cogan, *1 Kings*, AB 10 (New York: Doubleday, 2001), 375.

31. Walsh, *1 Kings*, 185. Walsh's commentary reflects this view more than his article, 'Contexts'. Walsh considers obedience to God's word as a central theme, but he also highlights the parallels between the prophet/man of God and Israel/Judah; see the fourth category below.

32. James A. Montgomery [ed. Henry Snyder Gehman], *The Books of Kings*, ICC (Edinburgh: T. & T. Clark, 1951), 261.

33. Lemke, 'The Way of Obedience', 306. Lemke 'cannot agree with those who see only one major theological theme in this story. This can only be done by subordinating drastically the one in favor of the other' (320 n. 32). I have therefore included him as a proponent of views two *and* three.

34. Rice, *1 Kings*, 115.

35. Robert Culley, *Themes and Variations: A Study of Action in Biblical Narrative* (Atlanta: Scholars Press, 1992), 89.

Donald Wiseman:	'the story...illustrate[s] the historian's main argument that judgment will inevitably befall those who defy God's word'.[36]
Choon-Leong Seow:	'The story of the man of God is...an illustration of what might happen when one does not obey the word of the Lord'.[37]
Lissa Wray Beal:	'the man of God faces an invitation to disobedience, which is the point of the whole narrative... Obedience to YHWH's word is paramount, regardless of alternative versions others offer'.[38]
Walter Gross:	'The author chose this structure and these categories and used them effectively to realize his didactic purpose, the inculcation of the obligation of obedience to YHWH's word'.[39]
James Mead:	'the Deuteronomistic Historians wanted to ensure that readers would have no confusion over the inviolability of Yahweh's word'.[40]
Steven McKenzie:	'the story in 1 Kgs 13:11-32a likely derives from Northern prophetic legends... It may have served as instruction for young prophets regarding obedience to the divine word.'[41]

A third interpretation sees *condemnation of Bethel* as the main thrust of the story. Again, this perspective is present in Barth's characterisation of Jeroboam and false prophecy in connection with the North:

> But confession is shown to be characteristic of the south, and profession of the north, and the light naturally falls upon the former, and the shadow upon the latter. The shadow which lies upon the professional *Nabi*-ism is... representative of the Israelite form of the Canaanite vitalism, the religion of blood and soil, which, according to the will of the God of Sinai and Jerusalem, is the very opposite of the life demanded of his people. It is thus no accident that this prophetic order has to the northern kingdom... the affinity which is proper to it in the story.[42]

Numerous scholars are convinced that this *anti-North polemic* is the main thrust of 1 Kings 13:

36. Donald J. Wiseman, *1 & 2 Kings*, TOTC (Leicester: IVP, 1993), 146.
37. Choon-Leong Seow, *The First and Second Books of Kings*, NIB 3 (Nashville: Abingdon, 1999), 105.
38. Lissa Wray Beal, *1 & 2 Kings*, Apollos OT Commentary 9 (Nottingham: Apollos, 2014), 193.
39. Gross, 'Lying Prophet', 125.
40. Mead, 'Kings and Prophets', 205.
41. Stephen L. McKenzie, *The Trouble with Kings: The Composition of the Book of Kings in the Deuteronomistic History*, VTSup 42 (Leiden: Brill, 1991), 55.
42. Barth, *CD* II.2, 400.

Gwilym Jones:	'The present deuteronomistic version has transformed a prophetical aetiological narrative, with all its legendary accretions, into a true expression of the deuteronomistic view that Bethel was cursed and could only provide a grave for an unfaithful Judean prophet'.[43]
Marvin Sweeney:	'The narrative...clearly serves the agenda of the DtrH, insofar as it condemns Jeroboam, the altar at Beth El, and even the city itself as the home of a lying prophet'.[44]
Walter Brueggemann:	'We may divide the narrative into five distinct units; all of them, however, seem fully focused on the theme of judgment against Bethel'.[45]
John Van Seters:	'the story is a vilification of the Bethel temple, which was still in use for some time in the exilic and post-exilic periods, and the Samaritan community'.[46]
Werner Lemke:	'this story revolves around two dominant motifs: a polemic against the cultic establishment of Jeroboam [vv. 1-10] and a discursive narrative about the importance of obedience to the divine word [vv. 11-32]'.[47]
Martin Noth:	'In the course of the eventful story both main actors, the man of God and the prophet, recognize the "rejection" of Bethel (and the "election" of Jerusalem).'[48]

The fourth perspective, which is directly derivative of Barth's exegesis, takes the view that this critical chapter functions in the books of Kings as an allegory or analogy, either for the political division of the kingdom or to draw parallels between Jeroboam and the man of God. The first two scholars below – each of whom explicitly acknowledges an indebtedness to Barth – note the political allegory between the prophets and the nations they represent:

---

43. Jones, *1 & 2 Kings*, 262.
44. Marvin Sweeney, *I and II Kings*, OTL (Louisville: Westminster John Knox, 2007), 179.
45. Brueggemann, *1 & 2 Kings*, 167.
46. Van Seters, 'On Reading', 233. On Van Seters' reading, see below.
47. Lemke, 'The Way of Obedience', 306. See n. 33 above.
48. Noth, *1 Könige 1*, 307. ('Zu der "Verwerfung" von Bethel [und der "Erwählung" von Jerusalem] bekennen sich im Verlauf der bewegten Geschichte die beiden Haupthandelnden, Gottesmann und Prophet.') Noth uses the terms 'election' (*Erwählung*) and 'rejection' (*Verwerfung*) here because he is responding to Barth's analysis.

Roland Boer:	'1 Kings 13 may then be described as an imaginary resolution to the contradictory situation of a North and South in the people of Israel'.[49]
David Bosworth:	'This prophetic story acts as a *mise-en-abyme* that emphasizes the theme of the relationship between Judah and Israel'.[50]

The following scholars also identify parallels between 1 Kings 13 and its wider context, but they place the analogical accent on the linkage between the man of God and Jeroboam:

Peter Leithart:	'The man of God's story offers a lesson for Jeroboam and also for all other kings of the north'.[51]
Jesse Long:	'The events are parabolic, a lesson for Jeroboam, for Israel and Judah, and for an exilic audience'.[52]
Keith Bodner:	'The author uses the allegory as a means of enlisting the reader to ponder Jeroboam's career path, as the major ideological lineaments of his story are refracted through the steps of the man of God'.[53]
James Mead:	'The literary elements in the four scenes of 1 Kings xiii serve to highlight what is central for the narrator, namely the way in which the man of God becomes an example of the king himself'.[54]
Robert Cohn:	'I see this tale as a kind of parable, a story within a story, that sets into relief the theological dynamics of the larger narrative… If the man of God, who is tricked into disobedience, pays the consequences, how much more so should Jeroboam who failed to walk in God's ways.'[55]

49. Roland Boer, 'National Allegory in the Hebrew Bible', *JSOT* 74 (1997): 110. It is difficult to find a representative quote from Boer's work on 1 Kgs 13 that encapsulates his view, in part because he is very self-aware about what he brings to the task of interpretation, and acknowledges repeatedly that other readings are also viable. His interpretation is discussed in further detail below.

50. Bosworth, *Story*, 156. The French term literally means 'put into [an] abyss' and is used in literary theory to designate a story-within-a-story. See Chapter 6 for a fuller discussion of *mise-en-abyme* and its development of Bosworth's thesis.

51. Leithart, *1 & 2 Kings*, 100. Leithart's theological commentary leans on the insights of Barth's analysis.

52. Jesse C. Long, Jr., *1 & 2 Kings, College Press NIV Commentary* (Joplin, MO: College Press, 2002), 177.

53. Keith Bodner, *Jeroboam's Royal Drama* (Oxford: Oxford University Press, 2012), 117.

54. Mead, 'Kings and Prophets', 197.

55. Robert L. Cohn, 'Literary Technique in the Jeroboam Narrative', *ZAW* 97 (1985): 33–4.

Finally, a handful of scholars do not easily fit any of the categories listed here. David Marcus interprets the story as 'a satire representing a sardonic comment on the curious ways and petty concerns of some prophets'[56] while Alexander Rofé treats it as an anti-angelological parable whose moral stresses 'the fundamental difference between the prophet [one who negates the existence of heavenly angels] and other people'[57] – which perhaps has affinities with the first category (prophetic discernment). A recent essay by Ellen Davis also resists categorisation; rather, she stresses four or five practical points of application for ministry, in keeping with the series title: *Interpretation: Resources for the Use of Scripture in the Church*.[58] Finally, in a psychological analysis of the story that focuses on the hidden motives and intentions of characters, Stuart Lasine concludes: 'The fact that Yahweh uses the lying prophet to relay his message of doom to the victim...should be construed as illustrating who is most likely to survive in this dangerous and deceptive story-world'.[59] Lasine's treatment is thought-provoking in its exploration of the many gaps in the narrative, though ultimately less helpful for understanding 1 Kings 13 within its broader literary and canonical context.

We will turn now to each of these themes in turn. First, the theme of prophetic discernment.

Discernment of True and False Prophecy: James Crenshaw (1971)

In his 1971 monograph entitled, *Prophetic Conflict*,[60] James Crenshaw examines the inherent difficulties in the nature of biblical prophecy that led to its decline and ultimately its demise. That Crenshaw's work has been widely cited and recently re-published is testament to its perceived significance for biblical scholarship.

The prophetic legend, or midrash, found in 1 Kings 13 is a critical text for the articulation of Crenshaw's thesis, since it depicts the 'failure of

---

56. David Marcus, *From Balaam to Jonah: Anti-prophetic Satire in the Hebrew Bible* (Atlanta: Scholars Press, 1995), 73.
57. Alexander Rofé, *The Prophetical Stories: The Narratives about the Prophets in the Hebrew Bible, Their Literary Types and History* (Jerusalem: Magnes, 1988), 180–1.
58. Ellen F. Davis, *Biblical Prophecy: Perspective for Christian Theology, Discipleship, and Ministry* (Louisville: Westminster John Knox, 2014), 179–84.
59. Stuart Lasine, *Weighing Hearts: Character, Judgment, and the Ethics of Reading the Bible*, LHBOTS 568 (New York: T. & T. Clark, 2012), 114.
60. Crenshaw, *Prophetic Conflict*, 38. This monograph was republished by SBL in 2007.

all criteria for distinguishing the true from false prophet'.[61] He stresses the importance of this chapter without reservation: 'The significance of 1 Kings 13 for a study of false prophecy has hitherto been overlooked as the decisive key to the understanding of prophetic aberrance'.[62]

Crenshaw's analysis of the phenomenon of prophecy in the Old Testament is based on a psychological consideration of prophetic experience whereby he links the prophetic conflict that arose between one prophet and another, or between a prophet and his or her community, with 'self-interrogation, a situation far more agonising than all the other battles. This inner struggle forced the prophet to ask whether the voice he "heard" was not the sound of thunder, the vision of a nightmare.'[63] Crenshaw's point is that 'prophetic conflict is inevitable, growing out of the nature of prophecy itself'[64] and that it is near impossible to resolve, regardless of whether one focuses on the message[65] or the man,[66] since none of the criteria mentioned in various Old Testament texts is ultimately sufficient for discerning true from false prophecy.[67]

His inquiry begins with a survey of biblical prophecies pertaining to prophetic conflict in order to place the phenomenon of false prophecy in perspective. At the same time, he reconstructs the *vox populi* of the eighth century, which is apparently 'crucial to the understanding of false prophecy',[68] and offers a sympathetic view of the 'positive aspects...of

---

61. Ibid., 38. J. Lindblom, *Prophecy in Ancient Israel* (Oxford: Blackwell, 1962), is more optimistic, though for him the moral of the story is directed at prophets: 'The object of the story was to give this lesson: when a revelation that you have received is contradicted by the revelation of another prophet, you have to obey the divine voice that you have heard yourself. The revelation of another may be untrustworthy. It is not prudent to rely on it' (64).

62. Crenshaw, *Prophetic Conflict*, 46.

63. Ibid., 3.

64. Ibid.

65. I.e., fulfilment or non-fulfilment; promise of weal or woe; revelatory form (i.e. ecstasy, dream, etc.); allegiance to Baal or Yahweh. Ibid., 49–56.

66. I.e., cultic/royal office vs. charismatic; im/moral conduct; commission (council of the LORD; cf. Jer. 23). Ibid., 56–60.

67. But see the valid criticism of Crenshaw in R. W. Moberly, *Prophecy and Discernment*, Cambridge Studies in Christian Doctrine (Cambridge: Cambridge University Press, 2006), 16: 'the question of whether they [i.e., the criteria] might be combined synthetically in such a way that the whole might be greater than the sum of its parts is not addressed'. I argue below that multiple criteria are combined in 1 Kgs 22, a comparable narrative which addresses the issue of prophetic discernment head-on.

68. Crenshaw, *Prophetic Conflict*, 23.

false prophets [and] of popular religion'.[69] Once it has been recognised that the religion of the people and of so-called false prophets was not unambiguously corrupt but in fact contained kernels of truth, Crenshaw posits that a re-examination of their theology may be illuminating for our grasp of what lay behind prophetic conflict.[70] However, his emphasis on the ecstatic and existential nature of prophecy in his survey of studies relating to prophetic discernment poses a methodological problem in that biblical exegesis is used to support a sociological theory about ancient Israel's deteriorating attitude towards prophecy. The Old Testament record consistently affirms that certain men and women were authenticated by God to speak his words during particular periods of Israel's history – quite in spite of their reception in Israel. In this sense, it matters not whether Crenshaw is right in claiming that 'the impact of prophecy upon Israelite society was negligible',[71] for the idea that prophecy had to authenticate itself by a means acceptable to the masses runs contrary to the canonical witness of Scripture. Crenshaw's thesis and his methodology are therefore not as compatible as they might be. As a result, it remains unclear whether the central issue that Crenshaw seeks to delineate and address is literary/canonical or historical/sociological in nature.

In any case, it is against this general background that Crenshaw turns to a detailed consideration of 1 Kings 13, which, in his view, addresses 'the Achilles-heel of ancient prophecy, namely the absence of any validation for a prophetic word'.[72] Crenshaw offers a brief summary of Barth's exegesis, adding that in spite of its apparent brilliance, it is 'only a pointer to the way, as Klopfenstein rightly perceives, for the narrative is not really concerned with election and rejection'.[73] Rather, because of the Bethel

---

69. Ibid., 24; also 35. The selected verses Crenshaw views as representational of 'the popular mind' seem questionable (ibid., 25–34). Moreover, as they stand, surely the prophetic books suggest that Israel ultimately accepted and trusted the judgment of the Deuteronomist (that Israel was deserving of judgment in exile). In any case, Israel's canonical record – the Hebrew Bible's own recounting of these events – presents the voice of Dtr justifying God's actions in punishing Israel, the prophets spelling out the implications to Israel (both in terms of immediate judgment and future hope), and the post-exilic community taking those prophetic warnings very seriously.

70. Ibid., 38.
71. Ibid., 103.
72. Ibid., 38.
73. Ibid., 41. Crenshaw's brief summary of Barth's two double-pictures on p. 40 is not entirely accurate. Moreover, he misrepresents Klopfenstein, for as we noted above, Klopfenstein ultimately concurs with Barth that true and false prophecy

prophet's claim in v. 18 – 'I also am a prophet as you are' – Crenshaw understands the conflicting oracles of the two anonymous prophets to indicate the theme of prophetic discernment. The man of God says he is under divine orders *not* to eat or drink, but the Bethel prophet tells him, allegedly on angelic authority, that he *may* eat and drink. 1 Kings 13 thus 'provides an example of two mutually exclusive words claiming divine origin...as well as one where no valid criterion between true and false prophecy exists'.[74] Crenshaw therefore makes this assertion: 'At the outset it must be declared that this passage deals the death knell to every attempt to specify absolute criteria by which to differentiate the true from the false prophet, for the ultimate criterion to which contemporary scholarship appeals (the charismatic intuition of a true prophet) fails in this instance'.[75] In order to assess the validity of Crenshaw's claim, we will briefly analyse a comparable text.

Another story containing 'two mutually exclusive words claiming divine origin' is that of Micaiah ben Imlah. Indeed, numerous commentators, including Crenshaw, make reference to 1 Kings 22 in their efforts to understand 1 Kings 13.[76] However, the decisive difference between the two narratives, in my view, is that the plot in 1 Kings 22 is *explicitly* driven by the issue of discernment; everything hinges on which prophet(s) can be trusted. Briefly, the narrative unfolds as follows.

Kings Ahab and Jehoshaphat, of the northern and southern kingdoms, together seek a reliable word from the LORD regarding an imminent battle. Ahab's 450 prophets are saying 'Go!', but Jehoshaphat rightly suspects their authenticity and asks for a second opinion. At this point Micaiah is summoned to the scene, although his reputation precedes him as one who 'never prophesies anything good...but only bad' – which is, of course, a strong indication that he is authentic. The messenger who summons Micaiah to the royal court pleads with him to speak טוב (well/good) and to ensure that his prophetic word matches that of the others. The report of this seemingly minor detail provides a second subtle indication to the reader concerning which prophet is true and which are false. When he

---

are presented in the Old Testament against the theological background of election and rejection. In fact, Klopfenstein concludes his essay by reformulating his own conclusions in precisely these terms. Klopfenstein, '1. Könige 13', 671–2.

74. Crenshaw, *Prophetic Conflict*, 48.
75. Ibid.
76. Ibid., passim, esp. 83–5. Also Lasine, *Weighing Hearts*, 93 n. 3; Leithart, *1 & 2 Kings*, 98; Provan, *1 and 2 Kings*, 114; Simon, *Reading Prophetic Narratives*, 137; etc.

is urged to tell the truth, Micaiah recounts a troubling heavenly vision, revealing that Ahab's 450 yes men are under the influence of a lying spirit. But Zedekiah, representing the cheerleaders, does not appreciate the prophetic insight. He strikes Micaiah and asks a question that goes to the heart of the issue: 'Which way did the spirit of the LORD go when he went from me to speak to you?' (1 Kgs 22.24) In other words, What makes you any different from the rest of us? Are you not inspired by the same spirit? Micaiah's reply to Zedekiah amounts to 'You'll see…' (ראה הנך, v. 25). And as he is taken to prison, his retort to King Ahab brings the theology of the Deuteronomist to the fore: 'If you return in peace, the LORD has not spoken by me' (v. 28b; cf. Deut. 18.22). The rest of the story makes the basic point that Ahab dies in battle, just as Micaiah prophesied, in spite of attempts to disguise himself. Thus, from beginning to end, 1 Kings 22 is presented as a story about prophetic discernment, and notably one in which a range of criteria provide critical clues for resolving the matter, including: the narrator's report; the morality (i.e. integrity) of the prophet; standing in the council of the LORD (cf. Jer. 22.23); and the Deuteronomic notion of fulfilment.

Crenshaw is right to notice a basic commonality between these episodes, but the differences between 1 Kings 13 and 22 are considerable when one acknowledges that prophetic *conflict* and prophetic *discernment* are distinct issues. In my judgment, 1 Kings 13 contains neither and 1 Kings 22 contains both.

First, regarding *prophetic conflict*, the contradictory words of the Judean man of God and the old Bethel prophet in 1 Kings 13 are not *prophecies*, but rather antithetical claims about what God has prohibited the man of God from doing while he is visiting Bethel. The threefold commandment is for the man of God alone (and was ostensibly given directly to him); it hardly compares to the oracle judging Jeroboam's altar, a prophecy that is introduced with the classic formulation, 'Thus says the LORD' (כה אמר יהוה). Similarly, the Bethelite claims to have received contrary instructions from an angelic messenger, but his words do not constitute a prophetic oracle either – especially since they are contrived! That the two anonymous figures are prophets does not mean that their disagreement constitutes a contest for prophetic authenticity. The story indeed contains 'two mutually exclusive words claiming divine origin', as Crenshaw describes it, but the conflict is over God's commandment to an individual, not the prophecy spoken in Bethel. In addition, 1 Kings 13 does not really reflect a mood of rivalry. There is deception, to be sure, but the stolid manner in which it occurs, as they are sitting together at a shared table, is yet another odd feature of the story. The cordial interaction between the anonymous prophets in 1 Kings 13 is very different from the prophetic conflict between Micaiah and the multitude in 1 Kings 22, which moves quickly to physical violence (cf. also Jer. 28.10).

Second, regarding *prophetic discernment*, the context of the royal court in 1 Kings 22 makes it obvious that Micaiah and Ahab's 400 prophets have an audience for whom the outcome of their prophetic conflict will mean the difference between life and death. Discernment is critical. In 1 Kings 13, however, no one is reported to be looking on when the Bethel prophet intercepts the Judean under the oak to challenge the threefold prohibition. Even if the Bethelite's purpose in inviting the Judean home is to test his prophetic authenticity (a point to which we shall return), what is at stake in their conflicting claims has no bearing on an immediate audience, but only on the man of God, who must choose whether to stay true to the original command or to believe that it has been rescinded.[77] To the reader or hearer of the story the issue is still less complicated, for the narrator cups his hand toward the audience and speaks two words at the end of v. 18 – כחש לו ('he lied to him') – that resolve the tension in black and white terms. In 1 Kings 13, the question of truth versus falsehood is resolved almost immediately using one of the most valid criteria known to Bible readers, though it is not one that is covered in Crenshaw's survey; namely, the evaluative judgment of the omniscient narrator.[78] The issue of discernment is clearly not in focus. Within the world of the text, the matter is perfectly straightforward: one prophet lies and the other

---

77. Moberly makes this point in connection with Jer. 28, mentioning Amos 7.10-17 and 1 Kgs 13 as further examples: 'If a narrative of prophetic conflict were supposed to be about discernment, then a prime question should be: Who is supposed to be doing the discerning? The most natural candidates would presumably be third-party hearers/onlookers within the story who have to decide which of the prophets to believe.' Moberly, *Prophecy*, 105.

78. Crenshaw's monograph was published just as the literary turn was taking place in the late 1960s and early 1970s, so it is perhaps understandable that his reading of 1 Kgs 13 does not include a discussion of narratological devices. Since that time, however, it has been a matter of general consensus among narrative critics that the omniscient narrator's judgments represent the divine point of view. See, e.g., Alter, *Art*, 158; Meir Sternberg, *The Poetics of Biblical Narrative: Ideological Literature and the Drama of Reading* (Bloomington: Indiana University Press, 1985), 84–99; Shimon Bar-Efrat, *Narrative Art in the Bible*, JSOTSup 70 (Sheffield: Almond, 1989), 17–18; Jerome Walsh, *Old Testament Narrative: A Guide to Interpretation* (Louisville: Westminster John Knox, 2010), 44–5. On the authoritative voice of the narrator in 1 Kgs 22, see my *Sharing God's Passion: Prophetic Spirituality* (Milton Keynes: Paternoster, 2012), 111–13.

is duped. Moreover, the narrative says nothing about whether the man of God deliberated over whether or not to trust his older colleague. He questions neither the older prophet's motives nor whether Yahweh has, in fact, changed his mind (as per 1 Kgs 21.29). The man of God simply trusts and is led astray – as a necessary development in the plot. At best, '[i]f the issue lying behind the episode is the question of false prophecy, then the message of the story was pertinent only to an audience of prophets, not to an audience of ordinary people'.[79]

In summary, then, while 1 Kings 13 recounts contradictory claims from two prophets, it is important to note that (a) their conflicting words are not prophetic oracles, and that (b) no deliberation is given in the text to discern between their claims. Therefore, since 1 Kings 13 is neither about prophetic conflict nor prophetic discernment, Crenshaw's assertion 'that this passage deals the death knell to every attempt to specify absolute criteria by which to differentiate the true from the false prophet'[80] does not hold up. His argument turns out to be a circular one; 1 Kings 13 only appears to deny the existence of a valid criterion for prophetic discernment because of the prior (and false) assumption that it addresses such matters in the first place.[81] Indeed, the simplest explanation is probably the best: 1 Kings 13 leaves the issue of a valid criterion unresolved because prophetic discernment is not in its purview. As we have seen, 1 Kings 13 is presented in different terms to 1 Kings 22, where the issue of discernment is pivotal to the story's outcome and meaning.

Nonetheless, since Crenshaw considers the story to be about discernment, he outlines the main criteria for validating a prophetic message (or man) in order to show that all these are inadequate, thereby affirming 'that the attempt to distinguish true from false prophecy in ancient Israel must be

---

79. Robert R. Wilson, *Prophecy and Society in Ancient Israel* (Philadelphia: Fortress, 1980), 191 n. 88. Similarly, McKenzie, *Trouble*, also notes that the story 'may have served as instruction for young prophets' (55).

80. Ibid., 47–8.

81. Roy Heller's monograph, *Power, Politics, and Prophecy*, about the Deuteronomist's evaluation of prophecy, contains a similar argument. Heller insists that 1 Kings has as its 'primary subject the nature of prophecy as an intermediary institution and the vexing question of the verifiability of true prophecy', but in the end concedes that the story has nothing to offer on this point. He concludes: 'The question which 1 Kgs 13 asks is "How can we know the word that YHWH has spoken?" The Deuteronomists, having again provoked the reader to ask this question, refuse to provide an answer.' Ibid., 37. Perhaps it is possible that the Deuteronomists posed a question that they then refused to answer, but it seems more likely that the text serves other purposes altogether.

abandoned'.[82] Crenshaw also draws the related conclusion that 'a degree of fluidity between the two [i.e. true and false] is inevitable', and that this assertion 'provides the stance from which K. Barth views 1 Kings 13'.[83] But Crenshaw's observation about fluidity between true and false prophecy, regardless of whether it is itself valid, should not be associated with Barth's position. Barth does indeed argue that the two prophets must be understood together, but he never speaks in terms of fluidity between truth and falsehood. On the contrary, Barth's entire schema is based upon clearly defined, antithetical roles being *exchanged*.

Crenshaw's reading of 1 Kings 13 critically informs his broader argument about the dwindling role of prophecy in ancient Israel, which may be summarised as follows. Prophecy went into decline in ancient Israel as a consequence of the exile, which for obvious reasons raised questions about God's justice. In turn, this theological crisis paved the way for prophecy's partial displacement by wisdom and apocalyptic.[84] As Crenshaw understands 1 Kings 13, this prophetic legend supports his theory concerning the emergence of the phenomenon of false prophecy because it highlights the fine line between true and false prophecy and demonstrates the difficulty, or impossibility, of discerning between them. Over time, as one prophetic word contradicted another, tensions arose within prophetic circles due to inherent difficulties in receiving God's mysterious word and articulating it effectively. These difficulties left prophets exposed to life-and-death situations on a regular basis, and since no criterion of validation functioned within the moment of decision (this was not helped by prophecies that took centuries to be fulfilled, as in the cases of 1 Kgs 13 or Jeremiah), the public eventually turned away from prophecy and toward wisdom and apocalyptic for spiritual direction.

The corollary of this was a shift from truth to falsehood in the prophet, undergirded by five causes, according to Crenshaw: the desire for success; compliance with the king; identification with popular theology; the extant power of past traditions; and the emergence of individualism.[85] These make up 'the human factor' in explaining false prophecy. But equally, Crenshaw avers, 'the dark side of God, the "demonic", must be taken into consideration, for the ultimate source of false prophecy is God himself!'[86] Referring again to the Micaiah narrative in 1 Kings 22, Crenshaw feels 'forced to conclude that prophetic tension cannot be explained solely in

82. Crenshaw, *Prophetic Conflict*, 61.
83. Ibid., 62.
84. Ibid., 22.
85. Ibid., 65–77.
86. Ibid., 77.

anthropological categories, for the likelihood of conflict within biblical prophecy was enhanced by the belief that Yahweh made use of men against their will or knowledge to accomplish his intentions, indeed on occasion sent deceptive visions to further the divine purpose for Israel'.[87] In relation to 1 Kings 13, since the fraudulent Bethel prophet goes on to receive a genuine prophetic word by divine inspiration, Crenshaw states conclusively that '1 Kings 13 points to the divine causality as the explanation of the phenomenon known as false prophecy'.[88]

My primary objection to Crenshaw's reading of these texts is that he seeks to draw isolated points from prophetic narratives and oracles without considering how those details make sense within the wider world of the text. This is particularly evident in his reading of 1 Kings 13, which is at the heart of many, if not all, of the book's theses. Crenshaw does not seek to understand the story in full, but rather draws on a few select details to drive his argument: namely, the contradictory words of two prophetic figures; the phrase, 'I am a prophet as you are'; and the genuine word that comes to the false Bethelite. Like a literary surgeon, Crenshaw incises the text to extract selected phrases from 1 Kings 13 that serve his purpose. But having done so, he leaves the rest of the narrative lying rather lifeless on the table. At best, this kind of approach fails to do justice to the text's integrity; at worst, it serves a questionable agenda via proof-texting.

The Efficacious Word of God: Jerome T. Walsh (1989, 1996)

Among scholars, the most popular construal of the message of 1 Kings 13 places the efficacious word of the LORD at the heart of the narrative. Whatever Jeroboam intends with his cultus, and however we interpret the details of the encounter between the prophets, it is the word of the LORD itself that emerges as the true hero of the story. Along such lines, the interpretive endeavours of Jerome Walsh are of particular interest for the present work, not just because he has written an important article on 1 Kings 13 and is responsible for an acclaimed commentary on 1 Kings, but also because his special interest in hermeneutical issues is often evidenced in his work.

Walsh has written three essays examining issues of methodology and interpretation, using texts from Kings as case studies. The essays pose interesting questions about the relationship between method and meaning,

---

87. Ibid., 110. It is somewhat misleading to call Micaiah's vision 'deceptive' as Crenshaw does here. The vision itself is not 'deceptive', but rather contains evidence of a conspiracy against Ahab that involves deceit. The difference is quite significant.

88. Ibid., 48.

as well as the interpreter's role in determining these. Walsh asks, for instance, 'What are the factors in the methods themselves that lead to such variety? Does each method retrieve only *part* of a text's meaning? Or does each method retrieve a more or less independent *whole* meaning that may or may not be compatible with other readings?'[89] 'The Contexts of 1 Kings XIII' (1989) was the first of these studies to be published. Here we examine this essay together with some additional insights on 1 Kings 13 from his 1996 commentary on Kings.

'The Contexts of I Kings XIII' (1989)

Walsh begins his essay with the observation that among a reader's first interpretive decisions is that of choosing among 'different unifying horizons, whether those horizons be source documents, redactional levels, or narrative or poetic units'.[90] From the outset, the reader is foregrounded in the interpretive process. Therefore, regarding his own approach to 1 Kings 13, Walsh articulates the hermeneutical decisions that undergird his study upfront:

> This essay is not historical, attempting to reconstruct events underlying our texts, nor is it historical-critical, in the sense of seeking to separate sources and redactional levels, even though some of its questions inhabit terrain usually claimed by redaction criticism. It is essentially a literary inquiry, and it will confine itself to the final form of the text... This essay will examine 1 Kgs xiii at three different contextual levels: as two self-contained narratives, as a component of the story of Jeroboam, and as an element in the Deuteronomistic History of the two kingdoms.[91]

With this established, Walsh outlines different elements that come to the fore when 1 Kings 13 is read on these three contextual levels.

First, as a self-contained narrative, '1 Kgs xiii falls clearly into three sections': vv. 1-10; vv. 11-32; and vv. 33-34.[92] In the first two sub-sections, Walsh detects parallelism and interprets the text accordingly. 'The symmetrical structures underlying the two narratives in 1 Kgs xiii provide an entrée to themes and motifs central to the stories'.[93] The dominant concern of vv. 1-10 is the rejection of the Bethel cult, which is stressed through the opposition of the man of God from the south and the

---

89. Jerome T. Walsh, 'Methods and Meanings: Multiple Studies of 1 Kings 21', *JBL* 111 (1992): 193 (original emphasis).
90. Walsh, 'Contexts', 355.
91. Ibid.
92. Ibid., 356.
93. Ibid., 361.

Israelite king.⁹⁴ And in vv. 11-32, the dominant concern is the reversal of fates between the two anonymous prophets: the Judean man of God 'moves from obedience through unwitting disobedience to death' while the Bethel prophet moves 'from narrow patriotism through sacrilege to true prophetic mission'.⁹⁵ Walsh says next to nothing about the final two verses (33-34), save that they require 'the larger context of Jeroboam's cultic innovations to be understood'.⁹⁶

The second context is broader, encapsulating what is often referred to as the Jeroboam cycle (i.e. 1 Kgs 11–14), within which Jeroboam's cultic innovations are pivotal (1 Kgs 12.26-31). This wider narrative frame serves to highlight certain shifts in the responses of northern and southern prophets toward Jeroboam. 'Ahijah's two oracles, one of election and one of rejection [note the inference to Barth], frame Jeroboam's career. Similarly the approval voiced by Shemaiah of Jerusalem is balanced by the condemnation announced by the unnamed man of God from Judah.'⁹⁷ The turning point in both cases, from approval to disproval, is Jeroboam's cult. Because of Jeroboam's cultic initiatives, 'the political disruption willed by Yahweh has begun to spread to the religious structures of the people'.⁹⁸ In Walsh's view, the chiastic repetition of words and phrases in 12.30-31 and 13.33-34 highlights the fact that Jeroboam's obduracy before Yahweh's prophets is as serious as the high places and their illegitimate priesthoods. It is noteworthy that Walsh's conclusions are again indebted to his interpretive method: 'the symmetrical structure of the literary unit provides the key to interpretation'.⁹⁹

Finally, the third context for understanding 1 Kings 13 is the entire history of the divided kingdoms. Rather than attempting a structural analysis or outline of 1–2 Kings in its entirety, Walsh points out 'ways in which individual elements of 1 Kgs xiii reappear elsewhere as significant motifs'.¹⁰⁰ He gives three examples, two specific and one general. First, the Deuteronomist's prophecy–fulfilment schema, famously identified by von Rad, links numerous details in the opening verses – the foretelling of Josiah, the defiled altar, and the burnt bones – with the statement

---

94. Ibid., 357.
95. Ibid., 360.
96. Ibid., 356. This is an odd statement in light of the fact that this first context supposedly takes 1 Kgs 13 (in its entirety) as a self-contained narrative. Here he intimates that a wider context is needed to make sense of the chapter's final verses.
97. Ibid., 363.
98. Ibid., 364.
99. Ibid., 361.
100. Ibid., 366.

concerning their fulfilment in 2 Kgs 23.17. Second, Walsh notes that the key phrase, 'the sin of Jeroboam' (12.30; 13.34), 'runs like a red thread through the history of the northern kingdom. It occurs in the condemnation of virtually every northern king and culminates in the epitaph of the northern kingdom in 2 Kgs xvii 21-3.'[101] Third, and more broadly, Walsh reiterates Barth's point about the prophets and their respective kingdoms:

> In the context of the history of the two kingdoms, the story of prophetic conflict is itself prophetic. The individuals mirror their kingdoms, and their tragedy portends the tragic destiny awaiting Israel and Judah. Israel has become unfaithful. Judah can still speak the word that Israel needs to hear; but if Judah, too, following Israel's lead, compromises its worship (as history shows it will), then both are doomed to overcome their separation only in death. Judah will be buried in an alien land, and Israel will be saved only so far as it is joined to Judah.[102]

Walsh links these last three observations with reading 1 Kings 13 as part of the history of the divided kingdoms. He thereby shows that different accents and nuances of the story can take precedence, depending upon the context in which they are considered. Additionally, a particular phrase or concept may have varying connotations as well. For instance, in the first and second reading contexts, the phrase 'the sin of the house of Jeroboam' refers to the king's obduracy in the face of prophetic warnings (i.e. 'Even after this event, Jeroboam did not turn from his evil way'; 13.33), but within the third, much wider context, its more natural referent is his cultic innovations, given the multiple repetitions of the phrase throughout the history of Israel's kings (i.e. 'he did not depart from the sins of Jeroboam son of Nebat, which he caused Israel to sin'; 2 Kgs 14.24; passim).

Walsh concludes with some observations. Most obviously, the reader's choice of a literary context predetermines interpretive possibilities by setting the parameters of the text under investigation. In turn, this framing also affects the relative importance of textual elements, regardless of whether the determination of context constituted a conscious or subconscious decision.[103] So far so good. But Walsh goes on to suggest that

---

101. Ibid., 368.

102. Ibid., 367–8. Walsh acknowledges his indebtedness to Barth on this point. Affirming that Barth's work 'remains a classic', he writes: 'The proleptic character of the narrative is fundamental to Barth's justly famous exposition of the chapter. My reading is similar to his' (368 n. 25) The paragraph quoted above is also repeated (not quite verbatim) in Walsh's commentary on 1 Kgs 13, where Barth's influence is readily discernible. Walsh, *1 Kings*, 205.

103. Walsh, 'Contexts', 369.

analysis of a text's surface structure can help to 'identify a basis in the text on which to build an interpretation of the unit and of its component parts'.[104] This observation is somewhat problematic, because it blurs the distinction between two distinct decisions made by the reader. One of these, as Walsh clearly shows, is the determination of literary boundaries for the task. But the other decision, derived directly from the interpretive aims of the reader, is the choice of an appropriate methodology. Walsh appears to suggest that one leads quite naturally – and consistently – to the other; namely, that a certain kind of structural analysis is the natural methodological choice for those interested in narrative-critical interpretation.[105] Whether Walsh thinks that ancient authors/editors were intentional about such patterning, or whether he believes chiasms to be inevitably present in any purposive writing, he does not say. However, he does assert that the kinds of concentric structures he identifies are superior to 'the outlines commonly offered in commentaries'.[106] Moreover, it is readily apparent from even a cursory glance at Walsh's articles, books and commentaries that symmetrical chiastic patterns abound in Hebrew narrative and that they apparently contribute much to determining a text's dominant motif. Not all students and scholars of biblical literature share Walsh's conviction, however, that ancient authors consistently arranged their compositions using such conventions. Symmetrical structures like these certainly seem most obvious to those who believe they are there to be discovered. Given that his work promotes a degree of hermeneutical self-awareness, Walsh's unwavering conviction that any narrative text's leading motif can be established via structural observations appears to be something of a blind spot.

Walsh's final reflection pertains to the relation between literary analysis and historical-critical analysis. Specifically, he asks whether structural and literary observations can raise helpful questions about sources and redaction seams. The suggestion is helpful, though again, 'the identification of symmetrical structure'[107] in 1 Kgs 12.32-33 is presented more as an assumption than a contention.

104. Ibid.
105. Bosworth's appraisal of Walsh makes similar judgments. Bosworth, 'Revisiting', 376.
106. Walsh, 'Contexts', 369: 'western analytical outlines are hard pressed to capture the type of symmetrical structure that is seen here as fundamental to the text. Commentators should use schematizations of the text that more accurately reflect its inherent articulation.'
107. Ibid., 370.

1 Kings (1996)

Walsh's commentary on 1 Kings reflects the same foci as his articles, offering exegetical insights via structural and narratological analyses of the text; in fact, he has published separate volumes on each of these methodologies.[108] His introduction to *Structural Issues* in the Kings commentary suggests that the concentric arrangement of a text's parts, resulting in chiastic symmetry, was fully intended by the ancient authors and editors. This, as I mentioned above, is a questionable assumption, not least because two interpreters who identify different chiasms in the same text may each wish to argue that their perceived chiasm was the author's way of making a deliberate point, and there are no failsafe criteria for choosing between them. In addition, as we will see below, one reader's proposed chiasm will inevitably fail to accentuate, or perhaps even draw attention *away* from, what another reader's chiasm has identified as most significant in the text.[109] Walsh's approach thus blurs the line between authorial intentions and interpretive aims.

Hermeneutical issues aside (for now), Walsh divides 1 Kings into four overarching narratives: the stories of Solomon (chs. 1–11); Jeroboam (11.26–14.20); Elijah (chs. 17–19); and Ahab (20.1–22.40).[110] Within the section on Jeroboam, Walsh divides 1 Kings 13 in two, treating 1 Kgs 12.26–13.10 in one chapter of his commentary and 13.11–14.20 in the next. This judgment, which determines the context(s) for his analysis (as per the discussion above), is again based on structural analysis.[111] It is a surprising interpretive decision, given his preference for understanding the text in its final form, but he consistently speaks of 'the two stories in chapter 13'.[112] This puts some strain on the fluidity of his exegesis and, oddly, he treats the enveloping frame (12.30-31; 13.33-34) of 1 Kings 13 separately, stating only that this 'adds another dimension to the unity of chapter 13'.[113]

Walsh is an attentive reader, offering numerous insights of value to students, scholars, and preachers alike throughout his treatment of 1 Kgs 13.1-10. As one might expect, he aims to offer a synchronic evaluation

---

108. Jerome T. Walsh, *Style and Structure in Biblical Hebrew Narrative* (Collegeville, MN: Michael Glazier, 2001); idem, *Old Testament Narrative*.

109. This criticism holds regardless of whether Walsh is arguing for an authorial hermeneutic or a text hermeneutic; see Chapter 5.

110. Cf. Jerome T. Walsh, *Ahab: The Construction of a King*, Interfaces (Collegeville, MN: Liturgical, 2006).

111. Ibid., 174–6, 182–3, 190.

112. Walsh, *1 Kings*, 190–1, passim.

113. Ibid., 191.

of narrative details rather than examining the compositional history of the story. For instance, regardless of whether or not the prophecy in 13.2 is a *vaticinium ex eventu*, as some scholars postulate, Walsh perceives the naming of Josiah as 'one end of a link that contributes to unifying all of 1–2 Kings... Perhaps the Davidic scion who will undo Jeroboam's religious deviations will also be able to repair the political division in which his reign began.'[114] Regardless of how Josiah came to be named in this story recounting events 300 years before his time, Walsh seeks to interpret the text as it stands rather than speculating about how it may have been put together.

As well as identifying how the prophecy in v. 2 directs the reader's attention to a distant future, Walsh observes that the prophetic oracle – 'he shall sacrifice on you the priests of the high places who offer incense upon you' – implicates Jeroboam in the present moment as well, since he is probably the only one to date who has undertaken the priestly function at the Bethel altar. 'In this way the oracle that pointedly ignores the king by addressing the altar nevertheless implicates him obliquely in the prophesied destruction.'[115]

Scholars are divided over whether the remarks about the altar in vv. 3 and 5 are immediate or parenthetical (i.e. retrospective). For his part, Walsh firmly asserts the latter because of 'the Hebrew grammatical form and the unnecessary introductory words... In other words, this parenthetical sign is not part of the scene; we hear it but Jeroboam does not.'[116] By way of explanation, Walsh surmises that since the spilling of the ashes is tantamount to a desecration of the sacrifice, it cannot have happened earlier than Josiah's northern reforms, 'since in that case the altar would already be desecrated and unusable, and Josiah's actions would be pointless'.[117]

Following Barth, Walsh perceives that a meal with the king would signify solidarity and thus interprets the man of God's refusal as a rejection of Bethel: 'he will not eat "in this place". Jeroboam is not the problem – Bethel is...the "house" of the golden calf, with its altar and its

---

114. Ibid., 177.
115. Ibid., 178.
116. Ibid. Walsh does not make it clear what he means by 'the Hebrew grammatsical form' and it is not self-evident. He makes a similar statement about the man of God 'coming' to Bethel in 13.1 (ibid., 176). He states that it is a participle, but does not explain how he reaches this conclusion, since the participial form and Qal (3ms) are identical (בָּא).
117. Walsh, *1 Kings*, 178. I shall address this further in Chapter 7.

priests, is irrevocably doomed.'[118] Therefore, when the man of God not only declines the invitation but also reveals that he was commanded by the LORD to avoid any fraternisation with Bethel, his public obedience to the threefold prohibition gains gravitas as an enacted prophetic sign, indicating his rejection of false worship in the north as well as the irrevocable nature of his mission.

The second prophetic story (1 Kgs 13.11-32) about the betrayal of a southern prophet by his northern colleague raises a number of questions – not just about the anonymous characters and their motives, but also about why this story is located here at all, since Jeroboam is never mentioned. According to Walsh, its structure is 'developmental':

A. The prophet hears news of the man of God (13:11)
  B. He speaks in reaction to the news (13:12)
    C. He has his sons saddle his donkey (13:13)
      D. He journeys and finds the man of God (13:14-18)
        E. The man of God comes back and eats with him (13:19)
          F. The prophet speaks the word of Yahweh (13:20-22)
            G. The word is fulfilled (13:23-25)
A'. The prophet hears news of the man of God (13:25)
  B'. He speaks in reaction to the news (13:26)
    C'. He has his sons saddle his donkey (13:27)
      D'. He journeys and finds the man of God's corpse (13:28)
        E'. He brings back the man of God, and honors him (13:29-30)
          F'. He confirms the word of Yahweh (13:31-32)
            G'. ... [119]

Walsh states that this structure 'focuses our attention on three dimensions of progression: from element to element (A to B to C, etc.), from parallel element to parallel element (from A to A', etc.), and from sequence to sequence (from A through G to A' through G')'.[120] But while Walsh's structural analysis brings certain repeated elements to the fore, it also (inevitably) fails to emphasise what other scholars consider to be of critical importance. For instance, Klopfenstein perceives v. 20 to be pivotal in the narrative's plot, since that is where the story's *single* reversal takes place. But where a scholar holding Klopfenstein's view might appeal to the *petuchah* [פ] in the middle of v. 20 (Masoretic punctuation, marking off

---

118. Ibid., 180.
119. Ibid., 182–3. (The ellipsis is part of the citation from Walsh's commentary; see my comments below.)
120. Ibid., 183.

a literary unit) as an indication that v. 20 contains a critical turning point in the narrative, Walsh emphasises instead the repetition in the narrative, claiming that the symmetrical structure he observes is 'fundamental to the text'.[121] In Walsh's outline, v. 20 comes under point F, which is neither structurally central nor of any particular significance. Consequently, his summary of 1 Kgs 13.20-22 – 'The prophet speaks the word of Yahweh' – bypasses the strangeness of an event that Klopfenstein considers critical: a *lying* prophet now receives and speaks a *genuine* prophetic word! The issue, of course, is that these two readers have identified different structural centres to the narrative, and any attempts to evaluate between them will not be aided by either one claiming to have identified a pattern that is 'fundamental to the text'. In any case, Walsh's structural analysis fails to account for G', where he simply inserts an ellipsis without explanation. Does G' fail to uphold the sequence?

However one resolves such differences, the point is not that one interpreter has understood the story's structure correctly and the other has it wrong. Rather, as Peter Leithart rightly observes, 'multiple structure is virtually inescapable, especially in narratives and poetry'.[122] Just as a reader's choice of context brings certain dimensions of the text into focus, so also do the reader's decisions concerning structural elements and patterns. Notwithstanding the limitations imposed by Walsh's strict adherence to chiastic structures and his unusual decision (as a narrative critic) to divide the narrative in 1 Kings 13 into two parts, his exegesis contains a number of illuminating insights.

Anti-North Polemic: Van Seters (1999, 2000)

Van Seters is well-known for his critical literary analysis of biblical texts and for his work in ancient Near Eastern historiography. He has published two short essays on 1 Kings 13 from entirely different points of view, though they both present the story as a post-Dtr composition, written to function as anti-Samaritan propaganda. Here we examine Van Seters (both his interpretation and his hermeneutics) as a representative of those who see 1 Kings 13 as an anti-north polemic.

In the first of these essays, 'On Reading the Story of the Man of God' (1999), Van Seters offers his views on the composition and purpose of 1 Kings 13; in the second, 'The Deuteronomistic History: Can it Avoid

---

121. Walsh, 'Contexts', 369.
122. Peter J. Leithart, *Deep Exegesis: The Mystery of Reading Scripture* (Waco, TX: Baylor University Press, 2009), 143.

Death by Redaction?' (2000), he challenges the way 1 Kings 13 has come to function within the F. M. Cross school.[123] Both works attend to 1 Kings 13, although they represent very different approaches, and the latter work is more cogent in its argumentation and thus more persuasive. It will therefore be appropriate to assess each essay separately before considering the sum of Van Seters' contribution.

'On Reading the Story of the Man of God' (1999)
'One of the most difficult stories in biblical prose narrative to read and interpret is this strange story of the man of God from Judah.'[124] So begins this essay by Van Seters, whose aim is neither to review nor add to the collection of interpretive options for this difficult text, but rather to suggest the incompetence of its author as the basic reason for its perplexity. A more recent essay repeats many of the so-called problems presented here and asserts once again that 1 Kings 13 is comprised of 'a pastiche of elements borrowed from many other narratives and put together in such a careless and confusing fashion that it is difficult to make out at any point in the story just what is actually going on'.[125]

Van Seters observes that numerous studies of this text 'limit the interpretation of the story to whatever lies within 1 Kgs 13:1-32 and assume that it was originally independent or that the redactional connections before and after are of little significance to its meaning'.[126] But, as he rightly points out, the story has clear links with both the preceding narrative concerning Jeroboam as well as with the prophecy's fulfilment in 2 Kings 23, so that 1 Kings 13 is well integrated as part of the DH, strategically located between Jeroboam's cultus and Josiah's reforms. More than that, Van Seters asserts (for reasons given in his second essay) that 1 Kings 13 and 2 Kgs 23.15-20 are actually two parts of the same story. Together – and he also groups 2 Kgs 17.24-34; 23.4b together with them[127] – these verses constitute a post-Dtr addition, composed for a specific purpose. Van Seters does not mean to say that these texts would

---

123. This includes also the contributions of Cross's students, such as Stephen McKenzie, Werner Lemke, and Richard Nelson (Nelson was a student of Pat Miller, who studied under Cross).

124. Van Seters, 'On Reading', 225.

125. John Van Seters, 'Prophecy as Prediction in Biblical Historiography', in *Prophets, Prophecy, and Ancient Israelite Historiography*, ed. Mark J. Boda and Lissa M. Wray Beal (Winona Lake, IN: Eisenbrauns, 2013), 100.

126. Van Seters, 'On Reading', 225.

127. Ibid., 226.

make sense on their own if they were extracted, but rather that they were written in order to make sense of their present contexts.[128]

Before arriving at his main point, Van Seters acknowledges that a more common explanation for the 'self-contained' character of this narrative is to posit a *pre*-Dtr source for 1 Kings 13 and to attribute anything un-Deuteronomistic or otherwise problematic to the work of later redactors.[129] But even in spite of having great difficulty himself in understanding the text as it stands, Van Seters is reluctant to blame its incoherence on redactors, since that only relegates problems 'to another level where they are just as difficult to explain'.[130] (As the title suggests, his second essay warns of the dangers of redaction criticism and articulates its proper place in biblical interpretation.) The bulk of Van Seters' essay argues that the best explanation for the story's proliferation of problems is really quite simple; troublesome details in the text 'are the result of a lack of literary skill by the author'.[131] To make his point, Van Seters presents a list (not exhaustive, mind you) of sixteen problematic aspects of the story in 1 Kings 13. For the sake of being thorough, I shall respond briefly to each of the sixteen problems:

(1) *The man of God does not address Jeroboam, nor call him to account for his sin; he only addresses the altar.* 'This is totally uncharacteristic of Dtr in his presentation of prophetic confrontation of evil rulers... '[132] It is indeed unusual in the DH for a prophet to address an inanimate object rather the person responsible for that object. However, surely the reader's task is not to rewrite the story by eradicating anomalous details, but in fact quite the opposite; to pay special attention when a writer or redactor deviates from the norm. (This is, of course, assuming that the primary aim of the interpreter is to understand rather than, say, demonstrate authorial incompetence.) Thus, it may prove more fruitful to ask what is inferred

128. John Van Seters, 'The Deuteronomistic History: Can it Avoid Death by Redaction?', in *The Future of the Deuteronomistic History*, ed. Thomas Römer, BEThL 147 (Leuven: Leuven University Press, 2000), 216–17.

129. This is more or less the approach adopted by Mark Dwayne Allen in his recent PhD dissertation, *The Man of God*. Allen treats 1 Kgs 13 in three contexts: 'first, in its pre-deuteronomistic form, second, in its setting within the Deuteronomistic History, and, finally, in its larger canonical context' (i). The existence of a pre-deuteronomistic form in part one is simply assumed.

130. Van Seters, 'On Reading', 226. His example draws on Uriel Simon's essay in *Reading Prophetic Narratives* (Bloomington: Indiana University Press, 1997).

131. Ibid., 233.

132. Ibid., 227.

by a prophetic utterance against the altar rather than the king? In addition, since Van Seters proposes that 1 Kings 13 was composed and inserted by a post-Dtr author, is it fair to criticise him for diverging from typically Deuteronomistic characteristics?

(2) *The text confuses a large altar that Jeroboam stands upon with the offering of incense, which is associated with a small altar/stand.* The Hebrew indeed suggests that Jeroboam is standing 'over' or 'upon' (על) the altar. However, the *hiphil* form of the verb (להקטיר) is not restricted to 'offering incense'. Most scholars see no problem here, since the plainest meaning of the verb is 'to make a burnt offering'.[133]

(3) *The prophecy that Josiah will sacrifice 'the priests of the high places' (13.2) upon this altar is 'grotesque' and 'inappropriate for the righteous Josiah'. Moreover, 'there is no suggestion that the idolatrous priests in Judah were treated in this way'.*[134] Within the world of the text, 2 Kgs 23.20 responds directly to (i.e. fulfils) 1 Kgs 13.2, regardless of how one envisages Josiah's righteousness. Moreover, this is certainly not a standalone Hebrew text in its association of violence with righteousness (cf. Phineas in Num. 25; Jael in Judg. 4; Samuel in 1 Sam. 15; etc). An alternative solution to this dissonance is the intertextual reading offered by Van Seters himself in a footnote: 'Is it influenced by the story of Elijah's slaughter of the prophets of Baal in 1 Kgs 18:40? The latter episode could have been construed by the author of 1 Kings 13 as a sacrifice.'[135]

(4) *The prophecy in v. 2, especially the naming of Josiah, is 'quite meaningless' within 1 Kings 13, and 'not the least in the style of a Dtr editor',*[136] *since nothing is said of Jeroboam's own household.* The naming of Josiah provides an explicit link to 2 Kings 23 and can hardly be considered meaningless, especially if Josiah's reforms are to be understood as a reversal of the division that occurs in 1 Kings 11–14 – a point that Van Seters himself makes. And it is certainly in keeping with 'the style of a Dtr editor' to accent the theme of prophecy and fulfilment, which is achieved by naming Josiah. Moreover, 1 Kings 14 deals in detail with the fate of Jeroboam's household, so there is no need to double up on that theme here.

(5) *The splitting of the altar 'seems totally pointless in relation to the prediction'.*[137] *And if its point is to authenticate the man of God, why the second miracle as well? Also: 'The narration of the two miracles is*

133. See, e.g., Gray, *I & II Kings*, 326.
134. Van Seters, 'On Reading', 227.
135. Ibid., 227 n. 5.
136. Ibid., 227.
137. Ibid., 228.

certainly muddled'. Van Seters resolves these problems himself when he states that the splitting of the altar is evidence 'that the one who speaks is a man of God', and that the second miracle occurs because 'the king seems to react even before the miracle can take effect'. Exactly how the narration of the miracles is 'muddled', Van Seters does not say.

(6) *Regarding the king's response, 'the total lack of concern about the altar and the extension of friendship...seems entirely inappropriate'.*[138] The king does not show a 'total lack of concern about the altar' at all. On the contrary, he is so offended by its destruction that he orders the man of God's arrest (v. 4)! Regarding the invitation to fellowship (v. 7), it seems clear (to me and a good number of other interpreters) that the king would like to have the kind of power he has just witnessed at his beck and call. Thus the invitation to fellowship. On both of these points, the logic of the narrative's development is clear.

(7) *The threefold command 'seems clear enough, if it means that the man of God is to refrain completely from association with the people of Bethel. This obvious sense, however, seems to be confused by the remark in v. 10 that he returned to Judah by a different route.'*[139] This is an issue that has caused confusion for a few interpreters. Van Seters cites Rofé for taking v. 10 as an interpretive clue for the whole,[140] and Marcus also makes more of this detail than seems warranted.[141] However, the majority of commentators, even those who acknowledge the possibility of ambiguity, do not see a problem. The command is to not return *to Judah* by the way that he came *to Bethel*, and this is precisely what v. 10 specifies.

(8) *If the terms 'man of God' and 'prophet' serve the purpose of distinguishing between these two anonymous figures, why must the author add 'tedious' qualifying clauses in addition? The author's 'tiresome repetition' surely indicates 'very limited narrative skills' and not 'literary artistry'.*[142] I agree with Van Seters regarding the purpose of the two designations, though it is unclear to me why the additional qualifying clause (presumably, 'the man of God *who came from Judah*') is considered to be 'tedious'. Repetition is no more a 'problematic aspect' of 1 Kings 13 than it is of Hebrew narrative generally. Perhaps the man of God's place of origin was important to the writer?

138. Ibid.
139. Ibid.
140. Rofé, *The Prophetical Stories*, 174–5.
141. Marcus, *From Balaam to Jonah*, 78–82.
142. Van Seters, 'On Reading', 228.

(9) *The narrative only ever speaks of one ass at a time: 'the ass'. The repetition of this 'stereotyped phrase...creates serious contradiction in the text'.*[143] From what I can tell, it is unclear to Van Seters whether there is one ass or two. In my judgment, it is clear that there are two, and it is difficult to see how 'only one ass mentioned at any one time, which is rendered with the definite article' creates any kind of serious contradiction or interpretive problem. How many asses there are and who they belong to generally receives a passing comment (at best) from commentators. How or why Van Seters regards 'the ass' (החמור) as a 'stereotyped phrase', I cannot say.

(10) *How can a miracle-working prophet show such little discernment and be so easily duped by the Bethel prophet? 'The man of God is not disobedient; he is merely stupid.'*[144] This comment is rather curious, given that the plot's central tension derives from this act of deception and its outcome. Moreover, the man of God can hardly be labelled 'merely stupid' when other texts make it clear that God does, on occasion, change his mind about prophetic words given (e.g., 1 Kgs 21.29; more broadly, Jer. 18.7-10). Indeed, as Stuart Lasine points out, another anonymous prophet is killed by a lion in 1 Kings 20 precisely because he does *not* do what a fellow prophet asks him to do![145] It is only the narrator's assertion in v. 20b that enables readers to know for certain that the man of God should not have trusted his hospitable, older colleague.

(11) *Why does the lying Bethel prophet receive the word of the LORD in v. 20 rather than the man of God? 'This makes a total mockery of any distinction between true and false, or obedient and disobedient, prophets. The author contradicts all of the norms of prophecy but still wants us to take the prophetic oracles seriously'.*[146] *What lesson can we possibly learn from such a tale?* This turning point is indeed one of the most troublesome details of the story, but the fact that it surprises us and demands interpretive rigour hardly means that its author is unskilled. In fact, for many readers, this conundrum is the very point of the narrative! Does Van Seters mean to suggest that biblical narratives containing an act of God that contradicts human expectations are not to be taken seriously? He is, of course, right to note that the role reversal has a confounding effect on readers, but perhaps this text serves a function beyond being reduced to a moral lesson.

---

143. Ibid.
144. Ibid., 229.
145. Lasine, *Weighing Hearts*, 104–5.
146. Van Seters, 'On Reading', 229.

(12) *Why is nothing said about 'the second miracle' wherein the lion permits the Bethel prophet to remove the Judean's corpse without attacking him or his ass?* Hebrew narrative is terse, and gaps abound, only some of which are significant. The withering and subsequent healing of Jeroboam's hand are also narrated with striking brevity, and the momentum and thrust of the story evidently do not require any further reflection upon 'the second miracle', either.

(13) *The 'sequel' or epilogue in 2 Kgs 23.15-20 is confusing. Are Jeroboam's altar and high place pulled down, burned, or crushed to dust? And how can this altar be used to burn human bones if it has been destroyed – whether during Josiah's reign or almost three hundred years earlier when it was torn down in 1 Kgs 13.5?* 2 Kings 23.15 may appear to be an 'ill-constructed sentence' (Gray), but the sense is clearly that these idolatrous objects were destroyed.[147] Perhaps the complex manner of description is the result of referencing Moses' actions toward the golden calf in Exod. 32.20 in addition to other potent verbs of destruction.[148] Regarding the destruction of the altar, two possibilities are present to the reader: either (a) 1 Kgs 13.5 presents a later perspective and is, in fact, reporting the same event as 2 Kgs 23.15 (i.e. the narrator is stating as an aside that this prophetic oracle will be fulfilled in due course); or (b) the rent altar of 1 Kings 13 was at some point rebuilt (due to its continuing usage), only to be torn down again in Josiah's day.

(14) *If the memory of the Judean (together with his prophetic oracle) was preserved by inhabitants of Bethel with a specially marked tomb, then 'why did they maintain the sanctuary as a place of worship?'* It is unclear whether the sanctuary is still being used as a place of worship when Josiah visits; the point is rather that he is burning bones from the tombs upon the idolatrous altar, and that he spares the shared tomb because of the legend behind it.

(15) *In connection with point 13 above regarding 2 Kgs 23.15-16, how can priests be slaughtered upon altars (v. 20) when those high places have been destroyed (v. 19)?* Verses 19-20 do not necessarily report sequential events, but rather collective details about Josiah's reforms. As Van Seters himself points out, the purpose of these recollections is to create a direct link back to the prophecies of 1 Kings 13. Given Van Seters' suggestion that a post-Dtr writer has composed these stories separately in order to insert them at these points, the details given are logically coherent and even what one might expect.

---

147. So Nelson, *First and Second Kings*, 258. See Chapter 7 on the interpretive possibilities for the author's use of multiple descriptions.

148. So J. Long, Jr, *1 & 2 Kings*, 515.

(16) *'The curious remark in 2 Kgs 23:4 that the king "carried their ashes to Bethel" makes no sense in its context and seems entirely motivated by the presentation in vv. 15-20.'*[149] From a redaction-critical perspective the phrase may appear as an addition,[150] but from a synchronic perspective it is certainly feasible (and makes perfect sense in its context) that Josiah carried ashes from the idolatrous artefacts of worship to Bethel, in order to accomplish the task of defiling Jeroboam's high places.[151]

This list of sixteen problems leads Van Seters to the conclusion 'that the story of the man of God from Judah is incoherent throughout'.[152] He then briefly explores three common strategies for making sense of the confusion.

The first strategy often adopted by scholars is to assume that the original story, prior to editorial interference, was probably more coherent; in other words, redactors may be blamed for any inconsistencies. But since Van Seters cannot discern a clear purpose behind the sixteen problems he has identified, he instead posits that the story's problems were inherent to the original version and places full culpability upon a hypothetical post-Dtr writer who composed the story in its entirety and inserted it untidily into the DH. Van Seters's best guess is that the author's *modus operandi* 'seems to have been the gleaning of motifs and elements from a body of earlier literature which included such late pieces as Jonah, the P Code and Chronicles. Such a collage of materials has created a very confusing text.'[153]

A second means of explaining the anomalous quality of the story takes the opposite approach. Rather than dismissing problematic aspects of the story as erroneous, some interpreters assign particular significance to those very details by appealing to rhetorical devices such as irony or parody. David Marcus presents such an approach in his monograph, *From Balaam to Jonah: Anti-prophetic Satire in the Hebrew Bible*, within which he interprets 1 Kings 13. However, Van Seters rightly points out that while elements in certain narratives, such as the Balaam and Jonah stories, do appear to contain greater doses of exaggeration and irony than other texts, it is difficult to see what the point of satirising prophecy in 1 Kings 13 might be. A parody of prophecy at this point in Kings would certainly undermine the seriousness of the man of God's oracle regarding Josiah's reforms.

149. Van Seters, 'On Reading', 229.
150. Gray, *I & II Kings*, 732.
151. Sweeney, *I & II Kings*, 447.
152. Van Seters, 'On Reading', 230.
153. Ibid., 233.

Yet a third method by which some scholars seek to make sense of the confusion is by reading 1 Kings 13 intertextually. As Van Seters puts it, 'the account may be enriched in its meaning by association with other texts with similar terminology and allusions to other stories. In this way also what is confusing and problematic may be clarified by the comparison.'[154] Van Seters considers five possible intertexts but ultimately concludes that an author who does not borrow skilfully from the materials at his disposal will inevitably compose an incoherent text, which is the most likely explanation for the problems in 1 Kings 13. In my judgment, however, the suggested intertexts put forward by Van Seters are limited in their heuristic value, and his means of analysis is rather unusual. In each instance, Van Seters highlights one parallel between 1 Kings 13 and the intertext, and then seeks to show that the parallel is not sufficiently sustained to be convincing or clear. In so doing, he gives the impression that the purpose of an intertextual relationship is less about being suggestive through nuance than it is about precise imitation. Narratives that show signs of semblance with another text but then diverge along their own course, are therefore labelled 'clumsy', 'confused' and 'muddled'.[155] Perhaps it would be more accurate, however, to say that Van Seters does not suggest the most illuminating intertextual links.

In any case, none of these three methods satisfactorily resolves Van Seters' efforts to make sense of 1 Kings 13. In his words: 'This leads me to the conclusion that the difficulties in reading this text cannot be blamed on incompetent editors or redactors; nor can they be solved by intertextuality. They are the result of a lack of literary skill by the author. The incoherence resides in the original text...'[156] On this basis, he suggests: 'If the text is not coherent and consistent then perhaps one should be very cautious about trying to discover what it is about and especially from drawing theological and moral lessons from it'.[157] In other words, if Van Seters is correct that the story's quandaries are the direct consequence of its author's incompetence, then one must be wary of interpreting those problematic details, lest meaning be found where none is present. In the end, Van Seters describes 1 Kings 13 in this way: 'It is a fairly crass piece of anti-Samaritan religious propaganda constructed with little narrative skill or sensitivity to religious and moral issues'.[158] (It seems entirely appropriate that the essay appears in a volume entitled, *The Labour of Reading*!) In addition, Van Seters maintains that it is highly unlikely

154. Ibid., 230.
155. Ibid., 231–2.
156. Ibid., 233.
157. Ibid.
158. Ibid.

that there was ever a pre-Dtr account of Jeroboam's apostasy or Josiah's reform, and in the final paragraph he abruptly adds that 'the story is a vilification of the Bethel temple, which was still in use for some time in the exilic and post-exilic periods, and the Samaritan community'.[159] He provides no argumentation for this assertion, but promises that it is forthcoming (see below).

In my judgment, and as I have sought to demonstrate, Van Seters' list of so-called problems are much less disconcerting than he would have us think. His use of phrases like 'totally pointless', 'entirely inappropriate', 'tiresome repetition', 'limited narrative skills', 'serious contradictions', 'makes no sense', and 'incoherent throughout' ultimately do little more than to expose Van Seters' exasperation with a text that is different to the one that he might prefer to have been written. It certainly seems ironic for Van Seters to be critical of Simon's reading – which suggests 'a rather clumsy and repetitive Dtr redactor' – for being 'highly speculative' and failing to reckon with problems![160] In my view, Van Seters' essay could be described in exactly those same terms. Although he succeeds in identifying some of the challenges for interpreting this chapter, they are, generally speaking, the kinds of challenges posed by many Hebrew narratives. Moreover, those very elements of the story that signify incompetence in Van Seters' mind (i.e. 'problems') are generally thought of as hermeneutically significant 'gaps' and plot drivers by narrative critics. As Randolph Tate rightly observes, 'hermeneutics must give appropriate attention to interpretive aims, for differences in interpretation may be due as much to differing aims as to textual ambiguity, interpretive competence, and matters of genre'.[161] In this case, since the interpretive aim of Van Seters' reading of 1 Kings 13 (in this essay) is to demonstrate the ancient author's incompetence, textual ambiguity is presented in a negative, even damning, light. By the same token, since methods (the how of reading) are adopted to suit aims (the why of reading), Van Seters looks *behind* the text to explain conundrums *within* the text.

---

159. Ibid. On the probability that there was never a pre-Dtr version of 1 Kgs 13, but that the exilic editor composed it for its present purpose, Van Seters cites Knoppers, *Two Nations Under God*, 2:25–44; Eynikel, 'Prophecy and Fulfillment'; his own *In Search of History*, 313–14, and his essay, 'The Deuteronomistic History: Can it Avoid Death by Redaction?', on which see below.

160. Van Seters, 'On Reading', 226.

161. W. Randolph Tate, *Biblical Interpretation: An Integrated Approach*, rev. ed. (Peabody, MA: Hendrickson, 1997), 195.

'The Deuteronomistic History: Can it Avoid Death by Redaction?' *(2000)*

In his second essay, as the title suggests, Van Seters seeks to defend Noth's thesis of a unified history (i.e. Deuteronomy–2 Kings)[162] by disproving the Cross school and questioning the gains of the Göttingen school. Because the prophecy in 1 Kgs 13.2-3 and its fulfilment in 2 Kgs 23.15-20 establish a frame for Dtr[1], 1 Kings 13 has come to function as a supporting text for the Cross school, which views 1 Kings 13–2 Kings 23 as the main body of a pre-exilic edition of the DH. Cross himself did little more than mention 1 Kings 13 in his well-known essay, but an important study by one of his students has argued convincingly 'that 1 Kings 13 forms an integral part of the structure and theology of the Deuteronomistic History'.[163] Van Seters argues to the contrary that 1 Kings 13 and 2 Kgs 23.15-20 (also 2 Kgs 17.24-34; 23.4b) are post-Dtr additions and cannot therefore have been part of a work of propaganda supporting Josiah's reforms. Since 'the whole of Cross's thesis rests on Josiah's northern campaign against the high places of Samaria', Van Seters concludes that 'the primary reason for dating DtrH to the time of Josiah is invalid'.[164] In addition, he stresses that redaction criticism might be better utilised to recover Noth's concept of a unified DH instead of dissolving it.[165]

The logic of Van Seters' argument for seeing 1 Kings 13 (and other selected verses) as a later text is as follows: 1 Kgs 12.33–13.33 has been inserted into the DH via resumptive repetition, or *Wiederaufnahme*.[166] The majority of scholars who hold this position think Dtr to be responsible

---

162. For his defence of Noth's unified DH, see the second part of John Van Seters' *Abraham in History and Tradition* (New Haven, CT: Yale University Press, 1975).

163. Lemke, 'Way of Obedience', 304. See also the more comprehensive defence of Cross's position in Knoppers, *Two Nations Under God*.

164. Van Seters, 'Death by Redaction?', 220–1. This is perhaps overstated by Van Seters. Cross provides a range of supporting arguments for why he thinks the primary edition of the DH (Dtr[1]) comes from the Josianic era; Cross, *Canaanite Myth*, 288–9.

165. Van Seters, 'Death by Redaction?', 214, 222.

166. I.e. 'resumptive repetition'. The German word literally means 'taking up again'. Where an interpolation has been made, the redactor uses a repeated phrase (or phrases) to draw the reader's attention back to the main subject matter; a literary device that effectively says, 'Now, where were we?' The repetition of the phrase 'and this thing became a sin' thus forms an *inclusio* around the story of the two prophets, suggesting that 1 Kgs 12.30–13.33 is an interpolation, a conclusion numerous scholars have drawn. On the similarities between *Wiederaufnahme* and ordinary conversation, see R. F. Person, 'A Reassessment of Wiederaufnahme from the Perspective of

for incorporating 1 Kings 13 in its pre-Dtr form (generally as a prophetic legend) into the larger corpus,[167] but Van Seters differs: 'The redactional seams are not part of Dtr's effort to integrate into his work an older prophetic story but rather the work of the later writer of 1 Kings 13 to tie his story into the DtrH'.[168] Van Seters thus affirms that 1 Kings 13 and 2 Kgs 23.15-20 are intrinsically linked as prophecy and fulfilment and cannot be understood without one another. Just as 1 Kings 13 makes no explicit mention of Jeroboam's apostasy but only makes sense within that assumed context, so the latter text has been composed and inserted into the record of Josiah's reform as one episode within it.[169] This explains why the altar mentioned in 1 Kings 13 and 2 Kgs 23.15-20 receives no mention outside of these two texts.

Van Seters cites the work of Alexander Rofé to support the notion that 1 Kings 13 is a late text due to its content and vocabulary.[170] In addition, he notes that certain characteristics of the story are very unlike Dtr: the phrase '*by* the word (בדבר) of the LORD';[171] a Yahwistic prophet interceding for an evil king; the absence of a pronouncement of judgment upon the evil king's dynasty; and the (anachronistic) mention of 'the cities of Samaria' in v. 32. Van Seters also considers 2 Kgs 17.24-34 to be a late text, since 'the idea…that there were no priests of Yahweh and no Israelites left in the northern province of Samaria after the fall of Samaria is obviously unhistorical'.[172] Moreover, he understands 2 Kgs 17.24-34 to function in much the same way as 1 Kings 13: 'this is merely

---

Conversation Analysis', *Biblische Zeitschrift* 43 (1999): 239–48. Also see Curt Kuhl, 'Die "Wiederaufnahme" – ein literarkritisches Prinzip?', *ZAW* 64 (2009): 1–11. We shall discuss this device further in Chapter 7.

167. So Lemke, 'Way of Obedience', 320 n. 31; Cohn, 'Literary Technique', 31 n. 15. Although McKenzie, *Trouble*, notes that the story has been inserted between references to the sin of Jeroboam (52–4), he nonetheless maintains that 'this theme is not at work in the intervening story' (54). Rather, he suggests that 'the story in 1 Kgs 13:11-32a likely derives from Northern prophetic legends like those of Elijah and Elisha and 1 Kings 20…and [was] inserted into Dtr's account of Jeroboam at a late date' (55).

168. Van Seters, 'Death by Redaction?', 216.

169. Ibid., 217.

170. Rofé, 'Classes in the Prophetical Stories', 158–63. Knoppers, however, *Two Nations Under God*, 2:51, considers Rofé's arguments to be weak. On the problematic nature of dating texts according to content and/or vocabulary, see the discussion in Chapter 5 under *Historical-critical and Canonical Approaches*.

171. 1 Sam. 3.21; 1 Kgs 13.1, 2, 5, 9, 17, 18, 32; 20.35. The typical Dtr formulation is '*according to* the word (כדבר) of the LORD'.

172. Van Seters, 'Death by Redaction?', 220.

anti-Samaritan propaganda to discredit any association with the northern worshippers of Yahweh'.[173] Van Seters agrees with Lemke concerning the close relation between 1 Kings 13 and 2 Kings 17, since both texts draw attention to Bethel and the failure of the north. But where Lemke wishes to show that they have been integrated by Dtr at critical junctures within the DH, Van Seters distinguishes these texts from the DH and asserts that they were written later and for a very different purpose. Presupposing a Judean author who wrote during the exilic period, Van Seters expresses the meaning, or moral, of 1 Kings 13 in this way:

> The author is no longer concerned about the fate of the northern kingdom as in Dtr but about the continuing existence of cult places in Samaria and especially the important temple in Bethel. The message of the unit is twofold. First, the altar was completely desecrated by divine decree so it is no longer an appropriate place of worship and the priesthood is entirely illegitimate from the beginning. Secondly, one is to have no further communal association (to eat and drink) with anyone in Bethel, even those who worship Yahweh, as represented by the old prophet. This reflects the same kind of anti-Samaritan vilification that is represent by 2 Kings 17,24-34, and since it shares so much of the same terminology it could actually stem from the same hand.[174]

Van Seters' argument that Josiah's reform never actually occurred in Bethel or the cities of Samaria[175] is dependent upon these texts (1 Kgs 13; 2 Kgs 17.24-34; 23.4b, 15-20) being bracketed out from the DH as later additions. Historically, he states that '[a]ny reform activity and cult centralization was entirely restricted to Judah "from Geba to Beersheba" [in accordance with 2 Kgs 23.8], and this was confirmed by the corresponding archaeological evidence'.[176] Van Seters thereby seeks to undermine the basic position of the Cross school, which understands these very texts to support Josiah's campaign in the north.[177]

173. Ibid.
174. Ibid.
175. Van Seters, 'On Reading', 233; idem, 'Death by Redaction?', 221.
176. Van Seters, 'Death by Redaction?', 221. But see William G. Dever, 'The Silence of the Text: An Archaeological Commentary on 2 Kings 23', in *Scripture and Other Artifacts: Essays on the Bible and Archaeology in Honor of Philip J. King*, ed. Michael D. Coogan, J. Cheryl Exum and Lawrence E. Stager (Louisville, KY: Westminster John Knox, 1994), 143-4.
177. Cross puts it thus: 'In fact, the juxtaposition of the two themes, of threat and promise, provide [*sic*] the platform of the Josianic reform. The Deuteronomistic history, insofar as these themes reflect its central concerns, may be described as a propaganda work of the Josianic reformation and imperial program. In particular, the

In summary, Van Seters asserts in these two essays that the author of 1 Kings 13 was a post-Dtr writer whose moral insensitivity and literary incompetence are evidenced in his work, and that the subject matter of the passages he composed and inserted into the DH are historically inaccurate regarding the reforms of Josiah. Whatever is made of these revisionist speculations, one is still left with the canonical record of Israel's history, which unambiguously upholds King Josiah – in both prophecy and fulfilment – as the one who rid the south and the north of the idolatrous activities that caused their division.[178] To my mind, if Van Seters is, in fact, right about a lack of historical precision in this record of Israel's past, the question why Israel recorded and preserved its past in this particular way becomes all the more urgent. To what end would Israel have preserved the memory of Josiah as an ideal monarch who reversed the sins of Jeroboam? When details in the narrative are difficult to reconcile with practical or historical realities, these only intensify questions about the literary record we have.

Political Allegory: Roland Boer (1996, 1997)

A fourth approach to 1 Kings 13 pays special attention to its literary placement within the Jeroboam narrative and judges on that basis that its significance reaches beyond what it might mean as a self-contained narrative (as per Walsh's observations above). Robert Cohn therefore describes 1 Kings 13, located within the Jeroboam story (1 Kgs 11–14), as 'a kind of parable, a story within a story, that sets into relief the theological dynamics of the larger narrative'.[179] The term 'story within a story' has also been adopted by David Bosworth, though he places 1 Kings 13 within the much broader context of 1 Kings 13–2 Kings 23 (see Chapter 6). Keith Bodner similarly refers to 1 Kings 13 as a *play-within-a-play*,[180] while

---

document speaks to the North, calling Israel to return to Judah and to Yahweh's sole legitimate shrine in Jerusalem, asserting the claims of the ancient Davidic monarchy upon all of Israel. Even the destruction of Bethel and the cults of the high places was predicted by the prophets, pointing to the centrality of Josiah's role for northern Israel.' *Canaanite Myth*, 284.

178. Note the divine promise made to Jeroboam via Ahijah in 1 Kgs 11.39: 'For this reason I will punish the descendants of David, but not forever'. Cross comments, 'In this statement we must understand that the oracle presumes an ultimate reunion of the two kingdoms under a Davidid'. Ibid., 279.

179. Cohn, 'Literary Technique', 33. For Cohn, 'the larger narrative' refers to 1 Kgs 11–14.

180. Bodner refers to the second part of the narrative (13.11-32) 'as a "play-within-a-play", a type of *political allegory* that functions as a subtle reflection on the fate of Jeroboam's kingship'. Bodner, *Jeroboam's Royal Drama*, 97–8 (original emphasis).

others use such terms as 'parable' (Rofé) and 'political allegory' (Boer). In spite of variations in terminology, what is being evoked and accented by these scholars is the nature of the story as one that utilises a system of referentiality to illuminate national and political themes. Bodner and Cohn argue (in their own ways) that the fate of the man of God reflects that of the king (Jeroboam), who in turn represents the nation of Israel.

In this vein, Roland Boer offers a stimulating analysis of 1 Kings 13 as a political allegory. In his doctoral dissertation (1993), published as a monograph under the title, *Jameson and Jeroboam*, Boer seeks to explore how the writings of prominent Marxist literary critic Fredric Jameson relate to biblical studies. The work has three substantial chapters. In the first, Boer sets out Jameson's twofold approach: 'the use of metacommentary [i.e. the consideration of other methods and interpretations, of the pluralism of methods in contemporary criticism] in the specific and limited capacity of identifying major ways in which biblical texts have been interpreted; and then the use of this phase of the analysis as a basis for a Marxist reading'.[181] For our purposes, however, it is the second chapter – 'Historical Determinism in 1 Kings 11–14' – that is of primary interest, wherein Boer explores how, in keeping with Marxist literary theory, the interpretation of the Jeroboam cycle reflects the ideological interests of the institution(s) from which the texts originated. He has selected these particular chapters from the DH because of their interest to theologians, literary/textual critics, and historical critics. That is to say, these biblical texts are well suited to Boer's approach via metacommentary because they are methodologically 'thick'.[182] In the second and third chapters of his work, then, Boer applies Jameson's approach by considering the wide range of scholarly work done on 1 Kings 11–14 (and related texts[183]) to determine which feature or features may be used as a basis for a Marxist reading. In the case of 1 Kings 11–14, he finds that 'national allegory' proves to be the dominant feature warranting further analysis. Here we shall examine the second chapter of *Jameson and Jeroboam* in conjunction with a related essay featuring 1 Kings 13 entitled, 'National Allegory in the Hebrew Bible' (1997).[184]

Boer's metacommentary begins with Barth, which he recognises as 'perhaps the most significant interpretation of this text (1 Kings 13)'.[185]

181. Boer, *James and Jeroboam*, 2.
182. Ibid., 101.
183. In Chapter 3, Boer compares his findings from Chapter 2 (on 1 Kgs 13) with studies of two other texts that also deal with the succession to the throne after Solomon's death; namely, 2 Chron. 10–13 and 3 Kgdms 11–14 (LXX).
184. Boer, 'National Allegory in the Hebrew Bible'.
185. Boer, *Jameson and Jeroboam*, 102.

He then proceeds to consider analyses that fall under the rubric of an historical-critical approach (source-, form- and redaction-criticism), literary studies of the text in its final form, and ideological or political (i.e. Marxist) approaches. Having established which elements might be useful for his project, Boer analyses the text according to the three levels of Jameson's Marxist allegorical method.

The first horizon is concerned with dissonant structural elements in the text and how variant structural motifs vie for control. Thus, contradictions are pertinent to Jameson's mode of political reading, be they formal, ideological or historical. Based on the work of source-critical scholarship, Boer distinguishes between 'prophetic' and 'annalistic' source materials.[186] He notes that it is somewhat ironic, however, that studies which seek to locate sources historically are of greater value (for Boer's purposes, at least) when they are read in their final form, for 'only the more amorphous situation of the final redaction – the exile – meets the requirements of a social situation with a real contradiction which is reflected in the ideological antinomy [i.e. the reliability, or lack thereof, of the word of Yahweh] and for which our text is an imaginary and formal resolution'.[187] Although attempts to determine the text's compositional history are fraught with pitfalls, Boer is convinced that the tensions in the text point to broader ideological issues.

The logic of his analysis is as follows. In Boer's judgment, the narrative and its literary context (1 Kgs 11–14) highlight the theme of the divine word, of which there are three distinct types. The *punishment* announced against Solomon in 11.11-13, 31-39 is fulfilled in 12.1-20, and Shemaiah's *prohibition* to Rehoboam is also obeyed and remains in force (12.21-24). In light of these affirmations of the efficacy of the divine word, Boer posits that Jeroboam's cultic activities, which constitute a *breach of the covenant*, also anticipate ideological closure through a further affirmation of the reliability of the divine word. Since readerly expectations have been established (regarding Solomon and Rehoboam), what happens next comes as something of a surprise, for in 1 Kings 13 the reliability of the word of the LORD comes 'under severe ideological attack'[188] when the Bethel prophet also claims divine authority for a word that contradicts the prohibition articulated by the Judean. In addition, when the Judean trusts the Bethelite and breaks the prohibition, yet another fulfilled announcement plays out, resulting in the Judean's death as foretold by his deceiving 'brother'. These events thereby call into question the reliability

---

186. On this distinction, see Montgomery, *Kings*, 38–9.
187. Boer, *Jameson and Jeroboam*, 146.
188. Ibid., 139.

of God's word: 'who bears the word? where may it be located? when is it genuine and when is it false? In the surrounding narrative the divine word seems to be in control, but in 1 Kings 13 this begins to disintegrate.'[189] Boer's reading seeks to show how the foundational Deuteronomistic theme of prophecy–fulfilment (cf. *the efficacious word of God* above) comes under fire in this text; 'in chapter 11, 12 and 14 the prophets act as media for a divine word which operates according to conventional patterns, all of which becomes problematical in the light of the uncertainties over the word of Yahweh in the intervening chapter'.[190] 1 Kings 13 thus places a question mark over the certainty of the divine word in a general sense, though it perhaps does so in a specific way as well.

The narrative is problematised by the last two words of v. 18: כחש לו ('he lied to him'), and the vast majority of commentators agree (or assume) that the subject of the verb כחש is the old prophet. But if the verb's subject is taken to be the angel who allegedly brought the word of the LORD to the old prophet, then the notion of divine deception comes to the fore:

> The questions are displaced from those of obedience and the veracity of prophecy to a more fundamental consideration of the workings of Yahweh. If Yahweh is the cause of the deception and subsequent destruction of the hapless man of God from Judah, then questions begin to arise concerning the reliability of the divine word in relationship to human activity. The sentence structure of 13:18 leaves open both possibilities, and both cause problems. But I would highlight the second option, that Yahweh is responsible, if for no other reason than that it has been neglected. The ambiguity is itself a sign of the difficult questions being entertained.[191]

Boer thus shows that 1 Kings 13 may be understood as a text that calls into question the reliability of the divine word, either by highlighting the contradictory words of the two prophets (in contrast to other prophetic words in the Jeroboam cycle), or via an alternative understanding of the subject in v. 18b.

Jameson's second horizon requires that this tension concerning the reliability of God's word, as depicted in 1 Kings 11–14, be examined further. In so doing, Boer determines that 'the major ideologeme of 1 Kgs 11–14 [is] historical determinism'[192] – i.e. 'the way in which the divine

---

189. Ibid.
190. Ibid., 142.
191. Ibid., 141–2.
192. Ibid., 149.

may be understood to be involved in human affairs'.¹⁹³ The same concept is elsewhere referred to as 'dual causality', wherein historical outcomes are attributed to divine influence in spite of the focus being on free human decisions in the relevant narratives.¹⁹⁴ Through this lens, Boer examines 1 Kings 13 as a national allegory that explores the tension between (human) voluntarism and (divine) determinism. He is particularly attentive to the oft-neglected divine prohibition against eating, drinking or returning by the same route since, in his view, this tripartite commandment 'contributes heavily to the narrative machinery'.¹⁹⁵ Specifically, the ideologeme of hospitality is utilised to simultaneously affirm and deny legitimacy to the north. Boer recognises the contradictory nature of this claim, but sees the conflict as providing an important perspective on the duality of Israel; '1 Kings 13 may then be described as an imaginary resolution to the contradictory situation of a North and South in the people of Israel'.¹⁹⁶

In order to consider the third horizon according to Jameson's hermeneutic, it will serve our purposes to explore Boer's article, which draws upon the second chapter of *Jameson and Jeroboam*, but focuses especially upon national allegory in 1 Kings 13. Boer begins his article with this definition:

> By 'national allegory' I mean a genre in which characters play out complex relationships that interpret and highlight what are felt to be the significant features of the national situation in past and present and project possibilities for the future; thus, national allegory connects public and private, society and individual, where public and society are constituted by a 'nation'.¹⁹⁷

Drawing on the work of Joel Rosenberg,¹⁹⁸ who introduced the term 'political allegory' to the study of the Hebrew Bible, Boer affirms that allegories in the Hebrew Bible very often have political connotations.¹⁹⁹ He

---

193. Ibid., 157.
194. See, e.g., Yairah Amit, 'The Dual Causality Principle and its Effects on Biblical Literature', *VT* 37 (1987): 387–90.
195. Boer, *Jameson and Jeroboam*, 172.
196. Ibid., 174.
197. Boer, 'National Allegory', 95.
198. Joel Rosenberg, *King and Kin: Political Allegory in the Hebrew Bible*, Indiana Studies in Biblical Literature (Bloomington, IN: Indiana University Press, 1986)
199. Rosenberg defines 'political' as that which pertains to the state, *viz.* Israel. He defends the use of 'allegory' to biblical scholars, for whom 'parable' and '*mashal*' are more readily acceptable terms than 'allegory'. In Rosenberg's judgment, the reason for this anti-allegorical attitude is that '[t]he allegorical correspondences are

also draws on Jameson, who introduced 'national allegory' as a rhetorical device in contemporary literature, to stress that 'national allegory is concerned with the nexus between the individual and the national situation: the individual story functions, in different and sometimes contradictory ways, as the source of a range of allegories of the nation in question'.[200]

Boer offers two examples of political allegory in the Hebrew Bible, 2 Sam. 12.1-4 as an obvious example, and 1 Kings 13 as a more nuanced one. From Nathan's parable of the poor man and his ewe, Boer 'tentatively suggest[s] that the repression of the political in political allegory is a signal feature of political allegory itself'.[201] To demonstrate this, he elucidates the allegorical function of other female figures (besides Bathsheba) in Judges and Samuel, informed by the works of David Jobling, Regina Schwartz and Mieke Bal.

Turning to 1 Kings 13, Boer notes that the first hint that we are dealing with a political allegory comes from the preceding chapter, where opposition is established between Rehoboam of the south and Jeroboam of the north.

> In 1 Kings 13 there is a slippage in which the conflict between Jeroboam and Rehoboam is replaced by that between Jeroboam and the man of God from Judah (vv. 1-10); and then a further slippage replaces Jeroboam with the old prophet from Bethel (vv. 11-13), giving us the opposition: man of God/Rehoboam/Judah versus old prophet/Jeroboam/Israel.[202]

As the representative or allegorical function of the anonymous prophets is being established through this 'slippage', the narrative's primary interpretive clue is also accented when Jeroboam asks the man of God to stay for a meal.

> It is precisely this prohibition against eating, drinking and travelling – an ideological unit or 'ideologeme'[203] relying on and informing the psychological, social, political, economic and spatial dimensions of hospitality – that provides the means of identifying the workings of political allegory in this

generally understood as a one-for-one homology – rather than as a dynamic system of syllogistic and dialectical transformation, in which words and figures change meaning across time'. Ibid., 21.

200. Boer, 'National Allegory', 98.
201. Ibid., 103.
202. Ibid., 107. Boer acknowledges Barth's influence on this point – although Barth highlights Josiah rather than Rehoboam in the first triplet.
203. Boer defines 'the "ideologeme" as the "smallest intelligible unit [conceptual or belief system, abstract value, opinion or prejudice] of the essentially antagonistic

text. It does so through a series of repetitions (11 in various forms) whose cumulative effect is to undermine the overt favouring of Judah by means of a slow separation of the unity between the man of God and Yahweh... and the subsequent condemnation of the former, providing thereby a much-desired legitimation of the north.[204]

Boer thus perceives the presence of a different kind of reversal in the narrative; not one of prophetic legitimation, as per Barth and Klopfenstein (see the preceding chapters), but rather a legitimation *crisis*. In the opening scene, the words and prophetic sign(s) of the man of God deny the northern cult any legitimation whatsoever, but as the same prohibition is picked up in the second story (vv. 11-32), and Jeroboam's role of 'enticing the man of God into his home'[205] is picked up by the Bethel prophet, the man of God's resistance to the north weakens and he relents. Whatever his motive, the Bethel prophet's determination to see the man of God accept his hospitality wins out, and when it does, his successful deception brings an announcement of divine punishment that includes a triple reference (vv. 22-23) to the broken command. Boer comments:

> The triplet marks a resolution of some sort, which I would suggest is the final breakage of identity between the man of God and God and the end of the opposition between the man of God and the prophet. This in turn leads to the gradual identification of the second pair which culminates in the anticipated burial of the northern prophet beside the bones of the man of God (the final dimension of the ideological unit of hospitality).[206]

Boer thus argues that 'the allegorical function of the prohibition and its transgression is to provide Bethel, and thus northern Israel, with the legitimacy sought in the preceding ch. 12'.[207] That is to say, the man of God's initial condemnation of Bethel ultimately gives way to hospitality – at a shared table and then in a shared grave. Boer is aware that this dimension of the narrative, in its legitimation of the north, runs counterpoint to the announcement of Jeroboam's sin and impending doom in 13.33-34, but in his view this does not detract from his suggested political reading. On the contrary, as mentioned above, 1 Kings 13 is further established as a

---

collective discourses of social classes"... The ideologeme mediates between abstract concepts and specific narratives, providing raw materials for the elaboration of both'. Ibid., 133.
   204. Ibid., 108.
   205. Ibid., 109.
   206. Ibid., 110.
   207. Ibid.

narrative that provides interpretive comment on the unusual co-existence and cultic independence of north and south in Israel.

The final step in Boer's interpretation of 1 Kings 13 pushes beyond the immediate political referents of the story (Israel and Judah) to the broader socio-economic clash between Judah and the empire in whose shadow it lived when these texts were composed; i.e. Babylon or Persia. Thus, the narrative includes a further 'slippage' from *national* to *natural*; 'Nature, more particularly the animals, function in this text as a figuration of a larger entity'.[208] Seen thus, the lion has a double allegorical reference, representing God as an agent of divine punishment, but also the Babylonian (or Persian) empire that 'exercises control by restraint'.[209]

Since this treatment of 1 Kings 13 is part of a broader project, utilising Fredric Jameson's notion of national allegory to enhance Rosenberg's work on political allegories in the Hebrew Bible, Boer goes on to consider (under the rubric of Jameson's third horizon) 1 Kings 11–14 as an example of the Asiatic mode of production (AMP), whose primary features are religious in nature. His reflections on modes of production are less relevant to this study, however.

Summary and Conclusions

In this chapter, we have examined four readings which have utilised a range of methodologies and understood the form of 1 Kings 13 in a variety of ways. As one would expect, these readings reflect a number of views concerning the *Sache* of 1 Kings 13. Moreover, it is not difficult to see that the stark difference between the exegeses of say, Barth and Klopfenstein, is a consequence not only of distinct interpretive methods, but also of divergent views on what Scripture actually *is*. This is an issue to which we shall return in the next chapter. We have also seen in our survey of the past seventy years of scholarship that the subject or moral of 1 Kings 13 is understood in terms directly related to the primary issue or question being brought to the text, and that in each case the methodology chosen for engaging with 1 Kings 13 has been appropriate to the interpretive aims. In theory, this is precisely what one would expect, but it is nonetheless interesting to see how it plays out in practice. Randolph Tate makes the point with unsettling simplicity: 'Interpreters use texts to fulfil their interests or aims'.[210]

---

208. Ibid., 111.
209. Ibid., 112.
210. Tate, *Biblical Interpretation*, 195.

In Crenshaw's monograph, 1 Kings 13 provides supporting evidence for his thesis concerning the decline of prophecy in ancient Israel. Thus, the story is taken to be about the issue of discernment – ostensibly demonstrating that no valid criteria for discernment exist. To make this point, Crenshaw adopts sociological and psychological approaches in order to establish his foundational premise that prophecy went into decline in ancient Israel because it became increasingly hard to know which words claiming divine inspiration were trustworthy. Granted, Crenshaw adopts other methods traditionally associated with literary/biblical studies, too. But in light of his main premise, it is fitting that emphasis is placed on the sociological and psychological dimensions of prophecy in ancient Israel.

Walsh's essay and commentary make use of literary and structural analyses to make the point that certain kinds of chiastic symmetry are preferable to 'the outlines commonly offered in commentaries'.[211] (He does not state this as his primary goal, but it is certainly a very strong subtext!) While his analysis in the essay is presented as a methodological exploration, his findings all stress the importance of concentric symmetry for a fruitful reading of Scripture. His book, *Style and Structure in Hebrew Narrative*, reinforces this theme more emphatically with more than thirty examples of structural patterns in the Bible. His use of literary and structural analysis are entirely suited to making this point. Indeed, one might draw the conclusion that the endorsement of structural methodology *is* his point.

In his essay, 'On Reading the Story of the Man of God' (1999), Van Seters wishes to highlight the incompetence of the author of 1 Kings 13, so he examines the text to expose the narrative's inconsistencies and thereby unveil the author's shortcomings. By highlighting sixteen apparent problems in the story, he hopes to persuade readers that the biblical author has drawn on source materials rather carelessly to compose a piece of religious propaganda in the post-exilic period. Van Seters makes numerous assumptions about what source materials were used and what the author's intentions were in composing the story found in 1 Kings 13 (together with its epilogue in 2 Kgs 23), but a kind of narrative/plot analysis is the method best-suited to making his point that the story has been poorly written. His second essay uses redaction-criticism to bracket out texts referring to Josiah from the DH, a methodology well-suited to his interpretive aim of countering Cross's double-redaction theory.

---

211. Walsh, 'Contexts', 369: 'western analytical outlines are hard pressed to capture the type of symmetrical structure that is seen here as fundamental to the text. Commentators should use schematizations of the text that more accurately reflect its inherent articulation.'

Of the four readings examined here, Boer is the most explicitly self-conscious with regards to his methods and goals. He observes the text from numerous angles, including 'theology, text criticism, historical social scientific approaches, and literary and poststructural approaches' and in so doing, states with refreshing candour: 'In each case I am interested in insights that assist in my own interpretation of the text'.[212] Boer's overarching goal – 'to read the Bible in the light of Jameson's textual theory'[213] – is thereby served by a political reading that is alert to dissonance (regarding the reliability of the divine word) within the logic of the story.

The methodological tensions between Barth and Klopfenstein in Chapters 2 and 3, and the wider range of interpretive possibilities that we have considered here, raise a number of important hermeneutical questions. Can synchronic and diachronic approaches be fruitfully utilised together? Does Barth's overtly christological reading sit comfortably with the concerns of Dtr? What criteria are appropriate for adjudicating between divergent readings of this (or any) text? To what extent must we determine or define what Scripture *is* when interpreting biblical texts? These are the kinds of questions that will occupy us in the next chapter.

---

212. Boer, *Jameson and Jeroboam*, 102.
213. Ibid., 193.

5

Hermeneutical and Methodological Issues

Barth and Klopfenstein: Divergent Approaches to Scripture

The divergence between Barth and Klopfenstein is illustrative of the polarisation that can, and often does, occur between literary-theological and historical-critical approaches. Whereas Barth reads election and rejection 'into' the text (and would readily admit to doing so) because his questions and his interpretive categories are informed by the entire counsel of Christian Scripture, Klopfenstein objects to this kind of exegetical maneuvering since, in his view, the importing of external categories is precisely what leads to Barth's problematic *Überinterpretation* of elements such as the 'lion of Judah' and the shared grave.

In the previous chapter, we examined the readings of other scholars who have more recently approached 1 Kings 13 from different (and sometimes multiple) angles of enquiry, including the psychological, sociological, structural, rhetorical, source-critical, redaction-critical, historical, theological, and so on. In order to address some of the issues at stake in evaluating these divergent approaches to Scripture, we shall in this chapter review some common hermeneutical dichotomies in biblical scholarship: between text-hermeneutics and author-hermeneutics; between synchronic and diachronic interests; and between canonical and historical priorities. Ultimately, we shall see that problems can often stem from a failure to differentiate between the notions of 'scripture is' and 'scripture as'.

It is not my intention to polarise interpreters such as Barth and Klopfenstein, nor the readings they proffer, by placing them in stark opposition to one another. Rather, my intention is to build on the previous chapter's claim, using examples from the readings we examined, to explore the notion that readerly questions (which, of course, can be multiple and varied) help to determine the most appropriate methodology/ies for the interpretive task. To do this, we shall consider three hermeneutical spectrums.

Author-Hermeneutics and Text-Hermeneutics

One of the more obvious polarities in hermeneutics has to do with perceptions of objectivity and subjectivity, where the former is often represented by a commitment to determining authorial intent. Stendahl's famous distinction between 'what it meant' and and 'what it means' sought to distinguish between attempts to determine an author's original, intended meaning and what other significations a text may derive over centuries of use (i.e. its *sensus plenior*).[1] Biblical scholarship today continues to be divided on this issue.

One might think that attempts to ascertain authorial intention would necessarily be held lightly, given the paucity of evidence that is available concerning the identities of those in question. This is especially the case with 1 Kings 13, which is often referred to as a 'prophetic legend' – the point being, no one knows its origins. Nonetheless, we observed in the previous chapter that it is indeed possible to give a very particular answer to the question of authorship! He was an incompetent writer and religiously insensitive Judean who tried to write a piece of anti-Samaritan religious propaganda during the sixth century BCE in an effort to discredit any association with worshippers of Yahweh in the north. This kind of assessment, which perceives a direct link between the author's identity and the meaning (or lack thereof) in the text, is a clear example of author-hermeneutics.

In contrast to Van Seters, Barth's exegesis is informed very little by conjecture about the identity and intentions of the author. All that Barth offers about the story's origins is that it appears to have come from a different source than its literary context, perhaps from something similar to the Elisha cycles at the beginning of 2 Kings.[2] Barth makes no claim whatsoever about the historical author. What is determinative for him is the text itself, and he certainly abides by the principle that meanings can transcend authorial intention. It was for this very reason that Barth was criticised by Noth and others for using the text to elucidate the doctrine of election. In Chapter 2, I delineated three primary elements of Barth's exegetical method – intertextuality, synchrony and christology. These do not need repeating here, except as a reminder that his exegesis utilises a text-hermeneutic. It will be clear by now that a key question – actually, *the* key question – for Barth in his reading of 1 Kings 13 (or any biblical text, for that matter) is, 'how is Christ revealed in this text?' In

---

1. Stendahl, 'Biblical Theology, Contemporary'.
2. Barth, *CD* II.2, 393.

his *Dogmatics*, under the heading, 'The Time of Expectation',[3] Barth describes the Old Testament as a witness to the revelation that is expected in Christ. 'Revelation itself takes place from beyond the peculiar context and content of the Old Testament'.[4] From this standpoint, he gives voice to a text-hermeneutic in the strongest language when he states that 'Jesus Christ is manifest in the Old Testament as the expected One'.[5] Does Barth see things in the text that were not intended by the author, such as a doctrine of election that is fully made known in Christ, who is both Elect and Rejected? Absolutely.

My purpose here is not to evaluate or prioritise these different kinds of enquiry but rather to stress the importance of consciously locating one's own work in one category or another. To grasp the importance of this, let us take an example from the previous chapter where the muddling of author- and text-hermeneutics led to some confusion.

Walsh is a biblical scholar whose essays and books are filled with sharp narratological insights gleaned from close reading of the final form of the text. In the opening pages of his commentary, he states: 'Interpretation of texts in terms of the real author requires an independent access to the historical person that is difficult, if not impossible, in the case of 1 Kings'.[6] From the outset, then, Walsh gives the impression that his work complies with the rubric of a text-hermeneutic approach. But as we noted in the previous chapter, Walsh sometimes intimates that his observations about concentric structures were, in fact, in the mind of the author, or at least the implied author. This leaves his readers with the impression that he is not just making readerly observations on a textual level, but that he wants to ascribe them to the mind of the author. For instance, Walsh offers the following categorical analysis of 1 Kgs 13.1-10 in his commentary:

The narrator arranged the scene chiastically, although the NRSV's translation is misleading in places and obscures the structure.

A. Introduction (13.1)
    B. Oracle (13.2)
        C1. Parenthesis: sign given (13.3)
        C2. King's reaction and punishment (13.4)
        C1'. Parenthesis: sign fulfilled (13.5)
        C2'. King's reaction and healing (13.6)
    B'. Invitation and oracle (13.7-9)
A'. Conclusion (13.10)

3. *CD* I.2 §14, 71–101.
4. *CD* I.2, 71.
5. *CD* II.2, 72.
6. Walsh, *1 Kings*, xviii.

Grammatical forms in vv. 3 and 5 mark those verses as parenthetical asides by the narrator to the reader.[7]

Here Walsh makes two broad observations and a judgment. He observes that 1 Kgs 13.1-10 has a chiastic structure, and that vv. 3 and 5 do not report events that occur within the flow of the narrative but are asides to the reader about future confirmations of the oracle. He also evaluates the NRSV translation, calling it 'misleading' because v. 1 is unfaithful to the Hebrew word order and because vv. 3 and 5 do not comply with Walsh's second observation. None of these points are without problems.

First, if one sees a chiasm here, it is certainly rather weak. There is no substantive correlation whatsoever between A and A', and the man of God's words in vv. 8-9 (B') do not comprise an 'oracle' to match B. In addition to this, the purpose of the proposed chiasm is unclear; i.e. what is brought into focus for the reader?

Regarding his second observation, Walsh's comments about vv. 3 and 5 being parenthetical statements represent only one possibility for interpretation and translation – a minority view among scholars – in spite of his dogmatic tone: 'Both the Hebrew grammatical form and the unnecessary introductory words show that we are not to read this statement as a continuation of the oracle in v. 2. Although the NRSV allows for this, its phrasing is not completely clear.'[8] The Berit Olam series of commentaries is not overly technical, but Walsh does not offer even a footnote to explain what aspect of 'the Hebrew grammatical form' has led him to this conclusion.[9] It is certainly not obvious. In connection with this, it is somewhat confusing that Walsh ascribes structural and grammatical decisions to the *narrator*, even in spite of being quite clear (in theory) about the distinctions between narrator, implied author and author.[10]

A more problematic aspect of Walsh's analysis presents itself in his discussion of symmetry (e.g. chiasms, envelope structures, alternating repetition) and *asymmetry*. The difficulty is already evident in Walsh's definition: 'The author can create a symmetrical pattern *with a flaw*...not an absence of symmetry, but a flawed symmetry'.[11] The problem is in the

---

7. Ibid., 176. It is unusual to speak of the narrator, rather than the author, as the one arranging the scenes of a narrative, but I will leave this quibble aside.

8. Ibid., 178.

9. Walsh does offer explanatory footnotes on linguistic and technical matters in other instances; e.g. 40, 248, 266, 316, etc. A few pages later, Walsh changes his tone somewhat and refers to his view about the later destruction of the altar as a 'surmise'. Ibid., 179.

10. E.g., Walsh, *Old Testament Narrative*, 9, 100–102.

11. Ibid., 117.

assumption that ancient readers were sufficiently familiar with chiastic structures (a device that remains questionable in modern scholarship) to be able to recognise an author's use of skewed symmetry as 'a powerful device for manipulating a reader's response to the text'.[12] A clear example of such asymmetry is where a subunit within a chiastic structure has no counterpart so that, for instance, ABCD is followed by D'C'A' (i.e. no B' is found to reflect B). In Walsh's analysis of 1 Kgs 13.11-32, an example of 'forward symmetry' that follows a 'developmental structure' (see p. 92 in Chapter 4), Walsh lists points A to G and then A' to G', but simply inserts an ellipsis at G' since no counterpart to G is present (presumably this is an excellent example of asymmetry?). Again, my point is not that it is inconceivable for ancient authors to have ever used such devices, but rather that *since we have no way of knowing*, we must settle for attributing what structures we find to our own imaginations, accepting that many other structures and devices (some of which may conflict with our own) are also identifiable in the same texts. In any case, Walsh's commentary is one of the best examples of a narrative-critical approach to Kings available, and although his approach is undergirded by an assumed correlation between structure and authorial intent, the merits of most of his observations do not actually require a move from text-hermeneutics to author-hermeneutics.[13]

Before a contemporary reader makes any judgments about the authorial intention behind a text composed in the distant past, it seems to me that a few things must be readily acknowledged: (a) the inevitable influence of conjecture and hypothesis from the reader, who reads with particular questions in mind and who plays a significant role in the interpretive process as the 'filter' or 'grid' through which meaning is determined; (b) the reality that even if the author was accessible to answer the question, *what did you mean by this?*, as Schökel notes, 'the author's psychology is far more complex than a scheme of intention in meaning';[14] (c) readers often discover meanings in texts – e.g., through symbolic

---

12. Ibid.

13. It is interesting to note that when Walsh directly addresses the subject of symmetrical forms in the Hebrew Bible in his more recent book, *Old Testament Narrative*, he appears appropriately cautious. Regarding rhetorical devices in Hebrew narrative, he concedes that 'there is still much to be done in this area of study; and so we must be aware that, to this point, most results remain more or less tentative'. Ibid., 108. In his earlier essays and commentary, Walsh seems to have expressed his opinions with greater certitude.

14. 'The text is full of meaning that comes from desire, from fantasy, from the author's subconscious, and which is indeed part of the meaning of the text, but which does not pass through the reflective activity of the author's intellect'. Luis Alonso Schökel, *A Manual of Hermeneutics*, The Biblical Seminar 54 (Sheffield: Sheffield

language or because of subsequent historical developments – that their original authors couldn't possibly have intended. As Chapman rightly states, 'texts *always* mean something they never could have meant to their authors and (first) readers!'[15]

As a concluding word to this discussion, it is important to note that a shift from author-hermeneutics to text-hermeneutics comprises a critical hermeneutical turn, but not one that ousts the significance of the author from the exegetical task. In Schökel's words, 'it is not correct to understand text-hermeneutics as an exact substitute for author-hermeneutics, where the primacy of the text would replace that of the author. Author, text, and others, are joint factors in an ample universe: they are correlative elements involved in a single whole, where other decisive factors coexist in literary interpretation'.[16] Exegetical attempts to ascertain authorial intent via historical-critical methods therefore remain worthwhile and potentially informative, especially if one seeks to balance the multiple perspectives of author, text, and reader.[17] The prioritisation of these factors depends, rather, on what the interpreter seeks to discover in her encounter with the text. Numerous lines of inquiry are available: 'The author's experience? The text as the author's objectivation? My existence at a critical juncture?'[18] Again, a self-conscious statement from the interpreter locating his or her work on the spectrum between author- and text-hermeneutics is of prime importance.

Historical-Critical and Canonical Approaches

Historical-critical approaches to interpretation tend not only to emphasise the importance of the author, but also to place significant weight on the date of a text's composition for the determination of meaning. Again, my purpose is not to set historical and canonical approaches against one

---

Academic, 1998), 35. Cf. Sandra M. Schneiders, *The Revelatory Text: Interpreting The New Testament as Sacred Scripture*, 2nd ed. (Collegeville, MN: Liturgical, 1999), 162-3.

15. Stephen B. Chapman, 'Reclaiming Inspiration for the Bible', in *Canon and Biblical Interpretation*, vol. 7, ed. Bartholomew et al. (Grand Rapids, MI: Zondervan, 2006), 183. Chapman is responding to the following statement made in Gordon D. Fee and Douglas Stuart, *How to Read the Bible the Bible for All its Worth* (Grand Rapids: Zondervan, 1981): '*a text cannot mean what it never could have meant to its author or his readers*' (60, emphasis original).

16. Schökel, *Manual*, 28.

17. Ibid., 34-9. Also see Tate, *Biblical Interpretation*, who endorses an approach that integrates these three perspectives.

18. Ibid., 28.

another. (This would not be possible at any rate, since any theory of canon formation is of necessity an historical formulation.) Rather, my purpose is to highlight some of the pitfalls in attempting to date texts such as 1 Kings 13 with any degree of certainty, and to evaluate the historicist assumptions that undergird many such attempts. We will then consider some of the hermeneutical implications of Childs' theory of canon formation.

The authors reviewed in the previous chapter present a range of viewpoints on the most probable date of composition for our narrative. Walsh's narrative-critical commentary notes the inaccessibility of the 'real author' and makes no attempt to date the composition of Kings. Instead, he begins his commentary by noting that the composition of Kings has its own history; 'a series of creative author-editors selected, rearranged, combined, and sometimes thoroughly reshaped the source materials to produce, eventually, a continuous text. Later editors revised this text in light of the concerns of subsequent generations…'[19] This summary has some clear affinities with Childs' theory of canon formation, as we shall see shortly. Given the synchronic nature of his commentary, there is little need for Walsh to venture beyond this general statement. Similarly, Boer offers a concise review of the three main views propagated since Noth, but does not push for a particular date. Of the search for a precise compositional history and context for the final form of the DH, he simply says:

> Such specific locations in time and place, and the search for ever more redactions or the fine-tuning of existing ones, rely on evidence that is far too meager and which the nature of the biblical text itself shortcircuits… Yet the texts with their tantalizing hints of compositional layers keep inducing people to pursue such studies.[20]

Boer, too, is content to identify the final shape of the DH with 'the more amorphous situation of the final redaction – the exile',[21] a social situation that adds a certain poignancy to his study of national and political allegory. Crenshaw's reading of 1 Kings 13 supports a sociological theory about the decline of prophecy in ancient Israel, but he does not tie the authorship of Kings to a particular date, either. He suggests loosely that an oral tradition 'has been added by the Deuteronomic compiler (or perhaps a subsequent editor) after Josiah's reform'.[22]

---

19. Walsh, *1 Kings*, xi.
20. Boer, *Jameson and Jeroboam*, 145.
21. Ibid., 146.
22. Crenshaw, *Prophetic Conflict*, 43.

Van Seters is the most precise, as we have seen. He insists on an exilic date for the composition of the DH, but a post-exilic date for both the composition *and* redaction of 1 Kings 13 and 2 Kgs 23.15-20 (as well as 2 Kgs 17.24-34; 23.4b). Contrary to the Cross school, which sees 1 Kings 13 as a pre-existing text (*viz.* midrash or legend) that was redacted into Kings to support Josiah's reforms,[23] Van Seters argues that these texts were written in the post-exilic period to vilify the Bethel temple and the Samaritan community because of the continuing use of Jeroboam's places of worship. Since Van Seters is the most particular in dating the composition of 1 Kings 13, I shall engage primarily with his arguments before also reviewing some of the hermeneutical suppositions undergirding his method. Van Seters gives the following three reasons for asserting that 1 Kings 13 is a post-exilic *composition*:

a. From a redaction-critical perspective, the repeated phrase, 'and this thing became a sin' (12.30; 13.34) indicates that the text between these references has been inserted into the DH via *Wiederaufnahme*.[24] And since 2 Kgs 23.15-20 forms a natural epilogue to 1 Kings 13, Van Seters regards both texts to have been inserted at the same time. In addition, since 2 Kgs 17.24-34 uses similar terminology and expresses the same anti-Samaritan sentiment, he considers that text also to have come from the same hand and to have been inserted at a similar late date.

b. Drawing on Rofé's work, Van Seters also argues for a late date on account of the content and vocabulary of these texts. Apparently, many of the phrases (e.g., בערי שמרון / בדבר יהוה; 'in the word of the LORD'/'in the cities of Samaria') and themes (e.g., a prophet interceding for an evil king rather than pronouncing judgment on him) are uncharacteristic of Dtr and thereby suggest a different author.

c. Van Seters insists also that Josiah's reforms never actually took place in Bethel or the surrounding cities of Samaria. He cites archaeological evidence in support of the view that cult centralisation and other reforms were restricted to Judah (i.e. 'from Geba to Beersheba' in accordance with 2 Kgs 23.8) and that since Josiah's northern reforms were not an historical reality, these later interpolations must serve a purpose other than religio-political propaganda for Josianic reform.

23. Cross, *Canaanite Myth*, 278–9. More explicit on this point is his student, Lemke, 'The Way of Obedience'.
24. See n. 166 in Chapter 4 and the beginning of Chapter 7.

Van Seters' arguments are internally coherent, and he is not the first to designate 1 Kings 13 as a secondary, post-Dtr interpolation.[25] But his reasoning is problematic. First, the identification of 1 Kings 13 as an instance of *Wiederaufnahme* is a neutral observation, which may be – and has been – used to argue for 1 Kings 13 as a pre-exilic *or* a post-exilic redaction.[26] Similarly, his second argument, citing a study of terminology that indicates post-exilic composition,[27] is debatable since the story's vocabulary has also been used to assign the final form of the redacted story to Josiah's day.[28] As Wellhausen observed, it is often very difficult to distinguish between what he called pre-canonical (*vorkanonischer*) and post-canonical (*nachkanonischer*) redactions,[29] and evidence can be garnered for either position. Thirdly, Van Seters cites archaeological

---

25. So Iain Provan, *Hezekiah and the Books of Kings: A Contribution to the Debate about the Composition of the Deuteronomistic History*, BZAW 172 (Berlin: de Gruyter, 1988), 81; McKenzie, *Trouble*, 55.

26. If the framing verses, which apparently contain Dtr language, are included with the intervening story, then 1 Kgs 12.30–13.34 may be seen as pre-exilic (i.e. Deuteronomistic). So Lemke, 'The Way of Obedience', 306. However, if the editor is understood to have made an interpolation without editing the surrounding verses, then 1 Kgs 13 (without 12.30-33 or 13.33-34) may be understood as a post-exilic redaction. So McKenzie, *Trouble*, 52–3. But scholars could also argue that a later editor, wishing to insert the story as smoothly as possible, copied the style of Dtr in the surrounding verses, resulting in an insertion that we hardly recognise as an insertion. Cf. the beginning of Chapter 7 on *Wiederaufnahme*.

27. Rofé, 'Classes in the Prophetical Stories', 143–64.

28. So Lemke, 'Way of Obedience', 303–4. Lemke's proposal for a Dtr redaction rests on the use of six phrases that he believes to be consistent with Dtr's theology and work: 'cities of Samaria'; 'priests of the high places'; 'shrines of the high places'; 'to rebel against the mouth of the LORD'; 'to keep the commandment'; and 'to turn [or return] from/by the way' (306–12). He thus argues that 1 Kgs 13 has been redacted into a pre-exilic version of the DH (Cross's Dtr[1]) in support of Josiah's northern reforms – the very position that Van Seters is seeking to undermine. Thus, some scholars use the style and vocabulary of 1 Kgs 13 to assert an early date, while others use precisely the same means to insist that it is a late text.

29. Julius Wellhausen, *Die Composition des Hexateuchs und der historischen Bücher des Alten Testaments*, 3rd ed. (Berlin: G. Reimer, 1899), 262: '…wie denn überhaupt zwischen vorkanonischer und nachkanonischer Diaskeue kaum eine Grenze zu ziehen ist'. Wellhausen (277–8) was of the view that 1 Kgs 13 represents a late addition to the corpus of material we now call the DH. He perceives 13.33 as the continuation (*Fortsetzung*) of 12.31 so that 12.32–13.31 are the boundaries of the redacted story, a midrash which is most likely an attempt to explain the grave of a Judean in Bethel.

evidence to deny that Josiah's reforms occurred, but archaeological evidence also exists in support of the opposite viewpoint.[30]

In any case, the problem is less with the claim that 1 Kings 13 was written in the post-exilic period, than with a certain brand of historicism. The three arguments offered by Van Seters constitute an attempt to establish 1 Kings 13 as a post-exilic text *in order to locate its meaning within a particular time and place*. But as Benjamin Sommer has shown in a percipient essay on the perils of pseudo-historicism,[31] it is a methodological fallacy to think 'that meaning must be correlated with a particular historical event, that history, and *only* history or at least *primarily* history, explains the theme of a literary text'.[32] This kind of approach binds texts to narrow historical windows and then reads them through thick, i.e. controlling, lenses.[33] Sommer points out a second, related assumption as well: 'when scholars claim that a text is obviously appropriate for a particular moment in history, they are often correct, but they fail to acknowledge that the idea or text is equally appropriate for some other moment as well'.[34] A problematic implication of this kind of historicism (Sommer calls it *pseudo-historicism*) is that ideas are perceived to 'belong' to moments in time.[35] But the process of canonisation itself resists the historicist assumption that dating a text will *ipso facto* expose its true meaning, when biblical texts have been preserved within the canon for the very purpose of resonating again – perhaps even more deeply – among future generations in contexts other than that in which they originated. Childs pinpoints the issue thus: 'Often the assumption that the theological point must be related to an original intention within a reconstructed historical context runs directly in the face of the literature's explicit statement of its

---

30. E.g., Dever, 'The Silence of the Text', 143–58; ibid., *What Did the Biblical Writers Know and When Did They Know It?* (Grand Rapids: Eerdmans, 2001), 159–243. See also Jesse Long, *1 & 2 Kings*, 509, and the source materials cited there.

31. B. Sommer, 'Dating Pentateuchal Texts and the Perils of Pseudo-Historicism', in *The Pentateuch: International Perspectives on Current Research*, ed. T. Dozeman et al. (Tübingen: Mohr Siebeck, 2011), 85–110.

32. Ibid., 90–1.

33. McKenzie acknowledges plainly, 'The question of the DH's purpose has always been treated in conjunction with its date'. *Trouble*, 149.

34. Sommer, 'Dating Pentateuchal Texts', 94. In addition: 'if we find a particular set of values in a text, does this mean that the text was written when those values were ascendant? Or does it mean that the text was written when those values were under attack – or even when they had been lost altogether?' (101)

35. Ibid., 98. Sommer also makes the related point that 'an eighth-century thinker may think a sixth-century thought' (104).

function within the final form of the biblical text'.³⁶ Childs' statement is especially relevant to interpreters who, like Van Seters, historicise texts like 1 Kings 13, leaving one with the impression that it can signify nothing other than what the hypothesised author intended. But the divergence between Childs and Van Seters on where meaning resides (in the text itself or its author) stems from their different views on the purpose of redaction criticism.

As the title of Van Seters' essay suggests – 'The Deuteronomistic History: Can it Avoid Death by Redaction?' – he wishes to address the dismantling of Noth's unified DH by those who identify redaction seams everywhere throughout the work (*viz.* the Göttingen school). In Van Seters' opinion, redaction criticism would be put to better use by identifying and bracketing out extraneous blocks of text that are non-Deuteronomistic in style and content (such as 1 Kgs 13) in order to gain 'much greater clarity about the limits and nature of DtrH'.³⁷ He therefore concludes his essay with this word of counsel:

> The first task of redaction criticism of the DtrH is not to continue to split it up into small fragments on the basis of rather dubious principles, but to identify the large amount of later additions and to retrieve the core work. It is only in this way that its unity and consistency of perspective will become apparent. Redaction criticism need not be the death of DtrH as Noth understood it. On the contrary, it can be the means by which to revive this important thesis to new life and vitality.³⁸

Van Seters thus opposes the Göttingen school's tendency to fragment the text through recourse to DtrP, DtrN, DtrG, and so on.³⁹ In support of Noth's thesis, he reinforces Dtr's competence as an historian capable of literary sophistication and multiple points of view over and against the notion that complexity must necessarily be the result of multiple redactions.⁴⁰ Van Seters' goal – 'to identify the large amount of later additions

---

36. Brevard S. Childs, *Introduction to the Old Testament as Scripture* (Philadelphia: Fortress, 1979), 75.

37. Van Seters, 'Death by Redaction?', 221. Similarly, McKenzie, *Trouble*, 147–50.

38. Van Seters, 'Death by Redaction?', 222.

39. For a summary of views on the development of the DH, see Provan, *Hezekiah*, 2–31.

40. See esp. John Van Seters, *The Edited Bible: The Curious History of the 'Editor' in Biblical Criticism* (Winona Lake, IN: Eisenbrauns, 2006), 260–76; Cf. J. Gordon McConville, 'Narrative and Meaning in the Books of Kings', *Biblica* 70 (1989): 31–49.

and to retrieve the core work' – which he helpfully makes explicit, is entirely legitimate. But there is some irony in the fact that he criticises the Cross school for bracketing out 2 Kgs 23.21–25.30 from the DH, even as he himself brackets out 1 Kings 13; 2 Kgs 17.24-34; 23.4b, 15-20, and does so on the basis of equally 'dubious principles'.

I do not wish to question Van Seters' supposition that *the DH's unity and consistency of perspective will become apparent only through retrieval of the core work*. That may well be true – were such a retrieval possible. However, his statement concerning 'the first task of redaction criticism' suggests that he views the redacted, canonical text as a problem to be fixed in order to have its meaning restored, and it is important to recognise that not all biblical scholars share this view regarding the purpose of redaction criticism, since not all view the recovery of a hypothetical 'core work' as the goal. For those seeking to understand the text in its received form, as 'an artist's final composition which transcends the sketches',[41] the goal is quite different. Certainly, this is true for Childs: 'The canonical approach is concerned to understand the nature of the theological shape of the text rather than to recover an original literary or aesthetic unity'.[42]

Since Childs aims to understand the canonical text as mature, theological reflection, he perceives the purpose of redaction criticism in entirely different terms; 'the canonical approach seeks to employ the tool of redaction criticism to the extent that it aids in a more precise hearing of the edited text, but at the same time seeking to understand the expressed intentionality of that interpreted text'.[43] Childs is less interested in working backwards, in an attempt to discover what shape 1 Kings 13 – or the entire DH for that matter – might have once had, let alone the precise origins of its source material.[44] Nonetheless, he maintains that synchronic readings of texts can be enriched by paying attention to redaction seams and compositional processes. The basic difference is that Childs uses redaction criticism to attain a better understanding of the text in its *final form* whereas Van Seters uses redaction criticism to retrieve a *core work* from 'beneath' it. At the risk of repeating myself, each of these lines of enquiry is legitimate, so long as interpreters are able to be clear about

---

41. R. W. L. Moberly, 'The Canon of the Old Testament from a Western Perspective: Some Historical and Hermeneutical Reflections from the Western Perspective', in *Das Alte Testament als christliche Bibel in orthodoxer und westlicher Sicht*, ed. I. Z. Dimitrou et al., WUNT 174 (Tübingen, Mohr Siebeck, 2004), 250.
42. Childs, *Introduction*, 74.
43. Ibid., 300.
44. Ibid., 301.

their reasons for reading. This is not to say, however, that there is no place for evaluating one approach over and against another. Not all approaches hold equal promise for fruitful readings and, to my mind at least, some approaches appear to read along the grain of Scripture more than others.[45]

Before concluding this section, it will be worthwhile to reflect for a moment on Childs' understanding of the nexus between these historical-critical and canonical dimensions of biblical studies. It is well known that Childs did not develop a theory about the compositional history of the biblical canon out of historical interest only, but also because of its theological and hermeneutical implications.[46] His fundamental observation in this regard was that Israel not only shaped the canon for future generations, but was also shaped *by* the canon.[47] In his words, 'the process of the canonisation of the Hebrew Bible was closely related to the concern to render the sacred tradition in such a way as to serve future generations of Israel as authoritative Scripture'.[48] As redactions were made over time, however, the evidence (or lack thereof) would suggest that the editors sought not to make their identities known, preferring rather to keep future readers focused on the sacred writings themselves.[49] As Childs famously put it, 'basic to the canonical process is that those responsible for the actual editing of the text did their best to obscure their own identity. Thus the actual process by which the text was reworked lies in almost total obscurity.'[50] Rather than reconstructing the

---

45. I borrow this phrase from Chapman who, it seems, borrowed it from C. S. Lewis. See the discussion in Stephen B. Chapman, *1 Samuel as Christian Scripture: A Theological Commentary* (Grand Rapids: Eerdmans, 2016), 27–8, where Chapman observes: 'The truly grave danger of a literary approach reveals itself most fully when biblical interpretation becomes a way of talking about texts rather than talking about God'.

46. See Childs, *Introduction*, 53–9; idem, 'Analysis of a Canonical Formula: "It shall be recorded for a future generation"', in *Die Hebräische Bibel und ihre zweifache Nachtgeschichte*, ed. E. Blum (Neukirchen-Vluyn: Neukirchener Verlag, 1990), 358–64.

47. Childs, *Introduction*, 41. Also see idem, 'A Study of the Formula "Until this Day"', *JBL* 82 (1963): 279–92, where he argues that what is at stake in surmising the nature of this canonical process is the very *definition* of canon. Cf. Chapman, 'Reclaiming Inspiration', 169; idem, *The Law and the Prophets: A Study in Old Testament Canon Formation*, FAT 27 (Tübingen: Mohr Siebeck, 2000), 45.

48. Childs, 'Analysis', 358.

49. Childs, *Introduction*, 59.

50. Ibid., 78. This kind of hypothesis bears similarities to Barton's notion of a 'disappearing redactor'. John Barton, *Reading the Old Testament: Method in Biblical Study* (London: Darton, Longman & Todd, 1984), 56–8.

text's compositional history, then, as Wellhausen sought to do, Childs' canonical approach places the emphasis upon *Israel's construal of her own history*. Reading the Old Testament *as Christian Scripture* therefore means resisting the historical-critical tendency to extract and de-canonise texts so as to place them in a particular historical context, since that kind of exegetical work effectively reverses the very process that gave shape and focus to the texts we have.

More than that, given the implicit 'canon-consciousness' (*Kanonbewußtsein*) of the entire process, Childs rightly stressed that the 'canonical process often assigned a function to the literature as a whole which transcended its parts. The collection acquired a theological role in instructing, admonishing, and edifying a community of faith, and that altered its original semantic level.'[51] From this canonical frame of reference, then, theocentric interpretation of Scripture ought not be seen simply as fideistic, since it takes its cues from an *historical* premise; namely, that the development of Israel's canon was itself governed by a theocentric perspective.[52] An important, prevailing implication of Childs' work is that interpretations of texts may be evaluated according to how well they resonate with this canon-conscious hermeneutical trajectory that is intrinsic to the canonical process.[53] As an example, we may note that Childs endorses Barth's reading of 1 Kings 13 for accenting the story's 'paradigmatic significance', based on its literary placement within the canon.[54]

---

51. Childs, *Old Testament Theology*, 22–3.

52. In evangelical terms, the theocentric perspective governing the canonical process is attributed to the people of God under the influence and guidance of the Holy Spirit. Chapman, 'Reclaiming Inspiration', explores the implications of the process of editing and canonisation for a Christian doctrine of inspiration. 'A canonically oriented view of inspiration, one that is suggested and even warranted by the historical study of canon formation, retains room for the transcendent but sees the divine–human encounter as occurring over a lengthier period of time and as including more people than just one author alone' (172).

53. Childs, 'Analysis', 363; cf. Chapman, *The Law and the Prophets*, 47. One may object, as James Barr has, that texts do not have intentions, people do, such that Childs appears to downplay *authorial* intention but then grant *canonical* intention. In Chapman's monograph, he resolves this issue to some extent in his development of the hermeneutical significance of canon-consciousness for understanding the subcollections of Law and Prophets in the Hebrew Bible. Chapman emphasises tensions (i.e. the multiplicity of voices) over singular, ideological motifs, stressing that 'canons *subvert* ideals just as much as they enshrine them' by preserving alternative viewpoints (95).

54. Childs, *Old Testament Theology*, 142.

Synchronic and Diachronic Priorities

Noth's landmark study of the Deuteronomistic History in 1943[55] was a diachronic work of *literarkritik*, focusing on 'stratum',[56] 'threads'[57] and 'source materials'[58] behind the editing and redaction of the DH. At the same time, however, Noth emphasised Dtr's 'carefully conceived plan'[59] for the entire history, so that in hindsight his monograph may be seen as an early sign of the shift that would later take place in Old Testament scholarship from diachronic to synchronic studies.[60] The only element of Noth's thesis that was original to him (which is now the most disputed) was that the entire work was pieced together by a single Deuteronomist, who 'was not simply an editor but the author'.[61] This focus on the homogeneity of the entire work paved the way for subsequent Deuteronomistic studies to focus less on the history's internal seams and more on overarching structural motifs, such as the speeches framework and certain *leitmotifs*. Indeed, the identification of such unifying concepts has been an important element in subsequent studies of the DH.[62] Noth's rather negative view of the DH as a theological rationale for exile has since been balanced by von Rad's emphasis on the promise-fulfilment schema,[63]

---

55. Martin Noth, *The Deuteronomistic History*, JSOTSup 15, 2nd ed. (Sheffield: JSOT, 1981) (trans. D. Clines et al. of pp. 1–110 of *Überlieferungsgeschichtliche Studien: Die Sammelnden und Bearbeitenden Geschichtswerke im Alten Testament*, 2nd ed. [Tübingen: Max Niemeyer, 1957]; original: 1943)

56. Ibid., 5.

57. Ibid., 8.

58. Ibid., 9.

59. Ibid., 10.

60. As early as 1938, von Rad lamented the apparent 'irreversibility' (*Nichtumkehrbarkeit*) of the 'process of disintegration' (*Auflösungsprozess*) that characterised Hexateuchal studies in his day, and the associated neglect of the text's 'final form' (*Letztgestalt*). Gerhard von Rad, *Das formgeschichtliche Problem des Hexateuchs* (Stuttgart: W. Kohlhammer, 1938), 1. On the roles played by Gunkel, Noth and von Rad in the shift from internal textual issues to overarching structural motifs, see Rolf Rendtorff, 'The Paradigm is Changing: Hopes – and Fears', *BibInt* 1 (1993): 34–53.

61. Noth, *The Deuteronomistic History*, 10.

62. See, e.g., Moshe Weinfeld, *Deuteronomy and the Deuteronomic School* (Oxford: Clarendon, 1972).

63. Gerhard von Rad, *Studies in Deuteronomy*, trans. David Stalker (London: SCM, 1953), 74–91.

Wolff's emphasis on the theme of repentance,[64] and Cross's observation that the promise to David and the sin of Jeroboam are twin themes throughout the history.[65]

Barth's exegetical work in the 1940s and 1950s focused on texts in their received form, but as we have seen, his exegetical endeavours were not well-received by Old Testament scholars due to his perceived hermeneutical naivety and lack of interest in historical-critical issues. In hindsight, however, it is clear that he was ahead of his time. Indeed, it would have been interesting to see the nature of Barth's engagement with the literary turn that began in the 1970s if he had lived a decade longer. By the early 1980s, a renewed focus on the final form of the text had been established, not least in Robert Alter's highly influential work, *The Art of Biblical Narrative* (1981), which was essentially a compilation of essays published between 1975 and 1980.[66] Jewish scholars, drawing on rabbinic exegesis which tends to emphasise the text's potential for imaginative linkage, have led the way in outlining a methodology for the new literary criticism.[67] But a certain sense of relief was expressed by numerous Old Testament scholars about the methodological shift taking place, because the historical-critical method was perceived in some circles as having failed to ascertain much about the world behind the text with any degree of certainty.[68] In an essay written at the end of the twentieth century, entitled, 'The Paradigm is Changing: Hopes and Fears', Rolf Rendtorff, a former student of von Rad, expressed his concerns about scholarship's ongoing obsession with dating texts and doing little that is innovative except perhaps finding new ways to get 'behind' the text:

> I want to stress that taking a synchronic approach to the text in its given shape is a task Old Testament scholarship has neglected too long and too intentionally. Scholars still seem to be proud of knowing things better than the final redactors or compilers. This is a kind of nineteenth-century hubris

---

64. Hans Walter Wolff, 'The Kerygma of the Deuteronomic Historical Work', in Walter Brueggemann and Hans Walter Wolff, *The Vitality of Old Testament Traditions*, 2nd ed. (Atlanta: John Knox, 1982), 83–100.

65. Cross, *Canaanite Myth*. But see Provan's insightful critique of these themes that undergird Cross's double-redaction hypothesis; *Hezekiah*, 28–9.

66. See Alter, *Art*, x–xi.

67. Alter, *Art*; Sternberg, *Poetics*; Adele Berlin, *Poetics and Interpretation of Biblical Narrative* (Sheffield: Almond, 1983); Bar-Efrat, *Narrative Art*.

68. See David M. Gunn, 'New Directions in the Study of Biblical Hebrew Narrative', *JSOT* 39 (1987): 65–75.

we should have left behind us. The last writers, whatever we want to call them, were, in any case, much closer to the original meaning of the text than we can ever be. From time to time we should remember what Franz Rosenzweig taught us: that the letter 'R', as usually taken for the 'redactor', actually should be read as 'Rabbenu', 'our master'. For we receive the text from the hands of these last writers, and they are the ones whose voice and message we have to hear first.[69]

The most radical shift with the transition from diachronic to synchronic analysis is what Sternberg describes as a change of focus from *genesis* to *poesis*. Regarding *The Poetics of Biblical Narrative: Ideological Literature and the Drama of Reading*, Sternberg states confidently, 'this book will repeatedly show that what has been decomposed by geneticists makes a poetic and purposive composition'.[70] His interpretive endeavours thus seek to elucidate a sophisticated scheme of poetics, i.e. how the text generates meaning (in a purposeful manner).

The distinction between these two modes of analysis is most evident when dealing with dissonance in the Hebrew Bible, since in many cases dissonance may be understood either in *diachronic* terms pertaining to its genesis (e.g., the redaction of conflicting sources), or in *synchronic* terms that illuminate the text's poetics (e.g., rhetorical devices whose significance readers can learn to identify and comprehend). To take one simple example from 1 Kings 13, the lack of any reference to King Jeroboam in vv. 11-32 has led some diachronic interpreters to the understanding that vv. 1-10 and vv. 11-32 were originally two independent legends that were at some stage amalgamated.[71] Synchronic readers, on the other hand (without necessarily discounting the possibility of multiple sources), focus on the way the threefold prohibition is distributed throughout the chapter as a whole (vv. 5, 9, 17) and the way in which the two parts of the story make little sense without one another.[72] We will consider a further example in greater detail – the widely recognised 'envelope' structure of 1 Kings 13 – in the next chapter.

Another key difference between synchronic and diachronic approaches pertains to the different 'worlds' they negotiate. Approaches dealing with the final form of the text focus on the world *within* (and *in front of*) the text, whereas diachronic methods are more interested in accessing the world *behind* the text. From this perspective, synchronic methods that

69. Rendtorff, 'The Paradigm is Changing', 52. Driver notes the wide-reaching impact of this citation from Rozenzweig in Childs, *Biblical Theologian*, 132.
70. Sternberg, *Poetics*, 517 n. 9.
71. So G. Jones, *I and II Kings*, 1:261; McKenzie, *Trouble*, 54.
72. So DeVries, *1 Kings*, 169–70.

engage the world within the text with full, imaginative seriousness necessarily place a significant degree of trust in the literary competence of the author or final editor, while diachronic analyses are more interested in reconstructing the historical world that gave rise to the text. Van Seters' diachronic approach to 1 Kings 13 thus leads him to conclude that the difficulties one has in reading the story 'are the result of a lack of literary skill by the author'.[73] Although he initially attempts to understand the text in its received form according to what he considers to be a reasonable *poetics*, Van Seters turns to a critical evaluation of its *genesis* when the text continues to perplex him. Seeking an explanation for his list of sixteen problems in 1 Kings 13, he offers three suggestions: (i) the author used a hodge-podge of sources (P, Chronicles, Jonah); (ii) the text is not regular historical narrative, but represents another genre (e.g., irony, parody, satire); (iii) the author tried his hand at intertextuality but lacked proficiency there, too. The point, in any case, is that Van Seters seeks to resolve the problematic nature of the text by recourse to the world behind it; i.e. to the author's inability to write well. He evidently does not share Rendtorff's sentiment about trusting 'R' that the final form of the text is a purposeful composition.[74]

In contrast, while Sternberg concedes (in principle) that literary analysis ought to include a serious grappling with the prehistory of a text, he expresses great frustration with 'geneticists' who take incongruities in the text and come up with fantastical hypotheses: 'Rarely has there been such a futile expense of spirit in a noble cause; rarely have such grandiose theories of origination been built and revised and pitted against one another on the evidential equivalent of the head of a pin; rarely have so many worked so long and so hard with so little to show for their trouble'.[75] Even the Deuteronomist, he says, leads only a speculative existence as a (widely accepted) construct of geneticism.[76]

The narrative-critical approach championed by Sternberg, among others, seeks evidence of intentionality in the narrative detail, even when it is not immediately apparent. Readers thereby place greater trust in the narrator's voice, and by implication in the author's literary competence. When a text befuddles the reader, a degree of sophistication is assumed

73. Van Seters, 'On Reading', 233.
74. This is not to say that theological tensions and discrepancies between source materials were smoothed over. As Chapman argues in *The Law and the Prophets*, the biblical tradents made redactions according to a 'theological grammar' that allowed – or rather, *ensured* – the expression of 'a range of ideals' (96).
75. Sternberg, *Poetics*, 13.
76. Ibid.

and the text is probed from various angles until an 'aha!' moment occurs. To put it otherwise, what Van Seters perceives as indicators of authorial incompetence, synchronic readers treat as 'narrative gaps', an aspect of Hebrew narrative that is considered crucial for engaging readers and thickening the plot. For most narratologists, this approach entails a high level of trust in the narrator, whom narrative critics consider 'omniscient'.[77] Sternberg, for his part, describes this 'absolutely and straightforwardly reliable'[78] narrator who is able to report from any character's point of view, as 'a textual reflex of the Israelite conception of unrestricted divine knowledge'.[79] It is inconceivable that Sternberg would ask, as Van Seters does, 'Why is it that the word of Yahweh does not come directly to the man of God?'[80] – except as a rhetorical question. Synchronic interpreters tend not to challenge or question the narrator (much less the author behind the narrator) when met with difficulty. Sternberg assumes, rather, that filling narrative gaps is an important part of the reader's contribution to the task of discovering (or making) meaning. To question an unexpected detail in the plot is like asking why Rumpelstiltskin is able to weave straw into gold. If a child inquires about the story in this way, we are likely to say, 'That's just a necessary part of the story, but it's not the point. Keep listening...'

Sternberg's level of confidence in the narrator is not without problems, however, for even among advocates of a narratological method, not all agree on the notion of an omniscient narrator. While in theory, Sternberg emphasises the importance of the reader for *poesis*, he has been squarely challenged about whether his schema places too much faith in the narrator and also whether he denies readers permission to entertain readings that differ from Sternberg's own. In an essay entitled, 'Reading Right: Reliable and Omniscient Narrator, Omniscient God, and Foolproof Composition in the Hebrew Bible',[81] David Gunn resists Sternberg's

77. Walsh, *Old Testament Narrative*, 44–5; Bar-Efrat, *Narrative Art*, 17–23; Berlin, *Poetics*, 52; Sternberg, *Poetics*, 84–128, 153–85, passim.

78. Sternberg, *Poetics*, 51.

79. Ibid., 26.

80. Van Seters, 'On Reading', 229. Van Seters laments further: 'The author contradicts all of the norms of prophecy but still wants us to take the prophetic oracles seriously. How the story can teach any "lessons" about true and false prophets of obedience to the word of God is hard to imagine.'

81. David Gunn, 'Reading Right: Reliable and Omniscient Narrator, Omniscient God, and Foolproof Composition in the Hebrew Bible', in *The Bible in Three Dimensions: Essays in Celebration of Forty Years of Biblical Studies in the University of Sheffield*, ed. David J. A. Clines, Stephen E. Fowl, and Stanley E. Porter, JSOTSup 87 (Sheffield: JSOT, 1990), 85–101.

notion of 'foolproof composition, whereby the discourse strives to open and bring home its essentials to all readers'.[82] Gunn does not agree with the premise that narrators are 'absolutely and straightforwardly reliable' nor with the ramification that readers will therefore always be able to grasp 'the point of it all'.[83] Sternberg's claim, which effectively equates the narrator's point of view with a divine perspective, leaves very little room for texts that are inconsistent with one another and even less for the notion of an ironic narrator. His *poetics* thereby preclude from the outset a reading like that of David Marcus, who interprets 1 Kings 13 as parody.[84] Even so, there remains a significant difference between Van Seters, whose questions press beneath or beyond the world of the text to the historical circumstances that gave rise to it, and Gunn, whose objection pertains to a proper understanding of the narrator's role within the world of the text.

Bernard Levinson also finds Sternberg's mode of synchronic interpretation problematic, though for different reasons to Gunn. In Levinson's view, insisting that all anomalies in texts can be explained as purposive, artistic *decisions* prevents the Bible's history of composition from having its own, distinct voice. As he puts it, 'the exclusive derivation of the text from a single author/narrator, even if only maintained for heuristic purposes, risks returning a modernizing scholarship to the pre-critical, midrashic method of the early rabbis who, for dogmatic reasons, were constrained to avoid the intimations of literary history within the Pentateuch'.[85] Levinson therefore warns against using diachronic analysis only to illuminate the world *behind* the text, since such a view fails to attend to the development of the canon and its implications for reading the Bible in its received form.[86] Rather, diachronic and synchronic methods should both come into consideration even when interpreting the text in its received form. Levinson's argument resonates in some sense with the canonical approach of Childs, for whom an exclusively synchronic approach risks detracting from 'the full history of revelation'.[87] As Childs famously put it: 'To work with the final stage of the text is not to lose the historical dimension, but it is rather to make a critical, theological judgment regarding the process. The depth dimension aids in

---

82. Sternberg, *Poetics*, 50.
83. Ibid., 51.
84. Marcus, 'Elements of Ridicule'.
85. Bernard Levinson, 'The Right Chorale: From the Poetics to the Hermeneutics of the Hebrew Bible', in *'The Right Chorale': Studies in Biblical Law and Interpretation*, FAT 54 (Tübingen: Mohr Siebeck, 2008), 24.
86. Ibid.
87. Childs, *Introduction*, 73.

understanding the interpreted text, and does not function independently of it.'[88] Levinson thus provides a helpful corrective to simplistic notions of the final form of the text as 'all that really matters', wherein the impact of the canonical process on the received form is effectively discounted. The critical issue here is that even if one gives a certain priority to the final form of the text because of its canonical status as the material with which every scholar must begin his or her program, problems arise when diachronic and synchronic approaches are seen to be mutually exclusive, or when the canonical text is rendered autonomous via excessive distanciation from its origins.[89]

Even if one exhibits a greater confidence in the author of 1 Kings 13 than Van Seters, he nonetheless raises the important question of how to read when an 'omniscient narrator' leaves such considerable gaps in the narrative that the story becomes exceedingly difficult to understand without some degree of psychologising or guesswork. And needless to say, 1 Kings 13 is exemplary in this regard![90] The making of meaning with regards to this story requires that numerous gaps in the plot be filled in by the reader. For instance: what motivates the Bethel prophet to act deceitfully toward the man of God?; why is the man of God killed for disobedience when he was responding obediently to a prophet's word? Where gaps appear too wide for readers to fill with confidence, interpretive possibilities are multiplied, and as Van Seters suggests, intertexts or inner-biblical allusions comprise one possibility for filling such gaps.[91]

It is evident from the preceding discussion that the divergence between synchronic and diachronic approaches is not a simple matter, but rather one that involves a range of factors. Nonetheless, since the divergence often arises because of dissonance between the world *within* the text

---

88. Ibid., 76.

89. See Paul Ricoeur, 'The Hermeneutical Function of Distanciation', in *Hermeneutics and the Human Sciences: Essays on Language, Action, and Interpretation*, ed. Paul Ricoeur and John B. Thompson (Cambridge: Cambridge University Press, 1981), 131–44.

90. For a recent interpretation that 'psychologises' both the man of God and the Bethel prophet, see Lasine, *Weighing Hearts*, 93–114.

91. Intertextuality is itself a major area of study within biblical studies. On the distinction between author-oriented and text-oriented intertexts, see Geoffrey Miller, 'Intertextuality in Old Testament Research', *CBR* 9 (2011): 283–309; on the reasons for an author's use of intertexts, see Benjamin D. Sommer, *A Prophet Reads Scripture: Allusion in Isaiah 40–66*, Contraversions: Jews and Other Differences (Stanford, CA: Stanford University Press, 1998). Note Sommer's assertion: 'The weighing of such evidence (and hence the identification of allusions) is an art, not a science' (35).

and the world *behind* the text, it is important (yet again) for the interpreter to be explicit about which of these takes priority for their project. Van Winkle exemplifies this clarity of intention when establishing a synchronic approach to 1 Kings 13:

> If our focus is the final form of the text, we cannot allow hypotheses about the history of Israelite religion to influence the interpretation of the text so that we ignore material in the text or introduce information into the text that is contrary to the viewpoint of the narrator. Thus the theory that Israel's cult was centralized later than the time of Jeroboam should not lead us to ignore the narrator's view that Jeroboam violated the law of the central sanctuary. Knowledge of the archaeology of Syria and Palestine should not lead us to read into the story that Jeroboam merely made a place for Yahweh to dwell rather than making idols. While the cult may have been centralized later, and while Jeroboam may have made a throne for Yahweh rather than an idol, since the narrator does not introduce these elements, since our attention is on the final form of the text, and since these hypotheses are contrary to the author's perspective, we ought not allow these views to color our interpretation.[92]

Van Winkle thus helpfully differentiates between questions pertaining to the world *within* and the world *behind* the text, and prioritises the narrator's assertions according to his purpose and interests. When interpreters lay their cards on the table like this, it certainly facilitates better understanding and dialogue among biblical scholars, even – or perhaps, *especially* – when their methodologies differ. As Moberly put it some years ago, 'the crucial question, which is prior to questions of method and sets the context for them, is that of purpose and goal. To put it simply, *how we use the Bible depends on why we use the Bible*. In practice, many of the disagreements about how are, in effect, disagreements about why, and failure to recognise this leads to endless confusion.'[93]

'Scripture is' and 'scripture as'

We began this chapter with a brief review of the methodological divergence between Barth's literary-theological priorities and Klopfenstein's historical-critical approach. We also noted in Klopfenstein's response to Barth that it is unreasonable to review another scholar's exegesis by a different set of standards than the ones they used to engage the text. For Barth and Klopfenstein, as indeed for the interpreters we examined

---

92. Van Winkle, '1 Kings XII 25–XIII 34', 101–2.
93. Moberly, *The Old Testament of the Old Testament*, 2.

in the preceding chapter, the reasons for their differences have less to do with academic competence than they have to do with the questions and priorities of each interpreter. Yet, a context of hermeneutical pluralism requires that biblical interpreters be able to evaluate between competing construals of any given text. How, then, can such judgments be made without students and scholars of the Bible speaking past one another due to different priorities and locations on the spectrums discussed above?

Addressing this state of affairs, Richard Briggs makes a simple but rather helpful suggestion. 'Rather than talking bluntly about what "scripture is"', he offers, 'we might better learn to speak of "scripture as" whenever we want to offer judgments or criteria regarding the responsible interpretation of scripture'.[94] If nothing else, this advice ought to ensure that interpreters are on the same page, so to speak, before engaging with one another's exegeses of biblical texts. As we have seen in previous chapters, and as Briggs also affirms, 'normative criteria with respect to hermeneutical engagement can only really exist, in anything but the broadest terms, when there is a goal or purpose in view for the reading'.[95]

In practice, this kind of honest acknowledgement permits readers to consider the variety of ways that Scripture (or the Bible, for those who would prefer a more neutral term) may legitimately be construed.[96] Different interpretations may then be weighed and measured against appropriate criteria, depending on the interpreter's agenda, with an eye towards collaboration rather than exclusion. As Briggs goes on to suggest, 'scriptural responsibility in the face of hermeneutical plurality is a responsibility to fostering dialogue between multiple competing construals of "*scripture as*", arrayed across the domains of the theological, the literary, the historical, the cultural, the psychological, and so forth'.[97]

With this in mind, it is obvious that the divergence between Barth and Klopfenstein is due not only to markedly different approaches to exegesis, but to distinct conceptions of Scripture. Barth, on one hand, construes all of Scripture, including 1 Kings 13, *as testimony concerning Jesus Christ*:

---

94. Briggs, 'Biblical Hermeneutics', 41. It may still be worthwhile to discuss the definition or nature of Scripture itself (i.e. what 'scripture is'), but those questions would take us beyond the bounds of this study.

95. Ibid., 37.

96. Briggs draws the line at construals which 'deliberately step outside of scripture's own self-presenting categories', e.g., 'amongst the angry who are determined only to show the incoherence of theistic claims; and amongst the would-be spiritual who feel that the Lord has spoken directly to them, in rather unmediated fashion, about how the text is to be construed today' (ibid., 40).

97. Ibid., 48.

> The Bible says all sort of things, certainly; but in all this multiplicity and variety, it says in truth only one thing – just this: the name of Jesus Christ concealed under the name Israel in the Old Testament, revealed under his own name in the New Testament, which therefore can be understood only as it has understood itself, as a commentary on the Old Testament. The Bible becomes clear when it is clear that it says this one thing: that it proclaims the name Jesus Christ and therefore proclaims God in his richness and mercy, and man in his need and helplessness… [W]e can properly interpret the Bible, in whole or in part, only when we perceive and show that what it says is said from the point of view of that concealed and revealed name of Jesus Christ.[98]

This conception of Scripture is what leads Barth to interpret parts (such as 1 Kgs 13) in light of the whole in an effort to show how Christ is being revealed throughout Old and New Testaments alike. To Barth, then, 1 Kings 13 is yet another piece of the christological puzzle (or mystery), and he sees no problem interpreting the text on such terms. The questions he brings to the interpretive task are, in light of this, unsurprising. Barth's exegesis concludes with three very different questions which, in his view, must be answered by any who find his exegesis implausible or unacceptable. Barth asks: 'Where else do they [the two prophets and the two Israels] remain [if not in Christ]? What else is chapter 1 K. 13 if it is not prophecy? Where else is its fulfilment to be found if not in Jesus Christ?'[99] These three questions are but variations on a theme, each one reinforcing his view of *scripture as* testimony to Jesus Christ. (For my part, as I indicated earlier, I am not opposed to christological interpretation, but my sense is that by skipping lightly over the story's epilogue in 2 Kings 23 in favour of Easter Sunday, Barth fails to attend to the story's own rather explicit cues for resolution in Josiah.)

Barth's interpretive method and categories are thus fundamentally different from those of Klopfenstein, who construes 1 Kings 13 *as an historical record* that identifies these two prophetic figures as the responsible agents of the north–south division.[100] The questions Klopfenstein brings to the text are therefore typically historical: whence this story and why has it been preserved? For him, the use of intertexts or 'external' theological categories to inform the interpretation of an historically grounded text lures interpreters away from the narrow path of *Einzelexegese* into

---

98. Barth, *CD* I.2, 720.
99. Barth, *CD* II.2, 409. On Barth's discovery of God as the true subject (*Sache*) of the Bible, see Burnett, *Barth's Theological Exegesis*, 74–7.
100. Klopfenstein, '1. Könige 13', 669: 'als einer Demonstration zuhanden der Vertreter einer kultischen Trennung zwischen Bethel und Jerusalem fest'.

unruly fields of *Überinterpretation*. For both exegetes, however, the point is 'that scripture is always scripture with a view; that hermeneutical approaches need to be measured against the overarching goals of why scripture is being read'.[101]

In addition to the accents placed on the narrative by Barth and Klopfenstein – *scripture as* witness to Christ and *scripture as* historical record – one might treat 1 Kings 13 in other ways as well;[102] for instance, scripture as political propaganda (i.e., for Josiah),[103] or scripture as anti-prophetic satire.[104] In any case, Moberly's insight holds true; 'that the meaning of the Bible cannot be separated from the questions and concerns of its interpreters'.[105]

---

101. Briggs, 'Biblical Hermeneutics', 42.

102. Briggs refers to a spectrum of ways in which scripture is construed, from scripture *as text* and *as bearing of meaning* at one end, to scripture *as raw data for interpretive freeplay* at the other. Between these, scripture *as functional, communicative act* (which Briggs commends for remaining within scripture's own self-presenting categories) can take various shapes: 'divine address, historical document, record of the testimonies of the faithful, partisan ideological construct', and so on. Ibid.

103. So Cross, *Canaanite Myth*, 287.

104. So Marcus, 'Elements of Ridicule', passim.

105. Moberly, *Old Testament*, 2; cf. Schneiders, *Revelatory Text*, esp. 151–4.

6

BOSWORTH: REVISITING BARTH

David Bosworth: Revisiting Barth

In Chapter 3 we observed that Barth's exegesis of 1 Kings 13 has largely been overlooked by historical-critical scholarship, and that this has been at least in part due to the critical responses of Klopfenstein and Noth. The recent proliferation of hermeneutical models and approaches, however, has seen a resurgence of Barth's influence, especially in theological and literary analyses, thus raising the question of whether Barth's reading might now be integrated more thoroughly with contemporary, mainstream scholarship. This chapter evaluates one attempt to do just that.

Notwithstanding those who have credited Barth for providing certain insights for their work on 1 Kings 13, David Bosworth is the only scholar, of whom I am aware, to take Barth's theological presentation of the story and consciously seek to develop it. In an article entitled, 'Revisiting Barth's Exegesis of 1 Kings 13' (2002), and then also in a chapter of his monograph, *The Story Within a Story in Biblical Hebrew Narrative* (2008), Bosworth not only seeks to present Barth's interpretation as viable, but also to provide additional supporting material that he says 'Barth neglected to include'.[1] In this chapter, I offer a summary and evaluation of Bosworth before we move on to consider another way that Barth's insights might be assimilated with studies in the DH.

Bosworth rightly notes that even if some scholars have shown positive regard for Barth's theological angle (e.g., Lemke and Walsh), most have failed to seriously engage with Barth. For instance, Bosworth is surprised (as am I) that so many commentators continue to treat the story as an isolated legend and fail to recognise its function as political commentary, an insight that is central to Barth's contribution.[2] Bosworth observes that

---

1. Bosworth, 'Revisiting', 382 (from the abstract).
2. Ibid., 377. Bosworth (*Story*, 118) avers that 'the strange story can only be explained by appeal to its context.'

Barth's reception among biblical scholars has probably been tentative due to perceptions about his hermeneutical naivety and apparent disregard for sources. However, in Bosworth's view, recent shifts in theological method suggest that 'biblical scholars are in a position to re-evaluate Barth's exegesis of 1 Kings 13'.[3] On this basis, he develops Barth's proposal in the hope of increasing its plausibility among scholars.

The article develops the central dynamic of 1 Kings 13 as it was articulated by Barth; namely, 'the manner in which the man of God and the prophet belong together, do not belong together, and eventually and finally do belong together; and how the same is true of Judah and Israel'.[4] Bosworth observes:

> Although Barth sees the history of the divided kingdom played out in this story, he does not specifically spell out the relationship between 1 Kings 13 and the history of the divided monarchy in 1 and 2 Kings. Although some scholars have borrowed this central insight from Barth, none has developed it in detail. Barth's failure to elaborate the analogy makes his work more vulnerable to criticism from exegetes.[5]

For the remainder of the paper, then, Bosworth builds on Barth's insight by explaining how the relationship between the man of God (representing Judah) and the old prophet (representing Israel) can be mapped onto the history of the divided kingdoms by identifying elements in 1 Kings 13 that appear to have parallels in the subsequent record. His purpose is to clarify the details of the analogy to which Barth alluded. Bosworth is quite right in stating that 'Barth did not make this analogy clear by explaining how the kingdoms mirror the individuals in 1 Kings 13',[6] so he outlines a number of consecutive parallels in order to indicate 'how Barth's claims concerning 1 Kings 13 may be supported by the evidence of the history of the divided kingdom as told in Kings'.[7] In his article, Bosworth lists four distinct 'stages' in this relationship; in his book, he includes five.[8] Here we review the table from his most recent work:[9]

---

3. Bosworth, 'Revisiting', 378.
4. Barth, *CD* II.2, 393; cited in Bosworth, 'Revisiting', 367.
5. Bosworth, 'Revisiting', 372.
6. Ibid., 381.
7. Ibid.
8. The fourth stage, 'resumption of hostility', was added to the 2008 publication.
9. This table (a summary) has been copied in its entirety from Bosworth, *Story*, 132–3. See 'Revisiting', 379–81, and *Story*, 132–49, for detail on each of the stages.

	Man of God and Prophet	Judah and Israel
Mutual Hostility	1 Kgs 13.11-18 The prophet seeks to undermine the judgment of the man of God (from 1 Kgs 13.1-2) by inviting the prophet to share a meal in Bethel and by lying about a divine revelation	1 Kgs 11–21 Judah and Israel are mutually hostile and engage in several border skirmishes
Friendship	1 Kgs 13.19 The two prophetic figures share a meal together against God's command (vv. 16-17)	1 Kgs 22–2 Kgs 8 Judah (under Jehoshaphat) makes an alliance with Israel (under the Omride dynasty) which is evaluated negatively
Role-Reversal	1 Kgs 13.20-23 The prophet announces the judgment of God on the man of God	2 Kgs 9–11 Jehu's coup initiates a reversal by which Baal worship is eliminated in Israel, but introduced in Judah (under Athaliah)
Resumption of Hostility	1 Kgs 13.24-34 The figures part company with the understanding that their shared meal was unfaithful to God and based on a lie. The old prophet buries the man of God in his own tomb, in fulfilment of the divine judgment	2 Kgs 12–17 Judah and Israel return to their mutual hostility, with their wars going beyond border skirmishing
Southern Partner Saves Northern One	2 Kgs 23.15-20 Josiah does not disturb the bones of the old prophets because they share a tomb with the man of God who predicted Josiah's reform of Bethel	2 Kgs 22–23 Josiah's reforms eliminate the causes of the division of Israel after Solomon [*sic*] death and create the conditions for a possible renewal of the united Monarchy

As the table clearly shows, Bosworth matches plot developments in 1 Kings 13, focusing especially on the two anonymous figures, with stages in the historical account of the two kingdoms, beginning with the Jeroboam cycle (1 Kgs 11–14) and concluding with the reforms of Josiah in 2 Kings 23 (these stages are elucidated below). Given Barth's emphasis on the relationship between the prophets as national representatives, Bosworth concludes his article with a proposal that further research be undertaken in an attempt to answer the question, *How does Kings present the relationship between Israel and Judah* (particularly in contrast to say, Chronicles, or a prophetic book such as Amos)?

Bosworth's objective is worthwhile, even if Barth did not have the same kind of literary analogies in mind as the ones suggested by Bosworth, but we will return to that issue below. In the first instance, however, we begin with Bosworth's theoretical delineation of this rhetorical device in Old Testament narrative, wherein a shorter narrative illuminates a larger one of which it is a part.

1 Kings 13 as mise-en-abyme *(2008)*

In a monograph entitled, *The Story Within a Story in Biblical Hebrew Narrative* (2008),[10] Bosworth focuses on the literary device that featured in his previous article and develops it more fully under the appellation, *mise-en-abyme* – a phrase which literally means 'placement in abyss'.[11] Although Bosworth recognises the device as 'a specific kind of narrative analogy' (a term that is more widely recognised by Old Testament scholars),[12] key characteristics of a *mise-en-abyme* are set out in the opening section of the book, where Bosworth introduces the term via extra-biblical examples and even via 'non-examples' to ensure that the term is rightly understood. Nine criteria are briefly adumbrated to formulate 'a description of the *mise-en-abyme* that is neither too broad nor too narrow'.[13] Acknowledging some variance in the use of the term, Bosworth offers this definition: 'In literary studies, a *mise-en-abyme* is a part of a literary work that duplicates pertinent aspects of the whole within which it is placed'.[14]

By Bosworth's reckoning, the device is used only three times in the Hebrew Bible, one of them being 1 Kgs 13.11-32 + 2 Kgs 23.15-20 within the history of the divided kingdom (1 Kgs 11–2 Kgs 23).[15] Here we shall

---

10. Bosworth, *Story*, esp. 118–57.

11. The term was introduced by French novelist and critic, André Gide, *Journals 1889–1949*, trans. J. O'Brien (London: Penguin, 1984).

12. Bosworth, *Story*, vii.

13. Ibid., 16. The nine criteria are totality, reflection, explicitness, isolatability, orientation, extent, distribution, general function and motivation. See ibid., 11–16.

14. Ibid., 35.

15. The other instances are Gen. 38 within Gen. 37–50 and 1 Sam. 25 within 1 Sam. 13.12–2 Sam. 5.3. The main reason so few texts qualify as *mises-en-abyme*

consider what significance the identification of 1 Kings 13 as a *mise-en-abyme* has for Bosworth's advocacy of Barth's exegesis.

As mentioned above, Bosworth appeals to Barth's observation that the story's immediate, literary context – the division of the kingdom – is critical for a proper understanding of 1 Kings 13. However, unlike Barth, Bosworth provides additional support for this claim beyond noting only that the two prophets hail from north and south. Scholarly efforts to establish a qualitative difference between 'man of God' and 'prophet' have been inconclusive, leaving the simplest explanation as the best one: the narrator consistently uses different terms in order to maintain a distinction between the two anonymous prophets. (On this point, Bosworth differs with Barth, who associated northern prophets with professionalism and falsehood.) That the prophets foreshadow their respective kingdoms is also indicated within the text by the fact that the two parts of the story (1 Kgs 13.11-32 and 2 Kgs 23.15-20) form an *inclusio* around the history and highlight its political thrust.[16] The motif of prophecy–fulfilment is a well-known feature of the DH, and Bosworth suggests that by delimiting a major textual unit, 1 Kgs 13.11-32 + 2 Kgs 23.15-20 perhaps serves a function other than simply affirming Yahweh as Lord of history.[17] This argument is further strengthened by the fact that almost every Israelite king (from 1 Kgs 13 to 2 Kgs 17) is evaluated with regards to the sin of Jeroboam, since the Bethel cult and altar persist until Josiah's reforms in 2 Kings 23. Bosworth also argues, drawing on the work of Nadav Na'aman,[18] that prophetic and political narratives ought to be read in conjunction with one another, and that 1 Kings 22 and 2 Kings 3 also have special importance as stories of prophetic-royal conflict. 'These narratives in which prophetic figures intersect with the histories of both nations parallel 1 Kings 13 and contribute to the articulation

---

is that Bosworth considers 'isolatability' a critical criterion. On that basis, neither Nathan's parable (2 Sam. 12.1-6) nor Jotham's fable (Judg. 9.7-15) qualify, because they cannot be read as independent narratives. 'Allegory, exemplum, fable, and parable are literary devices that may be distinguished from the *mise-en-abyme* because they are typically not sufficiently isolatable from their contexts due to the explanatory function they serve' (Bosworth, *Story*, 19). I would argue, however, that the two above-mentioned parables make as much, or as little, sense as does 1 Kgs 13.11-32 + 2 Kgs 23.15-20 when isolated from their context.

16. Bosworth, *Story*, 122.
17. Ibid., 129.
18. Nadav Na'aman, 'Prophetic Stories as Sources for the Histories of Jehoshaphat and the Omrides', *Biblica* 78 (1997): 153–73. For additional references, see Bosworth, *Story*, 127 n. 30.

of the *mise-en-abyme*.'[19] Moreover, Bosworth identifies a pattern in the distribution of prophetic stories throughout the History of the Divided Kingdom. In summary, most of the prophetic stories are set in the north, which in his view 'indicates that Israel is the less faithful nation that stands in greater need of prophets'.[20] (This observation finds support in the opening verses of 1 Kgs 13, but Bosworth does not emphasise this, presumably because – surprisingly – he doesn't include 1 Kgs 13.1-10 in the *mise-en-abyme*.) With these observations, Bosworth seeks to highlight, in ways Barth did not, that the 'story of the prophetic figures in 1 Kgs 13:11-32 and 2 Kgs 23:15-20 contributes to several key motifs in Kings, including the concern with cultic policy and the sin of Jeroboam, prophetic stories (including prophetic–royal conflict), and the prophecy-fulfillment schema'.[21] He thereby not only echoes Barth's notion of a reciprocal dynamic between north and south, but provides further support for it with the identification of various literary signposts throughout the History of the Divided Kingdom:

> The parallel history of both kingdoms, connected by synchronistic chronological notices, indicates the narrator's interest in "all Israel," not only Judah (as in Chronicles). Furthermore, some of the stories involving prophets comment directly on the relationship between the two kingdoms (1 Kings 22; 2 Kings 3). Although scholars agree that the history represents a Judean perspective, Judah is not represented as blameless; the negative evaluation of the alliance and consequent reversal following Jehu's coup indicates a criticism of Judah and parallel praise of Israel.[22]

Observations such as these establish for Bosworth that 1 Kgs 13.11-32 + 2 Kgs 23.15-20 comprises a *mise-en-abyme* that 'does not comment directly on the history, but creates an analogy within it. The analogy invites comparison between the two narratives such that the *mise-en-abyme* elucidates aspects of the larger history.'[23] The point is that 1 Kgs 13.11-32 + 2 Kgs 23.15-20 function as a kind of hermeneutical key for the history encapsulated by these two texts. When the story is read in isolation from its wider context, it is often assumed that a story about prophets must necessarily be about prophecy. But as Bosworth rightly observes:

---

19. Bosworth, *Story*, 128.
20. Ibid., 129.
21. Ibid., 130.
22. Ibid., 152.
23. Ibid..

Scholars have struggled to locate a didactic lesson in the seemingly unedifying story. Such efforts have not succeeded because the story has been read apart from its immediate context concerning the division of the kingdom and its larger context of the History of the Divided Kingdom. Those scholars who have interpreted the story within its political context have had less difficulty with the strangeness of the story.[24]

By the same token, given the way in which a *mise-en-abyme* functions, difficulties and anomalies within the *mise-en-abyme* are also more easily understood when read in light of their broader, literary (and political) context, since the *mise-en-abyme* duplicates important dynamics within the wider narrative. Here, I shall briefly outline some of Bosworth's more salient points concerning narrative details in 1 Kings 13 that become less perplexing when seen through that broader, historical-political lens.

(a) *The Threefold Command*

The divine prohibitions against eating, drinking, and returning by the same way are repeated three times in 1 Kings 13 (vv. 9, 17, 22) and the entire story clearly revolves around them. However, it is not a simple matter to discern Jeroboam's motive for inviting the man of God to share a meal, or the old prophet's motive for tricking him into breaking the threefold command. Within Bosworth's proposal, these elements of the story are best understood as indicators of the mutual hostility between north and south in the wider narrative (i.e. the commandments in 1 Kgs 13 prohibit hospitable engagement). After the division of the kingdom, there are ongoing 'border skirmishes' between Israel and Judah (1 Kgs 14.30; 15.6, 16). 'This skirmishing conforms to the limited hostility between the prophetic figures in 1 Kgs 13:11-18.'[25]

(b) *The Man of God Reneges*

In connection with the narrative gap regarding the old prophet's motive for deceiving the man of God, a related difficulty in 1 Kings 13 is the manner in which the Judean is so easily duped into reneging on the divine prohibition. Given the manner in which he forcefully reiterates the command in v. 17, it is surprising that he breaks all three parts of it in v. 19. Presumably, this is why Van Seters states with such candour that '[t]he man of God is not disobedient; he is merely stupid'.[26] Bosworth

---

24. Ibid., 155 n. 80. Bosworth cites as examples Barth, Lemke, Walsh, Van Winkle, and Gunneweg.
25. Ibid., 137.
26. Van Seters, 'On Reading', 229.

focuses instead on the Bethel prophet's means of deception in v. 18, through which he brings about a change in the man of God's disposition. By stating, 'I also am a prophet like you' (גם־אני נביא כמוך), the old prophet obfuscates the terminological distinction between them that the narrator has been careful to maintain. At the end of that same verse, however, the narrator interjects to clarify that the old prophet ought not be trusted. But how are we to understand the shift from hostility (between the king and the man of God in the opening scene) to hospitality (between the old prophet and the man of God)? What indicators in the wider history might serve to explain the Bethelite's (apparent) amicability? For Bosworth, a proper understanding of the wider narrative again illuminates details in the *mise-en-abyme*. Following the border skirmishes between Israel and Judah in 1 Kings 11–21, Judah and Israel collaborate for two joint military expeditions (1 Kgs 22; 2 Kgs 3) during a period of unwarranted alliance:

> Since Israel is the more powerful kingdom, it assumes the position of leadership in the alliance. Instead of drawing Israel away from the worship of Baal, the alliance leads Judah into it. Jehoshaphat's desire for unity is not necessarily wrong, but Judah can have no real friendship with Israel while Israel follows the sin of Jeroboam and also worships Baal. A precondition of real unity is the cultic centrality of Jerusalem and the political leadership of the house of David. The alliance, like the fellowship between the old prophet and the man of God, is based on a lie and cannot stand.[27]

Regarding the joint military expedition in 1 Kings 22, Bosworth perceives Jehoshaphat's claim, 'I am as you are, my army as your army, my horse as your horses' (1 Kgs 22.4), as an echo of the northern prophet's statement, 'I also am a prophet like you'. Moreover, Bosworth seeks to show that in 1 Kings 22 and 2 Kings 3, the prophetic figures in those narratives are the ones who expose the distinction between north and south and thereby undermine the proposed alliance. 'As with 1 Kings 13, the prophetic conflict [in 1 Kgs 22] serves to illuminate the problem of the divided monarchy, not the problem of false prophecy.'[28] Bosworth's point is that the alliance between Judah and Israel is doomed to fail. It is discredited by Micaiah in 1 Kings 22 and then again by Elisha in 2 Kings 3, and neither military effort meets with success. Attempts to unite north and south are thus denied, shedding light on 1 Kings 13, where the shared meal also has disastrous consequences. Seen thus, the man of God's decision to renege

---

27. Bosworth, *Story*, 139–40. Bosworth notes that the Chronicler negatively evaluates the north–south alliance more explicitly than Dtr (cf. 2 Chron. 19.2).

28. Ibid., 142.

on the divine command in 1 Kings 13 is due neither to disobedience *nor* stupidity, but – in a literary, symbolic sense – because he foreshadows Judah's compromise within the History of the Divided Kingdom.

(c) *Role-reversal*

Bosworth notes that a significant number of interpreters struggle with 1 Kings 13 because of its apparent immoral – or amoral – quality; at the heart of the narrative, the man of God is punished for being duped while the Bethel prophet who deceived him goes unpunished. To make matters worse, the lying prophet subsequently becomes God's vessel for proclaiming judgment upon the man of God. In this instance also, Bosworth draws on an analogous event in the history of the kingdoms to elucidate the significance of the odd reversal within the *mise-en-abyme*. Just as the prohibited, shared meal between the prophets is interrupted by a reversal (1 Kgs 13.20), so the alliance between north and south is interrupted and reversed by Jehu's rebellion in 2 Kings 9–10. Jehu ends the alliance and purifies Israel of Baal worship (2 Kgs 10.28). Athaliah remains on the throne, however, so that Baal worship is sustained in Judah. By analogy: 'The man of God, like Judah, appears to be the more faithful follower of Yhwh until this reversal. After the reversal, the North becomes more faithful to Yhwh and executes Yhwh's judgment on the now disobedient south.'[29] The confusing reversal of 1 Kgs 13.20 is thus interpreted according to the dynamics of 2 Kings 9–11, so that what happens at the table of the Bethel prophet reflects how '[t]he roles of the two kingdoms are reversed in Jehu's coup'.[30]

(d) *The Lion*

The same part of the history (2 Kgs 9–10) also explains the presence and behaviour of the enigmatic lion in 1 Kings 13. 'The lion prevents the man of God from returning safely home after he has dined in Israel. If he had returned to Judah, then his message against the altar would have been undermined by his communion with the North.'[31] Bosworth suggests that it is best to understand the lion, which punishes the man of God for his disobedience to the threefold command, in light of Jehu's actions. Since Jehu proceeds after destroying the house of Ahab to destroy the house of Ahaziah of Judah, including 42 of his relatives who are visiting Samaria, Bosworth avers that 'Jehu is like the lion that executes Yhwh's

---

29. Ibid., 143.
30. Ibid., 145.
31. Ibid., 143.

judgment concerning the man of God'.[32] These parallels do not account, however, for the unusual *restraint* of the lion, which is perhaps even more perplexing than its function as an instrument of judgment.

(e) *A Shared Grave*

A final oddity in the narrative is the Bethel prophet's request (made to his sons) that upon his death his bones be laid beside the bones of the man of God (1 Kgs 13.31). What can he possibly hope to gain from such an arrangement? The plain sense of the narrative seems to be that he has recognised the authenticity of the man of God (not least because of his own prophetic word against him!) and therefore confirms that the man of God's words shall indeed come to pass in due course. On that basis, he perhaps wishes to be identified with his 'brother' in death. But in light of 2 Kings 23, Bosworth explains, there is a deeper significance to his request:

> The story of the two prophetic figures continues to mirror the history of the two kingdoms. This reflection may be seen in two different ways. First, just as the man of God saves the old prophet's bones from desecration, so the king of Judah saves the remnant of the North from the sin of Jeroboam. This incident shows that Israel can hope for salvation only through Judah. Second, the two prophetic figures sharing a common tomb may be likened to the two nations sharing a common exile in Mesopotamia.[33]

Once again, the perplexing detail in the *mise-en-abyme* is illuminated by the history's climax in the reforms of Josiah.

In this brief summation of his argument, it is evident that Bosworth is less concerned about making sense of 1 Kings 13 as an isolated story than about the (far more complex) matter of apprehending the obscure details of 1 Kgs 13.11-32 and 2 Kgs 23.15-20 in light of the larger history of which it is a part. And generally speaking, he succeeds in offering an insightful reading of the whole that makes sense of some obscure details.

Appraisal of Bosworth

Bosworth's intention, explicitly stated in his article but implicit also in his monograph, is to expand 'Barth's interpretation in directions not previously developed in an attempt to make his exegesis more plausible

---

32. Ibid., 144.
33. Ibid., 147.

so that future research may explore its implications'.[34] Since Barth did not elaborate upon the details of this analogy, Bosworth has sought to fill this gap by showing 'how Barth's claims concerning 1 Kings 13 may be supported by the evidence of the history of the divided kingdom as told in Kings'.[35]

Bosworth is very clear about his goal, and there is much that is useful in his analysis. However, since Bosworth presents his work as being consistent, even a *development*, of Barth's exegetical project, it is important to distinguish between those aspects of Bosworth's work that follow the trajectory of Barth's reading from developments that are quite original to Bosworth. In my judgment, Bosworth's expansion of Barth's exegesis is interesting and significant in its own right, and it certainly complements Barth's reading in important ways, but ultimately Bosworth's interpretive aims and methodology are distinct from those of Barth.

A Literary or Theological Analogy?

First, Bosworth's understanding of 1 Kings 13 as a *mise-en-abyme* puts the focus on literary elements and their counterpoints rather than on a theological dialectic that undergirds the relational dynamic between north and south, which was surely what Barth sought to draw out. In his article, Bosworth rightly identifies Barth's central insight: 'that the man of God and the old prophet represent the kingdoms from which they come', and that the 'interactions between these two characters prefigure the relationship between the two kingdoms.[36] He then cites the following key sentence from the opening of Barth's exegesis:

> The peculiar theme of the chapter is the manner in which the man of God and the prophet belong together, do not belong together, and eventually and finally do belong together; and how the same is true of Judah and Israel.[37]

But what Barth describes as a theological and relational dynamic within the text, Bosworth develops as a chronological sequence. It is entirely legitimate for Bosworth to make this methodological move, of course, but from his stated intention I suspect that Bosworth considers his reading to be more consistent with Barth than it is. By mapping five shifts in the *mise-en-abyme*'s plot onto the history of the divided kingdom (as

34. Ibid., 360.
35. Ibid., 381.
36. Ibid., 367.
37. Barth, *CD* II.2, 393.

per the table above), Bosworth does not bring us closer to the substance of Barth's reading, which highlights election, but in fact leads us away from it – in a more literary and less theological direction, one might say. To be clear, I do not wish to undermine Bosworth's fascinating study, but only to point out that he is doing something quite different – and to be sure, many readers will find his literary emphasis more persuasive than the theological accent of Barth's exposition.

Barth's point in the sentence cited above does not refer to *sequential* or chronological shifts in the narrative; i.e. together, then not together, then together again. Rather, his point is that 'because of the division [between north and south] there are...authentic relations in the history of Israel'.[38] To Barth, the significance of the confrontations and exchanges between the representative figures in 1 Kings 13 is not that each reversal has its direct analogue in the history that follows, but rather that the reciprocal dynamic between the (elect and non-elect) prophets accentuates the same dynamic between the (elect and non-elect) nations in the Old Testament historical books. *The purpose of the analogical relationship between prophets from north and south on the one hand, and Israel and Judah on the other, is to show that although the two ultimately belong together, it is their divinely ordained division that in some sense makes unity possible.* The story's role reversals are thereby an expression of the way in which division between true and false Israel is what makes genuine 'speech and hearing' (i.e. love) possible.[39] God wills that Israel and Judah be one, but distinguishes between them for the sake of this very will. Within this conceptual framework, Barth is able to explain why the rejected and elect act on behalf of one another in numerous ways:

> The man of Judah has not ceased to be the elect, nor has the prophet of Bethel ceased to be the rejected. But in their union as elect and rejected they form together the whole Israel from which the grace of God is not turned away. For the rejected acts on behalf of the elect when he takes over the latter's mission. And the elect acts on behalf of the rejected when he suffers the latter's punishment. Similarly, at the end, the rejected acts for the elect by making his own grave a resting-place for the latter. While again the elect acts for the rejected in that the bones of the latter are kept and preserved for his sake, and together with his own bones. *It is exactly the same with the distinction and mission of the true Israel.* It is betrayed in this way by itself, and yet also honoured in this way by God. What better thing can overtake the true Israel than this humiliation and this exaltation?[40]

38. Barth, *CD* II.2, 403.
39. Ibid., 404.
40. Ibid., 406 (emphasis added).

Within Barth's broader argument concerning election in the Old Testament, the distinction between true and false within Israel coincides with the way in which David and Saul 'belong together, and together attest the one true king of Israel',[41] and similarly with the way in which 'the creatures of the sacrificial liturgy, the two goats and two birds, certainly attest together the sacrifice and priestly ministry entrusted to Israel, and yet remain two figures'.[42] The distinction between Israel and Judah in 1 Kings 13 is certainly decisive for Barth, but this is so because of the dialectical theology (of election) to which the story bears witness, not because it provides a series of veiled parallels to events in the historical record of Israel and Judah. The punchline of Barth's exegesis makes it very clear that the story ends with these two representative prophets together in a grave, sharing a common fate, and their bones represent the deaths of the two prophets and the two Israels, which are restored to life in the resurrection of Christ. 'In this one prophet the two prophets obviously live. And so, too, do the two Israels – the Israels which in our story can finally only die, only be buried, only persist for a time in their bones.'[43] Just as the prophets end up in a grave that points to Christ, so too, do the nations of Israel and Judah. In Barth's reading, their shared exilic grave is 'answered' and fulfilled in Jesus.

Thus, although Bosworth sets out to make Barth's exegesis more plausible, he takes it in a different direction. Bosworth's study proceeds from the observation that 'Barth did not make this analogy clear by explaining *how* the kingdoms mirror the individuals in 1 Kings 13',[44] but the most likely reason Barth did not delineate any such analogies is because Barth did not consider each turn in the narrative to have a corresponding turn in the larger history. Had Barth understood 1 Kings 13 in this way, it is more than likely that he would have made this clear. At the risk of repeating myself, it is perfectly legitimate for Bosworth to take Barth's work as a catalyst for exploration and to proceed in an alternative direction, but it is important to recognise that Bosworth's agenda and priorities differ from those of Barth.[45] In Barth's exegesis, the significance of the multiple reversals in the story is not that each turn in the plot has a distinct parallel in the history of the divided kingdom, but

---

41. Ibid., 408.
42. Ibid.
43. Ibid., 409.
44. Bosworth, 'Revisiting', 381 (emphasis added).
45. U. Simon also identifies 'multiple reversals' in 1 Kgs 13, based on his unique structural analysis of the story. Simon, 'Prophetic Sign', 130, 146. See the tables on 137–9.

rather that this dynamic of repeated reversals elucidates the relationship between Judah and Israel, whose interdependence makes genuine unity possible. Although Barth does describe 1 Kings 13 as a kind of introduction ('in title-form') to the history that follows, he consistently makes it clear that he is referring to the narrative's function according to his theological interpretation (i.e. regarding election and unity) rather than to a chronological sequence of events encoded into the history of Judah and Israel.

Having said all of this, Bosworth's detailed literary observations *can* serve to establish Barth's rather general suggestion of a correlation between the prophetic figures in 1 Kings 13 and the nations whence they come. The critical issue is what the reader infers from these parallels, according to their own interpretive interests. For Barth, the significance of the reciprocal dynamic, together with other similar Old Testament trajectories, is its delineation of a theological reality, whereas for Bosworth the reversals point to a literary pattern in the ensuing history of the kingdoms. So, while Bosworth has succeeded in substantiating Barth's core observation from a literary standpoint, each reader must decide for themselves whether to appropriate the evidence as Bosworth intends.

Christological Focus

A second way that Bosworth endeavours to make Barth's exegesis more viable to contemporary scholarship is by dissociating it from an explicitly christological accent. Thus, he states: 'Barth's interpretation of the Old Testament texts can not be characterised as christological. Christological statements are absent from the interpretation of 1 Kings 13.'[46] In saying this, Bosworth perhaps hopes to defend Barth against the charge of eisegesis – though it is doubtful that Barth would have seen the need to defend himself thus. However, it cannot be overlooked that in this section of the *Church Dogmatics* under Election, Barth's treatments of various Old Testament texts, culminating in 1 Kings 13, paves the way for a fuller understanding of Jesus Christ as the Elect and Rejected One. Indeed, Barth's theological – or christological – point is that 1 Kings 13, *as Christian Scripture*, points forward to a time when God's will for a unified Israel will be fulfilled and achieved by the death and resurrection of the Jesus, 'the Elect of God who is also the bearer of the divine rejection'.[47]

---

46. Bosworth, 'Revisiting', 373.
47. Barth, *CD* II.2, 409.

Significantly, Barth brings his lengthy treatment of 1 Kings 13 to a close with a series of explicit christological statements that show he understands the entire drama and all its constituent elements in the light of Christ:

> [T]he problem of the reality and unity of what is attested by the story is also raised and left unresolved. But this story too, does point to one real subject if Jesus Christ is also seen in it, if at the exact point where this story of the prophets breaks off a continuation is found in the Easter story. The Word of God, which abides for ever, in our flesh; the man of God from Bethlehem in Judah who was also the prophet of Nazareth; the Son of God who was also the king of the lost and lawless people of the north; the Elect of God who is also the bearer of the lost and lawless people of the north; the Elect of God who is also the bearer of the divine rejection; the One who was slain for the sins of others, which He took upon Himself, yet to whom there arose a witness, many witnesses, from the midst of sinners; the One lifted up in whose death all was lost, but who in His death was the consolation and refuge of all the lost – this One truly died and was buried, yet he was not forgotten and finished on the third day, but was raised from the dead by the power of God. In this one prophet the two prophets obviously live. And so, too, do the two Israels – the Israels which in our story can finally only die, only be buried, only persist for a time in their bones. They live in the reality and unity in which they never lived in the Old Testament, but could only be attested. They remain in Him, and in Him the Word of God proclaimed by them remains to all eternity.
>
> Where else do they remain? What else is chapter 1 K. 13 if it is not prophecy? Where else is its fulfilment to be found if not in Jesus Christ? These are the questions which must be answered by those for whom the suggested result of our investigation may for any reason by unacceptable.[48]

From Barth's concluding statements, it is unclear to me how Bosworth can state that 'Christological statements are absent from the interpretation of 1 Kings 13', though I suspect it is related to his advocacy of Barth. In any case, there is no need to defend Barth against those who would accuse him of a christological hermeneutic. He certainly did not feel compelled to do so himself! We noted in the previous section that Bosworth takes an aspect of Barth's interpretation that is viable for narrative-critical scholars (i.e. the multiple reversals in the story) and develops it in order to make Barth's reading more widely accessible and less subject to criticism. But, for better or worse, Bosworth offers something substantially different by disregarding the theological (election) and eschatological (christocentric) elements of Barth's presentation. Bosworth's structural hermeneutic is

48. Ibid.

markedly different from Barth's theological one, and he thereby steers the discussion away from the doctrine of election and its consummation in Christ to a literary consideration of how the relationship between Israel and Judah is depicted in Kings. This is a legitimate move as far as it goes – and Bosworth is entitled to develop Barth's work in a new direction – but it is doubtful that Bosworth ultimately makes *Barth's* exegesis more plausible when he avoids what turn out to the central thrusts of Barth's reading, namely, election and Christology. The problem is perhaps only a matter of awareness; Bosworth gives the impression that his work is consistent with that of Barth, or as he describes it, that he is filling in some of the gaps left by Barth. It may be more accurate to say that Bosworth has made excellent use of some key Barthian insights to develop his own structural analysis that remains within an Old Testament frame of reference.

Mise-en-abyme

A few words about Bosworth's designation of the narrative analogy as *mise-en-abyme* are also in order. What does the identification of 1 Kgs 13.11-32 + 2 Kgs 23.15-20 as a *mise-en-abyme* highlight for the reader? In Bosworth's judgment, the gains of identifying 1 Kings 13 as a 'story within a story' include the following:

i. the *mise-en-abyme* indicates the importance of the relationship between the two kingdoms in the DH; i.e. Dtr's interest in 'all Israel', as compared with the Chronicler's focus on Judah;[49]
ii. there is potential for improved diachronic treatments of the composition of Kings in light of what this synchronic study reveals about, e.g., the role of Josiah in the overall history;[50]
iii. Dtr's particular perspective on the divided kingdoms may be better understood in contradistinction to how other Old Testament books present the division of Israel and Judah. Consequently, this may help to explain what is included and/or excluded from the account in Kings (e.g., the lack of an explicit association between the man of God and the prophet Amos, in spite of numerous links);[51]

49. Bosworth, *Story*, 152.
50. Ibid., 153. Bosworth states that the *mise-en-abyme* 'may indicate that the tale was part of a Josianic edition of the Deuteronomistic History'. Incidentally, my reading of 1 Kgs 13 in Chapter 7 has an opposite diachronic implication, one that counters Cross's double-redaction hypothesis.
51. Ibid., 153–4.

iv. the development of the text as *mise-en-abyme* shows that prophetic and political strands of the DH are intertwined and not distinct;[52]
v. finally, as we noted above in some detail, many of the confusing details of 1 Kgs 13.11-32 are explicable when it is treated as a *mise-en-abyme* that mirrors 1 Kings 11–2 Kings 23.

Identification of genre is an essential step in biblical interpretation, and Bosworth's list of gains for reading the narrative as *mise-en-abyme* is impressive. By way of criticism, however, three points may briefly be noted. First, in my view, Bosworth's delimits his proposal significantly by restricting the *mise-en-abyme* to only the second part of the story in 1 Kings 13 (vv. 11-32) and omitting the final verses (vv. 33-34). For 1 Kgs 13.1-10 surely introduces the notion of *mutual hostility*, the first stage in Bosworth's schema. Moreover, vv. 1-10 and vv. 11-32 are bound together by numerous motifs, including: the repetition of the threefold command (vv. 9, 17, 22); the explanation of judgment in v. 26 that hearkens back to the prophecy of v. 2; and the reiteration of the original prophecy against Bethel in v. 32.[53] By the same token, vv. 33-34 surely provide a logical conclusion to the chapter (in spite of their explicit reference to Jeroboam) and inform the overall schema (e.g., the destruction of Jeroboam's house in v. 34 is fulfilled in 2 Kgs 17.21-23).

A second problem with this reading strategy is that large portions of the history do not fit easily within Bosworth's schema. For instance, the *resumption of hostility* (stage four) that occurs between Israel and Judah after Jehu's coup in 2 Kings 9–10 has no counterpart in the *mise-en-abyme*, as Bosworth acknowledges: 'This phase of the relationship as described in the History of the Divided Kingdom does not clearly correspond to anything in 1 Kgs 13 + 2 Kgs 23:15-20. This stretch of historiography (2 Kings 12–21) may lack a correspondence in 1 Kings 13 because it is not pertinent to the issue of the relationship between Israel and Judah.'[54] Or, from the opposite point of view, '[t]he *mise-en-abyme* duplicates pertinent aspects of the whole, and these wars seem not to be relevant to the presentation of the relations between the kingdoms because of their anomaly'.[55] Perhaps this is because Bosworth's proposal attempts to account for everything in a chronological and schematised way. His suggestions make sense of a number of the story's odd details, as we have seen. But to force a rigid template over 1 Kgs 13.11-32 + 2 Kgs 23.15-20

52. Ibid., 155.
53. DeVries, *1 Kings*, 169–70.
54. Bosworth, *Story*, 146.
55. Ibid.

and the History of the Divided Kingdom does not result in a perfect fit, as Bosworth himself acknowledges with regards to the ten-chapter block, 2 Kings 12–21. This is not to say that 1 Kings 13 fails to highlight features of the wider narrative, but the story perhaps does this in a less rigid way than is suggested by Bosworth.

Finally, I am not sure *mise-en-abyme* is the best, i.e. most appropriate, term. Bosworth defines a *mise-en-abyme* quite specifically in terms of 'isolatability', but at the same time, one of his strongest arguments for this literary device is that 1 Kings 13 is only comprehensible when it is read as a political story with wider implications beyond itself.[56] Bosworth's clear intention is to fill a gap in biblical studies, yet his work is arguably less accessible to other scholars because he uses a niche term that is not in wide circulation. In my view, the more widely recognised term, *narrative analogy*, meets all the necessary criteria as an appropriate designation for 1 Kings 13.

All in all, Bosworth's synchronic analysis of the *mise-en-abyme* and the history of the divided kingdom is illuminating. He is certainly right in saying that scholars who concern themselves only with reconstructing pre-Dtr sources behind the story tend to miss any connections it may have with its present context.[57] As well as sparking a renewed interest in Barth's exegesis of 1 Kings 13 (as he intended), Bosworth's suggestion that further research be undertaken regarding *the relationship between Israel and Judah in Kings* is well-placed, since recent studies suggest that this continues to be a fertile field in Old Testament scholarship.[58]

---

56. See esp. his discussion of the moral dilemma at the heart of the story. Ibid., 155–6.

57. Ibid., 120.

58. See, e.g., G. N. Knoppers and J. G. McConville, eds, *Reconsidering Israel and Judah: Recent Studies*, SBTS 8 (Winona Lake, IN: Eisenbrauns, 2000), and Albert de Pury, Thomas Römer, and Jean-Daniel Macchi, eds, *Israel Constructs its History: Deuteronomistic History in Recent Research*, JSOTSup 306 (Sheffield: Sheffield Academic, 2000). More specifically, regarding Israel's national identity as a kingdom divided, see Linville, *Israel in the Book of Kings*; E. T. Mullen, *Narrative History and Ethnic Boundaries: The Deuteronomistic Historian and the Creation of Israelite National Identity*, SemeiaSt 24 (Atlanta: Scholars Press, 1993; J. Gordon McConville, *God and Earthly Power: An Old Testament Political Theology Genesis–Kings* (New York: T&T Clark, 2008).

7

Anonymous Prophets and Archetypal Kings: A Literary-Theological Reading of 1 Kings 13

In this chapter, I offer a literary-theological reading of 1 Kings 13 that takes seriously the analogical dimension of the text that we have seen in the interpretive works of Barth and Bosworth.[1] In summary, I read the story as a proleptic parable that anticipates King Josiah of Judah as the ideological antithesis of King Jeroboam I of Israel. These two archetypal kings are juxtaposed in the narrative and its epilogue in a way that accents the theological significance of their actions for the people of Israel, and provides clear terms of evaluation for all the kings whose reigns occur in the intervening period. At the same time, the fates of their kingdoms are represented in 1 Kings 13 by two anonymous prophetic figures.

The synchronic reading offered here does not depend upon or require a particular view of the redaction of Kings, since it is offered on the level of a text-hermeneutic that prioritises the received text, notwithstanding the contours of its compositional history. Whether 1 Kings 13 represents pre-existing source material (i.e. a prophetic legend) utilised in the composition of the book of Kings, or whether the story was composed and inserted at a later date to serve a particular purpose (as per Van Seters), we cannot know. For my purposes, it does not matter. I agree with Levenson's assertion that attempts to restore textual units to their *historical* context

---

1. A number of readings of 1 Kgs 13 in recent years have suggested links between the man of God from Judah and Jeroboam, mainly that both Jeroboam and the man of God are disobedient and therefore subjected to judgment. E.g., Bodner, *Jeroboam's Royal Drama*, 117; Wray Beal, *1 & 2 Kings*, 115; Mead, 'Kings and Prophets', 197; Cohn, 'Literary Technique', 35. On the surface, this general linkage makes some sense, but it cuts against the prophet–king, north–south, legitimate–illegitimate dualisms in the story.

often result in a loss of *literary* context.² In light of this, my interpretive aim, most simply put, is to read along the grain of the received text, without collapsing its compositional history into a flat, final form. As such, my interpretation takes Israel's theological (re)construction of its own past seriously, à la Brevard Childs, assuming what Levenson has described as 'the literary simultaneity of Scripture';³ i.e. a synchronous engagement with originary (historical) context, literary redaction, and received canon. So while the following reading is guided primarily by literary details, it certainly does not preclude insights garnered from redaction criticism and/or historical evidence. As I have said in the preceding chapters, an emphasis on the text's *poesis* ought not imply a disinterest in matters relating to its *genesis*.

It is my intention to draw from a range of scholarly insights and a repertoire of methods (many of which will be familiar from Chapter 4) to assist in answering the questions I bring to the text. In keeping with my submission in previous chapters concerning the importance of being explicit about one's interpretive priorities and interests, I aim to be clear about my point of view regarding the historical, literary and theological dimensions of the narrative, and about my interpretive aims in reading 1 Kings 13. One methodological supposition I bring, and that I regularly offer students, is that theological insights are often (not always) the reward for being diligent with literary and historical lines of inquiry. It will be clear below that the historical frame of reference and the literary function of the text, as outlined, directly stimulate the theological reading that follows.

Historical Frame of Reference

While the reading offered here operates on the level of a text-hermeneutic, it is informed by some historical suppositions about its composition. This is not to contradict my earlier comments about the dangers of historicising, but rather, more simply, to acknowledge the historical dimension of the text. It will become clear, at any rate, that my historical assumptions are neither radical nor overly speculative.

First, while I acknowledge that the books of Deuteronomy and Kings show evidence of being compiled from various sources and having numerous layers of redaction, I adopt the common scholarly convention

2. Jon D. Levenson, 'The Eighth Principle of Judaism and the Literary Simultaneity of Scripture', *The Journal of Religion* 68, no. 2 (1988): 222.
3. Ibid., 205–25.

of referring to their author(s) as Dtr. Debates concerning the compositional history of the DH continue, and while a good number of scholars continue to think of it as the product of at least a double redaction,[4] no consensus on these matters has been reached.

A central idea for those who have followed Noth's interpretive schema has been that the post-exilic context of the final redactor(s) had a deep and profound impact on the shaping of the record of Israel's history; more precisely, that Josiah's revival of covenant loyalty to 'all the law of Moses' (2 Kgs 23.25) established an ideal in the collective memory of the people, an ideal that was written freely into the DH.[5] Noth observed, for instance, that after the introductory material, the first detailed commandments within the Deuteronomic Law (i.e. those concerning cult centralisation in Deut. 12) receive a large amount of attention throughout the DH because they 'had a disproportionate effect on the actions of Josiah'.[6] On this basis, Noth contends, Dtr came to regard Josiah's reforms as normative so that the prescriptions of the Deuteronomic Law[7] were recounted throughout the DH as the responsibility of kings.[8]

More recently, the pendulum has swung hard in the opposite direction, bringing Noth's conclusions and assumptions under fire.[9] With regards

---

4. E.g., Cross, *Canaanite Myth*, 274–89; Richard Nelson, *The Double Redaction of the Deuteronomistic History*, JSOTSup 18 (Sheffield: JSOT, 1981); idem, 'The Double Redaction of the Deuteronomistic History: The Case is Still Compelling', JSOT 29 (2005): 319–37.

5. Deut. 31.11-12; Josh. 1.8; 8.31-34; 23.6; 24.26; 1 Kgs 2.3; 2 Kgs 10.31; 14.6; 17.13, 34, 37; 21.8; 22.8, 11; 23.24-25. See, e.g., Noth, *The Deuteronomistic History*, 81–2; von Rad, *Studies*, 75–6.

6. Noth, *The Deuteronomistic History*, 81.

7. I.e. Deut. 4.44–30.20 (ibid., 16, passim).

8. A related example of the same principle is the depiction of Joshua as a Josianic figure who rids Canaan of any threats to the worship of Yahweh (e.g., Joshua leads a covenant renewal ceremony in Josh. 8.30-35). For further literature and argumentation, see Richard D. Nelson, 'Josiah in the Book of Joshua', *JBL* 100 (1981): 531–40; Lori L. Rowlett, *Joshua and the Rhetoric of Violence: A New Historicist Approach*, JSOTSup 226 (Sheffield: Sheffield Academic, 1996). Here too, the recent memory of Josiah is understood to have directly influenced the recollection of ancient memories in the life of Israel.

9. The literature can be overwhelming. See the essays in L. S. Schearing and S. L. McKenzie, eds, *Those Elusive Deuteronomists: The Phenomenon of Pan-Deuteronomism*, JSOTSup 268 (Sheffield: Sheffield Academic, 1999), esp. Norbert F. Lohfink, 'Was There a Deuteronomistic Movement?', 36–66; R. Coggins, 'What Does "Deuteronomistic" Mean?', 22–35; and A. G. Auld, 'The Deuteronomists and the Former Prophets, or What Makes the Former Prophets Deuteronomistic?',

to the point above – that Josiah's reforms were heavily influenced by (what we now call) Deuteronomy 12, and that this in turn impacted Dtr's composition of the DH in retrospect – a number of scholars now suggest that Deuteronomy was influenced by Josiah's reforms, and not the other way around.[10] In either case, Sweeney is surely not overstating when he says that '[t]he remarkable narrative about Josiah in the DtrH has proved to be a pivotal text in biblical scholarship and has shaped the entire discipline of Hebrew Bible. It provides the fundamental linchpin by which modern critical scholarship reconstructs the development of Israelite/ Judean religion and the compositional history of much of the biblical literature.'[11] The specifics of those debates lie beyond the aims of this chapter, however, and beyond the scope of this book as a whole, though I happily acknowledge that certain tensions exist between historical reconstructions and the literary record of the DH.[12] Historically, it is difficult to ascertain the extent to which kings were actually responsible for sustaining the relationship between God and the people (cf. Noth[13]),

116–26. Also see Ernst A. Knauf, 'Does "Deuteronomistic Historiography" (DtrH) Exist?', in de Pury, Römer, and Macchi, eds, *Israel Constructs its History*, 388–98; Garry N. Knoppers, 'Rethinking the Relationship between Deuteronomy and the Deuteronomistic History: The Case of Kings', *CBQ* 63 (2001): 393–415; idem, 'The Deuteronomist and the Deuteronomic Law of the King: A Reexamination of a Relationship', *ZAW* 108 (1996): 329–46; Bernard M. Levinson, 'The Reconceptualization of Kingship in Deuteronomy and the Deuteronomistic History's Transformation of Torah', *VT* 51 (2001): 511–34.

10. See Erik Eynikel, *The Reform of King Josiah and the Composition of the Deuteronomistic History* (Leiden: Brill, 1996); Lauren A. S. Monroe, *Josiah's Reform and the Dynamics of Defilement: Israelite Rites of Violence and the Making of a Biblical Text* (New York: Oxford University Press, 2011). Cf. Jon D. Levenson, 'Who Inserted the Book of the Torah?', *HTR* 68 (1975): 203–33.

11. Marvin A. Sweeney, *King Josiah of Judah: The Lost Messiah of Israel* (Oxford: Oxford University Press, 2001), 5.

12. Theories concerning the identity and goals of Dtr (either as an individual or a movement) are also complex. See, e.g., Schearing and McKenzie, eds, *Those Elusive Deuteronomists*; de Pury, Römer, and Macchi, eds, *Israel Constructs its History*; Römer, ed., *The Future of the Deuteronomistic History.*

13. Noth regards Dtr's depiction of kings in the DH, as the ones responsible for covenant adherence, to be 'inaccurate' (*The Deuteronomistic History*, 82). He states, rather, that it was the duty of the people to 'purge the evil from your midst', citing Deut. 13.5; 17.7; 19.19; 21.9, 21; 22.21, 24; 24.27. By the same token, von Rad asks whether 'objective justice was done to these kings' inasmuch as 'they were measured against a norm which did not in fact apply in their time'. Von Rad, *Studies*, 76. If these scholars are right, and Dtr's emphasis on regnal responsibility for the worship

or to verify the historical accuracy of accounts detailing Josiah's reforms (cf. Van Seters[14]). But regardless of where such historical inquiries might lead, what we have in the book of Kings is a nuanced, theological account of the history of the divided kingdom, within which the archetypal status of the two kings introduced in 1 Kings 13 play a vital role.

The key point is that Dtr saw Israel's history through what we might call a Josianic lens, such that Josiah becomes *the archetypal king* for humble obedience, righteous action, and godly leadership.[15] Looking back via Josiah's cultic reforms, Dtr perceived and documented the history of Israel, from Moses' mediatory role in promoting obedience to the law through to Josiah's mediatory role in doing the same.[16] In a sense, Josiah's untimely death made it possible for this repentant reformer to sustain a legacy in Israel through Dtr's record of Israel's history rather than through his short-lived reign.

Literary and Theological Shaping

Erich Auerbach's exploration of *figura* is pertinent to our study, wherein he states that figural interpretation 'establishes a connection between two events or persons in such a way that the first signifies not only itself but also the second, while the second involves or fulfils the first. The two poles of a figure are separated in time, but both, being real events or persons, are within temporality. They are both contained in the flowing stream which

---

practices of the people did not come from Deuteronomy, then it is possible that Dtr's view (especially in Kings) represents an attempt to synthesise Deuteronomic perspectives and sources with royal Jerusalem perspectives and sources, such as those found in the classical prophets and royal psalms.

14. See my engagement with Van Seters in Chapter 5. Also see Philip R. Davies, 'Josiah and the Law Book', in *Good Kings and Bad Kings: The Kingdom of Judah in the Seventh Century BCE*, ed. Lester L. Grabbe (London: T&T Clark, 2005), 65–77.

15. See Alison L. Joseph, *Portrait of the Kings: The Davidic Prototype in Deuteronomistic Poetics* (Minneapolis: Fortress, 2015), who proposes that Dtr uses 'a royal prototype strategy…to construct the portrait of his kings' (55). Joseph's work is stimulating, though her focus on a Davidic prototype, rather than Josianic one, feels somewhat forced when she acknowledges plainly that 'the prototypical David constructed in Kings is modelled on the figure of Josiah, the great reformer, the hero of the book of Kings, and out of whose court the history emerges' (103). See my detailed review in *VT* 67 (2017): 153–7.

16. Richard E. Friedman, *The Exile and Biblical Narrative: The Formation of the Deuteronomistic and Priestly Works*, HSM 22 (Chico, CA: Scholars Press, 1981), 8–10, argues that Moses as lawgiver and Josiah as law-enforcer form an *inclusio* around the first edition of the DH.

is historical life, and only the comprehension, the *intellectus spiritualis*, of their interdependence is a spiritual act.'[17] As for the compositional history that undergirds such figural interpretation, there is much to be gained from attending to Childs' concern with canonical *shaping* (over and against simplistic perceptions of a static final form).[18] To Childs, the forces shaping the canon over time not only drew on various source materials and historical data; they were distinctly *theological* influences, as tradents of the biblical text testified to God's actions in history by making further contributions to existing traditions. Neil MacDonald helpfully outlines the 'historical trajectory of textual redactors' in these terms:

> These redactors received as in a transmission process what turned out to be from the vantage point of the future (relative to them) an incomplete scriptural text. In reception of this text and in witness (sometimes reacting) to the unfolding of God's action in historical time…they added to, or augmented, the then extant but incomplete text. In doing so, they redacted the cumulative output of a historical tradition of previous redactors, who themselves had done exactly the same thing (in algorithmic terms, we have a recursive, historical process).[19]

The result of such a process is a composite final form with a vital depth dimension, as exhibited in 1 Kings 13 and its epilogue (2 Kgs 23.15-20). This pair of texts providing bookends to the history of the kingdoms lend themselves rather naturally to figural interpretation due to the historical trajectories evidenced in the (redacted) text; e.g., the naming of Josiah

---

17. Eric Auerbach, *Mimesis: The Representation of Reality in Western Literature*, trans. Willard R. Trask (Princeton: Princeton University Press, 1953 [German original 1946]), 73. Auerbach means by this latter phrase that a figurative interpretation does not thereby indicate only metaphorical or abstract realities, but also ontic or historical ones.

18. The complexity of Brevard S. Childs' approach has led to various misunderstandings; e.g., the perception that his focus on final form equates to an objection to diachronic approaches (cf. his response in *Biblical Theology of the Old and New Testaments: Theological Reflection on the Christian Bible* [Minneapolis: Fortress, 1992], 104), or that the term 'canonical intentionality' was just another way of talking about authorial intention. See the numerous exchanges between Childs and James Barr, who dubbed canonical intentionality a 'mystic phrase'. Cf. Barr, 'Childs' Introduction', 12–13.

19. Neil B. MacDonald, 'Theological Interpretation, the Historical Formation of Scripture, and God's Action in Time', in *The Bible as Scripture: The Work of Brevard S. Childs*, ed. Christopher R. Seitz and Kent Harold Richards, BSNA 25 (Atlanta: Society of Biblical Literature, 2013), 91–2.

300 years before his time (1 Kgs 13.2), or the anachronistic mention of Samaria (1 Kgs 13.32). In short, I simply understand the final form of Kings to be a product of the exile, written with the end in mind. There is nothing particularly new or startling about this observation since, after all, Kings concludes with Jehoiachin living in exile. But the implications for reading 1 Kings 13 are quite significant, for the man of God from Judah is depicted in ways that signify Josiah, and Josiah – in his life and death – draws out the deeper significance, or fulfilment, of narrative elements foreshadowed by the man of God. I will develop this argument in some detail below, but let us turn first to the framing and the function of 1 Kings 13.

Literary Function

In 1975, Robert Alter lamented the dominance of 'excavative scholarship' and the corresponding dearth of any 'serious literary analysis of the Hebrew Bible'.[20] Since that time, countless articles, books and commentaries have been written in this vein, some covering general questions of method, others offering close readings of Hebrew narratives. Alter's subsequent essays were so well-received that they were collated to form the substance of his now-classic work, *The Art of Biblical Narrative*, in which Alter describes a rhetorical device called 'narrative analogy, through which one part of the text provides oblique commentary on another'.[21] What Alter describes as *narrative analogy*, others have called *mise-en-abyme* (Bosworth[22]), *narrative duplication* (Garsiel[23]), *analogy* or *analogical patterning* (Sternberg[24]), *metaphor plot* (Berman[25]), and *double narratives* (Nahkola[26]). Barth employed none of these technical terms since his exegesis preceded the kind of literary analysis that in now run-of-the-mill in biblical studies. Admittedly, he speaks of

---

20. Alter, 'A Literary Approach to the Bible', *Commentary* 60, no. 6 (1975): 70.
21. Alter, *Art*, 21.
22. Bosworth, *Story*, passim. This French term literally means 'placement in abyss'.
23. Moshe Garsiel, *The First Book of Samuel: A Literary Study of Comparative Structures, Analogies and Parallels* (Ramat-Gan: Revivim, 1985), 28.
24. Sternberg, *Poetics*, 365, 479–80, 542–3.
25. Joshua Berman, *Narrative Analogy in the Hebrew Bible: Battle Stories and their Equivalent Non-battle Narratives*, VTSup 103 (Leiden: Brill, 2004), 6.
26. Aulikki Nahkola, *Double Narratives in the Old Testament: The Foundations of Method in Biblical Criticism* (Berlin: de Gruyter, 2001), passim.

'double-pictures' (*Doppelbildern*) and 'mirroring', but these are used to understand the coherence of 1 Kings 13 as a 'self-contained chapter' rather than to elucidate any parallelism between 1 Kings 13 and related texts.

In any case, as Garsiel rightly observes regarding literary structures, analogies and parallels, '[t]here is no single research approach to the varied material...nor are there clear cut methods for dealing with it'.[27] Rather, 'each case must be taken on its own merits; it would be presumptuous to suggest that a master key can be furnished to every instance throughout the Bible'.[28] By the same token, the selection of terminology often depends on which details the interpreter intends to emphasise when encountering repetition, and upon the exegetical outcomes. Given the nature of my own exegesis and where it leads, I would prefer the term *proleptic parable* to suggest that 1 Kings 13 is a symbolically rich narrative that anticipates Josiah (though I am reluctant to introduce yet another term into the discussion).

Two literary features of the text are of critical importance for understanding 1 Kings 13 as a proleptic parable. The first has to do with how 1 Kings 13 itself *is framed* as a 'self-contained chapter', and the second is concerned with how 1 Kings 13 operates *as a frame* within the book of Kings – the opening bookend, as it were, for the history of the divided kingdoms. We will examine each of these features in turn, noting also how they are related to one another.

The Framing of 1 Kings 13

One of the first things a reader notices about 1 Kings 13 is its formal dissonance, when compared to the preceding and ensuing chapters. It begins and ends with Jeroboam, and thus fits its context, but the episode also brings with it a dramatic shift in tone, language and subject matter. Suddenly this story about two anonymous prophets! One of them is tricked and abruptly killed. There is a lion, a donkey, confirmation of the deceased prophet's oracle, and then...Jeroboam again. The purpose of the narrative is easily lost on students and scholars alike, who thought they were reading an account of Jeroboam's policies upon the division of the kingdoms. Efforts to understand the sudden change in tone have led to manifold theories of redaction (understandably), based on subtleties in the text that might betray an editor's hand.

---

27. Garsiel, *Samuel*, 28.
28. Ibid.

The occurrence of the phrase ויהי הדבר הזה לחטאת ('and this thing became a sin') in 1 Kgs 12.30, and its repetition in 1 Kgs 13.34, is widely recognised as an instance of the rhetorical device known as *Wiederaufnahme*, as noted in Chapter 4.[29] The German word means 'resumptive repetition' and is used by redaction critics to identify seams in the text around an interpolation that functions as an aside.[30] (In classical rhetoric, the same device is known as *epanalepsis*.) The recurrence of this phrase in 1 Kgs 12.30; 13.34 is widely recognised, yet the appellation used to describe and interpret it often depends upon whether the reader prioritises source-oriented or discourse-oriented analysis. McKenzie uses the term *Wiederaufnahme* for his diachronic assessment,[31] whereas Walsh speaks of an *inclusio* according to the rubric of a synchronic approach.[32] This is not to say, however, that the *genesis–poesis* dichotomy is determinative for interpretation, because the question of rhetorical purpose persists, regardless.[33] Robert Cohn uses the term *Wiederaufnahme* to refer to the envelope structure around 1 Kings 13, but proposes that a single author has used 'purposeful repetition' as a literary device to frame the story of the man of God with Jeroboam's sin and its consequences.[34]

---

29. So McKenzie, *Trouble*, 51; Cogan, *1 Kings*, 367; Van Seters, *Death by Redaction?*, 216; Lemke, 'Way of Obedience', 320 n. 31; Knoppers, *Two Nations*, 2:50–1; Van Winkle, '1 Kings XII 25–XIII 34', 102–3; Thomas Römer, *The So-Called Deuteronomistic History: A Sociological, Historical and Literary Introduction* (London: T&T Clark, 2007), 153. The only difference between the two phrases is that in the second instance בַּדָּבָר, replaces הַדָּבָר. But since the ה in 1 Kgs 13.34 is attested in LXX, Syriac, and the Targum(s), and the ב appears at the end of a chapter that contains multiple instances of בְּדָבָר (on which see below), it seems likely that בְּדָבָר in 1 Kgs 13.34 presents a scribal error.

30. This literary-critical device was first explained in detail by C. Kuhl, 'Die "Wiederaufnahme"', though the term was already in use and had indeed been applied to 1 Kgs 13 by G. Hölscher, 'Das Buch der Könige, sein Quellen und seine Redaktion', in *Eucharisterion*, ed. H. Schmidt, FRLANT 36 (Göttingen: Vandenhoeck & Ruprecht, 1923), 387–9. For parade examples, see B. O. Long, 'Framing Repetitions in Biblical Historiography', *JBL* 106 (1987): 385–9.

31. McKenzie, *Trouble*, 53.

32. Walsh, *Old Testament Narrative*, 118.

33. See Shemaryahu Talmon, 'The Presentation of Synchroneity and Simultaneity in Biblical Narrative', in *Studies in Hebrew Narrative Art throughout the Ages*, ed. Joseph Heinemann and Shmuel Werses (Jerusalem: Magnes/Hebrew University Press, 1978), 9–26; Berlin, *Poetics and Interpretation*, 126; Long, 'Framing Repetitions', 386.

34. Cohn, 'Literary Technique', 31 n. 15. An essay by Burke Long considers how a framing (i.e. resumptive) repetition sometimes provides a commentarial excursus.

He thus understands the resumptive repetition to set the story within a particular theological framework – referred to throughout the ensuing history as *the sins of Jeroboam*.³⁵

Before we even get to the story proper, the literary device used to frame it labels Jeroboam as an archetypical evil king – evil because his religiopolitical shortcuts place his subjects directly in harm's way. For not only does Jeroboam set the (very low) standard against which subsequent northern kings are measured, but 'the sins of Jeroboam' (חטאות ירבעם) are consistently reported in such a way as to highlight *the monarch's responsibility for the worship practices of the people*. Significantly, both references to 'this thing' (הדבר הזה) in 12.30 and 13.33, for which Jeroboam is condemned, denote 'the people' (העם) specifically. In 1 Kgs 12.30, *the people* go to Dan and Bethel to worship at Jeroboam's behest, and in 13.33, Jeroboam sins by appointing anyone from among all *the people* to the priesthood. In other words, the narrative in 1 Kings 13 is not only framed by twin references to Jeroboam's sin, but in a way that denotes his ruinous influence over the populace. We will see that this motif of *monarchial responsibility* resonates with both of the archetypal kings mentioned in the story, in addition to its being applied to almost every other king throughout the ensuing history.³⁶

His analysis is especially pertinent to our understanding of 1 Kgs 13. See Long, 'Framing Repetitions', 397. Long's essay seeks to relate instances of resumptive repetition to synchronic narrative theory, beyond labelling them simply as secondary insertions.

35. Given the apparent redaction seams, one possibility is that 1 Kgs 13 existed as pre-Dtr source material that was assimilated into the book of Kings. However, it is equally feasible to view it – as Van Seters suggests – as a story composed at a later date and interpolated to serve a particular purpose. Van Seters, 'Death by Redaction?', 216–17.

36. For northern kings who walked in the way of Jeroboam (or failed to depart from the sin of Jeroboam), they are described as having 'caused Israel to sin' (חטא in the *hiphil*). This applies to Nadab (1 Kgs 15.26), Baasha (1 Kgs 15.34), Omri (1 Kgs 16.26), Ahab (1 Kgs 21.22), Ahaziah (1 Kgs 22.52), Joram (2 Kgs 3.3), Jehoahaz (2 Kgs 13.2, 6), and Jehoash (2 Kgs 13.11). Similarly, when qualifying the more positive evaluations of southern kings, the narrator never simply makes the caveat that 'the high places were not removed', but always goes on to state *why* this is problematic; *viz.* 'the people (העם) continued to sacrifice and make offerings at the high places'. This applies to Jehoshaphat (1 Kgs 22.43), Jehoash (2 Kgs 12.3), Amaziah (2 Kgs 14.4), Azariah (2 Kgs 15.4) and Jotham (2 Kgs 15.35). Hezekiah and Josiah are notable exceptions (2 Kgs 18.22-23).

The Function of 1 Kings 13

In Chapter 4, we observed that the question of multiple context(s), as raised by Walsh, is suggestive for considering how a text's *function* (as well as its meaning) may change in accordance with the range and substance of its referents. In this case, when 1 Kings 13 is treated as a parabolic tale that introduces the history of the divided kingdoms and anticipates Josiah's cultic reforms, it functions less as a self-contained story with a moral than as an interpretive key for the subsequent history. Every story requires its own internal logic, of course, but the literary placement of an episode can also suggest that it bears a hermeneutical function for a broader range of texts and ought therefore to be interpreted accordingly. Well-known in this regard is Wellhausen's list of programmatic speeches that simultaneously recollect the past while looking to the nation's future. The retrospective/prospective function of these texts, as described by Wellhausen and Noth, bears numerous similarities to the function that some scholars, following Barth's suggestive proposal, have attributed to 1 Kings 13. In order to grasp this point, since it provides a vital pre-context for the reading below, we will briefly review some key insights concerning this rhetorical device.

Wellhausen first identified the use of speeches as a unifying structural device appearing throughout the DH in his *Prolegomena zur Geschichte Israels*:

> The great period thus marked off and artificially divided into sub-periods, is surveyed and appraised at every important epoch in sermon-like discourses. These are much more frequent in Kings than in Judges and Samuel. It makes no difference whether the writer speaks in his own person, or by the mouth of another; in reviews of the past he speaks himself, 2 Kings xvii.; in anticipations of the future he makes another speak (1 Kings viii. ix.). A few examples must be cited to show what we mean.[37]

Wellhausen goes on to cite from Solomon's prayer in 1 Kings 8, the prophecy of Ahijah[38] in 1 Kgs 11.31-35, and 2 Kings 17, before commenting thus: 'The water accumulates, so to speak, at these gathering places of the

---

37. J. Wellhausen, *Prolegomena to the History of Ancient Israel* (Cambridge: Cambridge University Press, 2013 [1885]), 274.

38. The text [ET] reads, 'a prophecy of Abijah to the first Jeroboam' (ibid., 275), though it is quite obvious that 'Ahijah' is intended. The same error occurs on p. 279, and in both cases the German also erroneously reads 'Abijah'.

more important historical epochs; but from these reservoirs it finds its way in smaller channels on all sides'.[39] Sixty-five years later, Noth popularised this observation in his pivotal work, *Überlieferungsgeschichtliche Studien* (1943), where he observed Dtr's use of speeches, prayers (Josh. 1; 23; 1 Sam. 12; and 1 Kgs 8) and direct commentary (Josh. 12; Judg. 2.11-23; 2 Kgs 17.7-23) throughout the history to evaluate Israel's progress or regress in relation to God.[40]

In light of the strategic placement of these texts, scholars noticed an unusual hiatus around 1 Kings 11–14, which narrates one of the worst political debacles in Israelite history. Plöger, for instance, registers his surprise that 'in the presentation of the time extending from the dedication of the Temple to the Ephraimite catastrophe, no further summary homily from the pen of the Deuteronomist is to be found, although an event such as the so-called division of the kingdom under Solomon's successor, Rehoboam, would have been serious enough to warrant it'.[41] In an effort to justify or explain 'the absence of these introspective pieces' between 1 Kings 8 and 1 Kings 14, Plöger supposes that Dtr 'was probably satisfied with the prophetic proclamations...of the prophet Ahijah of Shiloh in 1 Kgs 11:29ff. and the man of God Shemaiah in 1 Kgs 12:22ff.'.[42] Taking his cues from Wellhausen and Noth, Plöger was convinced 'that the contemplative homilies of the deuteronomistic historian are set forth [exclusively] in the form of speeches'.[43] But it is unnecessary to delimit Dtr to the use of speech forms. To Plöger's concern regarding an apparent lack of theological commentary at a critical juncture in the DH, Lemke responds that 1 Kings 13

---

39. Ibid., 277. Earlier, Wellhausen postulates that 'the author of the Book of Kings himself wrote the prayer of Solomon and the epitome [2 Kgs 17], at least, without Former Prophets borrowing from another source' (223). Similarly, he identifies Judg. 2 and 1 Sam. 12 as the author's introductions to the periods of the judges and kings respectively (246–7).

40. Noth, *The Deuteronomistic History*, 5–6.

41. Otto Plöger, 'speech and Prayer in the Deuteronomistic and the Chronicler's Histories', in Knoppers and McConville, eds, *Reconsidering Israel and Judah*, 34.

42. Ibid. Wellhausen, as cited above, also defers to Ahijah's speech in 1 Kgs 11.31-35, in spite of the fact that these verses do not 'anticipate and recapitulate' in characteristic fashion. Cf. Noth, *The Deuteronomistic History*, 76.

43. Plöger, 'speech and Prayer', 35. Plöger considers it strange for the narrator to offer direct commentary in 2 Kgs 17.7-18, when in 2 Kgs 18 the prophet Isaiah would have provided a perfectly suitable voice for such reflection (34).

fills a vacuum which has been felt by many. It would be remarkable, to say the least, if as important an event in the history of Israel as the division of the kingdom, with its ensuing religious schism, and the establishment of those cultic practices which led to the eventual downfall of Israel should have received only passing attention from the Deuteronomistic Historian... If we are correct, however, I Kings 13 fulfills precisely the kind of function Plöger was looking for. To be sure, it is not a speech like I Sam. 12, nor a prayer like I Kings 8, nor a free commentary like II Kings 17:7-20. Rather, it is a narrative with considerable action, suspense and movement, but heavily interlaced with dialogue and speeches by its main characters. The particular vehicle chosen by the Deuteronomist to make his point was dictated, here as elsewhere, by his available sources.[44]

Some aspects of Lemke's arguments are less convincing,[45] but I fully agree with his overall judgment 'that 1 Kings 13 forms an integral part of the structure and theology of the Deuteronomistic History'.[46] Similarly, Steven McKenzie acknowledges the potential gains of adding 2 Samuel 7 and 1 Kings 13 'to the series of speeches and narratives in Deuteronomistic style which provide structure for the DH'[47] due to their location and content. For just as the well-intentioned man of God in 1 Kings 13 is deceived and killed in an unexpected fashion, so Josiah dies an untimely death and Judah is not spared from divine judgment. In Josiah – and by analogy, in the man of God from Judah – we see the unavoidable consequences of Israel's broken covenant with Yahweh. Like Israel's act of adultery on her 'wedding night' at Sinai (the memory of which is evoked by the golden calves), the period of the monarchy commences with law-breaking and is therefore destined for ruin. In this sense, 1 Kings 13 serves a retrospective and a prospective function, not unlike Dtr's speeches. In summary, then, the framing of the story (via 'resumptive repetition') and a consideration of its didactic function lead to the conclusion that 1 Kings 13 functions as a programmatic text, or hermeneutical key, within the book of Kings.

44. Lemke, 'The Way of Obedience', 325–6 n. 103.
45. E.g., Lemke dates particular words and phrases to ascertain authorship and assumes that 1 Kgs 13 is derived from source material, but it is equally plausible that Dtr *composed* the story to suit his purposes (cf. the methodological discussion in Chapter 5).
46. Lemke, 'Way of Obedience', 304.
47. S. McKenzie, *The Chronicler's Use of the Deuteronomistic History*, HSM 33 (Atlanta: Scholars Press, 1985), 2; Dennis McCarthy, 'II Samuel 7 and the Structure of the Deuteronomistic History', *JBL* 84 (1965): 131–8, argues that 2 Sam. 7 is such a text as well. Cf. Cross, *Canaanite Myth*, 241–64.

1 Kings 13 as Opening Bookend

The structural importance of the Jeroboam cycle (1 Kgs 11–14) at the beginning of the history of the divided kingdoms is self-evident, since the history hearkens back to 'the sin of Jeroboam' again and again in its evaluation of northern kings and in its explanation for the fall of the north (2 Kgs 17.21-22). Similarly, there is a general consensus among scholars about the structural significance of the Josiah narrative (2 Kgs 22–23) as a high point in the gloomy record of Israel's monarchy. When the narrative is framed (broadly) like this, these two figures provide 'bookends' to the history of the divided kingdom, and it is significant that each archetypal king is mentioned in the narrative focusing on the other (1 Kgs 13.2; 2 Kgs 23.16). Their antithetical modes of engagement with the book of the law are repeatedly juxtaposed to serve Dtr's theologically constructive task. As Everett Fox puts it, Jeroboam 'emerges as a kind of model sinner',[48] whereas Josiah has been described as 'the best king ever'![49]

In accordance with Cross's observation, that Dtr 'is fond of bracketing events and periods with an explicit theological framework',[50] the anonymous prophets and archetypal kings featured in 1 Kings 13 present a stylised account of the history of Israel and Judah that simultaneously presents the fates of the kingdoms whilst urging covenant-faithfulness from future leaders for the sake of the people. Jeroboam and Josiah are juxtaposed within this highly symbolic story at the beginning of the history of the kingdoms, providing the reader with a theological framework for evaluating the monarchy through the use of formulaic statements.[51] Northern kings are compared to Jeroboam with reference to 'the sin he caused Israel to commit', and southern kings are evaluated against Josiah's reforms with the more lengthy formula, 'But/yet/nonetheless/however/only (ו or רק) the high places were not removed; the people still sacrificed and made offerings on the high places'. In order to present these archetypes side by side from the outset, the man of God is depicted *as Josiah* and set against Jeroboam in a rather dramatic conflict. The table below highlights the use of the judgment formulae to evaluate kings against the archetypes of Jeroboam and Josiah:

---

48. Everett Fox, *The Early Prophets*, The Schocken Bible 2 (New York: Schocken, 2014), 631.
49. Nelson, *First and Second Kings*, 252.
50. Cross, *Canaanite Myth*, 288.
51. For a comprehensive redaction-critical treatment of the judgment formulae, see Provan, *Hezekiah*, 33–90. A more recent literary approach to evaluating the kings is Joseph, *Portrait of the Kings*.

NORTH	Evaluated against Jeroboam	SOUTH	Evaluated against Josiah
Jeroboam	[The LORD] will give Israel up because of **the sins of Jeroboam**, which he sinned and **which he caused Israel to commit**' (1 Kgs 14.16) (cf. 1 Kgs 12.30; 13.34)	**Josiah**	Moreover, the altar at Bethel, the high place erected by Jeroboam son of Nebat, who caused Israel to sin – **he pulled down that altar along with the high place. He burned the high place**, crushing it to dust... Moreover, **Josiah removed all the shrines of the high places** that were in the towns of Samaria, which kings of Israel had made (2 Kgs 23.15, 19a)
Nadab	He did what was evil in the sight of the LORD, **walking in the way of** his ancestor and **in the sin that he caused Israel to commit** (1 Kgs 15.26)		
Baasha	He did what was evil in the sight of the LORD, **walking in the way of Jeroboam** and **in the sin that he caused Israel to commit** (1 Kgs 15.34)		
Elah	because of all the sins of Baasha and the sins of his son Elah that they committed, and **that they caused Israel to commit**, provoking the LORD God of Israel to anger with their idols (1 Kgs 16.13)		

NORTH	Evaluated against Jeroboam	SOUTH	Evaluated against Josiah
Zimri	because of the sins that he committed, doing evil in the sight of the LORD, **walking in the way of Jeroboam**, and for the sin that he committed, **causing Israel to sin** (1 Kgs 16.19)		
Omri	For he **walked in all the way of Jeroboam** son of Nebat, and in **the sins that he caused Israel to commit**, provoking the LORD, the God of Israel, to anger by their idols (1 Kgs 16.26)		
	Elijah cycles (under Ahab)		
Ahab	and I will make your house like **the house of Jeroboam** son of Nebat, and like the house of Baasha son of Ahijah, because you have provoked me to anger and have **caused Israel to sin** (1 Kgs 21.22)	Jehoshaphat	He walked in all the way of his father Asa; he did not turn aside from it, doing what was right in the sight of the LORD; **yet the high places were not taken away, and the people still sacrificed and offered incense on the high places** (1 Kgs 22.43)
Ahaziah	He did what was evil in the sight of the LORD, and **walked in the way** of his father and mother, and **in the way of Jeroboam** son of Nebat, **who caused Israel to sin** (1 Kgs 22.52)		

7. Anonymous Prophets and Archetypal Kings 175

NORTH	Evaluated against Jeroboam	SOUTH	Evaluated against Josiah
Joram	Nevertheless he clung to **the sin of Jeroboam** son of Nebat, **which he caused Israel to commit**; he did not depart from it. (2 Kgs 3.3)		
	Elisha cycles (under Jehoshaphat)		
		Jehoram	He walked in the way of the kings of Israel, as the house of Ahab had done (2 Kgs 8.18a)
		Ahaziah	He also walked in the way of the house of Ahab, doing what was evil in the sight of the LORD (2 Kgs 8.27a)
Jehu	But Jehu was not careful to follow the law of the LORD the God of Israel with all his heart, he did not turn from **the sins of Jeroboam, which he caused Israel to commit** (2 Kgs 10.31)	Joash [Jehoash]	**Nevertheless the high places were not taken away; the people continued to sacrifice and make offerings on the high places** (2 Kgs 12.3)
Jehoahaz	He did what was evil in the sight of the LORD, and followed **the sins of Jeroboam** son of Nebat, **which he caused Israel to sin**; he did not depart from them (2 Kgs 13.2)		

NORTH	Evaluated against Jeroboam	SOUTH	Evaluated against Josiah
Jehoash	He also did what was evil in the sight of the LORD; <u>he did not depart from</u> all **the sins of Jeroboam** son of Nebat, **which he caused Israel to sin**, but **he walked in them** (2 Kgs 13.11)	Amaziah	**But the high places were not removed; the people still sacrificed and made offerings on the high places** (2 Kgs 14.4)
Jeroboam II	He did what was evil in the sight of the LORD; <u>he did not depart from</u> all **the sins of Jeroboam** son of Nebat, **which he caused Israel to sin** (2 Kgs 14.24)	Azariah	**Nevertheless the high places were not taken away; the people still sacrificed and made offerings on the high places** (2 Kgs 15.4)
Zechariah	He did what was evil in the sight of the LORD, as his ancestors had done. <u>He did not depart from</u> **the sins of Jeroboam** son of Nebat, **which he caused Israel to sin** (2 Kgs 15.9)		
Menahem	He did what was evil in the sight of the LORD; <u>he did not depart all his days from</u> any of **the sins of Jeroboam** son of Nebat, **which he caused Israel to sin** (2 Kgs 15.18) *Shallum's one-month reign prior to Menahem is not evaluated.		

NORTH	Evaluated against Jeroboam	SOUTH	Evaluated against Josiah
Pekahiah	He did what was evil in the sight of the LORD; <u>he did not turn away from</u> **the sins of Jeroboam** son of Nebat, **which he caused Israel to sin** (2 Kgs 15.24)		
Pekah	He did what was evil in the sight of the LORD; <u>he did not depart from</u> **the sins of Jeroboam** son of Nebat, **which he caused Israel to sin** (2 Kgs 15.28)	Jotham	**Nevertheless the high places were not removed; the people still sacrificed and made offerings on the high places** (2 Kgs 15.35a)
		Ahaz	**He sacrificed and made offerings on the high places, on the hills, and under every green tree** (2 Kgs 16.3-4)
Hoshea	Instead of evaluating Hoshea, the narrator concludes the record of Israel's kings by identifying Jeroboam as the root cause of its demise: 'When he had torn Israel from the house of David, they made Jeroboam son of Nebat king. Jeroboam drove Israel from following the LORD and **made them commit great sin. The people of Israel continued in all the sins that Jeroboam committed;** <u>they did not depart from them</u>' (2 Kgs 17.21-22)		

NORTH	Evaluated against Jeroboam	SOUTH	Evaluated against Josiah
		Hezekiah	Note that the report on Hezekiah is a reversal of the norm: '**He removed the high places**, broke down the pillars, and cut down the sacred pole. He broke in pieces the bronze serpent that Moses had made, for **until those days the people of Israel had made offerings to it**; it was called Nehushtan' (2 Kgs 18.4)
		Manasseh	The report on Manasseh reverses Hezekiah's reforms (see above) and even uses the northern formulation (an isolated occurrence): 'For **he rebuilt the high places** that his father Hezekiah had destroyed; he erected altars for Baal, made a sacred pole, as King Ahab of Israel had done…besides the sin **that he caused Judah to sin** so that they did what was evil in the sight of the LORD' (2 Kgs 21.3a, 16b)
		Amon	There is no evaluation of Amon's two-year reign; he is simply likened to his father
		Josiah	[see top of table]

7. *Anonymous Prophets and Archetypal Kings*

NORTH	Evaluated against Jeroboam	SOUTH	Evaluated against Josiah
		Jehoahaz, Jehoiakim, Jehoiachin, Zedekiah	As one might expect, there are no further comparisons with Josiah or references to the high places that he destroyed

The use of the judgment formulae throughout the history of the kingdoms clearly reinforces the notion that Jeroboam and Josiah provide an evaluative matrix for assessing Israel's and Judah's kings. A couple of observations merit our attention:[52]

The generic phrase, 'sins of Jeroboam', is used for assessing northern kings. The narrative does not attend to a new king's policies, nor the people's response; the only criterion that appears to matter is whether the king turned (סור) from sins of the past that continue to lead the people astray.[53] Jeroboam continues to be named and blamed for the systemic corruption of worship practices.

For Judean kings, the wording of the formula presupposes knowledge of Josiah. Often, the statement 'X did what was right in the sight of the LORD...' is followed immediately by the formulaic evaluation: '*However* (רק) the high places were not removed...' In other words, just as the northern formula evokes the sin of Jeroboam, the southern formula measures kings against the exact reforms for which Josiah was remembered; i.e. removing the high places. Moreover, the formula does not merely consist of the caveat, 'yet the high places were not removed', but also includes an explicative statement about *why* this is problematic: because 'the people continued to sacrifice and make offerings at the high places'.

Overall, it is clear that the two kings who feature in 1 Kings 13 are deliberately introduced as measuring sticks for the monarchial record. The repeated formulaic patterns are obvious enough, but the implications of

---

52. Of course, there are some exceptions to the norm (e.g., Hezekiah and Manasseh; Jehoram and Ahaziah), and many of these are of interest precisely *because* they deviate from the formula, though they are of limited value for my argument here. Such variations have typically been used to support redaction theories (cf. Provan, *Hezekiah*; but see Joseph, *Portrait*).

53. The idea is expressed in two ways. In 1 Kings, it tends to be described as 'walking in the way of Jeroboam' (e.g., 1 Kgs 16.19: ללכת בדרך ירבעם); in 2 Kings, with 'he did not depart from the sins of Jeroboam' (e.g., 2 Kgs 15.24: לא סר מחטאות ירבעם).

the particular phrases used also have significance.⁵⁴ We have seen that the framing repetition around 1 Kings 13 ('and this thing became a sin') not only establishes Jeroboam as the archetype of a bad king; it introduces a vital theological link between 1 Kings 13 and the ensuing history as the first sounding of a monotonous drum that will continue to beat throughout the history of the kingdoms with little variation, as 'the sin of Jeroboam, which he sinned and which he caused Israel to commit' (1 Kgs 14.16).⁵⁵

Structural observations about the importance of Josiah, on the other hand, have typically not offered much help for interpreting 1 Kings 13, but this is surely because the mention of Josiah's name in 1 Kgs 13.2 is so frequently glossed over as an anachronism rather than as an interpretive clue. In the reading below, I shall argue that Josiah is presented in 1 Kings 13 *via the man of God from Judah* as the archetype of a righteous king, with obvious implications for the ensuing history.

Following the exegetical treatment of the text(s) below, I will conclude this chapter by considering the implications of my reading for constructive theological interpretation. I would prefer not to separate theology from exegetical work (due in part to my convictions as a preacher), but in this particular case, the story's purpose has more to do with its hermeneutical function for understanding the book as a whole than with providing the

---

54. Attempts to discern whether Dtr understood the (northern) sins of Jeroboam to be intrinsically different from the (southern) sins committed at high places – i.e. was one more idolatrous than the other? – miss the theological point of these literary features. E.g., Provan, *Hezekiah*, 61–5.

55. On the significance of this phrase and its variations, which appear repeatedly throughout the history, see E. T. Mullen, 'The Sins of Jeroboam: A Redactional Assessment', *CBQ* 49 (1987): 213 n. 3; Van Winkle, '1 Kings XII 25–XIII 34', 105. Regarding the world of the text, there is no consensus on what is meant by הדבר הזה in 12.30 and 13.34. One could infer from 1 Kgs 12.30b that the phrase refers to those Israelites who have begun to worship in Bethel and Dan, so that 'this thing' (as well as the 20+ references in Kings to 'the sin that Jeroboam caused Israel to commit') is understood as 'the eschewing of Jerusalem' (Bodner, *Royal Drama*, 93). Alternatively, in light of what is common to both contexts (12.30; 13.33), one could understand 'this thing' to refer to Jeroboam's *ad hoc* appointment of priests. However, other texts seem less ambiguous about the precise nature of Jeroboam's sins. In 1 Kgs 14, Ahijah speaks directly of idolatry: 'you have done evil above all those who were before you and have gone and made for yourself other gods, and cast images, provoking me to anger, and have thrust me behind your back' (1 Kgs 14.9). Along similar lines, in 2 Kgs 10.29, 'the sins of Jeroboam son of Nebat, which he caused Israel to commit' are directly identified with 'the golden calves in Bethel and in Dan'. In these verses, the issue of centralisation is less in focus than that of false idols, though it may generally be said that in either case the issue pertains to right worship.

reader with a moral or theological lesson per se. (1 Kings 13 effectively illustrates how unhelpful it is to assume that all biblical passages serve the same purpose in this regard!) Having said this, the book of Kings is clearly a thoroughly theological work with vital implications for today's church and world, and to this we shall return. But first, to the text.

A Literary-Theological Reading of 1 Kings 13

In the following section, I continue to cite the NRSV. It is well-known that the DH presents the simplest Hebrew in the Hebrew Bible, and 1 Kings 13 is no exception. For the majority of these verses, then, my own translation differs very little from the NRSV, and there is no need to add yet another Bible translation to the proliferation of options already available. My purpose is not to offer a text-critical or philological analysis, but I shall nonetheless make it clear in my comments when an alternative translation of a word or phrase is preferred.

The story's boundaries are more complex than I have perhaps indicated thus far by referring simply to '1 Kings 13'. The closure of the pericope in 13.33-34 is clear, and 14.1 certainly marks the beginning of a new unit. But where our story begins is less straightforward, since 13.1 commences with והנה – 'But look!' – which signifies a change in perspective but never the beginning of a new textual unit.[56] More specifically, והנה is a *presentative exclamation* that serves 'as a bridge for a logical connection between [the] preceding clause and the clause it introduces'.[57] 1 Kings 12.33 appears to mark the beginning of a new section in that it repeats almost everything in v. 32, emphasising that the festival, the date and the sacrifice are all of Jeroboam's design. It therefore seems appropriate to treat 12.33–13.34 as a textual unit.[58] While this adds only a single verse to 1 Kings 13, it is a sentence that provides והנה with a preceding clause and places Jeroboam's actions within an interpretive frame of reference.

For our exegesis, it is equally important to gain a sense of the broader literary context into which the man of God suddenly arrives. The narrative about Rehoboam's intention to go to war concludes in 1 Kgs 12.24, and the pericope beginning in 12.25 narrates Jeroboam's building projects in Shechem and Penuel, undertaken to fortify himself against a removal

---

56. So Gross, 'Lying Prophet', 100.

57. Bruce K. Waltke and Michael P. O'Connor, *Introduction to Biblical Hebrew Syntax* (Winona Lake, IN: Eisenbrauns, 1990), §40.2.d (677). Cf. ibid., §40.2 (674f.) on the functions of *hinne* as a 'presentative exclamation'.

58. So Gray, *I & II Kings*, 318; DeVries, *1 Kings*, 164; Cogan, *1 Kings*, 365; B. Long, *1 Kings*, 143 et al.

from power. The theme of Jeroboam's insecurity is thereby introduced in both geographic and cultic terms in the episode directly preceding 1 Kgs 12.33–13.34. These verses, i.e. 1 Kgs 12.25-32, therefore require some consideration, since they set the scene for a proper understanding of our narrative, which commences in 12.33.[59]

1 Kings 12.25-32

> [25]Then Jeroboam built Shechem in the hill country of Ephraim, and resided there; he went out from there and built Penuel. [26]Then Jeroboam said to himself, 'Now the kingdom may well revert to the house of David. [27]If this people continues to go up to offer sacrifices in the house of the LORD at Jerusalem, the heart of this people will turn again to their master, King Rehoboam of Judah; they will kill me and return to King Rehoboam of Judah'.
>
> [28]So the king took counsel, and made two calves of gold. He said to the people, 'You have gone up to Jerusalem long enough. Here are your gods, O Israel, who brought you up out of the land of Egypt.' [29]He set one in Bethel, and the other he put in Dan. [30]And this thing became a sin, for the people went to worship before the one [at Bethel and before the other][60] as far as Dan.
>
> [31]He also made houses on high places, and appointed priests from among all the people, who were not Levites. [32]Jeroboam appointed a festival on the fifteenth day of the eighth month like the festival that was in Judah, and he offered sacrifices on the altar; so he did in Bethel, sacrificing to the calves that he had made. And he placed in Bethel the priests of the high places that he had made.

After Rehoboam's thwarted attempt to engage in civil war and thereby secure the kingdom for himself (1 Kgs 12.17-24), attention shifts to Jeroboam's efforts to secure his royal appointment. Verse 25 tells of building projects at Shechem and Penuel, strategic for ruling the central hill country and for maintaining a presence both east and west of the Jordan.[61] Then in vv. 26-29, cultic matters take the spotlight, though Jeroboam's

---

59. There are also numerous lexical reasons for treating 1 Kgs 12.25-32 together with 1 Kgs 12.33–13.34, for which see Van Winkle, '1 Kings XII 25–XIII 34'; Sweeney, *I & II Kings*, 178–9.

60. The MT is awkward in v. 30; literally, 'and the people went to worship before the one as far as Dan'. Most modern translations follow Lucian's recension of the Septuagint, which adds the phrase indicated (בית־אל ולפני האחד), following the antecedent in v. 29. Cf. C. F. Burney, *Notes on the Hebrew Text of the Book of Kings* (Oxford: Clarendon, 1902), 177.

61. See Sweeney, *I & II Kings*, 175–7, for geographical particulars.

intentions remain the same. Fearing the loss of his position, he seeks to provide the Israelites with a more convenient access to God, in much the same way that Aaron did. 'You have gone up to Jerusalem long enough!' he declares, as he inaugurates new cultic centres in Bethel and Dan. The DH generally presupposes the authority of Deuteronomic law, but here Jeroboam entirely disregards the commandment in Deut. 12.5 regarding 'the place that the LORD your God will choose'. The narrator's evaluation of these events in v. 30, therefore, is that 'this thing became a sin' precisely because of the information that follows: 'for the people went to worship before the one at Bethel and before the other as far as Dan'.[62] As the history of the kingdoms makes clear with its repeated use of חטא in the *hiphil*, Jeroboam's terrible evil is that he *caused* the people of Israel to sin.[63]

Regarding the theological motif of good/godly leadership, an urgent matter for the post-exilic community, we may also note the nature of (or perhaps the motive for) Jeroboam's sin, especially in connection with the sin of Aaron to which it is so obviously compared.[64] What is at stake in Jeroboam's cultic innovations (and in Aaron's) is the provision of easy access to a more manageable and familiar deity. The consistent demand upon Israel's kings, often communicated via the prophets, is that they must

---

62. See n. 60.

63. Differences of opinion abound on whether, historically speaking, Jeroboam's golden calves might have constituted idolatrous worship, a form of syncretism, or an attempt to revive ancient traditions. But whatever view one takes concerning the world behind the text, the writer's view is unambiguous: Jeroboam's contrived priesthood and festival led the entire nation into sin. For our purposes here, this is the world in focus.

64. It has long been a matter of discussion that these two incidents of golden calves are intertextually linked by the near verbatim citation of the phrase: הנה אלהיך ישראל אשר העלוך מארץ מצרים ('Look! [or: These are] your gods, who brought you up out of the land of Egypt!). Whichever way the borrowing may have occurred, readers are prompted to understand the actions of Aaron and Jeroboam in relation to one another. Martin Noth, *Exodus: A Commentary*, trans. J. Bowden, OTL [Philadelphia: Westminster, 1962], 246, suggests that the plural (referring to Bethel and Dan) indicates that the Exodus passage borrowed from Kings 'to cast aspersion on Jeroboam's cult'; cf. Gray, *I & II Kings*, 316. Moses Aberbach and Leivy Smolar, 'Aaron, Jeroboam and the Golden Calves', *JBL* 86 (1967): 129–40, list 13 points of similarity between Jeroboam and Aaron; Jesse Long, *1 & 2 Kings*, goes a step further, postulating that Jeroboam *consciously* sought to align himself with Aaron (e.g., by naming his sons with almost identical names to Aaron's sons) in order 'to establish a "more conservative" cult for Yahweh that would be anchored in the Exodus traditions and rival Solomon's grand temple in Jerusalem' (166).

not bring trouble upon their people by forsaking the law and worshipping foreign gods, as Ahab the 'troubler of Israel' did so memorably (cf. 1 Kgs 18.18). In keeping with this, 1 Kgs 12.31-32 stresses the lengths to which Jeroboam has gone in breaking the Deuteronomic law. The verses are thick with repetition in an attempt to make one thing abundantly clear: Jeroboam's cultic innovations stand in sharp conflict with the law. The phrase אשר־עשה ('that he had made') occurs four times in vv. 32-33, regarding the altar (×2), the calves, and the high places. The same idea is then communicated a fifth time in the phrase אשר־בדא ('that he had devised') with reference to the festival.[65] Jeroboam makes high places, the sin for which Solomon lost the kingdom; he appoints non-Levitical priests as he sees fit; he inaugurates a new festival 'like the one in Judah'; and he officiates as priest-king, offering sacrifices 'to the calves he had made' (1 Kgs 12.32). The verses preceding 1 Kings 13 thus characterise Jeroboam as a self-serving king whose actions lead his own flock astray, even to their demise.

1 Kings 12.33–13.5

> [33]He went up to the altar that he had made in Bethel on the fifteenth day in the eighth month, in the month that he alone had devised; he appointed a festival for the people of Israel, and he went up to the altar to offer incense – [1]But look![66] – a man of God came out of Judah by the word of the LORD to Bethel while Jeroboam was standing by the altar to offer incense, [2]and he proclaimed against the altar by the word of the LORD, and said, 'O altar, altar, thus says the LORD: "A son shall be born to the house of David, Josiah by name; and he shall sacrifice on you the priests of the high places who offer incense on you, and human bones shall be burned on you"'. [3]He gave a sign the same day, saying, 'This is the sign that the LORD has spoken: "The altar shall be torn down, and the ashes that are on it shall be poured out"'.
>
> [4]When the king heard what the man of God cried out against the altar at Bethel, Jeroboam stretched out his hand from the altar, saying, 'seize him!' But the hand that he stretched out against him withered so that he could not

---

65. All of these cultic improvisations are presented in a manner consistent with the Deuteronomic law's focus on preventing cultic distortions, rather than cultic observance; cf. Noth, *The Deuteronomistic History*, 93.

66. The NRSV and NIV do not capture the perspectival shift. Both translations switch the order of the clauses in 13.1 for a smoother reading, though this surely counters the force of the Hebrew interjection. I have added to the NRSV the words 'But look!' (והנה) and added a pronoun at the beginning of v. 2 to reflect the narrative's change of focus effected in v. 1. For the same reason, I have reversed the two clauses of v. 1 from the NRSV so that their order accurately reflects the Hebrew – which spotlights the man of God.

draw it back to himself. ⁵The altar also was torn down, and the ashes poured out from the altar, according to the sign that the man of God had given by the word of the LORD.

The story opens with Jeroboam ascending (עלה) a cultic monument of his own design at what he perhaps expected to be a climactic point in his career. Within an overall schema that highlights the rise and fall of this northern king, Cohn notes that 'the man of God attacks the centerpiece of Jeroboam's achievement'.⁶⁷ At the very moment of imagined triumph for Jeroboam, the narrative is interrupted by a dramatic shift in perspective: 'But look! – a man of God came out of Judah...'

The phrase often translated 'by the word of the LORD' (בדבר יהוה) is almost exclusive to 1 Kings 13, where it occurs seven times.⁶⁸ More typical in similar contexts is the phrase '*according* to the word...' (כדבר יהוה) which appears 27 times in the Old Testament, and 15 times in Kings, including the immediate context (e.g., 1 Kgs 14.18). Rofé seeks to explain the ב by suggesting that it is late usage/vocabulary, but perhaps the phrase is suggestive of something else.⁶⁹ How is the ב to be translated: by? in? through? with? The NRSV and NIV translate it 'by the word...' JPS translates it less literally: 'at the command of the Lord'. If it is read as a *beth* of identity, or *beth essentiae*, it may be understood to mean that the man of God comes, *in the capacity of* the word, or even *serving as* the word of the LORD.⁷⁰ Robert Alter best reflects the anomalous nature of the phrase by translating it in 13.1 (and 13.1 only⁷¹) as 'a man of God comes *through* the word of the Lord to Bethel', though he unfortunately offers no textual note or explanation.⁷²

On its own, the phrase is somewhat perplexing. Together with other clues in these opening verses, however, it suggests that the anonymous prophetic figure coming from Judah to condemn and tear down Jeroboam's altar represents something greater, something *beyond* the concerns of the

---

67. Cohn, 'Literary Technique', 32.
68. 1 Kgs 13.1, 2, 5, 9, 17, 18, 32. The exceptions are 1 Sam. 3.21; 2 Chron. 30.12; Ps. 33.6.
69. Rofé, 'Classes in the Prophetical Stories', 163.
70. Waltke and O'Connor, *Introduction to Biblical Hebrew Syntax*, 198, §11.2.5e. Cf. W. Gesenius, *Gesenius' Hebrew Grammar*, ed. and trans. E. Kautzsch, 2nd ed. (Oxford: Clarendon, 1910), 119.
71. Throughout the rest of the chapter, Alter translates the phrase, 'by the word of the LORD'.
72. Robert Alter, *Ancient Israel: The Former Prophets: Joshua, Judges, Samuel and Kings* (New York: Norton & Co., 2013), 674.

immediate story. He comes to Bethel not simply in accordance with (i.e. in obedience to) the word of the LORD, but *in* the word of the LORD, somehow embodying its characteristic authority and veracity, perhaps even its substance. Much of the Hebrew Bible could accurately be described as both historiography and literary artistry, and oftentimes the artistry elucidates the theological and political nuances of a narrative.[73] I suggest that the dramatic perspectival shift in v. 1 juxtaposes Jeroboam with the enigmatic man of God from Judah and prepares the reader to see Josiah in the narrative. Three further details in these opening verses reinforce this perspective: the man of God (a) condemns the altar (i.e. the cult) directly; (b) speaks explicitly of King Josiah; and (c) proceeds to do precisely that which Josiah will also do 300 years later. These details, in conjunction with others that follow, prompt the reader from the outset to perceive Josiah, Israel's archetypical law-keeping king, *within* the narrative.

The man of God's prophecy is as enigmatic as his presence in Bethel. He ignores the king and verbally assaults the altar itself, declaring that in due course, King Josiah of Judah will defile it with human bones and the corpses of illegitimate priests. Perhaps the significance of addressing the altar and not the king is that the man of God's words constitute a divine *decree* against false worship. That is to say, the prophecy is not directed against Jeroboam because it is not delimited to his particular context; rather, it stands for all time.

The explicit reference to David in v. 2 carries a certain sting, for according to Ahijah's prophecy in 1 Kgs 11.38, Jeroboam's kingdom had the potential to rival that of the great King David. Yet, according to the man of God who has come to Bethel, David will continue to be favoured – over and against Jeroboam. The names of both David and Josiah bring the theme of covenant obedience to the fore and suggest the reason for the man of God's coming 'in the word of the LORD': to remove Jeroboam's cultic perversions from Bethel.

The mention of Josiah 300 years before his reforms took place has typically been understood by scholars as a later redaction. As Cross put it, the man of God 'is made to give utterance to one of the most astonishing as well as rare instances of a *vaticinium post eventum* found in the Bible, obviously shaped by an overenthusiastic editor's hand'.[74]

---

73. See, e.g., Jon D. Levenson, '1 Samuel 25 as Literature and History', *CBQ* 40 (1978): 11–28. Incidentally, Levenson concludes that 1 Sam. 25, a narrative analogy not unlike 1 Kgs 13, offers 'a proleptic glimpse, within David's ascent, of his fall from grace' (24).

74. Cross, *Canaanite Myth*, 279.

However, judgments of this kind fail to grasp the symbolic potency of these so-called Deuteronomic accretions.[75] The explicit reference to Josiah provides an early clue that this narrative's concerns extend beyond a couple of odd confrontations involving a king and some prophets. The apparent anachronism enables the reader to grasp what the editor may in fact be overenthusiastic about; namely, the pointed juxtaposition of one archetypal king with another, of Jeroboam's cultic deviations with Josiah's cultic reforms. (The other so-called anachronism in the chapter, the reference to 'the cities of Samaria' in 13.32, serves a related purpose, as we shall see.[76]) The meaning of the entire narrative is considerably enriched when the man of God from Judah is understood to bespeak King Josiah in both word and deed.[77] Moreover, the figural presentation of the man of God from Judah suggests that the interpretive tasks of understanding his actions in this narrative and of conceptualising Josiah's significance within the larger scheme are actually two sides of the same coin.

The substance of the prophecy in v. 3 is striking on account of its detail. Indeed, '[t]he precision of the data is almost unique in prophetic oracles'.[78] However, there is some debate about whether the destruction of the altar occurs immediately in Jeroboam's presence, or whether v. 5 constitutes a report from the narrator's exilic context, confirming that the sign was ultimately fulfilled in Josiah's day. Some question whether the altar was destroyed immediately because of the report that it remains standing in Bethel 300 years later, in Josiah's day (cf. 2 Kgs 23.15),[79] though it is reasonable to imagine that a destroyed altar was repaired or rebuilt over three centuries so that the report of Josiah's actions in 2 Kgs 23.15 is also true.[80] As I understand it, v. 3 is carefully constructed, and offers some insight concerning the canonical shaping of the text discussed earlier:

75. Gray, *I & II Kings*, 321.
76. The same phrase (בערי שמרון) is found in 2 Kgs 17.24, 26; 23.19.
77. Brueggemann, *Kings*, agrees that the 'pivotal reference to Josiah suggests the artistic and deliberate way in which the entire narrative of Kings is arranged with great theological self-consciousness' (168). Nelson, 'Josiah in the Book of Joshua', 531–40, makes a similar point about the presentation of Joshua: 'The Joshua of Dtr is in many ways a thinly disguised Josianic figure who acts out the events of Dtr's own day on the stage of the classical past' (340).
78. Walsh, *1 Kings*, 177.
79. This is one of Van Seters' objections; cf. Chapter 4.
80. So Burke O. Long, *1 Kings*, 147. Uriel Simon makes the judgment that 'the two verses about the collapse of the altar (13:3 and 5) do not seem to belong to the original story (both linguistic and thematic arguments support their secondary

ונתן ביום ההוא מופת לאמר	He gave a **sign** the same day, saying,
זה המופת אשר דבר יהוה	'This is the **sign** that the LORD has spoken:
הנה המזבח נקרע ונשפך הדשן אשר־עליו:	<u>Look</u>! The altar *is* torn down, and the ashes that are on it [are] poured out.'

The opening phrase states that the man of God gave a sign (מופת) *on that day* (i.e. on the day that he stood before Jeroboam in Bethel), and this is immediately followed by the pronouncement of a *future* sign (מופת) by which the LORD will confirm what has been prophesied about Josiah. The final part of the verse then describes the sign, which occurs both in the present and in the future: 'Look! The altar is [being] torn down, and the ashes that are on it [are] poured out.'[81] Verse 5 states quite plainly that the sign is fulfilled then and there, in accordance with the oracle – 'The altar also was torn down, and the ashes poured out from the altar, *according to the sign that the man of God had given by the word of the LORD*' – and 2 Kgs 23.16 explicitly confirms that the same sign is also fulfilled in Josiah's time: 'and he sent and took the bones out of the tombs, and burned them on the altar, and defiled it, *according to the word of the LORD that the man of God proclaimed*, when Jeroboam stood by the altar at the festival…' The shared, or repeated, sign thereby serves an important purpose in these opening verses of the chapter, linking the man of God and Josiah across time by establishing the divine commission of each in his own context.[82] Moreover, while the מופת ('sign') refers primarily to

provenance)'. He expands on these arguments in a footnote (p. 140 n. 17). Simon, *Reading Prophetic Narratives,* 139–40. Walsh, for different reasons, argues that 'this parenthetical sign is not part of the scene; we hear it but Jeroboam does not'. Walsh, *1 Kings*, 178. Noth presents yet a third view: the announcement of the portent (v. 3) is immediate and original, but its subsequent fulfilment (v. 5) is a later redaction. Noth, *Könige*, 297.

81. Most translations of v. 3b ignore the perspectival shift indicated by הנה (*Look!* or *Behold!*) and use a simple future tense. The *niphal* participle (נקרע), however, is indeterminate.

82. Given Dtr's concerns as we have outlined them, it is quite feasible that vv. 3 and 5 are deliberately ambiguous, since precise chronology is less important within a symbolic context, and may even detract from the point – that the man of God's prophecy against Bethel is a true statement for all time; whether one views the history of the kingdoms from the beginning (1 Kgs 13) or the end (2 Kgs 23), Jeroboam's cult – together with his household and the nation he leads into sin – is doomed to destruction. From Dtr's post-exilic perspective, however, it is Josiah's actions that make the destruction of the altar significant in both contexts.

the altar's destruction, it is clear in light of the events that follow that the man of God *himself* might also be considered a portent of Judah's best king, arriving suddenly in Bethel to enforce *Kultuseinheit* (cultic unity) and *Kultusreinheit* (cultic purity).

Following the announcement of the altar's destruction, King Jeroboam interjects and demands the man of God's arrest. If the man of God stands for covenant fidelity in this opening scene (vv. 1-10), Jeroboam models stubbornness and arrogance. Upon hearing the prophetic indictment, his first words in the story are antagonistic: 'seize him!' But like Miriam, who dared to question the authority of the first prophet/man of God (Deut. 18.15; 33.1), the king's hand withers so that he is unable to control it. As is often the case in the DH, the confrontation between royal and prophetic agencies moves swiftly to a resolution that undermines the king. Moreover, the incident enforces a principle that Elijah's confrontation with the prophets of Baal on Mount Carmel also demonstrates a few chapters later; that compromised worshippers are crippled by their duality (cf. 1 Kgs 18.21). The theological inference of Jeroboam's withered hand is then balanced by its subsequent restoration, thereby establishing the man of God's authority and authenticity.

To summarise: in these first five verses, Jeroboam, whose desecration of the cultus will lead the nation into sin and ultimately destroy it from the face of the earth (Deut. 6.15; 1 Kgs 13.34), is set against Josiah, whose obedience to the Torah will be long-remembered, although it comes too late to save him or his people from a fate that was sealed 300 years earlier. (Ahijah first prophesies Israel's exile in 1 Kgs 14.15.) The sins of Jeroboam and the reforms of Josiah are herein established as interpretive clues for the reader.

1 Kings 13.6-10

> ⁶The king said to the man of God, 'Entreat now the favour of the LORD your God, and pray for me, so that my hand may be restored to me'. So the man of God entreated the LORD; and the king's hand was restored to him, and became as it was before. ⁷Then the king said to the man of God, 'Come home with me and dine, and I will give you a gift'. ⁸But the man of God said to the king, 'If you give me half your kingdom, I will not go in with you; nor will I eat food or drink water in this place. ⁹For thus I was commanded by the word of the LORD: You shall not eat food, or drink water, or return by the way that you came'. ¹⁰So he went another way, and did not return by the way that he had come to Bethel.

Unexpectedly, the same king who commanded the man of God's arrest now requests a prayer for healing. The ensuing prayer for restoration together with the favourable divine response perhaps indicates that this story follows the patterning of Numbers 12,[83] but it is also possible that the hand of the king is healed to reinforce the fact that the prophecy is not a personal matter against the king, but rather against the illegitimate cultus. The narrative suggests, however, that the healing risks being misunderstood as a sign of divine favour or lenience when the man of God is invited to a meal. The king's thoughts are unstated, though it seems reasonable to assume (as many commentators do) that he would like to have this kind of power on his side. Perhaps the invitation is offered to appease the man of God after trying to arrest him, or to lower his defences via some old-fashioned wining and dining. We cannot be sure because the narrator withholds this information. The more important point is that the offer of table fellowship is rejected outright. Jeroboam's motive may be ambiguous, but the man of God's response is not; no gift will be received, no bargain struck, and no alliance forged – not even for half the kingdom!

The merciful healing of the king's hand thus leads to a brief conversation between the man of God and the obstinate king, one that contains critical information for understanding the story. Having been offered a meal and a gift, the man of God reveals that he is under a divine prohibition not to eat bread, drink water or retrace his steps. Like Josiah, the man of God has crossed (or ignored) the boundary between north and south in an effort to rid the northern kingdom of the cultic deviations that caused the division, and like Josiah he has torn down Jeroboam's altar. Now the man of God also reveals that he has come to Bethel under obligation to a threefold commandment, just as Josiah also visits Bethel compelled by the book of the Law. The threefold command thereby further strengthens the figural link between the man of God and Josiah by evoking the motif of covenant fidelity.

As DeVries rightly points out, the threefold commandment is 'absolutely structural. It explains the king episode, it creates the point of tension in the Bethelite's hospitality episode, and it provides the hinge for the climactic oracle of judgement'.[84] There can be little doubt that the commandment is central to the story's structure and meaning. Yet DeVries goes on to call them 'strange prohibitions…[that] seemed trivial', 'a set of arbitrary and

---

83. John E. Harvey, *Retelling the Torah: The Deuteronomistic Historian's Use of Tetrateuchal Narratives*, JSOTSup 403 (London: T&T Clark, 2004), 2–3.

84. DeVries, *1 Kings*, 173.

aimless rules'.⁸⁵ On the contrary, I understand the particular details of the prohibitions to enrich the overall meaning of the narrative.

First, in a very general sense, the three commands given to the Judean man of God signify the covenant stipulations for the people of God, whilst placing the man of God's stark commitment to obedience in the limelight; 'For thus I was commanded (צוה) by the word of the LORD...' A large number of commentators stress the theme of obedience as primary for understanding 1 Kings 13 (cf. Chapter 4), but very few articulate what might be signified by eating bread, drinking water or returning by the same route. In my view, there is more to say about the commands than that they simply call for obedience.

Do not eat bread or drink water

The eating and drinking are generally taken as a hendiadys, a pair of commands expressing a single idea or message. Barth's suggestion that the prohibition from food and drink equates to a ban on fellowship with the north represents the consensus view among scholars.⁸⁶ In essence, the man of God's prophetic words against the altar are reinforced by his prophetic actions, as is often the case with enacted parables in the Old Testament (cf. Hos. 1; Isa. 20; Jer. 16.1-5; Ezek. 4–5; etc.).

However, when the prohibitions against food and water are read alongside the commandments concerning centralised worship in Deuteronomy, an additional nuance is worth noting. Of the LORD's chosen place of worship, Moses says, 'And you shall eat there in the presence of the LORD your God, you and your households together, rejoicing in all the undertakings in which the LORD your God has blessed you' (Deut. 12.7). In light of this intertext, the man of God's avoidance of food in Bethel equates to a denial of Jeroboam's implicit claim that the LORD's presence resides there. Bethel is an inappropriate place for cultic festivities. In light of our understanding that the man of God comes as a forerunner of Josiah, we note also that the directive to eat in the place of the LORD's choosing follows immediately upon the commandments against false worship that lie at the heart of Josiah's reforms (Deut. 12.2-6).

Yet a third possibility is to read the prohibition against food and water in the context of Deuteronomy 9, where Moses recounts his experience at Horeb after the people had worshipped the golden calf. 'Then I lay prostrate before the LORD as before, forty days and forty nights; I neither

---

85. Ibid., 174.
86. Uriel Simon offers a helpful summary of interpretations of the prohibition against food and drink in a footnote. Simon, *Reading Prophetic Narratives*, 302 n. 19.

ate bread nor drank water, because of all the sin you had committed, provoking the LORD by doing what was evil in his sight' (Deut. 9.18). Here, the intertextual resonance may suggest that the man of God's fasting is an expression of grief and condemnation over the idolatrous golden calves in Bethel and in Dan. In either case, what these intertextual references have in common (i.e. Deut. 9 and 12) is an accent on cultic purity.

Do not return by the way you went
Establishing what the third part of the command might signify is less straightforward, and consequently, fewer scholars have sought to explain its significance. (Barth says nothing of the third command.) David Marcus interprets it as a prohibition against returning *to Bethel* after delivering the prophetic word there.[87] That is, the man of God is not prohibited from returning to Judah by the same route, but from returning to Bethel after he has pronounced God's word there. Marcus' reading thereby supports an anti-Bethel polemic, but it is problematic in light of v. 10, which states quite clearly that after his confrontation with Jeroboam, the man of God 'went by another way, and did not return by the way that he had come *there to Bethel*'.

Uriel Simon's contribution is more helpful on this point. He explains, with support from a range of Dtr texts,[88] that 'just as returning to one's point of departure may be regarded as cancelling out the journey, retracing one's footsteps can be regarded as negating one's mission and abandoning its goal'.[89] Simon cites other texts that use similar language, arguing that going back on one's way is an idiomatic expression for retreat, notably: Deut. 17.16 (cf. Deut. 28.68), where returning to Egypt means rejecting the LORD's deliverance from that place;[90] and 1 Sam. 25.12, where David's men retrace their steps (i.e. retreat) when sent away by Nabal. Of particular interest are God's words concerning Sennacherib of Assyria in 1 Kings 19, spoken through the prophet Isaiah:

> Because you have raged against me
> > and your arrogance has come to my ears,
> I will put my hook in your nose
> > and my bit in your mouth;
> *I will turn you back on the way* / והשבתיך בדרך
> > *by which you came.* / אשר־באת בה (2 Kgs 19.28)

87. Marcus, *From Balaam to Jonah*, 78–82. Bosworth lends his support to this reading and gives three reasons for doing so. Bosworth, *Story*, 135.
88. Deut. 17.16; 28.68; 1 Sam. 25.12; 2 Kgs 19.33 (= Isa. 37.34).
89. Simon, *Reading Prophetic Narratives*, 140.
90. Ibid.

Divine judgment upon Sennacherib forces him to turn back upon the way he came, and the language of 2 Kgs 19.33 bears striking similarities to that of 1 Kgs 13.10:

By the way that he came, by the same he shall return; he shall not come into this city, says the LORD. (2 Kgs 19.33)	בדרך אשר־יבא בה ישוב ואל־העיר הזאת לא יבא נאם־יהוה:
So he went another way, and did not return by the way that he had come there to Bethel. (1 Kgs 13.10)	וילך בדרך אחר ולא־שב בדרך אשר בא בה אל־בית־אל:

In light of what appears to be idiomatic usage of the phrase in the DH, Simon seeks to show that the third commandment in 1 Kgs 13.9 is not arbitrary, but quite emphatically a command that the man of God *not retrace his steps in a way that would symbolically negate his very reason for going to Bethel* (cf. 13.26 below). The third commandment therefore serves a double purpose. On one hand, 'the ban on returning by the same route gives tangible expression to the final and irrevocable nature of the decree...the entire populace saw that the word of the Lord, as spoken by him, was inviolable'.[91] On the other hand, the command serves as a warning to the man of God himself, who must be clear and direct in his coming and going, and in his proclamation against the altar, for he comes *in* the word of the LORD. His words must be as unrelenting as Deuteronomy's commandments against idolatry, and he can afford neither to linger nor wander in any way that might jeopardise the singularity of his message. The man of God's actions must reflect the black and white nature of the commandment.

In summary, the three commands, far from being 'a set of arbitrary and aimless rules', are in fact highly symbolic and laden with significance for the world of the text. The prohibitions against consuming anything in Bethel testify against Jeroboam's false worship while the third command contains a dual warning. The prophet himself is warned not to retrace his steps lest he negate his mission, and his obedience to the command constitutes a public declaration that the indictment against Jeroboam's cultus is irrevocable. And so far, so good. At the conclusion of this opening scene (vv. 1-10), the commands have been kept. Jeroboam's offer of food and water has been declined and the man of God 'did not return by the way that he had come to Bethel' (v. 10).

---

91. Ibid., 141.

1 Kings 13.11-19

> [11]Now there lived an old prophet in Bethel. One of his sons came and told him all that the man of God had done that day in Bethel; the words also that he had spoken to the king, they told to their father. [12]Their father said to them, 'Which way did he go?' And his sons showed him the way that the man of God who came from Judah had gone. [13]Then he said to his sons, 'saddle a donkey for me'. So they saddled a donkey for him, and he mounted it. [14]He went after the man of God, and found him sitting under an oak tree. He said to him, 'Are you the man of God who came from Judah?' He answered, 'I am'. [15]Then he said to him, 'Come home with me and eat some food'. [16]But he said, 'I cannot return with you, or go in with you; nor will I eat food or drink water with you in this place; [17]for it was said to me by the word of the LORD: You shall not eat food or drink water there, or return by the way that you came.' [18]Then the other said to him, 'I also am a prophet as you are, and an angel spoke to me by the word of the LORD: Bring him back with you into your house so that he may eat food and drink water.' But he was deceiving him. [19]Then the man of God went back with him, and ate food and drank water in his house.

The transition from vv. 1-10 to 11-32 is often understood to entail a shift in source material.[92] Verse 10 rounds off the first part of the story and could lead quite naturally into v. 33, where the narrator states that 'even after this [thing], Jeroboam did not turn from his evil way'. In other words, were vv. 11-32 omitted, 'this thing' (הדבר הזה) in v. 33 could refer to the withering and subsequent healing of the king's hand, giving the brief episode of conflict between prophet and king a tidy conclusion, complete with a moral (vv. 33-34). But as many scholars observe,[93] the two main parts of the story are difficult to separate without detriment to the overall sense of the narrative. Especially important are the repeated references to the threefold command (vv. 9, 17, 22) that hold the entire narrative together.

Man of God and (Old) Prophet

The first issue that arises with the introduction of the old prophet in v. 11 pertains to the terminology used for the two anonymous figures in the story. While some have sought to delineate between what constitutes

---

92. In the first (1964) edition of Gray's commentary, he treats vv. 1-10 and vv. 11-32 separately, but in the second, following Fichtner, Noth and Klopfenstein, he acknowledges vv. 1-32 as a unity. See Gray, *I & II Kings: A Commentary*, OTL, rev. ed. (Philadelphia: Westminster, 1970), 320–1.

93. E.g., Lemke, 'Way of Obedience', 306; Simon, *Reading Prophetic Narratives*, 134–5; DeVries, *1 Kings*, 169–70.

7. *Anonymous Prophets and Archetypal Kings*   195

a man of God (איש־האלהים) and a prophet (נביא), no real advances have been made that impact upon the meaning of the story.[94] That neither term indicates prophetic authenticity is clear from the fact both the man of God and the old prophet fail in some respect and both also speak a genuine word of the LORD.[95] As discussed earlier, the narrative certainly does not differentiate between a 'true' and 'false' prophet.[96] The simplest explanation seems the best that the consistent use of different appellations throughout the story serves the simple purpose of avoiding confusion. Since the prophets are unnamed, it is only by their titles that a distinction between them is sustained.

In addition, the terms clearly associate the two anonymous prophets with their respective kingdoms and thereby reinforce their symbolic presentation of the divided kingdom. Each figure is introduced with reference to their place of origin: in v. 1, 'a man of God came out of Judah'; in v. 11, 'there lived an old prophet in Bethel'. As Barth notes, neither one features more predominantly than the other, and this balance is then upheld throughout the ensuing history as well. In the regnal accounts of 1 Kings 14–16 and 2 Kings 12–16,[97] the editor goes to considerable lengths to ensure that neither Judah nor Israel comes to the fore as the predominant focus. Walsh notes, for instance, that the final editing of the materials 'reveals a carefully balanced interest in the affairs of the two kingdoms. The kingdom of Judah is the subject of nineteen chapters…and the kingdom of Israel is the subject of nineteen chapters.'[98] We are again reminded of Barth's claim that 1 Kings 13 stands in title-form over the history of the divided kingdoms.

But while a philological study of the distinction between *prophet* and *man of God* does not go very far towards explaining the story, a narratological consideration of the same detail points to a central issue in the plot. In light of the narrator's consistent use of these terms, it is striking that the old prophet tricks the man of God precisely by confusing this distinction. When his invitation is declined in v. 15, the old prophet tries a second time

---

94. On these terms (as well as רֹאֶה and חֹזֶה), and the roles associated with them, see David L. Petersen, *The Roles of Israel's Prophets* (Sheffield: JSOT, 1981). But see Jay A. Holstein, 'The Case of "*'îš hā'ĕlōhîm*" Reconsidered: Philological Analysis versus Historical Reconstruction', *HUCA* 48 (1977): 69–81.

95. In addition, both terms are used of Elijah (1 Kgs 17.18; 18.22) and Elisha (1 Kgs 4.7; 9.1).

96. Lucian's recension of the Greek describes the Bethel prophet in v. 11 as 'another (אללי) prophet' rather than 'a certain [אחד] prophet'.

97. More precisely, 1 Kgs 14.21–16.34; 22.41-53; 2 Kgs 12.1–16.20.

98. Walsh, *1 Kings*, 373.

to appeal to the Judean man of God, this time by pointing out their shared vocation, 'I also am a prophet [נביא] as you are' (v. 18a). This is the only verse in the story where the Judean is referred to as נביא rather than איש־ האלהים and the old prophet's words are clearly intended to manipulate. The Bethelite wishes to give the impression that since he is a prophet of the same ilk and under the same divine authority, *viz.* בדבר יהוה (v. 18), he is authorised to revise the commandment given to the man of God. And it is precisely here, as the old prophet blurs the careful distinction made by the narrator, that the real issue in the chapter is raised; namely, the old prophet's motive for deceiving his 'brother'.

Before we turn our attention to consider this question of motive, it is worth pausing, even if briefly, to consider the significance of the Bethelite's old age (זקן) that is specified when he is introduced in v. 11. On one hand, as Klopfenstein suggests, the Bethel prophet's age may be taken to signify that he is specially equipped to deceive a younger, less experienced, colleague.[99] Alternatively, and conversely, the implication may be that the Bethelite's prophetic authority and calling preceded the inauguration of Jeroboam's new, indiscriminate priesthood, thus suggesting that he is one of the only prophets left in the north who is genuine and trustworthy. In either case, it is impossible to know simply from the word זקן and it is surely unreasonable to assess his moral character and motives on account of his age alone.

Moreover, the Old Testament contains numerous references to the LORD changing his mind, so that within the world of the text, the notion of God relenting or altering his command may not have seemed impossible to the man of God. However, the theological principle set out in Jer. 18.7-10, with which many other texts agree, entails a divine response to human repentance,[100] a dynamic that is entirely absent from the old prophet's speech under the oak tree near Bethel. He has not pursued the man of God in order to report that Jeroboam has come to see the error of his ways! On the contrary, the man of God surely ought to have been more discerning about this alternate word of the LORD since, as Simon argues, the third command constitutes a warning to the man of God, to guard against anything that might cause him to retrace his steps and thereby negate his mission.[101]

---

99. Klopfenstein, '1. Könige 13', 657.
100. E.g., Jon. 3.1-10; Ezek. 33.10-16; 1 Sam. 2.27-30; 15.11, 35; 1 Kgs 21.29. See the discussion in Moberly, *Prophecy and Discernment*, 48–55.
101. Simon, *Reading Prophetic Narratives*, 140–1.

The Bethelite's Motive

In terms of plot analysis, the story's most confounding gap is the Bethelite's motive for deceiving the man of God.[102] Why, upon hearing the report from his sons, does the old prophet immediately set out in pursuit of the man of God? And why, upon finding him, does he trick him into disobedience? What does he stand to gain from this deception?

In v. 11, the prophet's sons not only tell their father of the events that occurred in Bethel that day, but also, quite emphatically, 'the words also that [the man of God] had spoken to the king, they told their father' (את־הדברים אשר דבר אל־המלך ויספרום לאביהם, v. 11b)

Therefore, when the Bethel prophet asks his sons, 'which way did he go?' and proceeds to pursue the man of God on a donkey, he – like the reader – is already aware of the threefold commandment. That is to say, his invitation to the man of God, 'Come home with me and eat some food' (v. 15) is neither friendly nor innocent, but rather a deliberate attempt to lure the man of God into breaking the commands.[103] Moreover, the invitation itself, attributed to an angel, explicitly contradicts each part of the commandment: 'Bring him back with you into your house so that he may eat food and drink water' (v. 18b). But the clearest indication of malicious intent comes at the end of the verse, where the narrator states bluntly that the old prophet has resorted to deception in order to achieve his goal[104] (unless God is understood to be the subject of the verb, as Boer suggests[105]). In any event, these details merely establish that the old Bethel prophet has his heart set on causing the man of God to disobey the LORD's commandment; they do not suggest *why*. So to this question we

---

102. This section contains a summary of my more sustained reflection, 'Deceiving the Man of God from Judah', 83–102.

103. Contra Walsh, to whom the question is left open whether the old prophet is *for* Bethel or simply *in* Bethel. Walsh, *1 Kings*, 183–4.

104. C. F. Keil, *The Book of the Kings*, Biblical Commentary on the Old Testament, trans. J. Martin (Grand Rapids: Eerdmans, 1950), 206–7, argues that without the Bethel prophet's intentional act of deceit, it is possible to see him in a much more positive light. But whether or not one omits the phrase 'he lied to him', the tenor of the entire passage is one of deceit. Similarly, Klopfenstein understands the concluding phrase to refer to 'all his goal-oriented behaviour' in vv. 11-20a, and not just his words. He also notes that the angel, in contrast to the Judean's 'word of the LORD', is not even an 'angel of Yahweh' (658). See Klopfenstein, '1. Könige 13', 658, and his 1964 article referenced there; similarly, Van Winkle, '1 Kings XIII', 35.

105. See Boer's reading in Chapter 4 under 'Political Allegory' on p. 106. The context problematises Boer's suggestion, in my view, as per the preceding footnote.

must return: what does the Bethel prophet hope to achieve by causing the man of God to break the threefold command?

Certainly one of the more creative explanations of the man of God's motive comes from Dutch scholar Jaap van Dorp,[106] whose work has been explained and developed somewhat by Eynikel.[107] Van Dorp is to be commended for engaging with the story with full, imaginative seriousness, although some of his conjecture over-reaches, in my judgment. The logic of his argument is this: the Bethel prophet deliberately entraps the man of God because he learns from his sons that one day King Josiah will remove 'human bones' from the ground in order to desecrate illegal altars. 'From their report he realises that his grave will be desecrated too, unless he finds some way to prevent it.'[108] He must therefore find a way to prevent the desecration of his own grave, and the only imaginable way to do so is to ensure that his bones are buried with a Judean of sufficient piety to ward off Josiah's acts of purification. 'The old prophet therefore can do only one thing: get the man of God killed.'[109] The prophet therefore resorts to a cunning trap wherein the man of God becomes 'the victim of his own obedience'.[110] After successfully springing his trap, the Bethel prophet commands that his own bones be placed with those of the Judean for self-preservation, since the Judean's tomb will undoubtedly be respected when Josiah comes to fulfil the word of the LORD.

The strength of van Dorp's argument is that its impetus comes directly from the text. At the beginning of the story the old man hears of the prophecy spoken in Bethel (v. 11), and at the end of the story he asks to be buried with the man of God *because* (כי) 'the saying that he proclaimed by the word of the LORD against the altar in Bethel...shall surely come

---

106. Jaap van Dorp, 'Wat is die steenhoop daar? Het graf van de man Gods in 2 Koningen 23' [What is that pile of stone there? The grave of the man of God in 2 Kings 23], in *Amsterdamse Cahiers voor Exegese en Bijbelse Theologie* 8, ed. K. A. Deurloo et al. (Kampen: Kok, 1987), 64–97.

107. Eynikel, 'Prophecy and Fulfillment', 227–37. Eynikel devotes about five pages of his article to van Dorp's essay. I do not have direct access to van Dorp's work (in Dutch), so I am reliant upon Eynikel's citations and explanation. Van Dorp's purpose is to reinforce the close connection between 1 Kgs 13.11-32 and 2 Kgs 23.16-20 (232f.) and to show that 1 Kgs 13 is an original unit.

108. Eynikel, 'Prophecy and Fulfillment', 234.

109. Cited in ibid. Similarly, Eynikel (who supports van Dorp's position) writes: 'The simplest solution is to assume that the old prophet acted only to save his bones from desecration, because he was informed from the beginning (v. 11) what would happen with all the graves of Bethel'. Ibid., 234 n. 29.

110. Cited in ibid., 234.

to pass' (v. 32). But for the Bethelite to have heard the report from his sons and immediately drawn the conclusion that someday his own bones would be included in Josiah's defilement of the altar (which would only require a few bones at most) seems rather extreme – or paranoid. Moreover, the Bethelite is presumably willing to lead another man to his death in order to (possibly) preserve his own bones from defilement. The logic of van Dorp's argument thus leads to the characterisation of the Bethelite as a fearful and murderous old man, an evaluation that is not easy to justify from the text. Moreover, the Bethelite could not have known from the beginning that the man of God would die in a manner that kept his body intact. It is only *after* recovering the corpse that the Bethelite publicly declares the truth of the man of God's prophecy (v. 32). Thus, readers remain in the dark concerning the motive for his act of deception. All things considered, van Dorp's gap-filling seems rather generous.

Keil argues for an opposite assertion; namely, that the old prophet (who speaks a genuine word in v. 20) acts with good intentions.[111] Following Hengstenberg, Keil argues that that when Jeroboam inaugurated his cultus, the old prophet sinned by keeping silent and was then convicted of this sin when the man of God came from Judah to speak against the altar. In an effort to restore his honour (for himself and before others), the old prophet sought fellowship with 'this witness to the truth' and was even willing to lie to the man of God to attain it. In spite of the deception used to achieve the fellowship, however, Keil maintains that responsibility for breaking the threefold command rests entirely with the Judean, who 'allowed himself to be seduced to a transgression of the clear and definite prohibition of God simply by the sensual desire for bodily invigoration by meat and drink'.[112] In brief, Keil maintains that the old prophet's motive was honourable, even in spite of his deception. But too much is left unexplained if the story is essentially about one prophet's attempt to befriend another.

A simpler and more common explanation of the Bethelite's motive is that the elder prophet wished to test his younger colleague's prophetic authenticity.[113] If the man of God could be duped into disobedience and

---

111. Keil, *Book of the Kings*, 207. Keil acknowledges, however, 'that Josephus and the Chald., and most of the Rabbins and of the earlier commentators both Catholic and Protestant, have regarded him as a false prophet, who tried to lay a trap for the prophet from Judah, in order to counteract the effect of his prophecy upon the king and the people' (206).
112. Ibid., 207.
113. So Gray, *I & II Kings*, 322; DeVries, *1 Kings*, 173; Rice, *1 Kings*, 113.

no consequences ensued for breaking the threefold commandment, then the man of God's prophecy against Bethel could readily be dismissed. From this perspective, the Bethel prophet is seen to be deliberately testing the man of God, since he was not an eye witness to the signs reported by his sons, to determine just how serious is the prophetic word of condemnation against Jeroboam's cultic initiatives. Having established that the Judean's prophetic mandate is indeed authentic (proven by his death!), the Bethel prophet fetches his body, mourns his death and requests that they eventually be buried together. He is thus able to offer an explanation for the death of his fellow prophet in v. 26 and to affirm the prophetic word spoken in Bethel in v. 32. This interpretation of the old prophet's motives and actions makes rational sense of the world within the text to some extent, but it also seems *too* simple. Are we to think that the Bethel prophet did not trust what his sons had seen and reported 'that day'? Or that the destruction of the altar and the withering of the king's hand were insufficient evidence of the man of God's authenticity?

I am inclined to think that the Bethel prophet's pursuit of the man of God and his premeditated attempt to make him break the commands are intended not for selfish gain nor merely to test the younger prophet's authenticity, but rather to *subvert* the prophecy in Bethel. In fact, this is a point upon which Barth and Klopfenstein are agreed, despite their divergent approaches. Barth remarks that the old prophet from Bethel is well aware that the theological justification for the northern kingdom's cultus would be restored if only the man of God would eat and drink in Bethel.[114] Similarly, Klopfenstein speaks of a 'double victory' (*doppelten Sieg*) in the deception. That is, while the Bethelite may perhaps be testing the man of God's authenticity as many commentators suppose, his deliberate act of seduction also has a specific goal in mind. Since the Judean's visit to the Bethelite's home could not have been done in secret (Klopfenstein repeatedly – and in my judgment, rightly – stresses the public nature of all these events), their communion together would be perceived as confirmation that Jeroboam's syncretism was a legitimate form of worship, perhaps even as evidence of a 'transfer of religious rights from Jerusalem to Bethel'.[115] For the man of God to visit the old prophet in his home would almost certainly give the impression that Bethel and Jerusalem (and their prophets) stand on common ground.[116] In the public eye, the Judean's earlier actions in profaning the cult could

---

114. Barth, *CD* II.2, 400–401.
115. Klopfenstein, '1. Könige 13', 657–8: 'die Übertragung von Jerusalemer Kultrechten auf Bethel und damit die Gemeinschaft unter Gleichberechtigten'.
116. Ibid., 658.

be disregarded, or at the very least, relativised significantly. While this interpretation of the Bethelite's motives depicts him in a negative light and as someone loyal to Jeroboam's cause, it certainly does not warrant or necessitate the view (espoused by Barth) that *all* northern prophets were 'professional' or 'false'.

Perhaps Gross is correct in judging that '[t]he text remains impenetrable when it comes to the motivation of characters. It can, therefore, only lead to error if exegetes try to gain sense from the text by positing hypothetical intentions for the actors. If intentions of this sort were of decisive importance in 1 Kings 13, the text would provide them or give explicit references.'[117] This may be true, although I would argue that good exegesis requires serious, imaginative engagement with the world within the text, as each of the four proposals outlined above have done.

Ultimately, however, I agree with Gross that the old prophet's motive for deceiving the man of God from Judah is not necessarily a narrative gap that *must* be filled for the story's plot to make sense. For as I have argued, the story is set within a context of division and opposition between north and south (1 Kgs 12.19; 14.30) so that, in terms of the story's parabolic significance, it is surely to be expected that the Bethelite, a representative figure for Jeroboam and northern Israel, demonstrates loyalty to the north – for *whatever* reason. In its opening scene, the narrative has already led us to expect an alignment between the actions of Josiah and the man of God on one hand (representing right worship in God's chosen city of Jerusalem), and those of Jeroboam and the Bethel prophet on the other (representing false worship in the cities of Samaria). However the gap of motive is filled, this central tension between north and south is sustained in the unfolding of the narrative by virtue of the fact that the old Bethelite takes up Jeroboam's cause.

Breaking the Commandment
Another significant plot element pertains to the man of God's abrupt decision to break the threefold commandment in its entirety. Why, having turned down Jeroboam's offer of hospitality with such conviction, does he

---

117. Gross, 'Lying Prophet', 122. Approaching the text via role analysis, he argues: 'The roles are more important than the characters. For whatever reason, YHWH forbade the man of God to eat or drink in Bethel. Both the king and the nabi, again for whatever reasons, assume the role of opponent through their actions.' Gross's analysis of role structures leads him to the following conclusion: 'The lie [of the Bethelite] is only of interest because and to the degree that it is suited to move the plot forward. 1 Kings 13 is not about false prophecy... It is about obedience and disobedience' (123).

later renege on the commands? What are the consequences of his actions within the narrative world of 1 Kings 13, and what might this act of disobedience symbolise for Judah in the history of the kingdoms?

In Bethel, the man of God vehemently rejects the king's invitation, stating that even for half the kingdom he would not eat and drink 'in this place' (במקום הזה, v. 8). Moreover, the reason given for his refusal is that he has been 'commanded (צוה) by the word of the LORD' (v. 9). His response is one of unflinching obedience to the word of the LORD. A close reading of his encounter with the Bethel prophet, however, reveals that a change in the man of God's disposition is already apparent in the substance of his response as well as the justification given for it. In contrast to the refusal given to Jeroboam ('not even for half the kingdom!'), his response to the old prophet hints at reluctance, even regret: 'I am *not able* (לא אוכל) to return with you and come with you...' (v. 17). In addition, the man of God justifies his negative response in different terms. Instead of relaying the vital fact that this is a divine command (צוה), he recalls simply that 'it was *said* (דבר) to me by the word of the LORD...' (v. 17).[118] These clues hint at a shift in the man of God's resolve *vis-à-vis* his commission so that even before the old prophet resorts to deception, the careful reader has an impression of the direction this encounter will take.

Having been refused by the man of God, the Bethelite seeks to authorise his act of deception in the claim that both men share a common purpose: 'I also am a prophet as you are' [גם־אני נביא כמוך] (v. 18a). The unspoken implications of such a claim extend beyond their prophetic vocation. In Josephus's paraphrase: 'Certainly God did not forbid you to dine at my table, for I am a prophet as you are, and worship God in the same manner as you do, and am now come sent by him to bring you to my house, and make you my guest'.[119] Such expressions of sameness are often articulated as precursors, even as invitations, to shared acts of defiance or rebellion. 'It's ok. We're the same, you and me, and we're in this together.' Yet, as we noted earlier, the Bethelite's words contradict the distinction that the narrator has sustained throughout by using the terms 'man of God' and 'prophet'. Verse 19 concludes this section of the story with a taut summary of the tragic disobedience that ensues: the man of God returns, eats, and drinks with his duplicitous host.

For readers who understand the two figures from north and south to serve a representative function for Dtr's overarching historiographical project, the man of God's disobedience also evokes the narrator's report

---

118. Wray Beal, *1 & 2 Kings*, 193–4.
119. *The Works of Flavius Josephus: Antiquities of the Jews*, vol. 2, rev. A. R. Shilletto, trans. William Whiston (New York: Cosimo Classics, 2005), 115.

in 2 Kgs 17.19, that 'Judah also did not keep the commandments of the LORD their God but walked in the customs that Israel had introduced'. Again, our identification of the story's function (as narrative analogy) illuminates certain plot elements.[120]

This brings us to the main turning point in the story.

1 Kings 13.20-22

> [20]As they were sitting at the table, the word of the LORD came to the prophet who had brought him back; [21]and he proclaimed to the man of God who came from Judah, 'Thus says the LORD: Because you have disobeyed the word of the LORD, and have not kept the commandment that the LORD your God commanded you, [22]but have come back and have eaten food and drunk water in the place of which he said to you, "Eat no food, and drink no water", your body shall not come to your ancestral tomb'.

As Klopfenstein has stressed (see Chapter 3), the narrative's single turning point occurs in v. 20, where the two antithetical prophets sit at a shared table in Bethel. It is at this table of falsified fellowship[121] that the word of the LORD comes once more, this time to the deceptive prophet. Herein lies one of the most confounding turns in the story; God speaks a true word through a deceitful agent. Perplexing as it may be, however, this quandary has also been taken by many as a clue to the story's meaning, since the reversal makes it clear that God's word against Bethel shall be upheld even if its hearer turns out to be the very prophet who caused his 'brother' to sin. In other words, this twist in the narrative highlights the fact that neither the Bethelite nor the man of God emerges as the hero of the tale; rather, it is God's word that triumphs.[122] The centrepiece of the story is thus understood to reinforce Dtr's concern for the theme of prophecy and fulfilment; the prophetic word spoken at Bethel *must* be upheld one way or another, whether through the man of God or through the Bethel prophet.

Within the world of the text, the turning point in the narrative has enormous significance for the Bethel prophet, who set out to defend Jeroboam's cultus and to willingly deceive the man of God in order to subvert his prophecy. For in v. 20, when the Bethel prophet receives a

---

120. See below on v. 26. I explore different aspects of this analogy between 1 Kgs 13 and the history of the kingdoms in 'Deceiving the Man of God', 98–102.

121. Klopfenstein calls it 'selbstgemachte Gemeinschaft in der selbstgesetzten Gleichberechtigung' [homemade community of self-imposed equal status] ('1. Könige 13', 658).

122. See 'The Efficacious Word of God' in Chapter 4 (pp. 71–3).

true word from the LORD, he is forced to recognise that his efforts to subvert the prophecy against Bethel have failed. From his own lips now come an oracle confirming the true nature of the other's mission – and judging him for his failure to obey! It is indeed a 'most dramatic and surprising' twist, as Klopfenstein puts it.[123] Just as the man of God had cried out (קרא) against the altar, the old Bethelite now cries out (קרא) against the man of God, even using the same classic speech-formula: כה אמר יהוה ('Thus says the LORD', 13.2, 21). The rhetoric and Masoretic punctuation[124] indicate that the prophecy that follows is as authentic as the one spoken in Bethel.

Moreover, when the word of the LORD comes to the older prophet at the table, his proclamation (v. 21b) confirms that the threefold instruction was indeed a commandment (מצוה) from the mouth of the LORD, and nothing less (cf. vv. 9, 17; see above):[125]

כה אמר יהוה יען כי מרית פי יהוה ולא שמרת את־המצוה אשר צוך יהוה אלהיך

Not only does the double use of the root צוה affirm that the threefold commandment evokes the Deuteronomic Law, but the opening phrase – literally: 'Because you have rebelled against the mouth of the LORD' – is distinctly Deuteronomistic, recalling especially Moses' rebuke of the Israelites for their disobedience regarding entrance to the land.[126] In connection with this, Gross observes that this is an uncharacteristic use of the word מצוה in the DH, which always refers to the Decalogue or to the entire Deuteronomic Law, with only one other exception (1 Sam. 13.13).[127] He therefore posits that the author has used this term 'to refer both to the specific prohibition against eating and drinking addressed to the man of God and to the entire Deuteronomic law addressed to Israel'.[128] Again the narrative stresses that Torah observance, which Josiah will re-establish in the course of time, is of utmost importance for the life of these two kingdoms under God.

---

123. Klopfenstein, '1. Könige 13', 658.

124. The long spacing in the middle of v. 20 indicates that the statement to follow merits special attention. See Montgomery, *Kings*, 264; Burney, *Notes*, 182.

125. Wray Beal, *1 & 2 Kings*, 194.

126. Deut. 1.26, 43; 9.23. Also, Josh. 1.18; 1 Sam. 12.14-15; 1 Kgs 13.21, 26. See Lemke, 'Way of Obedience', 308–9.

127. Gross, 'Lying Prophet', 104.

128. Van Winkle, '1 Kings XIII', 41. Van Winkle notes that this ambiguity is further supported by the usage of מרית פי יהוה (see n. 125 above). Cf. Van Winkle, '1 Kings XII 25–XIII 34', 111.

At this critical turning point in the narrative, then, the old prophet's words carry significant weight both for the disobedient man of God *within* the world of the text and for Dtr's exilic audience *behind* the world of the text. The unusual use of the word מצוה in v. 21 also accents the Dtr theme of prophetic responsibility for promoting obedience to the Mosaic law.[129] Moses is the obvious foundation for this motif, though other thematically related texts in the DH where מצוה occurs include the narrator's reflection on the fall of Israel in 2 Kgs 17.13, where the prophets are deemed responsible for warning Israel and Judah to keep the LORD's commandments:

ויעד יהוה בישראל וביהודה ביד כל־נביאו [נביאי] כל־חזה לאמר שבו מדרכיכם הרעים ושמרו מצותי חקותי ככל־התורה אשר צויתי את־אבתיכם ואשר שלחתי אליכם ביד עבדי הנביאים:	Yet the LORD warned Israel and Judah by every prophet and every seer, saying, 'Turn from your evil ways and keep my commandments and my statutes, in accordance with all the law that I commanded your ancestors and that I sent to you by my servants the prophets'.

Similarly, Josiah's reforms in 2 Kings 22–23 hold the law and prophets together in an interesting way, not just with regards to Huldah's interpretation of the law for that particular moment in history, but also, as Levenson observes, how '[t]he role which Josiah plays in 2 Kings 23 is one which Dtn would be more likely to assign to a prophet'.[130] Each of these texts (including 1 Kgs 13) holds prophecy and obedience to the law together in ways that have heuristic value for communities of God's people in any time and place, although the penalty for the man of God's disobedience – 'your body shall not come to your ancestral tomb' (v. 22) – is especially apt for a post-exilic audience.

1 Kings 13.23-25

> [23]After the man of God had eaten food and had drunk, they saddled for him a donkey belonging to the prophet who had brought him back. [24]Then as he went away, a lion met him on the road and killed him. His body was thrown in the road, and the donkey stood beside it; the lion also stood beside the body. [25]People passed by and saw the body thrown in the road, with the lion standing by the body. And they came and told it in the town where the old prophet lived.

---

129. See Van Winkle, '1 Kings XIII', 42.
130. Levenson, 'Who Inserted the Book of the Torah?', 228. Note that Levenson refers to Dtn (the Deuteronomic corpus; i.e. Deut. 4.44–28.68) and not Dtr.

Apparently, nothing is said in response to the Bethelite's prophecy; the silence may be taken to imply shame and admission of guilt, or perhaps anger at being had. The narrator simply reports that following his meal, a donkey is prepared for his departure.

The old prophet's oracle did not stipulate that judgment would be immediate, but he did state that the man of God would not be buried in the tomb of his fathers. It was inferred, therefore, that he would never make it back to Judah. Verse 24, for all its surreal details, is narrated with a terseness that is characteristic of Hebrew narrative; 'as he went away, a lion met him on the road and killed him. His body was thrown in the road, and the donkey stood beside it; the lion also stood beside the body.' These few words paint a mesmerising picture, nonetheless! The painting by British painter James Northcote, commissioned in 1809 by Charles Grey (the second Earl Gray) offers a striking depiction of the scene, with due emphasis on the lion's restraint and the old prophet's response.

Private Collection © Look and Learn/Bridgeman Images.

The Lion's Restraint

It is well-documented that lions were a problem in ancient Palestine,[131] so that the mere presence of a lion in the narrative need not raise questions of plausibility. Regardless, interpretive questions are often focused around the lion's metaphorical or symbolic significance, in addition to the role it plays in the story.

If we look at Kings more broadly, we note that there are three stories involving lions (1 Kgs 13.24-27; 20.36; 2 Kgs 17.25-26) that all have one thing in common; *the appearance of lions in all three texts coincides with a refusal to comply with the prophetic word.* At the very least, it seems reasonable to deduce that the lion in 1 Kings 13, like other lions in the book of Kings, metes out divine judgment for disobedience to the prophetic word.[132] If our focus is widened still further to include prophetic and poetic texts (esp. Amos), then we are faced with an additional array of texts that use the image of a lion to denote God. Such texts presumably provide the impetus for Barth's claim that the lion is, in fact, the lion of Judah. James Mead also claims that the lion is to be equated with God, though his argument is based on the structure of 1 Kings 13.[133] While we do not have space here to explore all prophetic texts that speak of lions, we note that Brent Strawn's comprehensive study of leonine imagery in the Hebrew Bible affirms that the imagery of God as lion in the prophets, as one who metes out prophetic justice, is consistent with the role of lions in the book of Kings.[134]

However, there is one striking detail in 1 Kings 13 that makes this lion quite different from any others in Kings, as James Northcote's painting shows. After killing the man of God, it is stated no fewer than three times that this lion remained 'standing by the body' (vv. 24, 25, 28). So, while the notion of lions killing people is not particularly unusual, there is almost certainly something more at stake than prophetic judgment when a lion appears under unusual circumstances to kill – and then stands guard over its prey. The point is sharpened further by the fact that the lion attacks and kills the man of God but spares his donkey. Perhaps the more pertinent

---

131. E.g., Montgomery, *Kings*, 261; Gray, *I & II Kings* (1970), 331. Cf. Brent A. Strawn, *What Is Stronger than a Lion? Leonine Image and Metaphor in the Hebrew Bible and the Ancient Near East*, Orbis Biblicus et Orientalis 212 (Göttingen: Vandenhoeck & Ruprecht, 2005), 40–3.

132. E.g., Bodner, *The Theology of the Book of Kings* (Cambridge: Cambridge University Press, 2019), 97: 'the lion is a figure of judgment in the story, as in Jdg 14:8-9 and later in 1 Kgs 20:36 and 2 Kgs 17:25-26'.

133. Mead, 'Kings and Prophets'.

134. Strawn, *What Is Stronger?*, 64.

question for the interpreter is not simply, 'why a lion?' but rather, 'why a lion that shows restraint?' A lion who kills selectively, but does not eat is an unnatural lion, or at least one under supernatural influence (cf. Dan. 6), and this is surely a critical detail in 1 Kings 13, though there is certainly no consensus on its meaning.

Gressmann, among others, contrasts the disobedient man of God with the obedient animal of God, so that the lion's restraint reflects what the man of God *should* have shown when invited to eat.[135] Bosworth, given his more allegorical approach, sees in these verses an allusion to 2 Kings 9–10, where King Jehu (who shows little restraint!) executes judgment on the house of David for taking the path of Ahab. He therefore draws a parallel between the lion and Jehu; 'Jehu is like the lion that executes Yhwh's judgment concerning the man of God'.[136] Boer, reading the story as political allegory, suggests that the lion is an allegorical manifestation of 'the Babylonian (or Persian) empire, or rather emperor… [T]he lion exercises control by restraint; for at any moment the lion could attack and eat, in the same way that imperial control is exercised by the restraint of force.'[137] Sweeney perceives connections between the donkey (חמור) and Hamor the father of Shechem, who raped Dinah's daughter (Gen. 34.2) on one hand, and the lion as the symbol for the tribe of Judah (e.g. Gen. 49.9) on the other. He concludes:

> These associations suggest that the image of the ass and the lion standing by the body of the man of G-d is an important element in the interpretation of this narrative. These symbols reinforce the point that the northern kingdom, with its capital in Shechem and its sanctuary in Beth El is a place of deception and lies. Jerusalem, Judah and the house of David, by contrast, are identified with YHWH, who will act against those corrupted by their association with Beth El and the north.[138]

---

135. Gressmann, *Die älteste Geschichtsschreibung*, 243. Similarly, Simon, 'I Kings 13: A Prophetic Sign', 96 n. 37, and Wray Beal, *1 & 2 Kings*, 194: 'The lion is an illustration of what the prophet should have done'. Cf. also Marcus, *From Balaam to Jonah*, 75–6, who mentions other animals in the Old Testament that are also contrasted with disobedient people (Balaam, Jonah, Elisha's hecklers).

136. Bosworth, *Story*, 144, observes that in 2 Kgs 9–10, 'The North, like the old prophet, suddenly speaks the word of Yhwh, and Judah, much like the man of the God, suffers for disobedience' (144). In my view, a better case can be made for a parallel between the lion that kills the man of God and Pharaoh Necho who kills Josiah at Megiddo (2 Kgs 23.29). See below.

137. Boer, 'National Allegory', 111–12. Cf. Strawn, *What Is Stronger?*, 60.

138. Sweeney, *I & II Kings*, 182.

In Barth's theological reading, wherein the elect suffers on behalf of the rejected, the lion represents God who strikes his own (i.e. Judah) on behalf of sinful Israel.[139] Klopfenstein, as we have seen, rejects the suggestion that the Judean man of God's death is on behalf of northern Israel, since the notion of vicarious suffering draws upon the theology of Isaiah 53, which Klopfenstein considers to be far removed from this text.[140] In his view, the origin and background of the lion must be left open, as indeed the text leaves them open. What the text is clear about, says Klopfenstein, are two functions for the lion. In v. 26, the Bethel prophet states that 'the LORD has given him to the lion', and in vv. 24, 25, 28 the lion is said to be 'standing by the body'. That is to say, the lion kills the man of God as Yahweh's agent, and then draws attention to the scene by standing beside the body.[141] Klopfenstein perhaps does well to stay within the margins of the textual world, although the lion arguably has one other function as well. The restraint of the lion ensures that the man of God's corpse remains intact for its burial, and this is the critical detail that facilitates the link between 1 Kings 13 and its epilogue in 2 Kings 23. Were the man of God eaten or carried away, he could not be buried in the Bethelite's tomb. Only the lion's unusual behaviour makes their shared tomb possible. In addition to all of this, when read as a narrative analogy or parable, the unjust and sudden death of the man of God anticipates the untimely death of King Josiah at the hand of Pharaoh Necho (see below).

In conclusion, we may affirm three observations about the lion in 1 Kings 13. First, like other lions in the book of Kings (and in prophetic literature), this one enacts judgment for disobedience to the word of the LORD. Second, by standing passively beside the man of God's corpse, the lion draws – or demands – the attention of passers by, and this plays a key role in the story's development (cf. Klopfenstein). Third, within the larger plot, the lion's restraint from mauling or otherwise destroying the corpse makes it possible for the burial to take place so that the man of God's tomb may one day be discovered by King Josiah.

---

139. Barth, *CD* II.2, 407. Barth interfaces the reference to the lion with other key texts; Gen. 49.9; Amos 1.2; 3.8 (397).

140. Klopfenstein, '1. Könige 13', 669.

141. Ibid., 660–1. (Klopfenstein discusses lions at length; 660–5.) Keil, *Book of the Kings*, also places the accent on this point: 'The lion...remained standing by the corpse and by the ass, that the slaying of the prophet might not be regarded as a misfortune that had befallen him by accident, but that the hand of the Lord might be manifest therein, so that passers-by saw this marvel and related it in Bethel' (205–6).

The second of these functions seems most significant, in light of the whole. Moreover, the sole purpose of v. 25 is to convey the impact of this 'very unlionlike lion'[142] upon passers by. People traveling to and from Bethel see the corpse of a man guarded by two silent sentinels – namely, a lion and a donkey! It almost goes without saying that 'they came and told it in the town where the old prophet lived' (v. 25), but this report from the narrator spells out the purpose served by the lion's restraint. The unusual lion makes the people of Bethel aware that the man of God who spoke publicly against Jeroboam's cult and was prohibited by God from having any fellowship in Bethel, but who was subsequently seen going home with a local prophet, has been killed. Klopfenstein's emphasis on the public nature of all these events is surely well placed, including what happens throughout the rest of the narrative with the mourning and burial (vv. 29-30), the prophetic proclamation (vv. 31-32), and in due course, the old prophet's own burial. All of these events are witnessed by the people of Bethel (as evidenced by the manner in which word reaches the old prophet on two separate occasions; vv. 11, 25-26) so that the man of God's demise testifies both to the authenticity of his word against Bethel and to his own failure to obey. Ironically, the deceit of the old prophet achieves its end but simultaneously seals the fate of the northern cultus. For the Bethelite, the battle is won but the war is lost, since, after breaking the commandment, the man of God's demise only confirms the veracity of his oracle against Jeroboam's altar. Accordingly, in what follows, the old prophet takes it upon himself to proclaim the same message.

1 Kings 13.26-32

> [26]When the prophet who had brought him back from the way heard of it, he said, 'It is the man of God who disobeyed the word of the LORD; therefore the LORD has given him to the lion, which has torn him and killed him according to the word that the LORD spoke to him'.
> [27]Then he said to his sons, 'saddle a donkey for me'. So they saddled one, [28]and he went and found the body thrown in the road, with the donkey and the lion standing beside the body. The lion had not eaten the body or attacked the donkey. [29]The prophet took up the body of the man of God, laid it on the donkey, and brought it back to the city, to mourn and to bury him. [30]He laid the body in his own grave; and they mourned over him, saying, 'Alas, my brother!'
> [31]After he had buried him, he said to his sons, 'When I die, bury me in the grave in which the man of God is buried; lay my bones beside his bones.

---

142. DeVries, *1 Kings*, 171.

> ³²For the saying that he proclaimed by the word of the LORD against the altar in Bethel, and against all the houses of the high places that are in the cities of Samaria, shall surely come to pass.'

Having heard about the lion and the corpse, the Bethel prophet offers up an explanation for the man of God's death,[143] perhaps to those who brought him news of the spectacle. At this point in the story, the narrator describes him not as the prophet from Bethel, but as 'the prophet who turned him from the way' (הנביא אשר השיבו מן־הדרך, v. 26). With these words, the reader is not only reminded of the Bethelite's treacherous role in what has transpired, but also alerted to the symbolic significance of keywords such as שוב ('turn') and דרך ('way'). In v. 21, we noted the multivalence of מצוה with regards to the world within the text and the world behind it. Lemke notes a similar dynamic here: 'Quite conceivably the author of v. 26 intended to play on the various nuances of the meaning of *sub* [turn] in conjunction with *derek* [way], leaving it purposely ambiguous in order to facilitate the transition from the literal sense (as in vss 9, 10, 17) to the metaphorical one (as in vs. 33)'.[144] That is, the narrator's comment refers not only to the Judean's geographic path, but also to his moral path, to the way of obedience – from which he has been led astray. Lemke points out that the narrative thereby leans toward its conclusion, where Jeroboam is condemned for failing to turn from his evil way (v. 33). But in addition to these nuances, the representative function of the prophetic characters comes again to the fore. As the man of God's untimely and unusual death anticipates the death of Josiah, so the negative influence of the Bethel prophet is aligned with Jeroboam's enduring legacy. The Bethelite is dubbed the prophet 'who caused him to turn [*hiphil* of שוב] from the way' just as Jeroboam is forever remembered as the king 'who caused Israel to sin [*hiphil* of חטא]'.[145]

The substance of the old prophet's proclamation also merits close attention. The distinctly Deuteronomistic phrase ('to rebel against the mouth of the LORD') has already been spoken by the Bethelite in his oracle against the man of God in v. 21, but what was said in the privacy of his home now becomes public as the Bethelite explains the bizarre

---

143. The explanation in the latter part of v. 26 ('therefore the LORD has given him to the lion, which has torn him and killed him according to the word that the LORD spoke to him') is not in the LXX.

144. Lemke, 'Way of Obedience', 311; also independently, Dozeman, 'Way of the Man', 386–7.

145. 1 Kgs 22.52, passim.

string of events: the corpse belongs to the disobedient man of God, whose death-by-lion should be understood as divine judgment in accordance with the word of the LORD. The last phrase in v. 26 – 'according to the word of the LORD that he spoke to him' (כדבר יהוה אשר דבר־לו) – is used throughout Kings to highlight the fulfilment of prophecy, and this usage is no exception. The Bethelite affirms that the man of God has perished according to the word that was given him; the LORD has given him over to be broken (שבר) by the lion, just as he has broken the threefold commandment.

Having made this declaration, the old prophet sets out to retrieve the Judean's corpse and finds the body 'thrown' (שלך) on the ground before passers by. One is reminded of the manner in which Moses threw down the stone tablets before the eyes of the Israelites as a sign of their broken covenant (the same verb is used in Deut. 9.17). The intertextual resonance of these two scenes is especially illuminating since the man of God has come from Bethel 'in the word of the LORD' and under obligation to a threefold commandment. That is to say, his broken body upon the road before the eyes of all the people serves a similar purpose within his context as did the broken tablets at Sinai; as a sign of Israel's broken covenant with the LORD.[146]

The prophet returns to Bethel with the corpse laid upon his donkey and proceeds to mourn the man of God's death. As it turns out, the Bethelite provides the means by which his own prophecy is fulfilled. In addition, he requests that he himself be buried alongside the man of God for the following reason: 'For the saying that he proclaimed by the word of the LORD against the altar in Bethel, and against all the houses of the high places that are in the cities of Samaria, shall surely come to pass' (v. 32). As Klopfenstein suggests, the Bethelite likely wants to be identified with the man of God in death as in life for their shared proclamation against Bethel.[147] This is consistent with the way the Bethel prophet publicly affirms the cause of his 'brother' from Judah, even adding to his prophecy 'the cities of Samaria' and thereby acknowledging the

---

146. There are further points of similarity between the man of God in our narrative and Moses, the archetypal man of God in Deut. 9. In addition to a general shared context of golden calves and broken commandments, the verbs used of Moses' throwing (שלך) and breaking (שבר) the tablets are the same ones used of the man of God's body that is thrown and broken by the lion. Also, Moses declares twice that, because of the people's idolatry, he neither ate bread nor drank water upon the mountain (Deut. 9.9, 18).

147. Klopfenstein, '1. Könige 13', 666.

condemnation of his own local sanctuary. His efforts to undo the man of God's prophecy have themselves come undone, and he has himself been inspired to speak the same word against Bethel. If the story teaches anything about prophetic discernment, it surely shifts the focus from attempts to discern the quality of the prophet (i.e. true or false) by various criteria (i.e. moral character, accuracy of prediction, calling, etc.) to the reality that God's word always finds fulfilment, and will do so by any means necessary, including even ways that make a true prophet false or a false prophet true.

Anachronism and Ambiguity

The anachronistic reference to 'the cities of Samaria' (בערי שמרון) in v. 32 has been attributed to 'carelessness' on the part of the author,[148] but as I stated earlier regarding the naming of Josiah in v. 2, these kinds of judgments miss the symbolic potency of the reference. The phrase links 1 Kings 13 to other key texts in the history (2 Kgs 17; 23) that also recount divine judgment for false worship practices.[149] Equally, as the Judean's initial prophecy names Josiah as its referent in v. 2, so the Bethelite's affirmation of that same oracle adds a phrase that is picked up in 2 Kgs 23.19 with regards to the cultic reforms of Josiah: 'Moreover, Josiah removed all the shrines of the high places that were in the towns of Samaria (בערי שמרון), which kings of Israel had made, provoking the LORD to anger; he did to them just as he had done at Bethel'. Therefore, even if the reference to 'the cities of Samaria' is relatively meaningless within the world of the text (since Samaria has yet to be established under the Omrides), it again anticipates Josiah and permits us to see important trans-historical patterns in the narrative. From this perspective, the man of God's prophetic oracle in v. 2, and its reprise in v. 32 from the old Bethelite prophet, both use so-called anachronisms to establish a theological framework that points to Josiah as a hermeneutical key.

---

148. DeVries, *1 Kings*, 169.

149. Lemke, 'Way of Obedience', 316, observes that 'the cities of Samaria', is one of three phrases that occur only in 1 Kgs 13, 2 Kgs 17, and 2 Kgs 23. 'Cities of Samaria occurs three times: 1 Kgs 13.32; 2 Kgs 17.24-28; 23.19; 'priests of the high places' occurs seven times: 1 Kgs 12.32; 13.2, 33 (×2); 2 Kgs 17.32; 23.9, 20; 'shrines of the high places' occurs five times: 1 Kgs 12.31; 13.32; 2 Kgs 17.29, 32; 23.19. Van Seters agrees on the similarities between these three texts, but argues that they are all post-Dtr redactions; 'Death by Redaction?', 216–21; idem, 'On Reading', 226.

1 Kings 13.33-34

> ³³Even after this [saying], Jeroboam did not turn from his evil way, but made priests for the high places again from among all the people; any who wanted to be priests he consecrated for the high places. ³⁴This matter became sin to the house of Jeroboam, so as to cut it off and to destroy it from the face of the earth.

We have already noted the very public nature of the events narrated in this chapter: the inauguration ceremony for Jeroboam's cultus, attended (among others) by the Bethel prophet's sons; the declined invitation of the king, followed by the man of God's rationale for having to leave Bethel immediately; the table fellowship of the two prophets, which would have been difficult to keep secret, as Klopfenstein points out; the bizarre spectacle involving the lion, the donkey and the man of God's corpse; the old prophet's subsequent explanation of its significance; the Bethelite's retrieval of the Judean's body and his words at the latter's funeral; and ultimately, the Bethelite's own burial alongside his 'brother'. Given the way in which the plot's development presupposes a narrative world in which news travels fast (notably to the Bethel prophet in vv. 11, 25-26), it is reasonable to assume that the king was notified of all these unusual happenings in Bethel. And while any of the incidents listed above might reasonably have demanded the king's attention, the particular 'thing' (דבר) of which Jeroboam ought to have taken heed, in my judgment, is its immediate antecedent in the verse preceding; namely, the affirmation of the man of God's word against Bethel by a local, elderly (and by implication, *authoritative*) prophet (v. 32; cf. v. 2). I suggest, therefore, that 'this thing' (הדבר הזה) in v. 33 is best understood to mean what it means in the previous verse, where it is translated 'this saying' (NRSV) or 'this message' (NIV). That is, 'even after this [*viz.* a local prophet's condemnation of the Bethel cultus], Jeroboam did not turn from his evil way...' To put it otherwise, the prophecy against the altar in Bethel has now been proclaimed by *two* distinct, prophetic authorities – and still Jeroboam remains obstinate.

Also ambiguous is Jeroboam's 'evil way' in v. 33. Does the generic phrase refer to the fabricated calves, the illegitimate altar, his appointment of false priests, the eschewing of Jerusalem, or all of the above? In my view, the most natural referent is in what follows directly, where it is reported that Jeroboam 'made priests for the high places again from among all the people' (i.e. anyone at all). To anyone desiring it, Jeroboam 'filled his hand' (ימלא את־ידו) to be a priest of the high places. The unusual idiom probably refers to a rite wherein something like a sceptre is placed in the hand of the appointee (cf. the consecration of Aaron and his sons as priests in Exod. 28.41; also Judg. 17.5, 12). But the basic point is that Jeroboam's actions are unchanged. As Wray Beal puts it, 'Jeroboam continues to transgress the deuteronomic law of worship as he did in 12:26-33',[150] and he is for that reason destined for destruction.

In a similar fashion, v. 34 refers again to 'this thing' (בדבר הזה) and again, the most natural referent is probably found in the preceding verse: i.e. Jeroboam's false priesthood (see above). As the story concludes, the narrator insists upon the consequences of Jeroboam's sin, that Jeroboam's house would suffer the same fate that awaits all Israel: cut off and destroyed from the face of the earth.[151] The chapter's conclusion – only the story's 'provisional epilogue'[152] – thus enforces yet once more the devastating impact of Jeroboam's sin upon the nation.

1 Kings 13 as Interpretive Key

It will be clear by now that the narrative in 1 Kings 13 has tremendous import for interpreting the history of the kingdoms, up to and including the closing 'bookend' of 2 Kgs 23.15-20. Before we examine Josiah's reforms, however, let us consider briefly how the regnal accounts of the northern and southern kingdoms pick up on themes raised by the representative roles of the anonymous prophets, and the archetypal reigns of Jeroboam and Josiah, in 1 Kings 13.

Exile is prophesied for the first time in 1 Kings 14, when Ahijah declares: 'The LORD will strike Israel, as a reed is shaken in the water; he will root up Israel out of this good land that he gave to their ancestors, and scatter them beyond the Euphrates, because they have made their sacred poles, provoking the LORD to anger. He will give Israel up because of the sins of Jeroboam, which he sinned and which he caused Israel to commit' (1 Kgs 14.15-16). Only a few verses later, the narrator adds that in due course, Judah would also fall into the same sin: 'Judah did what was evil in the sight of the LORD; they provoked him to jealousy with their sins that they committed, more than all that their ancestors had done' (1 Kgs 14.22). Similarly, in 2 Kgs 17.21-23, when the blame for Israel's scattering is attributed to Jeroboam, the narrator also comments that 'Judah also did not keep the commandments of the LORD their God

---

150. Wray Beal, *1 & 2 Kings*, 195.

151. The same phrase appears in Zeph. 1.3, which is attributed to the days of Josiah of Judah (see Zeph. 1.1). See part II of Sweeney, *King Josiah of Judah*, on prophetic literature in relation to Josiah's reign.

152. Barth, *CD* II.2, 397.

but walked in the customs that Israel had introduced' (2 Kgs 17.19). In both of these important narratorial reports, the history of the kingdoms follows the pattern established in 1 Kings 13; not only are the fates of the kingdoms inextricably bound together, but Judah (the man of God) is led into sin by Israel (the Bethel prophet).

When accounting for Judah's exilic demise in the final chapters of Kings, the lion's share of the blame is placed squarely on Manasseh.[153] This is likely so because Manasseh provided Dtr with a means of explaining the sudden and tragic demise of the righteous Josiah. On one hand, Dtr perceived Josiah as the best example of a king who mediated (and even enforced) Torah observance in Israel. Yet, on the other hand, in light of the Deuteronomistic principle of just reward and punishment, the untimely death of Judah's most righteous king demanded some form of explanation.[154] The strictly theological account of Manasseh's reign goes a long way to closing this theological gap by providing a rationale for the fall of Judah even in spite of Josiah's exemplary covenant fidelity (cf. 2 Kgs 23.26; 24.3).[155] For our purposes, we note that the narrative analogy in 1 Kings 13 anticipates this theological conundrum in the DH by foreshadowing the historical reality that this promised son of David (1 Kgs 13.2) would be abruptly killed by a 'lion' (1 Kgs 13.24) – namely, Pharaoh Necho II, in 2 Kings 23.29.[156] In spite of the fact that Jeroboam

---

153. As with the reforms of Josiah, many historians and biblical scholars doubt the veracity (and extremity) of the biblical testimony concerning Manasseh. See, e.g., the following three essays in Grabbe, ed., *Good Kings and Bad Kings*: Ernst Axel Knauf, 'The Glorious Days of Manasseh', 164–88; Francesca Stavrakopoulou, 'The Blackballing of Manasseh', 248–63; Marvin A. Sweeney, 'King Manasseh of Judah and the Problem of Theodicy in the Deuteronomistic History', 264–78.

154. On the apparent futility of Josiah's reforms, see, e.g., Stanley Brice Frost, 'The Death of Josiah: A Conspiracy of Silence', *JBL* 87 (1968): 369–82. The Chronicler's account hints that Josiah was perhaps responsible for his own death (2 Chron. 35.21).

155. On Manasseh in Dtr's theology of history, see also Baruch Halpern, 'Why Manasseh is Blamed for the Babylonian Exile: The Evolution of a Biblical Tradition', *VT* 48 (1998): 473–514; David Janzen, 'The Sins of Josiah and Hezekiah: A Synchronic Reading of the Final Chapters of Kings', *JSOT* 37 (2013): 349–70, and the works cited there.

156. On the depiction of Egyptian monarchs as lions, see Strawn, *What Is Stronger?*, 174–5. An exhibit at The Met (Fifth Ave) in Gallery 127 depicts a rearing lion (of glazed steatite) with cartouches of the Pharaoh Necho II (610–595 BCE) on its shoulders. The accompanying description reads: 'The motif of the king as a lion dominating enemies is well-known in Egypt. Astonishingly, however, here it is rendered in a style that is indebted to the Near East. Details like the curls on the mane

I and Josiah represent antithetical ideals in Kings, the sins of one lead eventually to the fall of the other.[157] Thus, when the prophetess Huldah declares in 2 Kings 22 that the sickness runs so deep in Judah's veins (again, as exhibited by Manasseh) that the fate of the nation is sealed even in spite of Josiah's contrite heart and national reforms, a familiar theme is reiterated; namely, that Judah follows in Israel's footsteps.

This linkage, introduced in 1 Kings 13, is further strengthened by the ways in which Huldah's message for Josiah hearkens back in some ways to Ahijah's judgment regarding Jeroboam. The purpose of Huldah's oracle is clearly not to pronounce judgment upon Josiah for unfaithfulness to the covenant – quite the opposite! – yet the commonality between these prophetic announcements perhaps suggests that the penalty for Jeroboam's sins eventually impacts upon even the most righteous of Judah's kings. On a superficial level, both Ahijah and Huldah pronounce their unfavourable prophetic verdicts upon Jeroboam and Josiah via mediaries (Shaphan *et al* and Jeroboam's wife). But more significantly, their judgments share key vocabulary and content. At the heart of both oracles, the LORD proclaims, 'Behold, I will bring evil upon' (הנני מביא רעה אל-, 1 Kgs 14.9; 2 Kgs 22.16) the house of Jeroboam/this place, for fabricating and worshipping 'other gods' (אלהים אחרים, 1 Kgs 14.9; 2 Kgs 22.17) and thus 'provoking me to anger' (להכעיסני, 1 Kgs 14.9; 2 Kgs 22.17). Some commentators note in addition that only three judgments in Kings (1 Kgs 14.10; 21.21; 2 Kgs 22.16-17) use the *hiphil* participle (בוא) with the preposition אל-, indicating that 'the word against Jerusalem is as certain of fulfilment as that given Jeroboam and Ahab'.[158] The phrases common to Ahijah's and Huldah's prophecies draw a connection between the cultic sins of Jeroboam and the cultic reforms of Josiah, implying that Jeroboam's evil

---

and even covering the folded ears speak to the immediacy of Necho's immersion in the Near East as he warred alongside the Assyrians against the Neo-Babylonians'. Source: www.metmuseum.org/art/collection/search/828678.

157. In Bosworth's schema, this 'spreading' from north to south occurs especially through Ahab's daughter, Athaliah, who perverts worship in Judah. Bosworth, *Story*, 145.

158. Wray Beal, *1 Kings*, 504; similarly, Sweeney, *Josiah of Judah*, 49–50; idem, *I & II Kings*, 442. In addition, the parallels between the deaths of Ahab and Josiah (as recorded in 2 Chron. 35) are remarkable: both kings repent and are shown mercy by God; both go out to war in disguise after being warned against it; both are shot by archers in their chariots; and both die as a result of their arrow wounds. Sweeney concludes from these observations that 'the house of David, including Josiah, is condemned to punishment by virtue of its identification with the house of Omri'. Sweeney, *I & II Kings*, 441.

way is so deeply ingrained as to bring even the mercies of Yahweh to a temporary standstill in Josiah's day – three centuries later.

While the abrupt death of Josiah has evidently raised considerable difficulties for biblical tradents and interpreters alike, this tension is set in relief to some degree when Josiah's death in 2 Kings 23 is read alongside 1 Kings 13 as a counterpoint. The numerous points of narrative analogy between the man of God in 1 Kings 13 and King Josiah in 2 Kings 22–23 illuminate each story or 'bookend' in important ways. But let us turn now to a key passage describing Josiah's visit to Bethel, six verses that Barth described as 'the real epilogue' to 1 Kings 13.[159]

2 Kings 23.15-20

> [15]Moreover, the altar at Bethel, the high place erected by Jeroboam son of Nebat, who caused Israel to sin – he pulled down that altar along with the high place. He burned the high place, crushing it to dust; he also burned the sacred pole. [16]As Josiah turned, he saw the tombs there on the mount; and he sent and took the bones out of the tombs, and burned them on the altar, and defiled it, according to the word of the LORD that the man of God proclaimed, when Jeroboam stood by the altar at the festival; he turned and looked up at the tomb of the man of God who had predicted these things. [17]Then he said, 'What is that monument that I see?' The people of the city told him, 'It is the tomb of the man of God who came from Judah and predicted these things that you have done against the altar at Bethel'. [18]He said, 'Let him rest; let no one move his bones'. So they let his bones alone, with the bones of the prophet who came out of Samaria. [19]Moreover, Josiah removed all the shrines of the high places that were in the towns of Samaria, which kings of Israel had made, provoking the LORD to anger; he did to them just as he had done at Bethel. [20]He slaughtered on the altars all the priests of the high places who were there, and burned human bones on them. Then he returned to Jerusalem.

2 Kings 23.1-14 narrates Josiah's reforms in and around Jerusalem, with particular reference to the idolatrous sins of Manasseh and Solomon. The narrator then turns our attention to Bethel, and to Jeroboam's altar in particular. Verses 15-20 are considered by many scholars working with a diachronic approach to be a later redaction, attributed by some to DtrP (a prophetic editor).[160] The links with 1 Kings 13 are obvious in any case,

---

159. Barth, *CD* II.2, 397.

160. So G. Jones, *1 & 2 Kings*, 2:624. The tendency to attribute various passages to schools or editors with different interests is, in my view, simplistic. One of the main underlying assumptions is that ancient authors and editors were incapable of literary sophistication.

not just thematically but also in terms of vocabulary. As Brueggemann observes, 'we can see a profound, self-conscious practice of intertextuality operative here...moreover, that the three references to Jerusalem (23:13-14), Samaria (23:19-20), and Bethel (23:15-18) are not simply happenstance references to earlier texts, but that the earlier texts have been placed as they are in order to create a context for the distinctive work of Josiah'.[161] Actually, almost every detail in the short passage is clearly aimed at expressing the fulfilment of the prophecy before its abrupt conclusion in v. 20: 'Then he returned to Jerusalem'.

First, Jeroboam's altar is broken down, burnt, crushed to dust (v. 15). One might reasonably ask (as Van Seters does) how it is possible to break down, burn *and* crush an altar to dust, but the multiplicity of images is almost surely theologically driven. The breaking down of the altar recalls the man of God's sign from 1 Kgs 13.3, 5; the burning recalls stipulations given in Deuteronomy for the treatment of towns that have fallen into apostasy (Deut. 13.16); and the crushing to dust is reminiscent of Moses dispensing with the golden calf in Exodus (32.20). The symbolic potency of the language is reminiscent of 1 Kings 13, and a proper consideration of the account's historiographical function mitigates against attempts to delimit its meaning.

Although Josiah's actions comply directly with the words (and actions) of the anonymous man of God who preceded him, the narrator makes doubly sure that the prophecy–fulfilment schema is not missed: 'he sent and took the bones out of the tombs, and burned them on the altar, and defiled it, according to the word of the LORD that the man of God proclaimed, when Jeroboam stood by the altar at the festival' (v. 16). It is interesting that the fulfilment of the man of God's prophecy in these verses is depicted as something that occurs quite by chance, and certainly not with Josiah's prior knowledge. That is to say, Josiah does not act as he does *in order to* fulfil an ancient prophecy. Rather, after tearing down the altar, Josiah notices a particular monument or signpost (ציון) that gives him pause to inquire about it significance (v. 17). But even if Josiah is ignorant of the significance of his actions, the impression given by the narrative is that 'the people of the city' are only too familiar with the prophecy concerning Jeroboam's altar. (Even 300 years on, the public nature of the events that transpired in Bethel retains significance.) The inhabitants of Bethel explain the importance of the tomb and the ancient prophecy to the southern king, connecting the man of God's words from the past to the king's actions in the present. Upon learning that the tomb belongs to one

---

161. Brueggemann, *Kings*, 556.

who foretold his reforms, Josiah commands that the man of God's bones be permitted to rest, free from disturbance.

One aspect of the fulfilment report that stands out in particular is the accent placed by the narrator on the common fate of the two anonymous prophets. That is, they are presented in a way that accents their *togetherness* in the reporting of vv. 18-20. First, they are reintroduced in vv. 17-18 with identical phrasing:

איש־האלהים אשר־בא מיהודה   the man of God who came from Judah (v. 17)
הנביא אשר־בא משמרון   the prophet who came from Samaria (v. 18)

Then, following the explanation of the monument's significance, and Josiah's command to let the bones rest, the narrator is careful to add that the bones of 'the prophet who came out of Samaria' are also left alone (v. 18).[162] In the same vein, v. 19 confirms the fulfilment of the Bethelite's addition to the prophecy by citing the additional phrase verbatim from 1 Kgs 13.32, when the Bethelite/Samarian prophet expanded upon the man of God's oracle regarding 'all the shrines of the high places that were in the towns of Samaria' (כל־בתי הבמות אשר בערי שמרון). The narrator thereby specially makes the point that Josiah's actions fulfil the prophecies of *both* the man of God (vv. 15-16) and the Bethelite (v. 19). The reader is thus reminded of the odd dynamic in the first story wherein the Bethel prophet's disposition was completely reversed upon hearing of the man of God's death. The deceased prophet went from foe to family as the Bethelite fetched the corpse, returned it to his own grave in Bethel, and publicly mourned the death of his 'brother'! In hindsight, the inexplicable *togetherness* of the anonymous prophets, so clearly in view in 2 Kgs 23.15-20, began at the conclusion of 1 Kings 13 with their deaths and the request for a shared grave (v. 31). One is reminded of Barth's statement, that the 'peculiar theme of the chapter is the manner in which the man of God and the prophet belong together, do not belong together, and

---

162. The reference to Samaria does not contradict the Bethelite's northern origin, as some commentators think, but does appear to reflect an era when Samaria had become established as the name for the northern region as distinct from Judah (i.e. seventh century; see Cogan, *1 Kings*, 290). Some commentators regard the mention of 'the prophet who came out of Samaria' in v. 18 as a reference to the man of God from Judah, and thereby think this to reflect an error in the text. E.g., G. Jones, *1 & 2 Kings*, 2:625. But as with 1 Kgs 13, the narrator continues to differentiate between 'the man of God who came from Judah' (v. 17) and 'the prophet who came out of Samaria' (v. 18). *BHS* has a textual note, suggesting that 'from Samaria' may be read as 'from Bethel', presumably for greater clarity and consistency with 1 Kgs 13.

eventually and finally do belong together; and how the same is true of Judah and Israel'.[163]

Although the authenticity and gravity of the decree against false worship in Bethel is underscored yet again in these verses, the 'real epilogue' to 1 Kings 13 gives the dissonance and perplexity of the whole story a surprisingly hopeful denouement.[164] For these two anonymous prophets, whose story commenced in a context of war and opposition, and whose relationship was therefore characterised by deceit and disobedience, are in the end unified. Even as their bones lie side by side in death, their prophecies are fulfilled in tandem beyond the walls of their shared tomb by a Davidic king whose long-awaited coming promises to uproot the evil way of Jeroboam and undo the very cause of their division. Indeed, the fulfilment of ancient prophecy and this portent of reunification call to mind another enacted parable and its message of hope for exilic Israel:

> I will make them one nation in the land, on the mountains of Israel; and one king shall be king over them all. Never again shall they be two nations, and never again shall they be divided into two kingdoms. They shall never again defile themselves with their idols and their detestable things, or with any of their transgressions. I will save them from all the apostasies into which they have fallen, and will cleanse them. Then they shall be my people, and I will be their God. (Ezek. 37.22-23)

Conclusion: Anonymous Prophets and Archetypal Kings

Our consideration of Dtr's post-exilic frame of reference spotlights Josiah as a central figure for interpreting and understanding Israel's monarchic historiography. His cultic reforms and their impact upon the populace evidently had a critical impact on Dtr's theology of history and the shaping of 1 Kings 13 and 2 Kings 22–23 as 'bookends' to the history. The manner in which the history of the kingdoms reflects the events of 1 Kings 13 is especially brought to light by a consideration of the exilic author's Josianic lens. It is widely recognised that Josiah's reign is presented as

---

163. *CD* II.2, 393.
164. On the centrality of the theme of hope in debates concerning redaction hypotheses and the theology of Dtr, see Noth, *The Deuteronomistic History*, 79–80; von Rad, *Studies*, 74–9; Wolff, 'Kerygma'; Brueggemann, 'The Kerygma of the Deuteronomistic Historian', *Int* 22 (1968): 387–402; and more recently, Nathan Lovell, 'The Shape of Hope in the Book of Kings: The Resolution of Davidic Blessing and Mosaic Curse', *JESOT* 3 (2014): 3–27.

the climactic point in the history of the kingdoms. Not only does Josiah oversee the rediscovery of the book of the law, but his wholehearted obedience to the Torah is unprecedented and accords with Deuteronomy's expectation that Israel's monarchs turn neither to the right nor the left from its demands (Deut. 17.20; 2 Kgs 22.2). In addition to his outstanding personal piety, Josiah is depicted as a king who demonstrates enormous concern for the obedience and worship practices of the populace as well. His reforms centralise worship in Jerusalem through the removal of illegitimate worship sites in both the south and the north, and he conducts a renewal ceremony in which he reads all the words from the book of the covenant before the people, who renew their covenant with the LORD (2 Kgs 23.2-3) and celebrate the Passover once again (2 Kgs 23.21-23). Fulfilling the prophecy in 1 Kings 13, Josiah unknowingly resolves many of the problems created by Jeroboam I whilst also raising the bar for Dtr's evaluation of northern and southern kings.[165]

Theological Context

At the beginning of this chapter, I commented on the particular function of 1 Kings 13 as I have perceived it, saying that the story does not have a particularly obvious moral or point, in and of itself. Moreover, we have seen that readers seeking a moralistic exposition of the strange narrative often fail to account for numerous details in the text. Indeed, in its context, the narrative appears to serve a different purpose.

Walsh's conclusion – that the determination of literary context brings the reader to the fore in the interpretive process – applies also to the prioritisation of theological motifs. We have seen that Barth's exegesis of 1 Kings 13 is set under the heading of election in his *Dogmatics*, and that subsequent scholars have located their readings within other theological fields of interest, such as prophetic discernment (Crenshaw) and political theology (Boer). The range of interests and questions provided by reading communities is, in fact, so diverse that what emerges is confirmation of Tate's honest assertion: 'Interpreters use texts to fulfil their interests or aims'.[166] In turn, interpretive interests inform methodological decisions and investigative outcomes. But are any or all theological categories

---

165. On cultic reform as a structuring device for the DH, with special emphasis on Josiah, see Hans-Detlef Hoffmann, *Reform und Reformen: Untersuchungen zu einem Grundthema der deuteronomistischen Geschichtsschreibung*, ATANT 66 (Zurich: Theologischer Verlag), 1980; cf. Van Seters, *In Search of History*, 317–20.

166. Tate, *Biblical Interpretation*, 195. Such interests and aims are not a free for all; rather, they are determined by a host of factors, including the rule of faith, biblical theology/intertextual resonances, and relevant life or ministerial experience.

equally suited to the task of interpreting 1 Kings 13? Clearly this is not the general perception, since Barth's analysis has been sidelined, or indeed rejected outright, by much subsequent scholarship due to the perception that he has brought 'strange fire' to the altar.[167] How then, might one ensure that an appropriate theological motif is being utilised to apprehend the text?

We observed in Chapter 3 that there are some problems with Klopfenstein's evaluation of Barth, since every interpreter inevitably brings critical questions and theological concerns to the exegetical task. Yet it seems to me that Klopfenstein's 'main question' remains an important one. He asks 'whether the text itself [*der Text selber*] proves Barth right' in his interpretation of 1 Kings 13 as a story about election and rejection.[168] For both Klopfenstein and Noth, a central issue in their criticism of Barth is whether *the text itself* does justice to Barth's choice of interpretive categories.

Consider an example briefly. Barth's exegesis labels northern prophets as false (i.e. rejected) and southern prophets as true (i.e. elect). After all, a dichotomy such as this helps to establish election as a theme in the narrative, which in turn informs his delineation of Christ as both the elect and rejected. However, it is telling that Barth defers to Amos to bolster his argument,[169] presumably because it is difficult to develop the claim that northern prophets were 'professional' from the text itself when certain northern prophets are presented as exemplary figures in Kings (e.g., Elijah and Elisha), and no discernible difference in meaning between 'prophet' and 'man of God' is apparent. Ultimately, it would appear that the categorisation is made because it suits Barth's reading with all its polarities between north and south, false and true, Jeroboam and Josiah, rejected and elected. Perhaps Klopfenstein's criticism holds some weight after all: a dialectical scheme of thought, which insists on and moves toward a synthesis of thesis and antithesis, lies couched in Barth's interpretation.[170] Crenshaw, for his part, sought to interpret the story using a theological category found *within* it – i.e. prophetic discernment – but on closer

---

167. DeVries, *I Kings*, 173.

168. Klopfenstein, '1 Kings 13', 667. See Chapter 3, pp. 57–63, under 'Konfrontation und Würdigung'.

169. Of 'the prophetic profession in contrast to the prophetic confession of the man of God from Judah', Barth states: 'It is naturally no accident that the roles are allotted exactly as in Amos: on the one hand, the institution, the bare possibility; and on the other the reality of prophecy rooted in the freedom of God'. *CD* II.2, 400. Cf. Amos 7.10-17.

170. Klopfenstein, '1 Kings 13', 670.

inspection, we found that the story is not about discernment at all, and that Crenshaw's reading does not account for all the story's details, but only a select(ed) few. In the end, I am inclined to agree with Klopfenstein that the issue of election lies outside of the story's intrinsic logic (Chapter 3), just as the issue of prophetic discernment also does (Chapter 4).

What I have sought to do is to make sense of 1 Kings 13 within Dtr's literary world by using the categories evidenced in the text itself; namely, kings and prophets. Pushing beyond the mere recognition of these narrative elements, or plot structures, a primary theological motif arising from this reading strategy is that of leadership, or influence. As we have seen, the representative function of the anonymous prophets holds weight precisely in terms of Israel's influence upon Judah (i.e. 'the prophet who caused him to turn from the way' in 1 Kgs 13.26; cf. 2 Kgs 17.19) and the archetypal kings, who are established as benchmarks for the regnal account, are described with judgment formulae that refer explicitly to their influence – for better and worse – over the populace.

An accent on leadership arises not simply from an effort to say something 'relevant', but from Israel's own recollection of her past. In a fascinating biblical-theological study, Mark Boda has traced the theme of sin throughout the Old Testament, attending to the different remedies for sin presented within various books and key sections of the Bible. Of the Former Prophets, Boda contends that 'the first solution to the sin of the people of Israel is...*the provision of faithful leadership*'.[171] In part, this is due to the fact that Dtr's theology of sin, for which leadership provides a cure, is centred around cultic purity, an intergenerational sin with significant implications for the future of the kingdoms. The intergenerational effects of a king's choices are articulated not only in relation to Jeroboam and Josiah, but also Ahab, Hezekiah and Manasseh. Moreover, it is well-known that the inherent tension in Dtr's theology of sin, between personal responsibility (2 Kgs 22.18-20; cf. Deut. 24.16) and the sins of the fathers (e.g., 2 Kgs 23.26-27), comes to a head in King Josiah, who exemplifies a repentant response to the Law and Prophets (via Huldah), but is unable to disrupt the divine judgment that is coming.[172] Josiah thus presents a significant theological conundrum at the conclusion of the DH,

---

171. Mark J. Boda, *A Severe Mercy: Sin and Its Remedy in the Old Testament*, Siphrut: Literature and Theology of the Hebrew Scriptures 1 (Winona Lake, IN: Eisenbrauns, 2009), 186 (original emphasis). Sweeney, *King Josiah*, 318–23, also perceives leadership as a critical issue posed by the premature death of Josiah.

172. On Josiah's death as a theological problem, see e.g., Sweeney, 'King Manasseh of Judah and the Problem of Theodicy'.

and a poignant reminder that no single leader – even in spite of great charisma – can alter the fate of a people and turn the tide of history.[173] These kinds of observations, together with their undergirding theological suppositions regarding divine sovereignty, have profound implications for contemporary challenges in political and ecclesial leadership.

But perhaps the most valuable 'takeaway' of the reading offered in this chapter is the proleptic presentation of Josiah as the man of God from Judah, who provides an alternative royal archetype to Jeroboam. Building on Barth's observation that the story stands 'in title-form' over the history of the kingdoms, the narrative links between the man of God from Judah and Josiah create an interpretive matrix for evaluating the kings (see the table at the beginning of this chapter) and a reading strategy for 1 Kings 13. Although the theological import of such a proposal may not be immediately apparent, since the reading strategy highlights the story's hermeneutical function over its substantive content, numerous elements within 1 Kings 13 are illuminated by this interpretive approach. Literary parallels between the man of God from Judah and King Josiah proliferate, and the archetypal kings of Israel and Judah are starkly polarised ('the sins of Jeroboam' are set against the reforms of Josiah), even as the sins of Jeroboam ultimately pave the way for Josiah's death. Within the symbolism of the narrative, the old northern prophet leads his younger colleague to his demise, just as Israel's idolatry spreads from north to south in the subsequent account of the kingdoms. Moreover, the two bookends (1 Kgs 12.33 13.34; 2 Kgs 23.15-20) establish a prophecy–fulfilment schema that places a significant accent upon YHWH's sovereignty over history. The structure of the whole indicates that the word of the LORD, spoken at the inception of the history of the divided kingdom, has enduring efficacy. That both Israel and Judah are doomed from the outset is manifested in 1 Kings 13, where the anonymous kingdom representatives (i.e. the man of God and the old prophet), who prove to be disobedient and deceptive, die separate deaths but share a common grave. By the same token, Jeroboam and Josiah, within their own times and contexts, die in ways that bespeak the fates of their kingdoms, Israel and Judah. Between bookends that accentuate these two theological figures is an historical account wherein Israel and

---

173. From a consideration of numerous texts throughout the DH, Fretheim makes a compelling argument that 'a mechanistic notion of sin-consequence, or a fixed theory of retribution, cannot be ascribed to the Deuteronomic History'. Fretheim, 'Repentance in the Former Prophets', in *Repentance in Christian Theology*, ed. Mark Boda and Gordon T. Smith (Collegeville, MN: Liturgical, 2006), 38.

Judah also move steadily towards a shared, exilic grave under the rule of various wayward kings who lead their peoples into sin through cultic improprieties. The history consistently hearkens back to Jeroboam's failure (no fewer than 26 times) even as it anticipates its climax in Josiah, the incomparable son of David foretold in 1 Kgs 13.2. Finally, even as Dtr's account of the divided kingdoms nears the tragic end that was prophesied at its inception, a hopeful note is sounded – not just in the reign and reforms of Josiah, but also in the union of the two anonymous prophets who represent the nations whence they come.

The theological crux, or moral of the story in 1 Kings 13, if I may speak thus, is that Israel and Judah are both doomed before the history of division even begins, so deeply will the sins of Jeroboam infect the religious practices of north and south. The anonymous kingdom representatives within this parabolic story make this abundantly clear in that one proves to be disobedient and the other deceptive. As the narrative plot unfolds – both in 1 Kings 13 and in the subsequent history – it becomes clear that Israel and Judah are destined to share an exilic grave. From a post-exilic author's point of view (i.e. in hindsight), the literary placement of 1 Kings 13 thus permits a schema of prophecy and fulfilment to envelope the entire history of the divided kingdom, casting a shadow upon it from its inception. The archetypal figures of Jeroboam and Josiah are ideally suited in that both kings influence their subjects with religio-political actions that are remembered forever as 'the sins of Jeroboam' and 'the reforms of Josiah'. Thus, the narratives about these figures not only establish a prophecy–fulfilment schema that highlights the sovereignty of Yahweh over history,[174] but that also stresses the Dtr principle that dynastic stability is dependent upon cultic centralisation.

My purpose in all of this is to indicate how a theological context for reading 1 Kings 13 might take its cues from *the text itself*: first, by attending to the way the literary framing (via *Wiederaufnahme*) of 1 Kings 13 reinforces important certain motifs, such as cultic purity and regnal responsibility; and second, by noting that some of the clearest categories for constructive theological work are presented quite plainly (though not simply!) in the narrative; namely, in the anonymous prophets and archetypal kings.

---

174. Cf. von Rad, *Studies*, 79.

8

CONCLUSION

Summary

In this book, I have sought to present a coherent reading of 1 Kings 13 that is attentive to its literary, historical, and theological cues. As noted in the Introduction, my aims in doing so have been twofold: on one hand, to offer a detailed exegesis of 1 Kings 13 that engages with the work of other scholars, regardless of whether their approaches and interests are the same as my own; on the other hand, to reflect on some of the hermeneutical assumptions and theological priorities that influence interpreters in their work. By way of conclusion, then, I shall briefly summarise the ground covered in Chapters 1–7 and then indicate some of the implications this book may have for further study and research.

Our study of 1 Kings 13 began with Karl Barth's exegesis of the passage, as it appears in his *Church Dogmatics*, not least because it remains one of the most fascinating, provocative, and insightful readings available. Therefore, in Chapter 2 I offered a detailed summation of the form and content of Barth's exegesis, followed by an assessment of his hermeneutical and doctrinal frames of reference. Certain literary aspects of his reading were noted also for their ongoing impact upon narrative-critical readings and thematic studies in Kings.

In Chapter 3, Barth's reading was subjected to a strictly historical-critical evaluation, guided by the sharp insights and questions of Martin Klopfenstein. While there is significant overlap in the details of the two expositions, Klopfenstein took issue with Barth's tendencies to impose dialectic patterns upon the text and to read intertextually, both of which, in his view, lead to *Überinterpretation*. Similarly, Noth's primary criticism was that the theme of election is nowhere to be found in this particular text. These esteemed biblical scholars each had a significant negative impact on the reception of Barth's exegesis in Old Testament scholarship.

The past seventy years of scholarship came under brief review in Chapter 4 in order to assess the main ways in which the subject matter of 1 Kings 13 has been understood. The four main categories I identified are: the discernment of true and false prophecy; the efficacious Word of God; an anti-north polemic; and political allegory. These themes were investigated in turn by engaging with scholarly works representing a variety of disciplines: James Crenshaw for a psychological/sociological reading; Jerome Walsh for his literary/structural analysis; John Van Seters for a redaction- and source-critical approach; and Roland Boer for a political and allegorical interpretation. These distinct approaches to the text presented a range of insights and observations, though some interpretations were found to be more internally coherent and methodologically consistent than others. In any case, these four construals of 1 Kings 13 provided a range of examples and illustrative material for a more theoretical analysis of interpretive issues in Chapter 5.

Given the sheer size and scope of the discipline of hermeneutics, the inquiry in Chapter 5 was limited to three perceived dichotomies in the field of hermeneutics that have the potential to polarise scholars and their work and lead to misunderstandings: author- and text-hermeneutics; canonical and historical-critical approaches; and synchronic and diachronic priorities. These were discussed as spectrums within which interpreters are encouraged to explicitly locate their projects so as to avoid confusion about the aims and means of inquiry. One way to foster dialogue where competing construals appear to be mutually exclusive, suggested by Richard Briggs, is to contextualise judgments by speaking of '*scripture as...*' rather than arguing about what scripture *is*.

In Chapter 6, we returned again to Barth's exegesis, this time with a more favourable outlook from David Bosworth, who has sought to develop Barth's reading by filling in the gaps where Barth was suggestive but not forthcoming with detail. Although Bosworth's project was found to be methodologically different to Barth's, his mapping of the multiple reversals in 1 Kings 13 onto the history of the divided kingdoms is a stimulating and worthwhile endeavour in its own right that complements Barth's work in important ways.

Finally, in Chapter 7, I offer a fresh interpretation of 1 Kings 13 by drawing on two key observations from previous scholars, one being Barth's brilliant observation about the metaphorical dimension of the text, and the other being Childs's notion of canonical shaping that permits the entire historical record (in its final form) to be viewed in hindsight through a Josianic lens. Building on these insights, I also utilise the redactional framing and literary function of 1 Kings 13 to establish a context for interpretation. My proposal is that when 1 Kings 13 is read as a narrative analogy that understands the man of God from Judah to prefigure Josiah, this reading strategy untangles much of the complexity in the story. More precisely, I construe the chapter as a proleptic parable within which the kingdoms of Israel and Judah are represented by two anonymous prophetic figures and Josiah of Judah is presented as the ideological antithesis of Jeroboam I of Israel. These two archetypal kings are set against one another in the narrative in a way that makes sense of Dtr's thematic priorities throughout the regnal accounts (e.g., in the evaluation of other kings) and accents the impact of their leadership over the kingdoms. In this sense, 1 Kings 13 is found to be of considerable structural importance, not unlike Dtr's speeches in the works of Wellhausen and Noth.

Implications

I have maintained throughout that readerly choices directly impact the meanings drawn from engagement with a text, and that these hermeneutical decisions are often determined by one's interpretive aims (see esp. Chapter 4). For this reason, the implications of a study such as this will be perceived differently by other readers, each according to their distinct interpretive agendas. In these last few pages, then, I aim to briefly outline the implications of this book under headings that represent some of the distinct (though often related) sub-disciplines in biblical studies.

(a) *Hermeneutics*

While I by no means claim to have broken new ground in hermeneutical theory, this work provides a case study in hermeneutical pluralism that takes as its focus one of the most perplexing narratives in the Old Testament. This has heuristic value for weighing interpretations against one another, and for increasing scholarly self-awareness with regards to *how* we read the Bible. Accordingly, my own reading of 1 Kings 13 has not been offered in isolation from other readings, but has drawn on and built upon insights garnered from numerous angles of inquiry, including redaction-critical (e.g., *Wiederaufnahme* and the literary framing of the chapter), theological/doctrinal (e.g., Barth's insight concerning the prophets as representative figures for their kingdoms), narrative-critical (e.g., analysis of characterisation, gaps, and narrative analogy), historical-critical (e.g., the association between Pharaoh Necho II and lions), and canonical (e.g., intertextual nuances regarding the lion and the three-fold commandment). As a consequence, it is my hope that this study advances the notion of what hermeneutical pluralism actually entails, not through (yet another) theoretical discussion, but through numerous worked examples in the text.

(b) *Literary Approaches*

In the previous chapter, I sought to proffer a literary interpretation of 1 Kings 13 that remains within an Old Testament (and Dtr) frame of reference. Perhaps one of the most significant implications for literary studies is that the reading suggested has the potential to stimulate further studies on texts in the DH that are comparable in genre and style (e.g., Judg. 9; 1 Kgs 20).[1] Certainly, one of the primary gains of reading 1 Kings 13 through a 'Josianic lens' is the insight concerning the hermeneutical function of 1 Kings 13, and as I have sought to demonstrate, the interpretive framing of the story via *Wiederaufnahme* has implications for understanding the evaluations of kings throughout the history, the importance of cultic centralisation, and the canonical shaping of the DH. The study of narrative analogy in the Hebrew Bible is no longer new, and it could certainly benefit from some standardisation of terminology and criteria, but this also seems to me a very promising strand for further literary studies in the DH.[2]

(c) *Redaction Criticism*

If the suggestion that the man of God from Judah anticipates and mirrors King Josiah is taken to have been in the mind of the author-redactor(s) of 1 Kings 13, then such a view may present a challenge to the notion of a Josianic redaction. (To be clear, however, it has not been my intention to challenge or propose redaction theories for the DH.) As a broad, structural observation concerning the final shape of Kings and the DH, my reading of 1 Kings 13 suggests that Josiah is the highpoint, *but not the endpoint*, of this history. That is to say, in spite of his cultic reforms and the renewal of Israel's covenant, Josiah's untimely death and the exile of his people is clearly anticipated in 1 Kings 13. While I have not sought to offer a redactional assessment of 1 Kings 13 or 2 Kgs 23.15-20, this reading of the text in its final form potentially impacts upon the viability of Cross's double-redaction hypothesis.[3]

---

1. The story in 1 Kgs 20 (esp. vv. 35-43) is especially interesting for all its points of commonality with 1 Kgs 13.

2. See, e.g., Garsiel, *Samuel*; Berman, *Narrative Analogy*; Nahkola, *Double Narratives*; Peter Miscall, 'The Jacob and Joseph Stories as Analogies', *JSOT* 6 (1978): 28-40; idem, *The Workings of Old Testament Narrative*, Semeia Studies (Chico, CA: Scholars Press, 1983); James G. Williams, 'The Beautiful and the Barren: Conventions in Biblical Type-scenes', *JSOT* 17 (1980): 107-19.

3. Cf. Janzen, 'The Sins of Josiah and Hezekiah', which also challenges the double-redaction hypothesis on the basis of a synchronic reading.

8. Conclusion

In Cross's double-redaction theory, 1 Kings 13, together with 2 Kings 22–23, is considered to be part of Dtr¹, a piece of Josianic propaganda composed in the seventh century.[4] His hypothesis rests on the identification of two major themes in Dtr¹ – the sin of Jeroboam (1 Kgs 13.34) and the faithfulness of David (1 Kgs 13.2) – both of which are mentioned explicitly in 1 Kings 13. Moreover, Cross specifies that 'these themes must stem from a very specific setting having a specific social function. We shall argue that they belong properly to a Josianic edition of the Deuteronomistic history.'[5] But the themes of Jeroboam's sin and the faithfulness of David could have had social functions other than that of political propaganda for Josiah. Furthermore, it is a weakness of Cross's argument that he cites these verses from 1 Kings 13 without attending to the narrative development that occurs between them. The mention of Josiah in 13.2 surely requires an explanation that takes into account the story of which it is a part, but Cross says almost nothing about what 1 Kings 13 might mean as a whole; he simply notes that the prophecy of an unidentified prophet from Judah anticipates Josiah's reform, 'preparing the reader's mind for the coming climax'.[6] Cross is correct to see that 1 Kings 13 anticipates Josiah's reforms as a climactic point in the history, but he fails to note how the numerous parallels between the man of God and Josiah may have significance for a Josianic edition of the DH. The prophecy in 1 Kgs 13.2 indeed points to Josiah as the one who will provide a remedy to Jeroboam's cultic trespasses, but this by no means requires that the Josiah narrative be the last word in the history. On the contrary, if 1 Kings 13 and 2 Kings 22–23 provide bookends to the history of the kingdoms, wherein Josiah is presented as a climactic point in the history *but not the end* – since the exilic end is already in view in 1 Kings 13 – then the history of the kingdoms interpreted thus could hardly have served as propaganda for Josiah's reforms. Rather, Josiah is presented as a key figure within an historical record that interprets and depicts events not only in light of his life, but also of his untimely death. Thus, Provan is surely justified in asking 'whether there is any compelling evidence that Josiah was the hero of a pre-exilic, rather than an exilic edition of the books'.[7]

---

4. Cross, *Canaanite Myth*, 278–80.
5. Ibid., 279.
6. Ibid., 280, 283.
7. Provan, *Hezekiah*, 147. The Manasseh passage also remains problematic for the double redaction hypothesis since scholars are unable to remove 2 Kgs 21 from the narrative (especially vv. 10-15, which articulate the imminent destruction of Judah and

(d) Theology of the DH

Another related implication of this study is its potential contribution to the theological (some would prefer to say ideological) aims and interests of Dtr. Much time and effort has been spent on getting 'behind' the text on certain matters presented in Kings. But as we observed in Chapter 5, the dangers of historicism are that interpreters can miss Dtr's point when the meaning of a text is perceived to be bound up with specific events at the time of writing. Dtr's depictions of Jeroboam and Josiah as flagrant lawbreaker and fervent lawkeeper are actually rather hard to miss, and oftentimes tensions within the narrative can serve as indicators of Dtr's theology, not just as evidence of fictionalised history. For instance, Jeroboam is denigrated for acting as priest-king in 1 Kgs 12.30–13.5, whereas Josiah is celebrated for doing so when he leads the Passover celebration in 2 Kgs 23.21-23. Similarly, Dtr seems reluctant to posit blame upon Jeroboam for a specific misdeed such as syncretism, idolatry or apostasy. Rather, the terms throughout Kings remain generic as the 'way' (דרך) and 'sins' (חטאות) of Jeroboam. Whatever the precise nature of the wrongdoing might be, Dtr chooses to highlight (repeatedly!) that Jeroboam *caused* Israel to sin (1 Kgs 12.30; 13.33-34; 14.16, passim), thus shifting the focus from a particular misdeed to the king's influence over the community. In keep with this, we noted that Josiah is expressly praised for public actions that impact directly upon the populace, such as normalising true (i.e. centralised) worship and reinstating the Passover. These textual elements point to yet another structural motif that is illuminating for studies in the theology of the DH, namely, Dtr's use of royal archetypes.[8]

(e) Canonical Shaping

In light of Childs's accent on the importance of canonical shaping as a theological process that is correlative to the community-shaping work of Scripture, it is important to ask *how 1 Kings 13 is authoritative* for communities of faithful readers. This is a vital question that would seek to account for the driving forces that have given the story its manifest depth dimension. Building on the 'historical trajectory of textual redactors' outlined by McDonald in Chapter 7, further work on 1 Kings 13 might examine the central thesis put forward in my reading (that the man of

---

Jerusalem as judgment for the sins of Manasseh), and ascribe it to Dtr², as per Cross (*Canaanite Myth*, 285–7) without serious detriment to the meaning and message of the whole. Cf. Provan, *Hezekiah*, 145–7; Sweeney, *Josiah of Judah*, 10–12.

    8. See, e.g., Joseph, *Portrait of the Kings*, for development of a Davidic prototype.

God is a figure or prophetic stand-in for Josiah) in terms of its theocentric message to readers. If the canon was intentionally shaped to influence and transform the next generation(s) of readers – as I believe it was – then the literary characteristics of 1 Kings 13 as a narrative analogy and a framing device for the history of kings merit further consideration for their canon-conscious theological import.[9] To the point: what does this sophisticated structural schema say about God? And please note that this question is not suggested as an 'additional' point of interest only for those interested in *theological interpretation* per se, but rather – as Childs would affirm – as a further investigation into a text that is part of a canon that was collated and shaped *in order to* provide a witness to God's engagements with Israel and the church. The canon is as theologically intentional throughout as it is historically grounded or literarily rich, and although space does not permit an equal focus on all of these dimensions in this book, each of them certainly merits sustained attention.

(f) *Figural Reading*

My main point of contention with Barth's brilliant reading of 1 Kings 13 has been that he leaps abruptly from the shared grave of the two prophets to the resurrection of Christ. However, as I have indicated, my reasons for resisting this have been that Barth's exegesis is somewhat inconsistent with his own, clearly stated, methodological aim to stay within the world of the Old Testament witness unless 'the entity in question cannot be brought out or apprehended within the Old Testament world'.[10] Moreover, because of his jump to Jesus, Barth's interpretation gives insufficient attention to King Josiah, in spite of labelling 2 Kgs 23.15-20 'the real epilogue' to the story. As I have stated, I am not in principle opposed to figural readings of Scripture. In fact, I regret not having more space to develop my thoughts in this regard – and I suspect that I am not yet done writing about 1 Kings 13 for this very reason!

In my judgment, 1 Kings 13 lends itself to a figural mode of interpretation due to its parabolic presentation and the anonymity of its main protagonist. The pan-historical tenor of the story opens up interpretive options for various narrative details (such as the identity of the lion), and the anonymity of 'the man of God from Judah' evinces the possibility of considering other prominent 'men of God' in the Christian canon as potential figural referents. When the actions and fate of the man of God from Judah are perceived in connection with say, Moses, or Josiah, or

---

9. On canon consciousness (*Kanonbewußtsein*), see Driver, *Childs*, 160–205.
10. Barth, *CD* II.2, 389; also 408.

Jesus, certain patterns of divine action in human history come to the fore. As we noted in the previous chapter, Auerbach says of figural interpretation that it 'establishes a connection between two events or persons in such a way that the first signifies not only itself but also the second, while the second involves or fulfils the first'.[11] The purpose in suggesting that the text be further developed this way would be to unveil something of what God is doing in history, to ponder its expression in Scripture, and to identify with the text's referents in our present contexts.

In any case, these are questions and debates for other times and places. In the meantime, it is my hope that the survey of scholarship and the reading of 1 Kings 13 offered in this book will stimulate deeper and further engagement with the biblical text, and with colleagues whose path we share.

---

11. Auerbach, *Mimesis*, 73.

Bibliography

Aberbach, Moses, and Leivy Smolar. 'Aaron, Jeroboam & the Golden Calves'. *JBL* 86 (1967): 129–40.
Allen, Mark Dwayne. 'The Man of God, the Old Prophet, and the Word of the LORD'. PhD diss., University of Notre Dame, 2012.
Alter, Robert. *Ancient Israel: The Former Prophets: Joshua, Judges, Samuel and Kings*. New York: Norton & Co., 2013.
Alter, Robert. *The Art of Biblical Narrative*. New York: Basic, 1981.
Alter, Robert. 'A Literary Approach to the Bible'. *Commentary* 60, no. 6 (1975): 70–7.
Amit, Yairah. 'The Dual Causality Principle and its Effects on Biblical Literature'. *VT* 37 (1987): 385–400.
Auerbach, Eric. *Mimesis: The Representation of Reality in Western Literature*. Translated by Willard R. Trask. Princeton: Princeton University Press, 1953. [DT: 1946]
Bar-Efrat, Shimon. *Narrative Art in the Bible*. JSOTSup 70. Sheffield: Almond, 1989.
Barr, James. 'Childs' Introduction to the Old Testament as Scripture'. *JSOT* 16 (1980): 12–23.
Barth, Karl. *Church Dogmatics I.1: The Doctrine of the Word of God*. Translated by G. T. Thomson. Edinburgh: T. & T. Clark, 1936.
Barth, Karl. *Die Kirchliche Dogmatik II; Die Lehre von Gott 2*. Zollikon-Zurich: Evangelischer Verlag A.G., 1942.
Barth, Karl. 'Exegese von 1. Könige 13'. In *Biblische Studien, Heft 10*, edited by H.-J. Kraus, 12–56. Neukirchen-Vluyn: Neukirchener Verlag, 1955.
Barth, Karl. *Church Dogmatics II.2: The Doctrine of God*. Translated by G. W. Bromiley et al. Edinburgh: T. & T. Clark, 1957.
Bartholomew, Craig. 'Theological Interpretation'. In *The Oxford Handbook of Biblical Studies*, edited by Steven L. McKenzie. Oxford: Oxford University Press, 2013.
Barton, John. *Reading the Old Testament: Method in Biblical Study*. London: Darton, Longman & Todd, 1984.
Berlin, Adele. *Poetics and Interpretation of Biblical Narrative*. Bible and Literature Series 9. Sheffield: Almond, 1983.
Berman, Joshua A. *Narrative Analogy in the Hebrew Bible: Battle Stories and their Equivalent Non-battle Narratives*. VTSup 103. Leiden: Brill, 2004.
Blum, Erhard. 'Die Lüge des Propheten. Ein Lesevorschlag zu einer befremdlichen Geschichte (1 Kön 13)'. In *Textgestalt und Komposition: Exegetische Beiträge zu Tora und Vordere Propheten*, 319–20. Tübingen: Mohr Siebeck, 2010.
Boda, Mark J. *A Severe Mercy: Sin and Its Remedy in the Old Testament*. Siphrut: Literature and Theology of the Hebrew Scriptures 1. Winona Lake, IN: Eisenbrauns, 2009.
Bodner, Keith. *Jeroboam's Royal Drama*. Oxford: Oxford University Press, 2012.

Bodner, Keith. *The Theology of the Book of Kings*. Cambridge: Cambridge University Press, 2019.

Boer, Roland. *Jameson and Jeroboam*. Semeia Studies. Atlanta: Scholars Press, 1996.

Boer, Roland. 'National Allegory in the Hebrew Bible'. *JSOT* 74 (1997): 95–116.

Bosworth, David A. 'Revisiting Karl Barth's Exegesis of 1 Kings 13'. *BibInt* 10 (2002): 360–83.

Bosworth, David A. *The Story within a Story in Biblical Hebrew Narrative*. CBQMS 45. Washington: Catholic Biblical Association of America, 2008.

Briggs, Richard S. 'Biblical Hermeneutics and Scriptural Responsibility'. In *The Future of Biblical Interpretation: Responsible Plurality in Biblical Hermeneutics*, edited by Stanley E. Porter and Matthew R. Malcolm, 36–52. Milton Keynes: Paternoster, 2013.

Brueggemann, Walter. *1 and 2 Kings*. Macon, GA: Smyth & Helwys, 2000.

Brueggemann, Walter. 'The Kerygma of the Deuteronomistic Historian'. *Int* 22 (1968): 387–402.

Burnett, Richard E. *Karl Barth's Theological Exegesis: The Hermeneutical Principles of the* Römerbrief *Period*. Grand Rapids: Eerdmans, 2001.

Burney, C. F. *Notes on the Hebrew Text of the Book of Kings*. Oxford: Clarendon, 1902.

Busch, Eberhard. *Karl Barth: His Life from Letters and Autobiographical Texts*. Translated John Bowden. London: SCM, 1976.

Chapman, Stephen B. *1 Samuel as Christian Scripture: A Theological Commentary*. Grand Rapids: Eerdmans, 2016.

Chapman, Stephen B. *The Law and the Prophets: A Study in Old Testament Canon Formation*. FAT 27. Tübingen: Mohr Siebeck, 2000.

Chapman, Stephen B. 'Reclaiming Inspiration for the Bible'. In *Canon and Biblical Interpretation*, edited by Craig Bartholomew et al., 7:167–206. Grand Rapids, MI: Zondervan, 2006.

Childs, Brevard. 'Analysis of a Canonical Formula: "It shall be recorded for a future generation"'. In *Die Hebräische Bibel und ihre zweifache Nachtgeschichte*, edited by E. Blum, 358–64. Neukirchen-Vluyn: Neukirchener Verlag, 1990.

Childs, Brevard. *Biblical Theology of the Old and New Testaments: Theological Reflection on the Christian Bible*. Minneapolis: Fortress, 1992.

Childs, Brevard. *Introduction to the Old Testament as Scripture*. Philadelphia: Fortress, 1979.

Childs, Brevard. *Old Testament Theology in a Canonical Context*. Philadelphia: Fortress, 1985.

Childs, Brevard. 'A Study of the Formula "Until this Day"'. *JBL* 82 (1963): 279–92.

Cogan, Mordechai. *1 Kings*. AB 10. New York: Doubleday, 2001.

Cohn, Robert L. 'Literary Technique in the Jeroboam Narrative'. *ZAW* 97 (1985): 23–35.

Cosgrove, Charles H. 'Toward a Postmodern *Hermeneutica Sacra*: Guiding Considerations in Choosing between Competing Plausible Interpretations of Scripture'. In *The Meanings We Choose: Hermeneutical Ethics, Indeterminacy and the Conflict of Interpretations*, edited by Charles Cosgrove, 39–61. London: T&T Clark, 2004.

Crenshaw, James L. *Prophetic Conflict: Its Effect Upon Israelite Religion*. Berlin: de Gruyter, 1971.

Cross, Frank Moore. *Canaanite Myth and Hebrew Epic: Essays in the History of the Religion of Israel*. Cambridge, MA: Harvard University Press, 1973.

Culley, Robert C. *Themes and Variations: A Study of Action in Biblical Narrative*. Atlanta: Scholars Press, 1992.

Cunningham, Mary Kathleen. *What is Theological Exegesis? Interpretation and Use of Scripture in Barth's Doctrine of Election.* Valley Forge, PA: Trinity, 1995.

Davies, Philip R. 'Josiah and the Law Book'. In *Good Kings and Bad Kings: The Kingdom of Judah in the Seventh Century BCE*, edited by Lester L. Grabbe, 65–77. London: T&T Clark, 2005.

Davis, Ellen F. *Biblical Prophecy: Perspectives for Christian Theology, Discipleship, and Ministry.* Louisville: Westminster John Knox, 2014.

Dever, William G. 'The Silence of the Text: An Archaeological Commentary on 2 Kings 23'. In *Scripture and Other Artifacts: Essays on the Bible and Archaeology in Honor of Philip J. King*, edited by Michael D. Coogan et al., 143–4. Louisville, KY: Westminster John Knox, 1994.

Dever, William G. *What Did the Biblical Writers Know and When Did They Know It?* Grand Rapids: Eerdmans, 2001.

DeVries, Simon J. *1 Kings.* WBC 12. 2nd ed. Nashville: Nelson, 2003.

DeVries, Simon J. *Prophet Against Prophet: The Role of the Micaiah Narrative (1 Kings 22) in the Development of Early Prophetic Tradition.* Grand Rapids: Eerdmans, 1978.

Dorp, Jaap van. 'Wat is die steenhoop daar? Het graf van de man Gods in 2 Koningen 23' [What is that Pile of Stone There? The Grave of the Man of God in 2 Kings 23]. In *Amsterdamse Cahiers voor Exegese en Bijbelse Theologie* 8, edited by K. A. Deurloo et al., 64–97. Kampen: Kok, 1987.

Dozeman, Thomas B. 'The Way of the Man of God from Judah: True and False Prophecy in the Pre-Deuteronomic Legend of 1 Kings 13'. *CBQ* 44 (1982): 379–93.

Driver, Daniel R. *Brevard Childs, Biblical Theologian: For the Church's One Bible.* Tübingen: Mohr Siebeck, 2010.

Eynikel, Erik. 'Prophecy and Fulfillment in the Deuteronomistic History: 1 Kgs 13; 2 Kgs 23, 16-18'. In *Pentateuchal and Deuteronomistic Studies*, edited by C. Brekelmans and J. Lust, 227–37. BETL 94. Leuven: Leuven University Press, 1990.

Eynikel, Erik. *The Reform of King Josiah and the Composition of the Deuteronomistic History.* Leiden: Brill, 1996.

Fee, Gordon D., and Douglas Stuart. *How to Read the Bible the Bible for All its Worth.* Grand Rapids: Zondervan, 1981.

Fichtner, Joseph. *Das erste Buch von den Königen.* BAT 12/1. Stuttgart: Calwer, 1964.

Flavius Josephus, *The Works of Flavius Josephus: Antiquities of the Jews*, vol. 2. Revised by A. R. Shilletto. Translated by William Whiston. New York: Cosimo Classics, 2005.

Fox, Everett. *The Early Prophets.* The Schocken Bible 2. New York: Schocken, 2014.

Fretheim, Terence E. *First and Second Kings.* Westminster Bible Companion. Louisville: Westminster John Knox, 1999.

Fretheim, Terence E. 'Repentance in the Former Prophets'. In *Repentance in Christian Theology*, edited by Mark Boda and Gordon T. Smith, 47–66. Collegeville, MN: Liturgical, 2006.

Friedman, Richard E. *The Exile and Biblical Narrative: The Formation of the Deuteronomistic and Priestly Works.* HSM 22. Chico, CA: Scholars Press, 1981.

Frost, Stanley Brice. 'The Death of Josiah: A Conspiracy of Silence'. *JBL* 87 (1968): 369–82.

Garsiel, Moshe. *The First Book of Samuel: A Literary Study of Comparative Structures, Analogies and Parallels.* Ramat-Gan: Revivim, 1985.

Gesenius, Wilhelm. *Gesenius' Hebrew Grammar.* Edited by E Kautzsch. Translated by E. Kautzsch. 2nd ed. Oxford: Clarendon, 1910.

Gide, André. *Journals 1889–1949.* Translated by J. O'Brien. London: Penguin, 1984.

Gignilliat, Mark S. *Karl Barth and the Fifth Gospel: Barth's Theological Exegesis of Isaiah.* Aldershot, England: Ashgate, 2009.

Grabbe, Lester L., ed. *Good Kings and Bad Kings: The Kingdom of Judah in the Seventh Century BCE.* London: T&T Clark, 2005.

Gray, John. *I & II Kings.* OTL. London: SCM, 1964.

Gray, John. *I & II Kings: A Commentary.* OTL. 2nd ed. Philadelphia: Westminster, 1970.

Gressmann, Hugo. *Die älteste Geschichtsschreibung und Prophetie Israels (von Samuel bis Amos und Hosea).* Göttingen: Vandenhoeck & Ruprecht, 1921.

Gross, Walter. 'Lying Prophet and Disobedient Man of God in 1 Kings 13: Role Analysis as an Instrument of Theological Interpretation of an Old Testament Narrative Text'. *Semeia* 15 (1979): 97–129.

Gunn, David M. 'Narrative Patterns and Oral Tradition in Judges and Samuel'. *VT* 24 (1974): 286–317.

Gunn, David M. 'New Directions in the Study of Biblical Hebrew Narrative'. *JSOT* 39 (1987): 65–75.

Gunn, David M. 'Reading Right: Reliable and Omniscient Narrator, Omniscient God, and Foolproof Composition in the Hebrew Bible'. In *The Bible in Three Dimensions: Essays in Celebration of Forty Years of Biblical Studies in the University of Sheffield*, edited by David J. A. Clines et al., 85–101. JSOTSup 87. Sheffield: JSOT, 1990.

Gunneweg, A. H. J. 'Die Prophetenlegende 1 Reg 13 – Mißdeutung, Umdeutung, Bedeutung'. In *Prophet und Prophetenbuch: Festschrift für Otto Kaiser zum 65. Geburtstag*, 73–81. BZAW 185. Berlin: de Gruyter, 1989.

Halpern, Baruch. 'Why Manasseh is Blamed for the Babylonian Exile: The Evolution of a Biblical Tradition'. *VT* 48 (1998): 473–514.

Harvey, John E. *Retelling the Torah: The Deuteronomistic Historian's Use of Tetrateuchal Narratives.* JSOTSup 403. London: T&T Clark, 2004.

Heller, Roy. *Power, Politics, and Prophecy: The Character of Samuel and the Deuteronomistic Evaluation of Prophecy.* LHBOTS 440. New York: T&T Clark, 2006.

Hoffmann, Hans-Detlef. *Reform und Reformen: Untersuchungen zu einem Grundthema der deuteronomistischen Geschichtsschreibung.* ATANT 66. Zurich: Theologischer Verlag, 1980.

Hölscher, G. 'Das Buch der Könige, sein Quellen und seine Redaktion'. In *Eucharisterion.* Edited by H. Schmidt. FRLANT 36. Göttingen: Vandenhoeck & Ruprecht, 1923.

Holstein, Jay A. 'The Case of "*'îš hā'ĕlōhîm*" Reconsidered: Philological Analysis versus Historical Reconstruction'. *HUCA* 48 (1977): 69–81.

House, Paul R. *1, 2 Kings.* NAC 8. Nashville: Broadman & Holman, 1995.

Janzen, David. 'The Sins of Josiah and Hezekiah: A Synchronic Reading of the Final Chapters of Kings'. *JSOT* 37 (2013): 149–70.

Jepsen, Alfred. 'Gottesmann und Prophet: Anmerkungen zum Kapitel 1. Könige 13'. In *Probleme biblischer Theologie: Gerhard von Rad zum 70. Geburtstag*, edited by H. W. Wolff, 171–82. Munich: Kaiser, 1971.

Jepsen, Alfred. *Nabi: Soziologische Studien zur alttestamentlichen Literatur und Religionsgeschichte.* Munich: Beck, 1934.

Jones, Gwilym H. *1 and 2 Kings.* 2 vols. NCBC. Grand Rapids: Eerdmans, 1984.

Jones, Paul Hedley. 'Deceiving the Man of God from Judah: A Question of Motive'. In *Characters and Characterization in 1–2 Kings*, edited by Keith Bodner and Benjamin J. M. Johnson, 83–102. London: Bloomsbury, 2020.

Jones, Paul Hedley. *Sharing God's Passion: Prophetic Spirituality.* Milton Keynes: Paternoster, 2012.

Joseph, Alison L. *Portrait of the Kings: The Davidic Prototype in Deuteronomistic Poetics*. Minneapolis: Fortress, 2015.
Keil, C. F. *The Book of the Kings*. Biblical Commentary on the Old Testament. Translated by J. Martin. Grand Rapids: Eerdmans, 1950.
Kelsey, David H. *The Uses of Scripture in Recent Theology*. Philadelphia: Fortress, 1975.
Kissling, Paul J. *Reliable Characters in the Primary History: Profiles of Moses, Joshua, Elijah and Elisha*. JSOTSup 224. Sheffield: Sheffield Academic, 1996.
Klopfenstein, M. A. '1. Könige 13'. In *ΠΑΡΡΗΣΙΑ: K. Barth zum achtzigsten Geburtstag*, edited by E. Busch et al., 639–72. Zurich: EVZ-Verlag Zurich, 1966.
Knauf, Ernst A. 'Does "Deuteronomistic Historiography" (DtrH) Exist?' In *Israel Constructs its History: Deuteronomistic Historiography in Recent Research*, edited by Albert de Pury, Thomas Römer, and Jean-Daniel Macchi, 388–98. JSOTSup 306. Sheffield: Sheffield Academic, 2000.
Knoppers, Gary. 'The Deuteronomist and the Deuteronomic Law of the King: A Reexamination of a Relationship'. *ZAW* 108 (1996): 329–46.
Knoppers, Gary. 'Rethinking the Relationship between Deuteronomy and the Deuteronomistic History: The Case of Kings'. *CBQ* 63 (2001): 393–415.
Knoppers, Gary. *Two Nations Under God: The Deuteronomistic History of Solomon and the Dual Monarchies*. 2 vols. Atlanta: Scholars Press, 1994.
Knoppers, G. N., and J. G. McConville, eds. *Reconsidering Israel and Judah: Recent Studies*. SBTS 8. Winona Lake, IN: Eisenbrauns, 2000.
Kristeva, Julia. 'Bakhtin, le mot, le dialogue et le roman'. *Critique* 33 (1967): 438–65 [ET: 'Word, Dialogue and Novel'. In *Desire in Language: A Semiotic Approach to Literature and Art*, edited by Leon S. Roudiez, 64–91. Translated by Thomas Gora et al. New York: Columbia University Press, 1980.]
Kuhl, Curt. 'Die "Wiederaufnahme" – ein literarkritisches Prinzip?' *ZAW* 64 (1952): 1–11.
Lasine, Stuart. *Weighing Hearts: Character, Judgment, and the Ethics of Reading the Bible*. LHBOTS 568. New York: T&T Clark, 2012.
Leithart, Peter J. *1 & 2 Kings*. Brazos Theological Commentary on the Bible. Grand Rapids, MI: Brazos, 2006.
Leithart, Peter J. *Deep Exegesis: The Mystery of Reading Scripture*. Waco, TX: Baylor University Press, 2009.
Lemke, Werner E. 'The Way of Obedience: I Kings 13 and the Structure of the Deuteronomistic History'. In *Magnalia Dei: The Mighty Acts of God. Festschrift for G. E. Wright*, edited by F. M. Cross, W. E. Lemke, and P. D. Miller, Jr., 301–26. Garden City: Doubleday, 1976.
Levenson, Jon D. '1 Samuel 25 as Literature and History'. *CBQ* 40 (1978): 11–28.
Levenson, Jon D. 'The Eighth Principle of Judaism and the Literary Simultaneity of Scripture'. *The Journal of Religion* 68 (1988): 205–25.
Levenson, Jon D. 'Who Inserted the Book of the Torah?' *HTR* 68 (1975): 203–33.
Levinson, Bernard M. 'The Reconceptualization of Kingship in Deuteronomy and the Deuteronomistic History's Transformation of Torah'. *VT* 51 (2001): 511–34.
Levinson, Bernard M. 'The Right Chorale: From the Poetics to the Hermeneutics of the Hebrew Bible'. In *'The Right Chorale': Studies in Biblical Law and Interpretation*, 7–39. FAT 54. Tübingen, Mohr Siebeck, 2008.
Lindblom, Johannes. *Prophecy in Ancient Israel*. Oxford: Blackwell, 1962.
Linville, James Richard. *Israel in the Book of Kings: The Past as a Project of Social Identity*. JSOTSup 272. Sheffield: Sheffield Academic, 1998.

Long, Burke O. *I Kings with an Introduction to Historical Literature*. FOTL 9. Grand Rapids: Eerdmans, 1984.
Long, Burke O. 'Framing Repetitions in Biblical Historiography'. *JBL* 106 (1987): 385–99.
Long, Jesse C. Jr. *1 & 2 Kings*, College Press NIV Commentary. Joplin, MO: College Press, 2002.
Lovell, Nathan. 'The Shape of Hope in the Book of Kings: The Resolution of Davidic Blessing and Mosaic Curse'. *JESOT* 3 (2014): 3–27.
MacDonald, Neil B. 'Theological Interpretation, the Historical Formation of Scripture, and God's Action in Time'. In *The Bible as Scripture: The Work of Brevard S. Childs*, edited by Christopher R. Seitz and Kent Harold Richards. BSNA 25. Atlanta: Society of Biblical Literature, 2013.
Marcus, David. 'Elements of Ridicule and Parody in the Story of the Lying Prophet from Bethel'. In *Proceedings of the Eleventh World Congress of Jewish Studies, Jerusalem, 22–29 June 1993*, 67–74. [Reprinted in Marcus, *From Balaam to Jonah: Anti-Prophetic Satire in the Hebrew Bible*. Atlanta: Scholars Press, 1995.]
Marcus, David. *From Balaam to Jonah: Anti-Prophetic Satire in the Hebrew Bible*. Atlanta: Scholars Press, 1995.
McCarthy, Dennis. 'II Samuel 7 and the Structure of the Deuteronomistic History'. *JBL* 84 (1965): 131–8.
McConville, J. Gordon. *God and Earthly Power: An Old Testament Political Theology Genesis–Kings*. New York: T&T Clark, 2008.
McConville, J. Gordon. 'Narrative and Meaning in the Books of Kings'. *Biblica* 70 (1989): 31–49.
McGlasson, Paul. *Jesus and Judas: Biblical Exegesis in Barth*. Atlanta, GA: Scholars Press, 1991.
McKenzie, Stephen L. *The Chronicler's Use of the Deuteronomistic History*. HSM 33. Atlanta: Scholars Press, 1985.
McKenzie, Stephen L. *The Trouble with Kings: The Composition of the Book of Kings in the Deuteronomistic History*. VTSup 42. Leiden: Brill, 1991.
Mead, James. 'Kings and Prophets, Donkeys and Lions: Dramatic Shape and Deuteronomistic Rhetoric in 1 Kings XIII'. *VT* 49 (1999): 191–205.
Miller, Geoffrey. 'Intertextuality in Old Testament Research'. *CBR* 9 (2011): 283–309.
Miscall, Peter D. 'The Jacob and Joseph Stories as Analogies'. *JSOT* 6 (1978): 28–40.
Miscall, Peter D. *The Workings of Old Testament Narrative*. Semeia Studies. Chico, CA: Scholars Press, 1983.
Moberly, R. W. L. 'The Canon of the Old Testament from a Western Perspective: Some Historical and Hermeneutical Reflections from the Western Perspective'. In *Das Alte Testament als christliche Bibel in orthodoxer und westlicher Sicht*, edited by I. Z. Dimitrou et al., 239–57. WUNT 174. Tübingen, Mohr Siebeck, 2004.
Moberly, R. W. L. *The Old Testament of the Old Testament: Patriarchal Narratives and Mosaic Yahwism*. OBT. Minneapolis: Fortress, 1992.
Moberly, R. W. L. *Prophecy and Discernment*. Cambridge Studies in Christian Doctrine. Cambridge: Cambridge University Press, 2006.
Monroe, Lauren A. S. *Josiah's Reform and the Dynamics of Defilement: Israelite Rites of Violence and the Making of a Biblical Text*. New York: Oxford University Press, 2011.
Montgomery, James. *The Books of Kings*. Edited by Henry Snyder Gehman. ICC. Edinburgh: T. & T. Clark, 1951.

Mullen, E. T. *Narrative History and Ethnic Boundaries: The Deuteronomistic Historian and the Creation of Israelite National Identity.* SemeiaSt 24. Atlanta: Scholars Press, 1993.
Mullen, E. T. 'The Sins of Jeroboam: A Redactional Assessment'. *CBQ* 49 (1987): 212–32.
Na'aman, Nadav. 'Prophetic Stories as Sources for the Histories of Jehoshaphat and the Omrides'. *Biblica* 78 (1997): 153–73.
Nahkola, Aulikki. *Double Narratives in the Old Testament: The Foundations of Method in Biblical Criticism.* BZAW 290. Berlin: de Gruyter, 2001.
Nelson, Richard D. *The Double Redaction of the Deuteronomistic History.* JSOTSup 18. Sheffield: JSOT, 1981.
Nelson, Richard D. 'The Double Redaction of the Deuteronomistic History: The Case is Still Compelling'. *JSOT* 29 (2005): 319–37.
Nelson, Richard D. *First and Second Kings.* Interpretation. Louisville: John Knox, 1987.
Nelson, Richard D. 'Josiah in the Book of Joshua'. *JBL* 100 (1981): 531–40.
Noth, Martin. *1 Könige, 1.* BKAT 9. Neukirchen-Vluyn: Neukirchener Verlag, 1968.
Noth, Martin. *The Deuteronomistic History.* JSOTSup 15. 2nd ed. Sheffield: JSOT, 1981. [Translated by D. J. A. Clines et al. of pp. 1–110 of *Überlieferungsgeschichtliche Studien: Die Sammelnden und Bearbeitenden Geschichtswerke im Alten Testament.* 2nd ed. Tübingen: Max Niemeyer, 1957. Original 1943.]
Noth, Martin. *The History of Israel.* Translated by P. R. Ackroyd. 2nd ed. London: A. & C. Black, 1960.
Person, R. F. 'A Reassessment of Wiederaufnahme from the Perspective of Conversation Analysis'. *Biblische Zeitschrift* 43 (1999): 239–48.
Petersen, David L. *The Roles of Israel's Prophets.* Sheffield: JSOT, 1981.
Plöger, Otto. 'Speech and Prayer in the Deuteronomistic and the Chronicler's Histories'. In *Reconsidering Israel and Judah: Recent Studies on the Deuteronomistic History*, edited by Gary N. Knoppers and J. Gordon McConville, 31–46. Winona Lake, IN: Eisenbrauns, 2000. [Translated by Peter T. Daniels from Otto Plöger, 'Reden und Gebete im deuteronomistischen und chronistischen Geschichtswerk'. In *Festschrift für Günther Dehn zum 75. Geburtstag*, edited by W. Schneemelcher, 35–49; Neukirchen-Vluyn: Neukirchener Verlag, 1957.]
Porter, S., and M. Malcolm, eds. *The Future of Biblical Interpretation: Responsible Plurality in Biblical Hermeneutics.* Downers Grove, IL: InterVarsity, 2013.
Provan, Iain W. *1 and 2 Kings.* NIBC. Peabody, MA: Hendrickson, 1995.
Provan, Iain W. *Hezekiah and the Books of Kings: A Contribution to the Debate about the Composition of the Deuteronomistic History.* BZAW 172. Berlin: de Gruyter, 1988.
Pury, Albert de, et al., eds. *Deuteronomistic History in Recent Research.* JSOTSup 306. Sheffield: Sheffield Academic, 2000.
Rad, Gerhard von. *Das formgeschichtliche Problem des Hexateuchs.* Stuttgart: W. Kohlhammer, 1938. ET: 'The Form-Critical Problem of the Hexateuch'. In *The Problem of the Hexateuch and Other Essays.* Edinburgh: Oliver & Boyd, 1966.
Rad, Gerhard von. *Studies in Deuteronomy.* Translated by David Stalker. London: SCM, 1953.
Rendtorff, Rolf. 'The Paradigm is Changing: Hopes – and Fears'. *BibInt* 1 (1993): 34–53.
Rice, Gene. *1 Kings: Nations Under God.* ITC. Grand Rapids: Eerdmans, 1990.
Ricoeur, Paul. 'The Hermeneutical Function of Distanciation'. In *Hermeneutics and the Human Sciences: Essays on Language, Action, and Interpretation*, edited by Paul Ricoeur and John B. Thompson, 131–44. Cambridge: Cambridge University Press, 1981.

Robinson, Joseph. *The First Book of Kings*. Cambridge: Cambridge University Press, 1972.
Rofé, Alexander. 'Classes in the Prophetical Stories: Didactic Legenda and Parable'. In *Studies on Prophecy*, 143–64. VTSup 26. Leiden: Brill, 1974.
Rofé, Alexander. 'The Classification of the Prophetical Stories'. *JBL* 89 (1974): 427–40.
Rofé, Alexander. *The Prophetical Stories: The Narratives about the Prophets in the Hebrew Bible, Their Literary Types and History*. Jerusalem: Magnes, 1988.
Römer, Thomas. *The So-Called Deuteronomistic History: A Sociological, Historical and Literary Introduction*. London: T&T Clark, 2007.
Römer, Thomas, ed. *The Future of the Deuteronomistic History*. BEThL 147. Leuven: Leuven University Press, 2000.
Rosenberg, Joel. *King and Kin: Political Allegory in the Hebrew Bible*. Indiana Studies in Biblical Literature. Bloomington, IN: Indiana University Press, 1986.
Rowlett, Lori L. *Joshua and the Rhetoric of Violence: A New Historicist Approach*. JSOTSup 226. Sheffield: Sheffield Academic, 1996.
Schearing, L. S., and S. L. McKenzie, eds. *Those Elusive Deuteronomists: The Phenomenon of Pan-Deuteronomism*. JSOTSup 268. Sheffield: JSOT, 1999.
Schneiders, Sandra M. *The Revelatory Text: Interpreting the New Testament as Sacred Scripture*. 2nd ed. Collegeville, MN: Liturgical, 1999.
Schökel, Luis Alonso. *A Manual of Hermeneutics*. The Biblical Seminar 54. Sheffield: Sheffield Academic, 1998.
Seow, Choon-Leong. *The First and Second Books of Kings*. NIB 3. Nashville: Abingdon, 1999.
Simon, Uriel. 'I Kings 13: A Prophetic Sign – Denial and Persistence'. *HUCA* 47 (1976): 81–117. [Revised and republished as 'A Prophetic Sign Overcomes Those Who Would Defy It: The King of Israel, the Prophet from Bethel, and the Man of God from Judah'. In *Reading Prophetic Narratives*, 130–54. Translated by Lenn J. Schramm. Bloomington: Indiana University Press, 1997.
Smend, Rudolf. 'Karl Barth and Walter Baumgartner: Ein Briefwechsel über das Alte Testament'. In *Zeitschrift für Theologie und Kirche, Beiheft 6: Zur Theologie Karl Barths Beiträge aus Anlass seines 100. Geburstags*, edited by Eberhard Jüngel, 240–71. Tübingen: Mohr Siebeck, 1986.
Sommer, Benjamin D. 'Dating Pentateuchal Texts and the Perils of Pseudo-Historicism'. In *The Pentateuch: International Perspectives on Current Research*, edited by T. Dozeman et al., 85–110. Tübingen: Mohr Siebeck, 2011.
Sommer, Benjamin D. *A Prophet Reads Scripture: Allusion in Isaiah 40–66*. Contraversions: Jews and Other Differences. Stanford, CA: Stanford University Press, 1998.
Stendahl, Krister. 'Biblical Theology, Contemporary'. In *Interpreter's Dictionary of the Bible* (1962): 418–32.
Sternberg, Meir. *The Poetics of Biblical Narrative: Ideological Literature and the Drama of Reading*. Bloomington: Indiana University Press, 1985.
Strawn, Brent A. *What is Stronger than a Lion? Leonine Image and Metaphor in the Hebrew Bible and the Ancient Near East*. Orbis Biblicus et Orientalis 212. Göttingen: Vandenhoeck & Ruprecht, 2005.
Sweeney, Marvin A. *I & II Kings*, OTL. Louisville: Westminster John Knox, 2007.
Sweeney, Marvin A. *King Josiah of Judah: The Lost Messiah of Israel*. Oxford: Oxford University Press, 2001.

Talmon, Shemaryahu. 'The Presentation of Synchroneity and Simultaneity in Biblical Narrative'. In *Studies in Hebrew Narrative Art throughout the Ages*, edited by Joseph Heinemann. Jerusalem: Magnes/Hebrew University, 1978.
Tate, Randolph. *Biblical Interpretation: An Integrated Approach*. Rev. ed. Peabody, MA: Hendrickson, 1997.
Van Seters, John. *Abraham in History and Tradition*. New Haven, CT: Yale University Press, 1975.
Van Seters, John. 'The Deuteronomistic History: Can it Avoid Death by Redaction?' In *The Future of the Deuteronomistic History*, edited by Thomas Römer, 213–22. BEThL 147. Leuven: Leuven University Press, 2000.
Van Seters, John. *The Edited Bible: The Curious History of the 'Editor' in Biblical Criticism*. Winona Lake, IN: Eisenbrauns, 2006.
Van Seters, John. *In Search of History: Historiography in the Ancient World and the Origins of Biblical History*. London: Yale University Press, 1983.
Van Seters, John. 'On Reading the Story of the Man of God from Judah in 1 Kings 13'. In *The Labour of Reading: Desire, Alienation and Biblical Interpretation*, edited by Robert C. Culley et al., 225–34. Semeia St 36. Atlanta: Scholars Press, 1999.
Van Seters, John. 'Prophecy as Prediction in Biblical Historiography'. In *Prophets, Prophecy, and Ancient Israelite Historiography*, edited by Mark J. Boda and Lissa M. Wray Beal, 93–103. Winona Lake, IN: Eisenbrauns, 2013.
Van Winkle, D. W. '1 Kings XII 25–XIII 34: Jeroboam's Cultic Innovations and the Man of God from Judah'. *VT* 46 (1996): 101–14.
Van Winkle, D. W. '1 Kings XIII: True and False Prophecy'. *VT* 29 (1989): 31–43.
Wellhausen, Julius. *Die Composition des Hexateuchs und der historischen Bücher des Alten Testaments*. 3rd ed. Berlin: G. Reimer, 1899.
Wellhausen, Julius. *Die kleinen Propheten übersetzt underklärt*. 4th ed. Berlin: de Gruyter, 1963.
Wellhausen, Julius. *Prolegomena to the History of Ancient Israel*. Cambridge: Cambridge University Press, 2013 [1885]. Translation of *Prolegomena zur Geschichte Israels*. 2nd ed. Berlin: G. Reimer, 1883.
Wallace, Mark I. *The Second Naiveté: Barth, Ricoeur, and the New Yale Theology*. 2nd ed. Macon, GA: Mercer University Press, 1995.
Walsh, Jerome T. *Ahab: The Construction of a King*. Interfaces. Collegeville, MN: Liturgical, 2006.
Walsh, Jerome T. *1 Kings*. BO. Collegeville, MN: Liturgical, 1996.
Walsh, Jerome T. 'The Contexts of 1 Kings xiii'. *VT* 39 (1989): 355–70.
Walsh, Jerome T. 'Methods and Meanings: Multiple Studies of 1 Kings 21'. *JBL* 111 (1992): 193–211.
Walsh, Jerome T. *Old Testament Narrative: A Guide to Interpretation*. Louisville: Westminster John Knox, 2010.
Walsh, Jerome T. *Style and Structure in Biblical Hebrew Narrative*. Collegeville, MN: Michael Glazier, 2001.
Waltke, Bruce K., and Michael P. O'Connor. *Introduction to Biblical Hebrew Syntax*. Winona Lake, IN: Eisenbrauns, 1990.
Webster, John, ed. *The Cambridge Companion to Karl Barth*. Cambridge: Cambridge University Press, 2000.
Weinfeld, Moshe. *Deuteronomy and the Deuteronomic School*. Oxford: Clarendon, 1972.

Williams, James G. 'The Beautiful and the Barren: Conventions in Biblical Type-scenes'. *JSOT* 17 (1980): 107–19.
Wilson, Robert R. *Prophecy and Society in Ancient Israel*. Philadelphia: Fortress, 1980.
Wiseman, Donald J. *1 & 2 Kings*. TOTC. Leicester: IVP, 1993.
Wolff, Hans Walter. 'The Kerygma of the Deuteronomic Historical Work'. In *The Vitality of Old Testament Traditions*. Walter Brueggemann and Hans Walter Wolff, 83–100. 2nd ed. Atlanta: John Knox, 1982.
Wray Beal, Lissa M. *1 & 2 Kings*. Apollos OT Commentary 9. Nottingham: Apollos, 2014.

Index of References

Hebrew Bible/Old Testament

Genesis
4	33, 41
34.2	208
37–50	144
38	41, 144
49.9	56, 208, 209

Exodus
28.41	215
32.20	99, 219

Leviticus
14	31, 32, 36, 40–2, 44
14.4-7	42
14.15	42
16	31, 32, 36, 40–2, 44
16.5-10	42
16.8	42

Numbers
12	190
25	96

Deuteronomy
1.26	204
1.43	204
4.44–30.20	161
4.44–28.68	205
6.15	189
9	191, 192, 212
9.9	212
9.17	212
9.18	192, 212
9.23	204
12	161, 162, 192
12.2-6	191
12.5	183
12.7	191
13.5	162
13.16	219
17.7	162
17.16	192
17.20	222
18.15	189
19.19	162
21.9	162
21.21	162
22.21	162
22.24	162
24.16	224
24.27	162
28.68	192
31.11-12	161
33.1	189

Joshua
1	170
1.8	161
1.18	204
8.30-35	161
8.31-34	161
12	170
23	170
23.6	161
24.26	161

Judges
2	170
2.11-23	170
4	96
9	10, 230
9.7-15	145
17.5	215
17.12	215
19–21	42

1 Samuel
2.27-30	196
3.21	104, 185
9.2	43
12	170, 171
12.14-15	204
13.12	144
13.13	204
15	96
15.11	196
15.35	196
25	10, 144, 186
25.12	192

2 Samuel
2.1	42
5.3	144
7	171
12.1-6	145
12.1-4	111

1 Kings
1–11	90
2.3	161
4.7	195
8	169-71
8.9	169
9.1	195
11–21	143, 148
11–14	7, 87, 96, 106–9, 113, 143, 170, 172

11–14 LXX	107	13	1, 2, 4-20,		172, 180,
11	17, 32,		22, 26, 27,		184–6,
	109, 144		29–37,		204, 213,
11.11-13	108		39–49,		214, 216,
11.13	42		51–5, 57,		226, 231
11.26–14.20	90		58, 60,	13.3	91, 118,
11.29	170		62, 63,		119, 187,
11.31-39	108		65, 67–74,		188, 219
11.31-35	169, 170		76–88, 90,	13.4	97, 118
11.38	186		93–5, 97,	13.5	91, 99,
11.39	106		99–114,		104, 118,
12	18, 48, 65,		116, 117,		119, 132,
	109, 112		122–5,		185, 187,
12.1-20	108		127, 129,		188, 219
12.17-24	182		132,	13.6-10	12, 189
12.19	201		133, 135,	13.6	118
12.20	42		137–48,	13.7-9	118
12.21-24	108		149–60,	13.7	19, 97
12.22	170		164–72,	13.8-9	119
12.24	181		179–81,	13.8	202
12.25-32	182		185, 186,	13.9	3, 54, 104,
12.25	181, 182		188, 191,		132, 147,
12.26–13.10	90		195, 198,		157, 185,
12.26-33	215		201–3,		193, 194,
12.26-31	87		205, 207–		202, 204,
12.26-29	182		9, 213,		211
12.29	182		215–34	13.10	97, 118,
12.30–13.34	124	13.1-32	94, 194		192–4,
12.30–13.33	103	13.1-10	3, 28, 65,		211
12.30–13.5	232		73, 75, 86,	13.11–14.20	90
12.30-33	124		90, 111,	13.11-32	29, 59,
12.30-31	87, 90		118, 119,		65, 73–5,
12.30	88, 123,		132, 146,		86, 87,
	167, 168,		157, 189,		92, 104,
	173, 180,		193, 194		106, 112,
	182, 232	13.1-5	12		120, 132,
12.31-32	184	13.1-2	143		144–6,
12.31	124, 213	13.1	91, 104,		150, 156,
12.32–13.31	124		118, 119,		157, 194,
12.32-33	89, 184		181, 184,		198
12.32	181, 184,		185, 195	13.11-20	197
	213	13.2-3	103	13.11-19	13, 194
12.33–13.34	181, 182,	13.2	4, 39, 40,	13.11-18	143, 147
	225		54, 91,	13.11-13	111
12.33–13.33	103		96, 104,	13.11	3, 17, 92,
12.33–13.5	184		118, 119,		194–8,
12.33	181, 182		157, 165,		210, 214

13.12	92		209, 211,	15.34	168, 173
13.13	92		212, 224	16.13	173
13.14-18	92	13.27-32	13	16.19	174
13.15-20	100	13.27	92	16.26	168, 174
13.15	195, 197	13.28	56, 92,	17–19	90
13.17	54, 104,		207, 209	17.18	195
	132, 147,	13.29-30	92, 210	18.18	184
	157, 185,	13.31-32	92, 210	18.21	189
	194, 202,	13.31	150, 220	18.22	195
	204, 211	13.32	4, 55, 72,	18.40	96
13.18	80, 82,		104, 157,	19	192
	104, 109,		165, 185,	20	10, 98,
	148, 185,		187, 199,		104, 230
	196, 197,		200, 212–	20.1–22.40	90
	202		14, 220	20.35-43	230
13.19-20	99	13.33-34	13, 86, 87,	20.35	104
13.19	92, 143,		90, 112,	20.36	207
	147, 202		124, 157,	21.21	217
13.20-32	55		181, 194,	21.22	168, 174
13.20-26	13		214, 232	21.29	83, 98,
13.20-23	143	13.33	88, 124,		196
13.20-22	92, 93,		168, 180,	22	20, 78,
	203		194, 211,		80–4, 143,
13.20	6, 58, 59,		213, 214		145, 146,
	92, 93, 98,	13.34	88, 123,		148
	99, 149,		157, 167,	22.4	148
	199, 203		173, 180,	22.24	81
13.21-22	3		189, 231	22.25	81
13.21	55, 204,	14–16	195	22.28	81
	205, 211	14	17, 19, 48,	22.41-53	195
13.22-23	112		65, 96,	22.43	168, 174
13.22	147, 157,		109, 170,	22.52	168, 174,
	194, 205		180, 215		211
13.23-25	92, 205	14.1	181		
13.24-34	143	14.9	180, 217	2 Kings	
13.24-27	207	14.10	217	3	20, 145,
13.24	56, 206,	14.15-16	215		146, 148
	207, 209,	14.15	189	3.3	168, 175
	216	14.16	173, 180,	8	143
13.25-26	210, 214		232	8.18	175
13.25	3, 92, 207,	14.18	185	8.27	175
	209, 210	14.21–16.34	195	9–11	143, 149
13.26-32	210	14.22	215	9–10	149, 157,
13.26	3, 56, 57,	14.30	147, 201		208
	92, 157,	15.6	147	10.28	149
	193, 200,	15.16	147	10.29	180
	203, 204,	15.26	173	10.31	175

12–21	157, 158	21.3	178	23.17-18	220
12–17	143	21.8	161	23.17	4, 88, 219,
12–16	195	21.10-15	231		220
12.1–16.20	195	21.16	178	23.18-20	220
12.3	168, 175	22–23	143, 172,	23.18	220
13.2	168, 175		205, 218,	23.19-20	219
13.6	168		221, 231	23.19	173, 187,
13.11	168, 176	22	217		213, 220
13.31	161	22.2	222	23.20	4, 96, 213,
14.4	168, 176	22.8	161		219
14.6	161	22.11	161	23.21–25.30	127
14.24	88, 176	22.16-17	217	23.21-23	222, 232
15.4	168, 176	22.16	217	23.24-25	161
15.9	176	22.17	217	23.25	161
15.18	176	22.18-20	224	23.26-27	224
15.24	177, 179	23	39, 47, 94,	23.26	216
15.28	177		103, 106,	23.29	208, 216
15.35	168, 177		114, 143,	24.3	216
16.3-4	177		144, 150,		
17	105, 145,		157, 188,	*2 Chronicles*	
	169, 170,		205, 209,	10–13	107
	213		213, 218	19.2	148
17.7-23	170	23.1-14	218	30.12	185
17.7-20	171	23.2-3	222	35	217
17.7-18	170	23.4	94, 100,	35.21	216
17.13	161, 205		103, 105,		
17.19	203, 216,		123, 127	*Psalms*	
	224	23.8	105, 123	33.6	185
17.21-23	88, 157,	23.9	213		
	215	23.13-14	219	*Isaiah*	
17.21-22	172, 177	23.15-20	2, 7, 9, 13,	20	191
17.24-34	94, 103,		39, 45, 94,	37.34	192
	105, 123,		99, 103–5,	53	60, 209
	127		123, 127,		
17.24	187		144–6,	*Jeremiah*	
17.25-26	207		150, 156,	16.1-5	191
17.26	187		157, 164,	18.7-10	98, 196
17.29	213		215, 218,	22.23	81
17.32	213		220, 225,	23	78
17.34-34	104		230, 233	28	82
17.34	161	23.15-18	219	28.10	82
17.37	161	23.15-16	99, 220		
18	170	23.15	99, 173,	*Ezekiel*	
18.4	178		187, 219	4–5	191
18.22-23	168	23.16-20	198	33.10-16	196
19.33	192, 193	23.16	172, 188,	37.22-23	221
21	48, 231		219		

Daniel
6   208

Hosea
1   191

Amos
1.2   56, 209
3.8   56, 209
7.10-17   82, 223

Jonah
3.1-10   196

Zephaniah
1.1   215
1.3   215

NEW TESTAMENT
Matthew
23.9   38
23.27   38

Luke
12   23

John
1.1-2   31
5.39   33

Ephesians
1.4   31

INDEX OF AUTHORS

Aberbach, M. 183
Allen, M. D. 49
Alter, R. 14, 82, 131, 165, 185
Amit, Y. 110
Auerbach, E. 164, 234
Auld, A. G. 161

Bar-Efrat, S. 82, 131, 134
Barr, J. 164
Barth, K. 1, 4, 5, 9, 11, 12, 14–30, 32–47, 49, 56, 61, 63, 70–2, 74, 117, 118, 139, 142, 151–5, 200, 209, 215, 218, 233
Bartholomew, C. 67
Barton, J. 128
Beal, L. M. W. 74
Berlin, A. 131, 134, 167
Berman, J. A. 165, 230
Blum, E. 27, 64, 69
Boda, M. J. 224
Bodner, K. 76, 106, 159, 180, 207
Boer, R. 7, 76, 107–13, 115, 122, 208
Bosworth, D. A. 14, 37, 64, 65, 76, 89, 141, 142, 144–51, 153, 154, 156–8, 165, 192, 208, 217
Briggs, R. S. 8, 138, 140
Brueggemann, W. 2, 75, 131, 187, 219, 221
Burnett, R. E. 1, 30, 34, 35, 139
Burney, C. F. 182, 204
Busch, E. 38

Chapman, S. B. 121, 128, 129, 133
Childs, B. 12, 72, 126, 127, 129, 132, 135, 136, 164
Cogan, M. 73, 167, 181, 220
Coggins, R. 161
Cohn, R. L. 76, 106, 159, 167, 185
Cosgrove, C. H. 68
Crenshaw, J. L. 6, 51, 70, 71, 77–80, 84, 85, 122

Cross, F. M. 53, 103, 106, 123, 131, 140, 161, 171, 172, 186, 231, 232
Culley, R. C. 73
Cunningham, M. K. 30, 31, 34

Davies, P. R. 163
Davis, E. F. 77
DeVries, S. J. 65, 70, 71, 132, 157, 181, 190, 191, 194, 199, 210, 213, 223
Dever, W. G. 105, 125
Dorp, J. van 198, 199
Dozeman, T. B. 49, 68, 71, 211
Driver, D. R. 49, 233

Eynikel, E. 48, 70, 102, 162, 198

Fee, G. D. 121
Fichtner, J. 53
Fox, E. 172
Fretheim, T. E. 72, 225
Friedman, R. E. 163
Frost, S. B. 216

Garsiel, M. 165, 166, 230
Gesenius, W. 185
Gide, A. 144
Gignilliat, M. S. 37
Grabbe, L. L. 216
Gray, J. 53, 70, 96, 100, 181, 183, 187, 194, 199, 207
Gressmann, H. 68, 208
Gross, W. 49, 69, 74, 181, 201, 204
Gunn, D. M. 131, 134
Gunneweg, A. H. J. 64

Halpern, B. 216
Harvey, J. E. 190
Heller, R. 71, 83
Hoffmann, H.-D. 222
Hölscher, G. 167

Index of Authors

Holstein, J. A. 195
House, P. R. 71

Janzen, D. 216, 230
Jepsen, A. 63
Jones, G. H. 70, 75, 132, 218, 220
Jones, P. H. 3, 82, 163, 203
Joseph, A. L. 163, 172, 179, 232

Keil, C. F. 197, 199, 209
Kelsey, D. H. 999
Kissling, P. J. 999
Klopfenstein, M. A. 5, 6, 14, 50–63, 70, 80, 139, 196, 197, 200, 203, 204, 209, 212, 223
Knauf, E. A. 162, 216
Knoppers, G. 69, 72, 102, 103, 158, 162, 167
Kristeva, J. 31
Kuhl, C. 104, 167

Lasine, S. 77, 80, 98, 136
Leithart, P. J. 14, 76, 80, 93
Lemke, W. E. 49, 70, 73, 75, 103, 104, 123, 124, 167, 171, 194, 204, 211, 213
Levenson, J. D. 41, 160, 162, 186, 205
Levinson, B. M. 135, 162
Lindblom, J. 78
Linville, J. R. 43, 158
Lohfink, N. F. 161
Long Jr., J. C. 999
Long, B. O. 70, 72, 167, 168, 181, 187, 188
Long, J. C., Jr. 76, 99, 125, 183
Lovell, N. 221

MacDonald, N. B. 164
Macchi, J.-D. 158, 162
Malcolm, M. 67
Marcus, D. 70, 77, 97, 135, 140, 192, 208
McCarthy, D. 171
McConville, J. G. 126, 158
McGlasson, P. 30, 31
McKenzie, S. L. 74, 83, 104, 124–6, 132, 161, 162, 167, 171
Mead, J. 69, 74, 76, 159, 207
Miller, G. 136
Miscall, P. D. 230
Moberly, R. W. L. 41, 78, 82, 127, 137, 140, 196

Monroe, L. A. S. 162
Montgomery, J. 73, 108, 204, 207
Mullen, E. T. 158, 180

Na'aman, N. 145
Nahkola, A. 165, 230
Nelson, R. D. 72, 99, 161, 172, 187
Noth, M. 18, 64, 65, 68, 75, 130, 161, 162, 170, 183, 184, 188, 221

O'Connor, M. P. 181, 185

Person, R. F. 103, 104
Petersen, D. L. 195
Plöger, O. 170
Porter, S. 67
Provan, I. W. 73, 80, 124, 126, 172, 179, 180, 231, 232
Pury, A. de 158, 162

Rad, G. von 130, 161, 162, 221, 226
Rendtorff, R. 130, 132
Rice, G. 2, 73, 199
Ricoeur, P. 136
Robinson, J. 68, 70
Rofé, A. 70, 77, 97, 104, 124, 185
Römer, T. 158, 162, 167
Rosenberg, J. 110
Rowlett, L. L. 161

Schearing, L. S. 161, 162
Schneiders, S. M. 121, 140
Schökel, L. A. 120, 121
Seow, C.-L. 74
Simon, U. 64, 72, 80, 95, 153, 188, 191–4, 196, 208
Smend, R. 52
Smolar, L. 183
Sommer, B. D. 125, 136
Stendahl, K. 49, 117
Sternberg, M. 82, 131–5, 165
Stavrakopoulou, F. 216
Strawn, B. A. 207, 208, 216
Stuart, D. 121
Sweeney, M. A. 75, 100, 162, 182, 208, 215–17, 224, 232

Talmon, S. 167
Tate, R. 102, 113, 121, 222

Van Seters, J. 2, 7, 70, 75, 94, 96–8, 100–105, 126, 133, 134, 147, 167, 168, 222
Van Winkle, D. W. 70, 71, 137, 167, 180, 182, 197, 204, 205

Wallace, M. I. 31, 42
Walsh, J. T. 7, 13, 14, 29, 51, 73, 82, 86–93, 114, 118–20, 122, 134, 167, 187, 188, 195, 197
Waltke, B. K. 181, 185
Webster, J. 32
Weinfeld, M. 130
Wellhausen, J. 70, 124, 169, 170
Williams, J. G. 230
Wilson, R. R. 83
Wiseman, D. J. 74
Wolff, H. W. 131, 221
Wray Beal, L. M. 159, 202, 208, 215, 217

www.ingramcontent.com/pod-product-compliance
Lightning Source LLC
Chambersburg PA
CBHW072134290426
44111CB00012B/1875